The Only Land They Knew

The Only Land They Knew

The Tragic Story of the American Indians in the Old South

J. Leitch Wright, Jr.

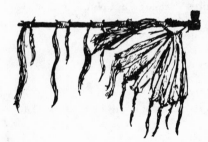

THE FREE PRESS
A Division of Macmillan Publishing Co., Inc.
NEW YORK

Collier Macmillan Publishers
LONDON

The Free Press
A Division of Macmillan Publishing Co., Inc.
866 Third Avenue, New York, N.Y. 10022

Collier Macmillan Canada, Ltd.

Library of Congress Catalog Card Number: 80-1854

Printed in the United States of America

printing number
1 2 3 4 5 6 7 8 9 10

Library of Congress Cataloging in Publication Data

Wright, James Leitch.
  The only land they knew, the tragic story of the
American Indians in the Old South.

    Bibliography: p.
    Includes index.
    1. Indians of North America—Southern States—History.
2. Southern States—History. 3. Southern States—Race
relations.   I. Title.
E78.S65W74   975'.00497   80-1854
ISBN 0-02-935790-X

To Lucy

Contents

Maps and Illustrations

Preface and Acknowledgments

For a long time after white contact Indians, Europeans, and
Africans lived in the South, interacting with one another and
altering the culture of each. This book is part of that story, which
in important respects differs from the experiences of these three
groups elsewhere in the United States and in the Western Hemisphere. I have focused on the Indians in the South, although the
narrative wanders off to the West Indies, Mexico, South America,
Europe, and Africa. Part of my consideration of areas outside the
South and of Europeans and Africans is by design, and partly it
reflects the nature of or, better said, the lack of sources. Since the
Southern Indians did not write, one often has to wonder what
they were thinking as opposed to what missionaries, traders,
and merchants reported was on their minds. To compensate for
the lack of traditional historical sources I have turned to scholars
in other disciplines, including archaeology, linguistics, ethnography, anthropology, oral history, demography, and geography.

Even using this broader ethnohistorical approach it is apparent
that important aspects of Indian history are obscure, perhaps lost
forever. When Spaniards, Englishmen, and Frenchmen first ex-

plored the South, they sometimes portrayed the Indians as shadowy figures, silently observing from their forest sanctuary or relentlessly stalking and assaulting the intruders before withdrawing into the fastness of the woods. This brings to mind Plato's parable, where in antiquity a group sat huddled and chained in the dimly lit recesses of a cave. The philosopher-leader stepped outside and, seeing the sun's full brilliance—the truth—subsequently returned and attempted to pass on this knowledge to his listeners. But never having left the cave and only seeing the dim light at its entrance or shadows on the wall, his audience, mere mortals, could only partially comprehend what the philosopher was saying. Today we also are trapped and chained in a cave when trying to comprehend the Indians' history. I do not expect to lead readers out of this cave; I only hope that this work will allow them to loosen their chains and shift their seats a bit closer to the entrance.

Because of the wide scope of this study it has often been necessary to generalize about Indians who were no more uniform or a single people than their European and African counterparts. To ease the reader's journey through the text, I have deliberately not used "in most instances," "probably," and other qualifiers as much as the subject matter would dictate. The terms race, tribe, mestizo, Negro, zambo, and mulatto, often employed in the narrative, are all subject to different interpretations. In some instances the confusion is more than semantic and in fact is one reason I undertook this work. In any case, I hope the text makes it clear in what sense I am using these terms. All too frequently it is difficult if not impossible to determine with a reasonable degree of confidence whether Indians of an earlier day are responsible for particular aspects of our contemporary culture. Uncertainty repeatedly arises over whether a custom originated with the Indians exclusively, was simultaneously invented by them and others, or was transmitted to them after Columbus's voyage.

My debt to colleagues is great. Particular mention should be made to those at Florida State University: Professors Kathleen A. Deagan and James Anthony Paredes in the Department of Anthropology, and Joe M. Richardson and Robert L. Hall in the Department of History. John W. Walker and his associates at the Southeast Archaeological Center, National Park Service, also located at Florida State University, afforded useful advice and the use of their library. The archaeologists B. Calvin Jones, Curtiss E. Peterson, and Wilburn A. Cockrell at the Florida Division of Archives, History, and Records Management; Frank T. Schnell at the Columbus Museum of Arts and Sciences; and Charles H. Fairbanks and Jerald T. Milanich at the University of Florida were most helpful, as was Charles M. Hudson in the Department of Anthropology at the University of Georgia. Those colleagues who read various chapters include Richardson, Hall, Paredes, Fairbanks, Hudson, and Jones. This book is much improved because of their criticisms. William C. Sturtevant and his associates at the Center for the Study of Man, Smithsonian Institution, and Francis Jennings and his colleagues in the Newberry Library's Center for the History of the American Indian all were gracious and accommodating hosts on my research visits. I cannot fail to mention the many courtesies extended by the staffs of the Virginia State Library in Richmond and the South Carolina Department of Archives and History in Columbia. Grants from the Rockefeller–Florida State University Center for the Study of Southern Culture and Religion and the Florida State University President's Club helped make possible the necessary research travel, and a sabbatical leave from Florida State University afforded indispensable time for writing. Typing was carefully done by Nancy Mann Wright, Margaret Leitch Wright, Helen Lee Wright, Sylvia Tomberlin, Mary E. Kirlin, and especially Barbara A. Presgrove. Richard S. Dawdy of the Department of Geography at Florida State University prepared the maps. As always, I and this book owe more to Beth than it is possible to acknowledge.

1
The Original Southerners

During the first part of the sixteenth century English, French, Spanish, and Portuguese mariners sailed along the North American Atlantic Coast and sometimes were shipwrecked or went ashore for refreshment. Ponce de León, Verrazzano, and the Cabots skirted the shoreline, and occasionally a De Soto penetrated deep into the interior. From their accounts it is possible to catch a glimpse of the Indians they found and of their life-style and culture. But these natives had not suddenly appeared on the scene. Where had they come from, and what cultural changes had they undergone over the centuries? For this there is not a single eyewitness account, and it is necessary to rely on the archaeologist, linguist, folklorist, and ethnologist. Although a few little-understood petroglyphs and pictographs are scattered throughout parts of the South, these Indians were clearly a nonliterate people.

The geographic area covered by this study is roughly that of the old Confederacy, excluding the trans-Mississippi West—that is, the bounds are the Ohio and Mississippi rivers, the Atlantic Ocean, and the Gulf of Mexico. Emphasis is on the eastern Tide-

1

water or Atlantic Coastal part and to a lesser extent on the Gulf Coast and its hinterland. It was primarily along the Atlantic Coast that Europeans first confronted the Indians, and these Europeans more often than not were Englishmen or Spaniards. One cannot ignore the sixteenth-century French presence on the Atlantic Coast. The Valois ensign flew briefly over settlements at present-day Port Royal, South Carolina, and on the St. Johns River in Florida, and countless French ships followed the Gulf Stream along the coast before returning to Europe. But this early French influence proved transitory because of the campaigns of the ruthless Spanish captain, Menéndez de Avilés, which destroyed the French posts. Almost a century and a half later Frenchmen pushed southward down the Mississippi River from Canada and about 1700 founded Biloxi, Mobile, and New Orleans on or near the Gulf of Mexico. French missionaries, officials, and *courieurs des bois* left abundant records describing their relations with the Natchez, Choctaw, and other Indians in the lower Mississippi Valley. With few exceptions these are eighteenth-century accounts, written some two hundred years after the Southern Indians had first encountered whites, and much had changed. That is why this work emphasizes the Spanish and English presence on the Atlantic Coast rather than the French influence in Louisiana.

We have gotten ahead of our story, and it is necessary to return to the Indians—and not to those natives depicted in the accounts of De Soto's expedition or those portrayed by the artist John White at Sir Walter Raleigh's Roanoke Island colony. One thing is certain: The culture of the original Indians differed drastically from that delineated in White's sixteenth-century drawings.

It has not been ascertained with certainty when or from where man first arrived in the South. Archaeologists have uncovered as much of the story as is known. While not ruling out intrusions from Europe, Africa, or the Orient, there is a consensus, or nearly so, that man crossed the ice bridge over the Bering Strait and spread over much of North and South America. Recent archaeological evidence suggests the traditional date of twenty thousand years ago is possibly too late and that man first crossed the Bering Strait perhaps forty thousand or more years ago.[1] The latest archaeological excavations in the Eastern woodlands have supported this theory.

By radiocarbon measurement and other scientific means of dating it has been shown that man has been around not just for a few thousand years but for sixteen thousand or more. Discoveries at Russell Cave in northeastern Alabama disclose an aboriginal occupation extending back about eight thousand years, and excavations at Flint Run, Virginia (near Front Royal), push the date back to 11,500 years.[2] A similar site at Meadowcroft in southwestern Pennsylvania dates back to fourteen thousand B.C.[3] One of the most significant discoveries in the South has been made 47 feet below the surface at Warm Mineral Springs near the Gulf in southwestern Florida. Here divers have retrieved a ten-thousand-year-old human skull from a submerged cave. Subsequent discoveries at an even lower depth suggest the presence of man for up to thirteen thousand years. The latter date, if verified, represents the earliest proven existence of man in the South, and there are indications that even this date will have to be pushed back further.[4]

Little is known about earliest man in the South. His religion, language, and social and political relationships are almost a complete mystery. To help describe how Indians advanced from one level of social complexity to another, anthropologists have identified four major cultural periods or traditions: Paleo, Archaic, Woodland, and Mississippian. A minority of contemporary archaeologists contend that a fifth period, Early Man, is emerging, which includes the most ancient Indians such as those at Warm Mineral Springs and Meadowcroft. At this point little is known about Early Man, and it may well be that in fact he did not exist. Paleo man was a nomadic hunter, best known for killing large, now extinct animals with stone-tipped spears or by stampeding them into various kinds of traps to their deaths. Life for Indians in the Archaic tradition was more sophisticated. Depending far less on large game animals, instead they exploited their environment more intensively. They hunted smaller animals with darts thrown from an *atlatl* or spear thrower; gathered nuts, berries, and shellfish; and became more sedentary. In some places they made a crude pottery tempered with vegetable fibers. In the Woodland Period, ca. 1000 B.C. to A.D. 700, the aborigines continued to rely primarily on hunting and gathering. But the use of pottery became widespread, and rudimentary agriculture supplemented their diet. Artifacts recovered from Woodland Period burial mounds, including pipes, stone and copper gorgets, wooden carvings, pottery effigies, and earrings, indicate the cultural advance. Such exotic materials as obsidian, shells from the Gulf of Mexico, and mica reveal that the Woodland Indians were more "cosmopolitan" or had more wide-flung relationships than did Archaic people. Burial mounds up to 40 or more feet in height scattered throughout the South perhaps best separate the Woodland Indians from their predecessors.

The Mississippian tradition, one of the most notable Indian cultures, beginning sometime after A.D. 700 and lasting up to or after white contact, is important for our purposes. This was the era of the mound builders, who constructed truncated platform temple mounds up to 100 feet tall, with religious and political structures on their flat tops. Frequently there was not just a single isolated temple mound but several spread over acres in planned clusters. From the top of the principal mound the priest could see villagers working in outlying fields. Indians brought in countless basketloads of dirt on their backs to construct the mounds, and villages provided the agricultural surplus to support a priestly and political elite.[5]

The organized labor necessary to construct these mounds implies a structured political organization. At the time of white contact an indeterminate number of powerful tribes, chiefdoms, or confederations existed. Some of the better known are the Powhatan Confederation (Tsenacommacah) in Tidewater Virginia, the Natchez on the lower Mississippi River, the Calusa Kingdom in southern Florida, the Apalachee in northern Florida, and the Cofitachiqui in South Carolina. The Natchez, the Apalachee, and the Cofitachiqui were in the mainstream of the Mississippian tradition, while the Algonquians in Virginia, who had no temple mounds, and the Calusa in southern Florida, a maritime people, were on the fringe of Mississippian culture.

The Cofitachiqui chiefdom, occupying a central position in present-day South Carolina, was one of the most powerful societies in the South. De Soto visited the celebrated Queen of Cofitachiqui, the seat of whose domain was perhaps at Silver Bluff on the Savannah River below Augusta or more likely on the Wateree River near Camden. De Soto's chroniclers were clearly impressed by the numerous houses, large mounds, and the grand wooden, mat-covered temple containing bones of deceased natives, whose entrance was defended by intricately carved armed wooden giants. The Queen and her attendants wore long pearl necklaces; the Spaniards and their horses to-

4

The Original Southerners

SOUTHERN   INDIANS

R.S. DAWDY

gether could not possibly carry all of the pearls, reputedly weighing thousands of pounds. The Queen's armory held an enormous quantity of copper-tipped pikes, maces, battle axes, and, according to some accounts, fifty thousand bows and quivers. For all the known opulence and size of Cofitachiqui, it is not at all clear today whether the Indians there spoke a Siouan, Muskhogean, or some other language, what the bounds of the Queen's realm were, and where her capital was located.[6]

In addition to the Indians of Cofitachiqui, from the earliest times whites also came into direct or indirect contact with the Yuchi at one or another place in the South. In the folk history of these people, who comprised a separate linguistic family, there is the tradition that they had descended from a powerful empire. Yet almost nothing is known about this elusive Indian society.[7] Even more mystery surrounds the Westos and Ricahecrians, who appeared so menacingly on the South Carolina and Virginia frontiers in the seventeenth century. Were they Iroquoian, Muskhogean, or Siouan speakers? Were they different or perhaps the same people? What was the extent and nature of their chiefdom?[8] Spaniards and Frenchmen encountered, painted, and described Timucuans on the Atlantic Coast of present-day northern Florida and southern Georgia. Whether these Indians belonged in the Muskhogean family, as seems likely, or whether it is more proper to link them with Arawakan speakers of the Caribbean and northern South America is still not clear.[9] An appalling number of Southern Indian languages became extinct without having been recorded; it is probable, in fact, that whole families of languages have disappeared without a trace.

Such linguistic diversity, which was greater than that of modern Western Europe, should not obscure the fact that remarkable cultural similarities existed throughout the South. Sixteenth-century Indians were essentially farmers and as such lived far more complicated lives than the hunter-gatherers associated with Russell Cave and Warm Mineral Springs. Maize—Indian corn—was the staff of life. Developed in South America and Mexico, it had made its way north during the Woodland Period. Northern flint corn spread into New England and the Mid-Atlantic states, and varieties of flint corn or popcorn early appeared in the South. Adapted to a warm, moist climate and proceeding along the Gulf of Mexico, southern dent (gourd seed) corn at a much later date, perhaps even after contact, also began to be grown in the South.

It had a larger ear and produced a higher yield than flint. Dent and other varieties of corn assumed greater importance in native life and culture.[10] During the Mississippian Period it was difficult to imagine either a large palisaded town containing houses and temple mounds or an isolated residence without an adjoining maize field. Maize itself, along with the Corn Mother goddess and the annual Green Corn festival, played a vital role in the lives of Mississippian people. They did not rely solely on maize. Beans, varieties of peas indigenous to America, squash, and sunflowers were grown. Tobacco culture was widespread not only in the South but throughout North and South America. It was not normally smoked for pleasure but was used in religious and political ceremonies and for medicinal purposes. Countless stone and clay pipes, some finely wrought, attest to tobacco's importance. Aware of the narcotic qualities of this plant, medicine men carried its leaves in their bundles and administered it internally or externally to their patients.

Since the beginnings of agriculture in the South around 1000 B.C. in the early Woodland Period, Indians had perfected farming techniques. By the sixteenth century they had progressed far beyond any primitive slash-and-burn type of agriculture. After Europeans arrived, whether Spaniards in Florida or Englishmen at Jamestown, when they attempted to grow crops, they often turned to the natives for advice. Excavations of middens (trash heaps), fire pits, and an occasional cornfield itself have disclosed much about aboriginal agriculture. An equally important source, perhaps the best one for the sixteenth century, consists of written and pictorial accounts made by the whites. These include narratives of the De Soto expedition and drawings made by the French Huguenot Jacques Le Moyne of the Florida Indians and by the English artist John White at Roanoke Island. An impression frequently derived from such sources is that women performed most of the labor, that agriculture was "squaw" work, while the men lounged about except when off to war or away hunting. This point of view is pervasive and has been perpetuated in numerous works, including Edmund S. Morgan's recent study of seventeenth-century Virginia. The author characterizes the natives of Raleigh's Roanoke Island and of John Smith's Jamestown as "idle" and compares them with the English settlers, whom he regards as equally indolent.[11]

This perception distorts the fact that the sixteenth-century natives were agriculturalists and had been for centuries. They usually lived in towns and had their fields in the countryside. What European observers frequently saw and commented on and what White and Le Moyne painted were the small town garden plots, perhaps 100 by 200 feet, which, tended by women, were relied upon until crops in the main fields ripened. Men did much of the work in the principal fields. They cleared them, no easy task, as any white farmer carving out a homestead on the frontier could testify. They girdled large trees with stone axes and knives and used fire and stone implements to help fell the trunks. Time and fire disposed of stumps. In one sense it was easier for Indians than whites to clear an area, because before contact large trees were likely to be farther apart. The natives deliberately burned the forests when lightning did not do the work for them. The effect was to keep down the underbrush, make the woods more open, and facilitate the hunting of larger animals. Even so, the effort required to clear forests for cultivation was enormous, and countless Indian "old fields" scattered throughout the South attest to the Indians' toil. Whites eagerly sought out these clearings to escape such backbreaking work. Natives did not have plows or beasts of burden and broke the ground with hoes consisting of wooden handles with stones, conch shells, or large animal bones at the ends. Available evidence indicates that men with such implements did the heavy work and prepared the ground while women with baskets of corn and beans made holes with pointed sticks and dropped in the seeds.

Maize was the staple, and over centuries the aborigines had learned how to cultivate it more efficiently. Whereas not until the eighteenth-century agricultural revolution did Europeans normally stop sowing broadcast and begin planting in rows, Indians at a much earlier date grew crops in a regular fashion. That is what the women with pointed sticks were doing. Natives planted maize at stated intervals and hilled it; as the stalk grew they piled up more dirt. This helped establish a better root system, strengthened the stalk, trapped moisture in the soil, kept down weeds, and ensured a higher yield. Native practices of not disturbing the soil between hills, planting different crops in the same field, and relying heavily on bottom lands, which presumably were flooded and naturally fertilized, allowed them to use the same field for a long period before exhausting the soil.[12] Beans often were grown in the same field as maize. The corn stalk became a natural support for these "pole" beans, and together maize and beans provided most of the vegetable protein necessary for a balanced diet. Beans also restored nitrogen to the soil, which corn had depleted.[13] King Carter in Virginia and Abraham Lincoln's ancestors in the Mississippi Valley were relentlessly driven westward in search of virgin lands. Indians did not confront those pressures to such a degree, though in time they abandoned some fields and opened up new ones.

The first European observers sometimes remarked that the aborigines harvested two or even three crops of maize a year, but unfortunately they did not usually explain how.[14] A Timucuan practice in Florida was to plant one crop in the early spring and another in the summer on the same ground. It was also possible to grow dent, sweet, pop, and other varieties of corn, which matured at different intervals. In some fashion natives harvested maize throughout much of the summer and fall.

Large fields were owned communally, and vital decisions on what and when to plant were made by the village chief and elders. Agricultural labor was organized and disciplined as it had been for the erection of temple mounds. Any surplus was stored for use until the next harvest or to feed visitors. Granaries took several forms. Some were wattle-and-daub buildings with tightly thatched roofs and sunken clay-lined floors; others were log "corn cribs" raised off the ground on poles; and shallow clay-lined storage pits filled with food and covered with earth and stones at times were used. Indians did not build fences and hedgerows to ward off predators; with no roaming horses, cattle, or swine until after white arrival, they were not as necessary. But birds, deer, and raccoons provided indigenous enemies enough. During the growing season Indian women and children guarded the fields. Le Moyne's and White's pictures portray granaries, fields, planting techniques, and the simple wooden structures used to house sentinels protecting crops.[15]

If sixteenth-century Southern Indians were agriculturalists, they nevertheless had not completely abandoned hunting. For centuries their ancestors had hunted and gathered, and Indians of the late Mississippian tradition still hunted for food, clothed themselves with furs and skins, and collected acorns, walnuts, tuckahoe, chinquapins, and strawberries. It would be impossible to explain or to comprehend native religious beliefs and clan structure without taking into account this hunting tradition.

Even so, hunting and gathering clearly were secondary to agriculture, and game merely supplemented maize and beans. Much of the earliest information on aboriginal hunting practices concerns tribes living on the Atlantic Coast, such as the Timucuans in Florida or the Powhatans in Virginia. To a degree they were on the periphery of the great maize-growing centers in the interior, and there is some question as to how typical their experience was. But if these sixteenth- and early-seventeenth-century Timucuans and Algonquians provide any example at all, the continuing importance of hunting is obvious. White described how, after crops were harvested in the fall, able-bodied men and at least some of the women moved to temporary quarters in the interior and hunted for one to three months. During these winter months meat may have become more of a staple than maize.[16]

Natives pursued all types of game but especially deer, which abounded. Venison more than any other meat was cooked over Indian fires, and it was doe or buckskin that was likely to clothe a Southern Indian of either sex. In addition to their symbolic importance, bears were valued partly for their fur and meat and especially for their oil. It was used as a condiment with food or rubbed over the body as protection against insects, as a cosmetic, sometimes scented, and as a ritual unguent. Europeans noted that the coarse black hair of many a young female glistened as a result of being greased with bear oil. Meat not consumed immediately was smoked, though rarely salted, and taken to the village for future use. Indians stalked game with bows and arrows, sometimes concealing themselves under a deer's skin in order to get within range. Continuing an ancient practice, natives sometimes made a ring of fire, driving all game, large and small, to the center or to the end of a peninsula, where they could easily be dispatched. The aborigines also fashioned ingenious traps to snare their quarry. Whatever their method, the natives did not slaughter game indiscriminately but killed only that necessary for food and clothing. They lived close to—and regarded themselves as inseparable from—nature, considering the deer, bear, eagle, fox, buffalo, and other animals to be their brothers.

Maize culture and the higher civilization and greater population density associated with it had flowed into the South from an even more southerly region, namely, Meso-America. Perhaps this culture had advanced overland from Mexico via Texas, perhaps by water through the West Indies, or probably by both

routes. It may well be that important aspects of Southern culture
had evolved locally. In any case, many features of a higher civilization had progressed from somewhere to the south toward the
north. At the time of white contact hunting remained far more
important for those Indians who lived in the northern part of
what was to become the United States. The Algonquians are a
case in point. Having first spread over Canada, they thrust themselves southward into New England, the mid-Atlantic states, and
finally into the Virginia and North Carolina Tidewater. In general
they depended as much on hunting as on agriculture, if not
more, for subsistence. The Algonquians of Powhatan's Confederacy in Virginia and the Pamlico and Machapunga of eastern
North Carolina had not been on the scene too many centuries
before the Europeans arrived.

It is in the Virginia and Carolina Tidewater where the mixing
of the Northern hunting-oriented culture with the Southern
maize-agrarian civilization can best be documented. Powhatan's
subjects had much in common with the Algonquian Delaware,
Mohegan, and Pequot to the north. But they had just as much
and probably more in common with the Mississippian temple
mound civilization to the south. This included the busk or Green
Corn ceremony, fire hunting, "bone houses" for the remains of
important chiefs, bamboo knives, woven feather mantles, basket
traps for fish, cranial deformation, and fish poisoning. A feature
conspicuously missing in the Tidewater was the temple platform
mound. There is one essential point to keep in mind, however.
James Fenimore Cooper's characterization of the Mohegans in
New York, the Puritans' description of the New England Indians,
and the French portrayal of Algonquian life in the St. Lawrence
Valley, all emphasizing the Indians as hunters, becomes more
distorted the farther south one looks along the Atlantic Coast.[17]

So far only incidental mention has been made of fishing. A
reliance on shellfish dates back to the earliest period, as excavations at Muscle Shoals on the Tennessee River attest. Shell
middens many feet tall along the Atlantic and Gulf coasts
demonstrate the importance of clams and oysters. One need only
glance at Le Moyne's and White's drawings to realize that the
Indians did more than gather these mollusks. They fished with
spears, bows and arrows, and bone hooks; built rock weirs and
channeled fish into basket traps; and threw pounded walnut bark
or roots of the devil's shoestring (*Tephrosia*) into a stream to

stupefy fish so they could be easily caught.[18] Part of the catch was smoked and preserved. Until Franciscans established missions and promoted agriculture, Guale Indians in coastal Georgia still depended primarily on marine life from tidal waters.[19]

In most respects European fishing techniques were superior to those of the aborigines, though in regard to the Calusa one wonders. They were a maritime folk whose large canoes ranged the open sea. The Calusa were not typical Southern Indians, and in any case much of their remarkable history remains to be told.[20] As has been seen, the Powhatans were closer to the Mississippian culture. During the winter of 1609–10 Jamestown settlers living right on the river experienced the rigorous "starving time," when their numbers shrank from some five hundred to sixty. The Jamestown experience made it obvious that whites had much to learn from the natives.

The spread of agriculture and adoption of a sedentary life-style allowed time for artisans to perfect their crafts. Indians became proficient in basket-making, carpentry, woodworking, pipe-making, weaving, pottery, certain kinds of metal work, and tanning. Both sexes were artisans, though some crafts seemed to be identified with one or the other. Over the centuries Indians had perfected the art of basketry, making a wide range of colorful and utilitarian split-cane baskets. Some were flat, shallow ones employed in preparing and serving food; a considerable number were large and tightly woven with lids for storage; others were used for gathering nuts and berries; special types of baskets were containers or hampers for bones of deceased ancestors; and porters utilized large ones with arm straps or more likely with tumplines for their chests or foreheads to carry heavy loads of clay and foodstuffs. Basket-makers also made large utilitarian mats and tightly woven shields for warriors.

Scrutiny of early maps turns up such names as "pipemaker's bluff" or "pipemaker's field," which identifies another aboriginal craft. Tobacco cultivation created a demand for pipes. Some of the clay bowls were finely wrought and decorated and were attached to long cane stems that sometimes were adorned with eagle feathers. Clay pipes, along with magnificent stone effigy platform pipes, were widespread in the precontact era, and the effigy pipes, or at least the stone from which they were manufactured, were common trade items.

Because of the perishable nature of wood, much knowledge of

aboriginal woodcarving and carpentry has been lost. But from flukes of nature where wood has been preserved in the muck or in some lake or spring, and from early white written and pictorial accounts, it is obvious that the natives—apparently men—had developed their woodcarving talents. They fashioned spoons, bowls, platters, chests, totem or effigy posts, masks, and animal representations. Many structures in aboriginal towns were wood, reflecting the abilities of carpenters. They erected the post and rafter framework of wattle-and-daub thatch houses, built wooden palisades and fortified entrances, constructed frames for low wooden beds, and with fire and stone implements laboriously made large dugout canoes, some of which, such as those of the Calusa, were seaworthy and would hold up to eighty men.

Europeans repeatedly commented on the elaborately decorated, fringed deerskins worn by the Indians. Men clearly were the hunters, but either men or women skinned the deer, scraped off the hair, and soaked, dried, and smoked the skins. If aboriginal mantles were not of deerskin they might have been made of feathers; and multicolored feather mantles, held together by a fiber net base and perhaps embroidered with shells and copper beads, were prized by Mississippians.[21]

Pottery had appeared in the South around 2000 B.C. in the Georgia–Florida region during the late Archaic era. Indians never discovered the pottery wheel, but over the centuries they perfected techniques of tempering and firing. Most ceramics were utilitarian pots and bowls, though by the Mississippian era many were artistically formed, decorated, and painted. Other types of pottery included water bottles, beads, human and animal effigies, pipes, ear spools, ear bobs, burial urns, and storage vessels.[22]

The few surviving textiles from burials and textile impressions deliberately made on pottery give some indication of the ability of aboriginal weavers. They wove animal hair and vegetable and bark fibers into clothes, sandals, and nets.

Just before white contact Southern Indians still relied heavily on stone implements such as projectile points, scrapers, knives, mortars, and pestles. Stoneworkers who chiseled, flaked, ground, and polished stone were highly skilled, as were artisans who engraved elaborate designs on shells or manufactured various types of wampum. It would be erroneous to assume, however, that Indians knew nothing of metal. They made a number of decorative and utilitarian objects out of lead, and for centuries they had acquired and used copper from local sources, the Great Lakes region, or west of the Mississippi River. Hammering and incising with stone or bone tools and annealing the copper with skill, they fashioned beads, bracelets, earrings, ceremonial knives and axes, gorgets, and breast plates. Surviving examples of the latter, almost a foot by two feet in size, with component parts riveted together, are elaborately decorated with an eagle, hawk, or similar motif. These artifacts, some of which were up to five hundred years old at the time of contact and were associated with the Southeastern Ceremonial Complex, reflected a far greater knowledge of metallurgy than is commonly ascribed to the Southern Indians.[23]

The typical Indian at the time of contact was sedentary, living in a town. Scattered throughout the South, villages frequently were palisaded, containing from only a handful up to hundreds of houses. Population ranged from under a hundred to thousands, and over the long span of history the Mississippian was the typical Southern townsman. At the time of the American Revolution Charleston, the largest city south of Philadelphia, contained but twelve thousand inhabitants; Williamsburg, even when the legislature was in session, numbered less than two thousand; and Spanish St. Augustine, whose population numbered almost three thousand in 1763, for most of the eighteenth century was the second largest city south of Philadelphia. Even in 1861 Wilmington, North Carolina, with not quite ten thousand people, was the largest city in the entire state. By almost any standard the white South was rural. But it had not always been that way. For centuries before contact and for some time afterward towns dotted this region, and it is improper to refer to a rural South until after Europeans arrived. One reason for confusion is that we know a good deal about the development of Williamsburg, Norfolk, Charleston, Savannah, and St. Augustine,[24] whereas, in contrast, we are not even sure of the locations of such Indian centers as Cofitachiqui, Mabila, and the capital of the province of Apalachee, each of whose populations numbered in the thousands.

Towns varied in size and appearance. Those that were palisaded and fortified were likely to be on a tribe's or chiefdom's exposed frontier. Larger urban centers in the maize-growing Mississippian area probably contained one or a series of platform temple mounds with houses on top. The typical rectangular or round dwelling was of wattle-and-daub construction and had a thatch roof. Sometimes bark or mats covered the sides and roof, and the floor might be made of puddled clay. Towns generally shared certain key features. One was the square ground. Located in a level, well-defined area, it was enclosed by four wooden shedlike structures. Here elders and clan leaders sat in assigned spots as they conducted business, participated in rituals, or listened to a visiting dignitary.[25] Important towns were likely to have a large circular town house. Perhaps located on a platform mound close by the square ground, it had clay walls and an enormous roof, more often than not with a hole in the center for smoke, and contained scores or even hundreds of seats. Used more extensively in winter than in summer, this "rotunda" was the scene of important business and rituals.[26] A visitor on approaching a town saw first not a cathedral spire but a pole 50 or more feet in height erected on a small mound in the ceremonial ground for use in ball games, which, as will be seen, were so important in the Indians' culture. Eagle effigies, animal skulls, and sometimes enemy scalps graced the top of this ball pole. When Spanish missionaries arrived on the scene, they did not approve of the ball game or perhaps even understand its vital role in village life. All they saw was monstrous phallic symbols dotting the landscape.[27] An ossuary or bone house might be found in or close to the towns. Certain mortuary practices were similar throughout the South. Bones of the deceased, particularly those of leaders, were cleaned and at the appropriate time removed to a sacred charnel house and stored in boxes or baskets.[28] As has been mentioned, granaries were commonplace. Any town of consequence had a hot house, like a sauna. To an extent the large rotunda might serve this purpose. More properly the hot house or sweat house was a small, separate, tightly sealed structure where stones were heated and thrown into water. Indians regularly purged and cleansed themselves by first sweating and then plunging into a nearby cold stream.

Early white explorers and modern ethnologists and archaeologists have disclosed numerous characteristics of aboriginal towns. But they have had less to say about, or have almost completely ignored, those natives who lived in the countryside. Early narratives fleetingly mention habitations sprinkled about. Numerous houses outside Mabila reportedly were scattered through the fields a crossbow shot or two from each other.[29] As De Soto traveled up the center of the Florida peninsula, from time to time he encountered houses strung out over four leagues.[30] When in the mid-seventeenth century the English began to settle Carolina and in the early eighteenth century the French arrived in Louisiana, natives were reported to be living in straggling, dispersed houses.[31] The problem with these latter sources is that they refer to a century and a half to two centuries after white contact, and there is no assurance that they accurately depict earlier patterns of settlement. Before Europeans arrived towns were obviously numerous and important, but the extent of the nonurban settlements at that time is not at all clear. Knowledge about rural dwellers is important for a number of reasons, certainly if one is trying to count the total population.

Much is known about the social and political relationships of the surviving historical Southern Indians. As one moves back to the period of contact, however, the story becomes more obscure. The first Europeans were closer to the mark than is generally realized in referring to Indian "kings" and "emperors." These designations in time became so overworked and outdated as to be almost meaningless. But at the time of contact powerful chiefdoms existed, including the Cofitachiqui, Powhatan, Natchez, and Calusa. Powhatan had but to snap his fingers and an unfortunate Indian or the captive John Smith would be brought before him for execution. When the Natchez Sun died, his subjects staged an elaborate funeral which included immolation of his wives. De Soto's chroniclers recount how the Queen of Cofitachiqui was carried about in state in her litter and how her word was law over a large area. The sway of the Calusa chief Carlos was felt over much of southern Florida from the Gulf to the Atlantic Coast. In the eighteenth and nineteenth centuries much was made of the Creek Confederacy centered in the states of Alabama and Georgia. Although many chiefs claimed to be absolute king or ruler, in fact there never was any counterpart to a Carlos, Natchez Sun, or Queen of Cofitachiqui. In the sixteenth century, however, powerful, cohesive regional chiefdoms seemed to have been the norm. But if any ruler of the Aztec or Inca type had ever combined them into a larger state, we do not know about it.

Politically no far-flung polity existed in the South, yet culturally one did. Before white contact a new phenomenon known variously as the eagle, hawk, buzzard, or Southern cult, or the Southeastern Ceremonial Complex, spread over much of the region. Its origins and progress are debatable. It may have been transmitted from Meso-America or evolved locally. Some specialists argue that it suddenly swept over the South just before contact in the same fashion the Ghost Dance religion later galloped over the plains in the nineteenth century. It seems probable, especially in light of recent archaeological evidence, that the Southeastern Ceremonial Complex had evolved and flourished over a long time and had been around three, four, or even more centuries before Columbus's voyage. Associated with this complex were fire and sun worship and such motifs as the eagle, hawk, or buzzard; sun circles, bi-lobed arrow, forked eye, hand and eye, and cross, which can be found engraved on copper and shell. The great platform temple mounds of the Mississippian tradition are also identified with the Southeastern Ceremonial Complex. The highest point of this culture apparently was just before or at the time of white contact.[32]

More important than religion or anything else in regulating an Indian's conduct was clan membership. In no way can aboriginal culture be understood without taking this into account. Sharp differences existed between whites and Indians, and the fact that Southern Indians typically traced their lineage through females was as responsible as anything for the confusion. Both whites and Indians used such familiar terms as father, mother, sister, and brother, but with entirely different meanings. Europeans, raised in the tradition of primogeniture and entail, had difficulty comprehending that when an Indian spoke of his father in fact he might be referring to one of his uncles, and when speaking of his sister he might really mean his first or second cousin. It was difficult, if not impossible, for a father to hand down his possessions and office to his natural son, but he could to his nephew, that is, his sister's son.

All of this makes sense only when one comprehends the fact that clan membership was matrilineal. The mother's brother was more important to a child than his biological father, who was of a different clan. The child's eldest uncle of the same "blood" assumed responsibility for educating and disciplining the child. An Indian youth had brothers and sisters in the same sense as Europeans did, but this same Indian youth also called the children of his mother's sisters his own brothers and sisters. Clans

17

were a related group tracing their lineage in an intricate fashion through the female line, and they were symbolically associated with such totems as turtle, snake, bear, wind, deer, and raccoon. Various clans were represented in any given town. Clan membership determined one's conduct in rituals and political gatherings, prescribed where one sat at the square ground, and decreed whom one should treat with respect or familiarity and whom one could court. Indians visiting a remote town for the first time could expect to be housed and entertained by fellow clansmen, even if they were perfect strangers.[33]

Aboriginal economic concepts and methods of property holding differed markedly from those of Europeans. Knowledge of precontact native thought and practices is naturally incomplete, but certain characteristics seem obvious. At the lowest level individual Indians or families "owned" or enjoyed the use of small tracts, while at the village or tribal level land was normally owned communally; and capitalism, the profit motive, and the Protestant work ethic were largely foreign to the aborigines.[34] Hunting grounds seem to have had definite bounds and were regulated by towns or possibly chiefdoms. Clothing, arms, ornaments, and similar personal effects were owned individually, but no strong tradition of storing up treasures on this earth was apparent. Those who had surplus wealth were expected to distribute it generously, and much of what remained—fortunately for archaeologists—was buried with the deceased.

Southern Indians looked and dressed quite differently from the whites, and much is known about this thanks to Le Moyne's and White's drawings and contemporary written accounts. Although posterity has referred to the natives as red men, in fact, as the earliest Europeans noted, pigmentation might be brown, tawny, olive, yellow, or copper.

Indians—at least the men—were comparatively tall, usually around 5 feet, 6 inches, and sometimes 6 feet or more, and thus taller than their European counterparts. Women were likely to be shorter, averaging not much more than 5 feet. Both sexes were well proportioned, with athletic builds and few deformities.[35] Early English Puritan types in Virginia, either with Freudian perversity or in an attempt to attract more immigrants, enthusiastically described young Indian women with white teeth and twinkling eyes, smooth skins, and loose deerskin mantles exposing well-formed breasts.[36] A deerskin breechcloth for the men and a skirt for the women was the universal attire. At times, especially for use in the summer or in the semitropical lower South, women's skirts and men's breechcloths were delicately woven or plaited out of fiber. For the colder months mantles of deer, bear, or buffalo skins, woven feathers, and Spanish moss provided warmth. Leggings, leather moccasins, and woven sandals protected legs and feet.[37] Coarse black hair grew long, and women and occasionally men let it hang down in the back or to one side. Males sometimes tucked all of their hair on top and at other times shaved part of their heads, leaving a crown or some hair as a potential scalp to tempt any enterprising enemy warrior. Elaborate tattooing was widespread, and the amount of one's body covered seemed to have varied with one's status. Ornaments, worn by men and women alike, included earbobs, necklaces, bracelets, and gorgets fashioned out of clay, copper, bone, and shell.

Contemporary written sources and modern ethnographic studies give some idea about native religious beliefs. The Cherokees can be used as an example, not because they necessarily represented typical Southern Indians, but because more information about them is available. They divided the cosmos into three parts: the Upper World, the Earth, and the Under World. The Sun, Moon, Thunder, and other spirits of the Upper World represented the most important and powerful gods. Below them were men, plants, and animals of this world, while snakes, frogs, underground springs, and so forth were identified with the frightful monster Uktena of the nether regions. A complex system of symbols, rites, and taboos was associated with native religions. For example the eagle, who was of this world, soared and came into contact with the Upper World. Indians venerated this bird, and the eagle, his feathers, and the eagle tail dance figured prominently in religious and political ceremonies. Only after elaborate purification could a picked warrior be sent to hunt and kill an eagle. Anything else would bring down the wrath of the gods.[38]

The Sun and the closely related Corn God lived in the Upper World. The annual Green Corn festival or busk lasted for several days after the new corn ripened. Homage was paid to the Sun, Corn, and similar deities as Indians began their new year. Led by a singer intoning sacred chants, Indians purged themselves with emetics, fortified themselves with herbal medicines, extin-

guished old fires, laid logs at the cardinal points, and, in homage
to the Sun God, kindled a fire by friction. This new fire was taken
to each house in town. At the busk ceremonies young boys received war names; unpunished crimes, with a few exceptions,
were pardoned; and spouses of either sex could with little difficulty discard their partners. Dancing, celebrating, and feasting
on roasted ears of new corn and other food followed the lighting
of the new fire.[39]

Indians lived essentially in a law-abiding society. Not that
there was an absence of crime and punishment, but they were
innocent of a number of the moral lapses of which they were
accused. Whites charged young Indian girls with being lascivi-
ous and promiscuous, as most certainly they were by European
standards. If they could afford it, men might have as many wives
as they chose. Despite these differences, Indians had clear notions about marriage and adultery. Young girls normally had
sexual relations before marriage, and divorce was easy, yet once
a marriage had been agreed upon by the partners and clans involved, it was binding. Husbands and wives who committed
adultery could show bruises, broken bones, missing noses, ears,
and hair, or worse. These punishments, and those for murder
and the like, were meted out by the clan. If the culprit could not
be caught, another member of the offending clan had to pay.
Clan or blood vengeance was the mainstay of criminal justice
and, though harsh, worked reasonably well.[40]

Warfare played an important role in Indian life. Based on the
skimpy evidence available it appears to have been of less significance before whites arrived. Indians fought each other in ways
familiar to Europeans. A chief commanded his massed army of
warriors equipped with spears, war clubs, and bows and protected by leather or woven shields. Forces met in the open field;
ambushes, raids by small parties, a single warrior slipping into
the heart of an enemy town, and fighting from cover played a
role, but a subordinate one, in native warfare.

There seems little question that Indians scalped their victims
before Europeans arrived and that they burned at least some of
their captives. It has been argued that Europeans, who had been
burning witches and heretics for centuries, introduced this practice into America. That is unlikely. Guiding colonists into the
Carolina back country early in the eighteenth century, Saponi
Indians pointed out large mounds of rocks alongside the trail as

they added still another stone to each pile. It marked the place where valiant warriors had been burned or otherwise killed in the past. The spot was well known, and Indians passing by still heard voices, taunts, and cries.[41] How many were burned and how many enslaved or adopted is unclear.

Medicine was inseparable from native religion. The priest was religious leader and doctor at the same time. Over the centuries Indians had determined the curative and painkilling properties of assorted plants, including the narcotics tobacco and Jimson weed; yaupon holly leaves as a stimulant; willow bark, similar to aspirin, as a painkiller; dogwood bark, chinquapins, and persimmons as astringents; magnolia bark and ginseng as general cure-alls; wild cherry for coughs; sassafras as a tonic, salve, and "blood purifier," and so on. The list is long. Medicine men were skilled in treating wounds and snakebites, sucking out impurities with a hollow reed or bone and subsequently treating the victim with drugs. Patients were often diagnosed as being out of harmony with the gods and forces of the universe. Medicine men, who were also conjurers, sang and chanted at the patient's bedside, attempting to appease or drive out the appropriate spirit.[42] By today's standards Indian medical practices were primitive, but so too was European medicine. It was not always clear how a decoction of feces, urine, or stag's penis promoted a white patient's recovery. The Virginian William Byrd had good reason to want to escape from eighteenth-century doctors, to treat himself, and not to pay a fee to prolong his agony, and some of the better practitioners of the age hurried George Washington into the grave.[43]

Europeans portrayed the Indians as taciturn and not given to emotional outbursts, which was partly true. In public meetings they were respectful and attentive, not given to interrupting or quarreling directly with a speaker. This is not to imply that the aborigines never laughed or enjoyed themselves. Based on evidence of a later period it seems obvious they had a keen sense of humor, sometimes wry and subtle, sometimes bawdy. Indians of both sexes and all ages played games; gambled with wooden dice, straws, and seeds; or wagered on the outcome of a footrace or ball game. It was unlikely that a town would go for long without a dance. Led by the singer who had a drum or gourd rattle, men and women, the latter with tortoise-shell rattles attached to their legs, followed the leader in single or double file in various dances, perhaps one honoring the exploits of a war or hunting party, perhaps a formal eagletail dance, or perhaps a frolic having little symbolism.[44]

Numerous excavated chunky stones testify how popular the game of chunky was. Indians threw spears at rolling stones to see who could come closest to where the stone stopped. The ball games, one a forerunner of modern day lacrosse and the other pelota, rivaled chunky in popularity. Using the ball pole as a goal, neighboring towns played one another, and for days beforehand men trained, took medicine, and participated in traditional rites. Rules were simple, and serious injuries common. These games were usually but not always less bloody than open warfare and at times were a substitute for hostilities. In pelota an aggressive player might swallow the buckskin ball, only slightly larger than a musket ball, before dashing off to the goal. If he were discovered, opponents stomped on the victim's stomach until he coughed it up.[45]

Music played a role in precontact culture, and natives used several instruments, including drums, flutes, and rattles. Flutes were recorder-like instruments made of thick, hard cane; deep wooden platters and hollow logs covered with skins served as drums; while gourd or turtle shells filled with pebbles were made into rattles.[46] Natchez musicians in the eighteenth century reportedly used a banjo-like instrument, but whether this was indigenous or imported from Africa is unclear.[47] The singer, an important official in most ceremonies, sometimes accompanied by drums, rattles, and flutes, sang while villagers danced. But the lyrics and melodies of these early chants and songs for the most part have been lost.[48]

One of the most controversial questions is how numerous the Southern Indians were when whites arrived. A dense population suggests intensive agriculture, a high culture, and also a frightful population decline after contact. If the population was relatively sparse, it indicates that the mortality rate, though high because of exposure to new diseases, was not out of line with that of Europeans, who also were regularly swept away by pestilences. A small population made the question of appropriating native lands less bothersome, because if there were few Indians around, obviously there was room enough for everyone.

James Mooney, a distinguished anthropologist of the Bureau of American Ethnology at the Smithsonian Institution, made an intensive study of native population at the time of white contact of all the United States, including the South. He counted those tribes which had survived into the nineteenth century, along with the Occaneechee, Machapunga, Congaree, Mobile, Calusa, and others that for all practical purposes had become extinct. Mooney died in 1921, and his colleague John R. Swanton revised and refined Mooney's data and in 1928 published it.[49] No one but Mooney has so thoroughly studied the Southern Indian population, and his published findings, as slightly modified by Swanton, are a convenient and frequently the only source available. Historians and ethnologists have relied heavily on Mooney; American history textbooks, for example, have not deviated far from his estimates.

Despite Mooney's thoroughness, erudition, and prodigious scholarly contributions, there is a flaw in his method, because for the most part he did not start counting Indians until after 1600. He assumed that the destruction of the aborigines by De Soto and similar explorers was too early to document, and in any case the natives had probably recovered by the time of permanent English setttlement at Jamestown.[50] This view reflects both the paucity of sources and Mooney's ethnocentrism. Mooney in effect has written off a century of white—largely Spanish, but also English and French—contact with the Southern Indians and has implied that little of consequence happened to them before Jamestown. As will be discussed more fully in the next chapter, this is a fundamental error. From at least 1513 and possibly earlier, Europeans, accompanied by Africans, explored large parts of the South, repeatedly stopped along the Gulf and Atlantic coasts for wood and water or were shipwrecked, and in time established settlements over a wide area.

Taking this into account, one must conclude that Mooney's figures are far out of line and should be increased five, ten, or even twenty times. The key to the catastrophic sixteenth-century depopulation was pandemics set off by white and African newcomers. Mooney and his contemporaries recognized that new diseases wiped out multitudes of Indians, and the controversy is merely over the extent of this destruction. Since Mooney's death, scholars have been increasingly aware of the role diseases have played in the development of civilization, especially the appalling effect European and African contact had on the American natives. Unfortunately these specialists have emphasized regions in the New World outside the South.

Even so, it can be instructive to consider modern demographic studies of neighboring areas. Woodrow Borah and Sherburne Cook analyzed extant sixteenth-century Spanish records for the island of Hispaniola. They contend that the population of this island, containing the oldest European settlements in the New World, was almost four million in 1496 and only one hundred twenty-five in 1570.[51] Their findings for Central Mexico are similar: about twenty-five million in 1518 and slightly more than one million in 1608.[52] Studies of Indians in Brazil indicate a comparable abrupt population decline. The anthropologist Henry Dobyns has studied New World populations, and his conclusions generally agree with those of Borah and Cook. Dobyns assumes a New World depopulation ratio of twenty to one from the time of initial contact until a later era when native populations stabilized and began to revive. Unlike other scholars, Dobyns, at least to a limited extent, has studied the Southern Indians. His results suggest that the Powhatans in the Virginia Tidewater were the most densely populated of any in the South, and their depopulation ratio of twenty to one followed the Western Hemisphere norm. This means that Mooney's estimate of 8,500 to 9,000 should be increased to 170,000 and perhaps considerably more.[53] Considering the South as a whole, Dobyns calculates that in 1650, well over a century after contact, 1,357,000 Indians still survived.[54] Merely looking at the large number of aboriginal sites throughout the South recorded by archaeologists suggests the validity of a high population density.[55]

Dobyns's, Borah's, and Cook's results are based on sixteenth-century documents, comparative studies of the effects of virgin soil epidemics, native agricultural practices, soil fertility, and the theoretical population a given area could sustain. To a limited degree it is possible to corroborate such findings by casual observations of the earliest white explorers and colonists. Spanish chroniclers reported that an army of ten thousand Timucuans contested De Soto's passage through Florida and that up to seven thousand warriors assaulted him in Mabila.[56] Three thousand natives manned Chiaha on the upper Tennessee River against Juan Pardo.[57] Carlos's council house reputedly seated more than two thousand Indians "without being very crowded,"[58] and similar structures in Apalachee, Timucua, and Guale (coastal Georgia) held considerably more.[59] Supposedly Cofitachiqui contained at least five hundred houses, as did Caxa in Alabama and Ocale in Florida.[60]

At least some of these houses might hold twenty, fifty, or a hundred or more Indians, though the typical Mississippian dwelling was undoubtedly smaller. A Spanish missionary visited Tidewater Virginia in 1572, finding it even more populous than Carolina.[61] Yet the elderly Powhatan, not long after the founding of Jamestown, told the English he had seen the death of his people thrice in his lifetime and that none of his childhood companions was left.[62] The evidence is not conclusive and probably never will be, but it is apparent that more Indians first confronted the Europeans than is generally recognized.

New diseases, of course, were responsible for the depopulation. There is some question as to whether the Indians were friendly or hostile to Columbus and his contemporaries, but there is little debate that native bodies were gracious hosts to strange viruses and bacteria. For centuries, and for all practical purposes apparently forever, the American Indians had been isolated. Suddenly they were exposed to such scourges as smallpox, measles, chicken pox, scarlet fever, typhus, influenza, and whooping cough from Europe and malaria, yellow fever, and dengue fever from Africa. Over the years Old World inhabitants had built up immunity to many of these maladies, and in time they became less virulent "childhood diseases." But in America, where there was no immunity, the diseases raged with all their pristine fury. Their effect can be compared to the Black Death (bubonic and pneumonic plague), which in the fourteenth century reduced Europe's populace by almost one-third. The difference in America was that the Indians suddenly had to confront not just one alien disease but a variety of microparasites coming simultaneously from both Europe and Africa.

These facts, then, call Mooney's figures into question. Considering the United States in its entirety, his research discloses that Indian seminomadic hunters of the Plains and other Western Indians had a denser population than did the Southern agriculturalists, which may be correct for the eighteenth century. But the very fact that the Southern Indians were agriculturalists and lived in towns and villages made them all the more vulnerable to new diseases. Epidemics rapidly spread from one urban center to another, sweeping away a high percentage of the population. Smallpox, although in the 1970s finally eradicated throughout the world, at an earlier period was the greatest killer and one of the more loathsome diseases for the Indians. It was caused by a virus that spread from person to person in minute droplets expelled from mouth and nose. In the sixteenth century hardly ever was a European on hand to record the victims' high fevers, pains, and pus-filled blisters and the ensuing unprecedented mortality. But for the aborigines this and similar diseases were terrifying. For good reason Mooney did not find so many Southern Indians when he began counting.

If one accepts the higher population figures it is easier to recognize and appreciate the culture and civilization of the Southern Indians. By the time of contact they had not advanced as far as the Aztecs. The latter were literate to a limited extent, had a calendar more accurate than the Europeans had, were skilled in working gold, copper, and bronze, and had magnificent ceremonial centers and a well-organized empire. In the South the Queen of Cofitachiqui, Chief Carlos, or the Natchez Sun reckoned their subjects in the tens of thousands rather than millions; for all practical purposes the Southern Indians were nonliterate; their knowledge of metalworking did not extend beyond lead and copper; and their temple mounds, though individually quite large, did not rival the grandeur of those in the Valley of Mexico. The Southern Indians, along with those in the Greater Antilles, the Isthmus of Panama, and northern South America had achieved remarkable cultural advances and in time presumably would have moved on to the levels achieved by the Aztecs and Incas.[63] But Ponce de León, De Soto, and John Smith could not wait.

2
The Intruders

A mounted Castilian in armor or a ragged shipwreck survivor was usually the first European to startle Southern Indians. Spanish expeditions to what is now the United States are well known; to make the point one need look no further than the enormous literature of the De Soto expedition. The United States government in 1935 commissioned scholars to gather evidence for a definitive account of this Spanish undertaking. Sources unfortunately are limited, sometimes conflicting, causing specialists and chambers of commerce still to argue about the exact site of De Soto's landfall and his subsequent route.[1] Boosters in Memphis insist that De Soto crossed the Mississippi there, while those in Tallahassee, Florida, petitioned postal authorities to issue a stamp commemorating the first Christmas in the United States, celebrated near their city.[2] Ponce de León's quest for the fountain of youth in 1513 is a standard part of American folklore, and history texts seldom fail to note that St. Augustine, founded in 1565, became the oldest permanent settlement in the United States.

Despite widespread general knowledge about Spanish exploits

in the South, it is paradoxical that more often than not Spain's presence has been neglected or put out of mind by scholars and the general public. Twentieth-century Americans might do this, but sixteenth-century Southern Indians could not. During the century before Jamestown's founding in 1607 an increasing number of aborigines had the opportunity to see Europeans at first hand. These intruders were not necessarily all Spaniards. If accounts of English and other promoters are to be believed, John Cabot or his son Sebastian in the late 1490s skirted the Atlantic Coast from Newfoundland to the tip of Florida.[3] Sailing for France in the 1520s, Giovanni da Verrazzano came to North Carolina's Outer Banks, kidnapped an unsuspecting Indian from the Chesapeake Bay area, and described—the first European to do so—the aborigines of the Eastern Seaboard.[4] The number of Englishmen, Frenchmen, Dutch, and Portuguese visiting the South later on in the sixteenth century can be greatly expanded. Yet after taking this into consideration, the fact remains that when a Southern Algonquian, Muskhogean, Sioux, or Iroquois, looking up from his cornfield or gazing in the distance from atop a temple mound, saw a white foreigner approach, that intruder was usually a Spaniard.

Initial contacts between aborigines and whites were crucial, but unfortunately far less is known about European–Indian relations in the sixteenth century than later. Geographical misconceptions partly explain confusion and lack of appreciation of the Spanish influence. Modern readers sometimes assume when mention is made of Spanish exploits in Florida that the present-day state of Florida is meant, when in fact the area in question comprised Georgia, Virginia, Alabama, Mississippi, and possibly more. Sixteenth-century la Florida's boundaries stretched to Canada: Jacán (Tidewater Virginia) was a province of la Florida, as was Guale (coastal Georgia). For a few years Santa Elena (Port Royal, South Carolina) was the capital of an expansive la Florida. For whatever reason, the Spanish presence has been largely discounted. E. S. Morgan in his recent, and for the most part scholarly and discerning, book on colonial Virginia insists that Raleigh's failure at Roanoke Island in the 1580s at least made local Indians realize that Europeans were not gods.[5] This concept might have had validity concerning the Aztec perception of Cortez in 1519 but was time-worn and outdated by the 1580s. For well over half a century before Raleigh's time, North Carolina aborigines had had numerous contacts with Europeans; when English colonists eventually arrived, natives were not awestruck by large ships with billowy sails and bearded foreigners.

Throughout the sixteenth century Spain, not England or France, was the most active power in the New World, and it will be necessary to digress briefly and review what had been happening in Castile since 1492. Elation had swept the Iberian peninsula in that year as Ferdinand's and Isabella's troops captured Granada, the last Moorish outpost. In her enthusiasm the Queen, assisted by hopeful merchants, commissioned and outfitted Columbus's ships, and he began his momentous voyage, first making his way from Palos in southwestern Spain to the Canary Islands, which Castile had recently subdued. Sailing westward with the prevailing trade winds, Columbus began the most perilous part of his expedition, which after five weeks led to a landfall in the Bahamas. In his series of four voyages between 1492 and 1506 he explored most of the West Indian Islands, especially the Greater Antilles, examined the coastline of Central America and northern South America, and in 1496 founded Santo Domingo on Hispaniola, the oldest European settlement in the New World. Until his death Columbus maintained that he had reached the fringes of Cathay, that the seat of the Grand Khan could not be far off, and that he was justified in calling the natives Indians.

But when Columbus returned from his first voyage in 1493 there were those who suspected he had not sailed far enough west and that the Indians he brought back were entirely different from those described by Marco Polo. This touched off a squabble between the kingdoms of Castile and Portugal, because the latter, which previously had taken the lead in maritime expansion, felt that Isabella was encroaching on Portugal's preserve. To help settle this dispute the Pope intervened, issuing his famous bulls —four in 1493 and still another in 1506.[6] The net effect was to establish a north–south line of demarcation giving almost all of the New World to Spain.

The papal bulls were of great importance for Castile and Portugal, but other European countries, Catholic and Protestant alike, denounced or ignored them. They refused to concede that the Pope or anyone else had the right to parcel out the unknown world. Nevertheless the bulls, emphasizing that the foremost reason for Castilians to come to the New World was to convert the pagans, represented Castile's primary claim to America. Throughout the sixteenth century theologians, jurists, historians, friars, and administrators debated in Spanish courts, pulpits, and universities and before the monarch exactly what rights and prerogatives accompanied this charge to convert the aborigines. Bartolomé de las Casas, Antonio de Montesinos, Gines de Sepúlveda, and Francisco de Vitoria, among others, disputed whether the Indians had any title to the soil, whether they were naturally inferior, and whether if they refused to accept the beneficence of "lumbre y doctrina," Castilians could legally turn on them with fire and sword and enslave them.[7]

Controversies over interpretation of the papal bulls are but one manifestation of the role the Catholic Church played in lives of sixteenth-century Spaniards. When the Protestant revolt began in 1517, Castile remained the bulwark of orthodoxy, and her previous history helps exemplify her uniqueness. For seven centuries before Granada's fall, Castilians had waged the *reconquista*, almost a continuous crusade against Moors in the Iberian peninsula. Still very much alive in 1492, this crusading spirit was transferred to America as pagan Indians in a sense replaced the Moors. Other reasons beyond the *reconquista* explain Catholicism's dominant role. For centuries three religions had coexisted in Castile. In the sixteenth century the Christian majority perceived the two minority sects—Islam and Judaism—with some justification as threatening to their religious, economic, and political status. In response Catholics insisted that Jews and Moors adopt Christianity or leave and emphasized to an almost irrational degree *limpieza de sangre*—untainted Christian ancestry—as a requisite for holding office. Catholicism was associated with patriotism and national honor as never before. Officials at the Casa de Contratación, or House of Trade, established at Seville in 1503 went to great lengths to see that no heretic and no one of doubtful orthodoxy embarked for the New World. It was inevitable when Castilians arrived in the greater Florida and elsewhere in America that missionaries accompanied explorers, churches were raised immediately, and steps were taken to convert the heathen through force or reason.[8]

If surviving documents tell the true story, Castilians did not reach Florida until 1513, twenty-one years after Columbus's initial voyage. During those first two decades Castilians for the most part settled in the Greater Antilles. Santo Domingo was founded on Hispaniola, the largest of these islands. Before long other islands were occupied and new cities begun: San Juan, Puerto Rico, in 1511; New Seville, Jamaica, in 1509; and Santiago, Cuba, in 1511.

It is essential to be aware of Spain's experience in the West Indies if one is to interpret what happened later in Florida. The Antilles were important for two reasons. With a temperate climate, fertile soil, and at least some precious metals, they could be exploited in their own right like the Canary Islands. Whether the Antilles were on the fringes of Cathay or of some new continent, they provided a base for further explorations. Hispaniola, the most important island, affords the earliest documentary accounts of the Indians. Spaniards relied almost exclusively on aboriginal labor. In addition to domestic service, Indians tilled fields, which produced maize, cassava, or recently introduced wheat. Natives tended flocks of cattle and swine and panned for gold in streams, discovering just enough of the precious metal to whet Spanish appetites. Gold, hides, and tallow were shipped to Europe, while surplus foodstuffs were marketed locally. Indians were allotted to Spanish masters according to the *repartimiento*. At the outset, Columbus began this practice on his own authority, and in 1503 the crown gave its official approval. Theoretically there were reciprocal benefits: In return for labor and tribute, the natives received protection and conversion.[9]

As has been seen, microparasites introduced by whites and blacks were catastrophic for the aborigines. Earliest demographic estimates for Hispaniola reveal a dense population. The contemporary las Casas and such modern scholars as Cook and Borah estimate some four million in 1496. Four years earlier, at the time of Columbus's first voyage, Cook and Borah reckon the island's population as seven or eight million. Other estimates for just before 1500 are in the one million to two million range; the lowest is five hundred thousand. Despite the variance of early enumerations, there is little argument that long before 1600 the Arawakan-speaking Tainos had essentially disappeared.[10] For our purposes it does not make much difference whether the one million, four million, or even eight million estimate is correct. There is every indication that quick destruction of the Indians was repeated in the remaining Greater Antilles. The Cuban governor's 1530 report that one-third of the island's natives died "last year"[11] was probably as close to the mark as had been the dispatch from Hispanola in 1519 that a "grandisima enfermedad" had just swept away one-fourth of the island's populace.[12]

With certain modifications, demographic changes occurring in the Antilles were later duplicated in the South, and as the aborigines disappeared, whites and blacks in both areas took their place. Demands for a dependable source of labor along with concern over the plight of the natives were responsible for Spain's introducing African slaves into the West Indies soon after, if not before, 1500, and the new viruses and bacteria they brought with them accelerated aboriginal depopulation. In less than a century after 1492 the inhabitants of the Greater Antilles were Europeans and Africans. From the beginning a search for additional workers had spurred Spanish expansion throughout the West Indies. Spaniards captured natives from Cuba, Puerto Rico, and Jamaica, sending them back to Hispaniola, before long following up raids with permanent settlements. European newcomers even stripped the Bahamas, or Lucayos as they were called, bringing over thousands to Hispaniola and Cuba. Transplanted Lucayoans and those who remained behind quickly died, and the Bahamas, like the Greater Antilles, were soon depopulated.[13]

Ponce de León, Florida's discoverer, was almost as much a West Indian as an Iberian. Having come to Hispaniola in 1493, he had spent most of his adult life in the islands, in 1511 founding San Juan and for a period serving as governor of the entire island of Puerto Rico. It was Ponce who named Florida in 1513; as far as the documents clearly show, it was he who discovered this land. There are suspicions that Ponce was not the first Spaniard to set foot in Florida. In his general history or chronicle of the Spanish Indies, Antonio de Herrera y Tordesillas, writing in the late sixteenth and early seventeenth centuries, relates that when Ponce arrived at Charlotte Harbor on the Gulf side of the Florida peninsula, a Spanish-speaking Indian greeted him.[14] This native might have previously escaped from a passing Spanish ship or come from the Antilles on his own. Archaeological and linguistic evidence discloses numerous pre-Columbian contacts between the Greater Antilles and Florida. Herrera's Indian easily could have piloted his dugout canoe over to Hispaniola and back again. This native also might have accompanied West Indian slave raiders who had come to Florida before 1513. All this, of course, is speculation.

What is clear is that the veteran Ponce sailed over to Florida to capture slaves, not that he did not want to find a fountain of youth and discover precious metals. But a cargo of Indians would make his voyage, as a close reading of his royal commission discloses. He was authorized to make war if necessary on aborigines in the Lucayos, allocating them to himself and his associates. Florida was erroneously regarded as just another island, and the term Lucayos (or Bimini) frequently included Florida. It was some years before this geographical misconception was cleared up, and even after it was, Spaniards frequently referred to "la isla Florida."[15]

Sailing along the Florida coast from the vicinity of Jacksonville on the east to Charlotte Harbor on the west, Ponce was not successful in his 1513 voyage, having little more than a handful of Indians, some of whom were to be trained as interpreters, to show for his efforts. He set out for Castile to secure another commission authorizing him and his associates to exploit *la Florida*. Despite the flowery rhetoric, it was clear he was still after slaves. Upon returning to Florida he was to read the requirement to the aborigines three times. Expounding on the Petrine theory and papal donation, the Spanish rulers in 1512 had decreed that pagans must submit to Christian authority and receive religious instruction. If they refused, Castilians could wage a just war and enslave them. The crown would get its share, the royal fifth, of all such chattels.[16] Before setting out on his second voyage, Ponce denounced Spanish interlopers for illegally appropriating his pagans.[17] He eventually returned to Florida in 1521, but when he opened his just war against the Calusa, they impertinently waged their own and killed him. By the time of Ponce's death it was obvious that "la isla Florida" was part of an enormous land mass. The civilization and riches of the Mississippian interior, however, remained a mystery.

Lucas Vásquez de Ayllón was the first to follow Ponce to the greater Florida. Arriving at Hispaniola in 1502, the Licentiate Ayllón had risen rapidly in the civil service, had been awarded hundreds of Indians in *repartimiento* to work his plantations and mines, and had seen at first hand the dying off of his own and the island's natives. It was as clear to him as to other aspiring Spaniards that a dependable labor supply was essential in order to make one's fortune. In 1520, before completion of Cortez's great triumphs over the Aztecs, Ayllón commissioned Francisco Gordillo to sail to the northerly part of *la Florida*, and Gordillo

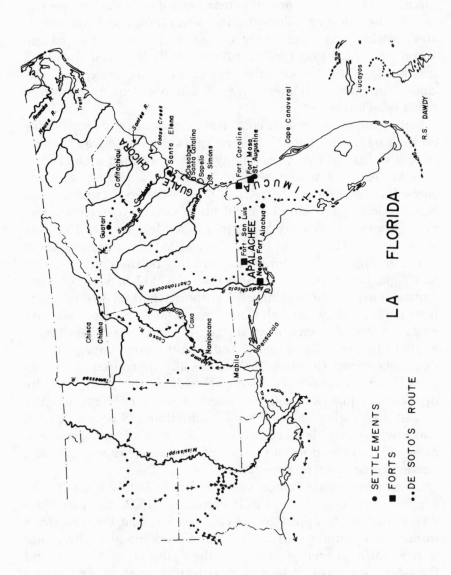

explored the Atlantic Coast from approximately Santa Elena to Chesapeake Bay. Making a slaving voyage on his own in the West Indies, Pedro de Quexós in time joined Gordillo, and together they landed on the Carolina coast at or in the vicinity of Pawley's Island. Remaining in this land, which they called Chicora, for some weeks, they examined at least part of the interior, though how far inland they penetrated is uncertain. Eventually they departed with almost one hundred and fifty previously unsuspecting natives imprisoned below deck. A hot dispute greeted the Spaniards in Hispaniola. Influenced by the polemics of Las Casas and other Dominicans, the crown insisted that these peaceful aborigines had been illegally enslaved, and Ayllón publicly concurred, swearing that Gordillo had exceeded his instructions. The outcome of this controversy, which dragged on for years, is unknown. For most of the Indians it made little difference, because they soon died; the last glimpses of survivors show them still in the possession of Ayllón, who continued to deplore their illegal capture. But considering it better for Indians to be "slave men" rather than remain "free beasts," Ayllón was really not so distressed.[18]

Chicora, this more northerly province of *la Florida*, was part of the coastal area of the two Carolinas. An Indian brought to Hispaniola who survived was Francisco Chicora. Ayllón taught Francisco Spanish, took him to Spain—where with great ceremony he was baptized—and pointed out to the King that Francisco was but the first of thousands to be rescued from paganism. Charles I was impressed and granted Chicora, along with other coastal provinces, to Ayllón. The royal concession in most respects was typical: Ayllón was to explore these provinces, search for a Northwest Passage, found towns, establish civil government, and take special care of the Indians' spiritual and physical well-being. With Hispaniola's experience in mind, the King decreed that the aborigines be not arbitrarily distributed by *repartimiento* but paid wages for voluntary labor. Those captured in a just war, however, could still be enslaved.[19] Francisco had described Chicora, perhaps thinking of the high Mississippian civilization of Cofitachiqui, as populous and opulent. Whether free or slave, workers enough sufficed for Ayllón and his backers to make their fortunes in producing foodstuffs and naval stores, establish a silk industry, and collect pearls.

Soon after receiving his grant in 1523, Ayllón returned to Hispaniola, where news of Spanish successes in Mexico made him eager to set out. But interruptions repeatedly delayed the departure of his expedition until 1526. In the interval he dispatched ships to reconnoiter further, and again they explored the coast, including Chicora, apparently the Bahía de Santa María (Chesapeake Bay), and perhaps even farther north. Spaniards picked up Indians from Chicora, Xapiracta, Auricatuye, Cayo, Xoxi, Nuaq, Ouxa, Anoxa, and other coastal provinces of *la Florida* in the Carolinas and perhaps Georgia and Virginia, bringing these unwilling passengers to Hispaniola for training as interpreters. Finally all was in readiness. With seven ships, some five hundred men, one hundred women and Negroes, eighty-nine horses, and Francisco Chicora and the other interpreters, the expedition departed. Ayllón's force was almost the size of the one Cortez had commanded when he set out to conquer Mexico, and Ayllón had in his party five times the number of people the English had when they later founded Jamestown.

Sixteenth-century navigators calculated latitude with reasonable accuracy, and it appears likely that Ayllón sailed to either the Cape Fear River or the Santee River, one or the other which might have been known as the River Jordan. This was Francisco's homeland, but he was not of much service because he immediately ran off. The other interpreters' fates are unknown, but it seems clear that they had little desire to substitute Jehovah for the sun, corn mother, and animal deities. The enterprise did not prosper: A provision ship wrecked and sank, and Ayllón died after an extended sickness. Survivors relocated to the south, presumably not far from the future George Town, South Carolina, where misfortune continued. Those who had not succumbed to disease, drowning, or Indian warfare after a few months returned downcast to Hispaniola, and Spain relinquished its tenuous hold over Chicora and neighboring provinces.[20]

Hardly any accounts tell exactly what the Spaniards did in their relations with the aborigines. But enough documentation has survived to make it clear that each learned a good deal about the other. Mariners sent out by Ayllón and Francisco and other Indian interpreters disclosed much about the land, and Spaniards saw at first hand large circular council houses and square grounds in coastal villages. It is not known how far inland Spanish foot soldiers or horsemen penetrated, but some of them must have seen the temple mounds and the more impressive interior towns with their caches of pearls. One reason for hostilities was the hungry Spaniards' practice of appropriating maize stored in aboriginal granaries. Despite Ayllón's failure, enough was learned about the villages and civilization of Chicora and adjoining provinces to tantalize the Spaniards further, even if accounts of giants and men with tails were not true.

For hundreds of miles along the Atlantic Coast and a considerable distance into the interior, Indians discovered a good deal about these newcomers. It is possible only to speculate about the aboriginal reaction to horses, armor, firearms, and manufactures introduced by foreigners, who were usually white but sometimes black. One can only wonder about what Indians, in their deliberations in the square ground or council house, thought about accounts of Spanish civilization in Hispaniola and Castile. Natives had seen European ships long before Ayllón ever set foot ashore at Chicora in 1526. Documents and archaelogical evidence disclose that Spanish slavers had cruised along the coast and that some of them, as well as other vessels, had been shipwrecked.

One indication of this is that early in the sixteenth century the Southern aborigines began to use silver. After salvaging wrecks, local craftsmen shaped silver coins and jewelry into pendants, gorgets, and beads, and in time these articles spread over the interior in the same fashion that columnella pendants, made from the columnella and terminal whorl of large conchs, previously had been widely disseminated, becoming a typical ceremonial object of the Southeastern Ceremonial Complex. It is possible that some silver had made its way into the South from Mexico or that the Southern aborigines had mined it themselves. Evidence, however, strongly favors the wrecks.[21] All of this means that Alonquians, Siouans, Muskhogeans, and Iroquoians living by the ocean and inland knew a great deal about the Europeans before Ayllón and his horses arrived. Whether Spanish, English, Dutch, French, or Portuguese, many, and probably most, ships sailing along the coast were not large cargo ships but small decked caravels, with a crew of from fewer than twenty to forty or more men. They obviously differed from aboriginal oceangoing dugouts, some of which were lashed together in catamaran fashion. It should be kept in mind, however, that these caravels were inordinately cramped, by modern standards seeming little larger than rowboats. The natives may not have been as awed as has been generally presumed.[22]

In 1526, three years after Ayllón received his patent for Chicora and neighboring provinces, the crown granted his rival, Pánfilo de Narváez, the Gulf coast portion of *la Florida*, that is, the region between the Río de las Palmas (Mexico) and the peninsula itself. Narváez could enslave pagans captured in war and purchase those who already were bona fide slaves of other Indians; unlike Ayllón, Narváez could also distribute natives in *repartimiento*.[23] Having been with Cortez in Mexico, unsuccessfully trying to supplant him, Narváez had seen the Aztec wealth of Tenochtitlán at first hand. When he came to *la Florida* his sights were set higher than on just the aborigines. With a party of four hundred, including soldiers, colonists, and a sprinkling of women and Negroes, almost all recruited in Castile, Narváez sailed to the West Indies, and in 1528 he landed at or in the vicinity of Tampa Bay. Indians, who had had unpleasant contacts with Spaniards for almost a decade and a half, stayed away as much as possible.

Narváez's sharp eye detected gold, which presumably had been obtained in trade with Mexico or from Spanish wrecks. Natives asserted they got it from Apalachee, a bountiful province many miles to the north. In these early years Apalachee's bounds were far more extensive than later, initially extending inland to include a large part of the Appalachian Mountains. And there was gold in those mountains. Before the 1849 California gold rush the center of gold mining in the United States was at Dahlonega, Georgia, where the national government founded a mint. Possibly Indians around Tampa told Narváez the truth about Apalachee, but more evidence is required to be certain. Archaeologists so far have disclosed that precontact aboriginal metallurgical knowledge did not extend beyond copper and lead, making it as risky to assume that Mississippians were working gold as were their contemporaries in Meso-America and South America.

What is important for the moment is not whether the Southern aborigines had gold but that Narváez thought they did. He split his command at Tampa: Soldiers marched overland northward while supplies were forwarded by sea to a rendezvous in Apalachee Bay. Narváez proved no more successful than had Ayllón. Timucuans and Apalachees fled or contested his passage; supply ships could not find Narváez; and the Indians had temple mounds, towns, and fields of maize, but no gold. Retiring to the coast, Narváez built makeshift boats to take his party to Mexico, all the while fighting the Apalachees and confiscating as much maize from them as possible. The Spaniards finally set sail but were lost at sea or killed by coastal Indians except for Cabeza de Vaca, the Negro Estéban, and a few others who survived for years in Louisiana and Texas. Cabeza and two Spaniards eventually reached Mexico to recount the disaster.[24]

Hernando de Soto became the most famous of all conquistadors to march across *la Florida*'s interior. Having served as Pizarro's lieutenant in Peru, he, like Narváez, had seen with his own eyes the wealth of the Indies. His share of the Inca booty helped De Soto obtain a grant to Florida, which included both the region on the Atlantic Coast formerly awarded to Ayllón and Narváez's area on the Gulf. De Soto assumed that somewhere another Inca empire lay in the interior, and the many provisions of his *asiento* or royal grant dealt primarily with booty and the distribution of Indians rather than conversion.[25] With some six hundred men and more than two hundred horses he sailed first to Cuba and then to the vicinity of Tampa Bay. Following Narváez's route up the Florida peninsula and wintering in Apalachee, he then struck out northward to Cofitachiqui, westward to present-day Alabama, and across the Mississippi into Arkansas before finally dying and being buried in the Mississippi River.

Both Ayllón's and Narváez's descriptions of *la Florida*'s interior are incomplete or nonexistent. As a result of the De Soto *entrada*, however, for the first time posterity gets a glimpse of the Mississippian maize culture of the heartland. De Soto's chroniclers described how they rode horses up broad steps to the tops of temple mounds, stooped to go through small entrances into large council houses, parleyed with the aborigines outside fortified towns or in square grounds, and saw, in addition to the productive fields, peltry, pearls, feather work, grotesque wood carvings, and other works of art. To be sure, accounts do not always agree, and some are more detailed than others. Despite hardships and failure, De Soto's survivors retained an appreciation for the Mississippian culture and wealth, recognizing that God had smiled more on fertile, gently rolling, extensive *la Florida* than on arid, windswept Castile. This vision continued to motivate Spaniards until they finally made a permanent settlement in Florida—and for many years afterward.[26]

La Florida's potential and strategic position inspired the Mexican viceroy to send still another expedition. Tristán de Luna with fifteen hundred men, women, and Negro slaves was to make two settlements, one at Pensacola on the Gulf and the other at Santa Elena (Port Royal) on the Atlantic. These two ports were to protect shipping routes and become the nuclei of profitable colonies. His undertaking, Spain's largest up to that time anywhere in America, proved no more successful than his predecessors'. After landing at Pensacola a large party moved forty leagues into the interior, appropriating the Indian town of Nanipacana on the Alabama River. From here, to some extent following De Soto's footsteps, soldiers revisited Alabama towns whose populations were smaller, searched for the pearls and furs De Soto's survivors had described, and assisted friendly Indians in wars against their enemies. But lack of supplies, disease, internal bickering, and native hostility took their toll. The Spaniards withdrew from Nanipacana and before long from Pensacola. The feeble attempt by Ángel de Villafañe, Luna's successor, to make a settlement on the Atlantic Coast at Santa Elena bore no fruit. By the end of 1561 it was apparent that the high expectations of 1559 had come to nought; Spain still had no settlement anywhere in *la Florida*.[27]

The Mexican viceroy was disappointed, because maritime routes connecting New Spain with the mother country remained exposed. Wind, currents, and royal decrees all prescribed that ships going to and from the Indies follow specified courses, and it is necessary to take a closer look at them because of their considerable effect on the Southern Indians. Spain's mercantilistic regulations decreed that ships sail from Spain south to the Canary Islands, where they picked up westerly trade winds to carry them into the Caribbean. Here the convoy divided, part going to the monopoly port of Nombre de Díos and the rest to Vera Cruz. After completion of the trade fairs, which involved most of the commerce of New Spain and Peru, returning ships assembled at Havana and then, propelled through the Bahama Channel by the Gulf Stream, sailed along the coast to the Carolinas, where westerly winds returned them to Spain. Ships coming from Vera Cruz to the Havana rendezvous frequently sailed close by the Gulf Coast. From the sixteenth century on Spanish ships regularly were wrecked on Florida's Atlantic and Gulf coasts, while others sought refuge from storms or sent parties ashore for wood and water.[28]

Paying little attention to Spain's exclusive claim to the Indies, French, English, and other foreign vessels encroached in increas-

ing numbers. Prevailing winds and currents dictated that interlopers also follow these same general routes. Raleigh's expedition
to Roanoke Island sailed through the West Indies before the Gulf
Stream carried his ships northward; and the *Susan Constant, Discovery*, and *Godspeed*, bringing English settlers to Jamestown,
followed approximately the same course. Spaniards in 1611 sent
a vessel to Chesapeake Bay. When its commander told English
colonists he was searching for a wrecked galleon, he was not
telling the truth.[29] Nevertheless, it is significant that in 1611, or
at any time in the sixteenth century, it was not unusual to expect
a shipwreck in Chesapeake Bay, off Cape Hatteras or Cape Cana-
veral, or anywhere along the Atlantic Coast.

After Columbus's voyage European mariners confronted
Southern aborigines who frequently welcomed the appearance
of a strange sail. A French (or possibly English) ship returning
home in 1546 briefly stopped at upper Florida in the vicinity of
Chesapeake Bay, and immediately thirty canoes containing fifteen to twenty Indians each set out to barter.[30] After Spaniards
in 1570 established a mission in Jacán, Powhatans began exchanging ears of corn for European manufactures.[31] One reason
Raleigh never ascertained the fate of his Roanoke colony was that
the vessels he dispatched to look for it spent more time trading
with the Carolina Indians than searching for survivors.[32]

The aborigines were delighted when news arrived of a European shipwreck. The vessel might be a small caravel on an ex-
ploring mission or an unwieldy galleon returning to Spain with
the wealth of the Indies and two hundred or more passengers
and crewmen. Centuries before 1492 Indians had perfected an
extensive commercial network, and now hardware, glass, textiles, and gold and silver from these wrecks made their way into
interior Mississippian towns. An untold number of Spaniards
survived storms, finding refuge ashore. The fate of almost all is
unknown or remains buried in obscure documents, though
sometimes a figure such as Hernando de Escalante Fontaneda
emerges. If his account is to be trusted, he was wrecked in the
mid-sixteenth century in southern Florida and lived for seven-
teen years among the Calusa and their neighbors. Again and
again he refers to Spaniards who had been wrecked and were
held prisoners by the natives.[33] One of the reasons Pedro Menéndez de Avilés, the founder of St. Augustine, was so anxious to
settle and explore the greater Florida was that his son had been

lost on a return voyage to Europe, and Menéndez vainly hoped he was still alive among the Indians.[34]

An enterprising scholar with a statistical or cliometric bent might ransack Spanish, English, French, and Dutch archives, estimating the number of sixteenth-century wrecks and their survivors. This figure might be compared with the more easily reckoned total of European explorers and colonists who are known to have come to *la Florida* in this same century. The latter figure is not likely to exceed ten thousand.[35] Data for the number of shipwreck survivors are simply not available, but there are many indications that it was greater than ten thousand. This of course does not include the many mariners who of their own volition put in at Florida ports for repairs and supplies. After the English founded Jamestown, rumors abounded of blond, blue-eyed Indians to the south. It was assumed then, as it generally still is today, that they must have come from Raleigh's Lost Colony. But shipwreck survivors or sailors who did more than cut firewood and fill water casks can just as easily account for blue-eyed Indians.

Fifty-two years after Ponce de León's discovery, Spain made a permanent settlement in *la Florida*. Menéndez led more than a thousand soldiers, farmers, artisans, their wives, and Negroes to America, in 1565 founding St. Augustine. In the beginning it was no more than a military base from which to attack the thousand or so French Huguenots who had fortified Fort Caroline just to the north on the St. Johns River. Fortune smiled on Menéndez, who at first captured the fort and subsequently Jean Ribault and his soldiers. They previously had left Fort Caroline to attack Menéndez but unfortunately had been shipwrecked below St. Augustine. Perhaps a score of Frenchmen not killed or who did not escape to French ships fled to Timucuan and other neighboring Indians. In the ensuing months many turned themselves in, agreeing to serve Menéndez as interpreters in return for their lives. Repeatedly returning to the Georgia and South Carolina areas, French and also English mariners for the balance of the sixteenth century continued to trade with, live among, and intrigue with the natives. More is known about late-sixteenth-century contact with the Indians here than elsewhere.

Even before realizing they had to deal with the French at Fort Caroline, Menéndez and his backers expected to settle and exploit *la Florida*, and the *adelantado*'s *asiento* superseded those of

Luna, De Soto, and other predecessors. His Florida, like theirs, extended almost to Canada, and he and his associates thought in ambitious terms. From one or both of the principal settlements at Santa Elena and Jacán, Spaniards could exploit the hinterland, perhaps even find a Northwest Passage. As it turned out, Santa Elena became *la Florida's* main port and for a time even the capital of the province. After expulsion of the French Huguenots, St. Augustine, with only a mediocre harbor and sandy, relatively unproductive soil, declined in significance.[36] From Santa Elena soldiers and missionaries trekked into the interior, partly retracing De Soto's footsteps. Captain Juan Pardo marched more than 700 miles, planting at least five garrisons in the Carolina back country and on the western side of the mountains. Accompanying Pardo, Jesuits established at least one mission, that being at Guatari on the Saluda River in the heartland of Cofitachiqui, and possibly others. For six years Father Sebastian Montero lived among the pagans, teaching them Spanish and the rudiments of Christianity.

Menéndez envisioned a road dotted with missions and blockhouses stretching from Santa Elena to Mexico. If this seems fantastic, one must keep in mind the successes of Cortez, the Pizarros, and their contemporaries.[37] In addition to missions at Santa Elena, Guatari, Jacán, and Guale, Jesuits founded others on the Florida peninsula at Charlotte Harbor, Miami, and elsewhere. Yet by 1572 they were abandoned, and the Jesuits themselves retired from *la Florida,* soon to be replaced by Franciscans. In 1586 the garrison at Santa Elena was withdrawn and moved to St. Augustine, the bustling town of Santa Elena reverting to just another mission guarded by a few soldiers. Spain also gave up her posts in the back country and on the coast north of Santa Elena. Nevertheless, through scattered missions and blockhouses; the exploits of Menéndez, De Soto, Ayllón, and others; and mariners who were shipwrecked or voluntarily came ashore, sixteenth-century Spaniards made an enormous impact on the Southern Indians—and not just on those who lived near the coast.

Not all the foreigners were Spaniards or even Europeans. As has been mentioned, Negroes appeared in the New World almost as soon as whites. They accompanied Ayllon and Narváez in the 1520s. Some escaped from De Soto in 1540, vanishing in Cofitachiqui.[38] One was shipwrecked on the Florida peninsula with

Escalante in mid-century,[39] and seven Negroes in 1603 ran away from St. Augustine, some keeping their freedom and marrying Indian women.[40] After the Franciscans arrived in Florida they repeatedly admonished the aborigines that it was an unclean thing to keep Negro mistresses.[41] Both blacks and whites introduced the killer smallpox, but Negroes were primarily responsible for unleashing malaria and yellow fever. On balance, African microparasites seemed more destructive than European ones.

Both shared responsibility for the frightful destruction of the aborigines. For example, Cabeza de Vaca, accompanied by the Negro Estéban, wandered throughout Louisiana and Texas in the late 1520s and early 1530s, noting that perhaps one-half of the local Indians died. Panicked natives blamed Cabeza, assuming that since he caused the disease he must have been able to cure it. They brought their chief to him, making it clear that if their leader died so would Cabeza. He was no doctor and had no cure, but Cabeza did not let the aborigines in on the secret. Natives passed this white "doctor" around; fervently chanting and praying, he miraculously cured the sick, and this was partly responsible for Cabeza's survival.[42] When De Soto came to Florida in 1539 the Calusas had already been depleted, and to the north settlements and temple mounds at Crystal River had been abandoned.[43] We can only speculate that disease was the cause. Upon reaching the heart of Cofitachiqui, De Soto saw that Talomeco, one of the principal towns, containing five hundred houses, lay deserted, the few native survivors refusing to return home. Soldiers silently rummaged through the town and temple, marveling at the copper artifacts, wood carvings, and implements of war and appropriating a portion of the pearls.[44] The pestilence that had recently swept away most natives could have been introduced by Narváez or Ayllón or by shipwrecks. There is another possibility. Spanish chroniclers reported that in 1530 a plague carried off one-half of Mexico City's aboriginal population. By land or in oceangoing canoes, terrified survivors might have fled and infested Cofitachiqui.[45] Whatever the origin, a plague had devastated the chiefdom even before De Soto arrived to impress Indians and carry off pearls.

By the time St. Augustine was founded, most of Cuba's aboriginal population had vanished, and long before 1565 Spaniards had tried to sustain the island's disappearing populace with infusions of Indians from *la Florida*. Menéndez not only established

St. Augustine and Santa Elena but at the same time also was active in Cuban affairs, including the fortifying of Havana. Aware of the island's labor shortage, he advocated enslaving recalcitrant Florida Indians and transporting them to Cuba or other West Indian islands. Spanish masters were to Christianize these workers, while the financially pressed *adelantado* could reap a tidy profit.[46]

Before and after Menéndez's time Florida Indians arrived in Cuba either against their will or voluntarily, as in the case of the Calusas, who made the voyage in their dugouts. These natives died off about as fast as had the Cuban aborigines. Menéndez saw this at first hand. While making peace with the warlike Calusas, Menéndez, as part of the overall conciliation, married Doña Antonia, Chief Carlos's sister. She and her attendants returned with the *adelantado* to Havana, where most of them expired, and the distraught Doña Antonia begged to be sent back before it was too late.[47] Menéndez forwarded other Florida Indians to Spain, where they were baptized with great pomp in Seville's massive Gothic cathedral. Unfortunately they too succumbed.[48] A few aborigines brought to Cuba by force returned home. In their many wars with the Spaniards Florida Indians had captured a number of whites who in time were exchanged for those Indians who had been carried off to Cuba.[49] Incomplete and skimpy as it is, the evidence indicates that Florida—that is, Southern—Indians were killed off almost as rapidly as those in the West Indies. *La Florida's* size and the fact that whites and blacks were less numerous on the mainland provided some protection. It is doubtful, however, that Southern aborigines appreciated their good fortune.

Spain's principal method of dealing with the Florida natives was through the missions. Mendicant orders flourished in Spain and, roused by the Protestant threat, attempted with renewed zeal to stamp out heresy and win over pagans. Approximately one out of every twenty-five Spaniards was a member of the regular or secular clergy. Columbus's discoveries made Dominicans, Franciscans, and Jesuits eager to come to America to spread the faith and enhance the effectiveness and prestige of their respective orders. Missionaries accompanied conquistadors when they marched across *la Florida*, and occasionally padres came on their own. It was not until after St. Augustine's founding that they could show much for their labors. Taking the broad view, it can be seen that Spain established two major mission chains: one stretching hundreds of miles along the Atlantic Coast and the other centering in the province of Apalachee.

The Atlantic coastal chain, close by the Gulf Stream, was in the regions explored by Ponce de León, Ayllón, and Villafañe. Most of the missions lay north of St. Augustine, but a few dotted the coastline to the south. The most northerly one was at Jacán, where between 1570 and 1572 nine Jesuits futilely attempted to win over the Powhatans. In those early years after 1565 Santa Elena was *la Florida*'s capital, in many respects containing Spain's most important mission. Menéndez envisioned building a road from Santa Elena, which had Florida's best port, to Mexico. As has been seen, Jesuits for at least six years planted one or more missions in the South Carolina back country on or in the vicinity of this road. Coastal missions and the ones in South Carolina's interior at least superficially brought the Christian message to tens of thousands of Mississippians. That is not to say that they suddenly exchanged worship of the eagle and corn mother for Jehovah. Jesuits and Franciscans alike realized that to convert these pagans considerable time was necessary—like a stream of water relentlessly wearing against a rock.[50] Within a decade after 1565, missions in the South Carolina back country, at Jacán, and with few exceptions on both sides of the peninsula south of St. Augustine were abandoned. As a result for most of the sixteenth century the Atlantic Coast chain of missions stretched from just below St. Augustine 200 miles north to Santa Elena. Spain established these missions at existing towns on coastal islands or near the mouths of rivers, where she maintained easy water communications. After Spaniards arrived, coastal Indian towns became relatively more populous and important.[51] Disruption of traditional Mississippian life in the interior caused some natives to move to the coast for protection. The aboriginal culture and life-style were modified. A large hewn wooden cross now stood out as prominently as the ball pole in the square ground. Wattle-and-daub churches and similar religious structures took their places not far from the council house and temple mound, while missionaries regularly catechized and instructed their charges.

Spain did not begin establishing her second great mission system (concentrated in the province of Apalachee) until the 1630s, well after the founding of Jamestown. In Apalachee, as along the

Atlantic Coast, the padres settled in or near existing towns. The peak of Franciscan effectiveness came in the 1670s. Some twenty smaller missions radiated from the principal mission and fort at San Luis (Tallahassee), and a road, dotted with additional *doctrinas* and *visitas,* connected this province with St. Augustine.[52]

Few indications remain today of the Apalachee and Atlantic Coast missions and of the neophytes who came forward to kiss the cross, recite the Hail Mary and Creed, and receive the sacraments. Pestilence, and to a lesser extent warfare and enslavement, destroyed the aborigines. A handful of surviving Christian Indians abandoned Florida in 1763, retiring with the Spaniards to Cuba or Mexico; those few remaining in Florida in all likelihood were absorbed by the emerging Seminoles. When Americans arrived in California during the nineteenth century missions were very much in evidence, but none greeted Americans who came to Florida in that same century. This should not obscure the fact that each of Florida's mission chains had flourished for longer than the one in California. Having been founded a century and a half to two centuries earlier, their day had long passed when American settlers arrived in Apalachee in the 1820s. The tendency has been to forget that they existed.

Contemporary Southern Indians could not ignore these missions. In many respects a more appropriate question is not why the Franciscans ultimately failed but why they were successful for such a long period. Spain's grasp on *la Florida* during the First Spanish Period (1565–1763) was weak. Her garrison, averaging three hundred to four hundred men, was scattered among St. Augustine, Apalachee, Pensacola (after 1698), and smaller outposts. The soldiers were not the flower of the Spanish army and had not volunteered to come to Florida. Spanish Florida's total non-Indian population was in the neighborhood of four thousand souls. Whatever their number at a particular time, natives vastly outnumbered Spaniards. Spain did not usually require Indians to move to a mission; instead it was established in or close to an existing town. Occasionally Spanish garrisons were on hand, such as at Santa Elena, Santa Catalina (St. Catherines Island), and San Luis (Tallahassee). More often than not no soldiers were about, just one or more Franciscans representing Spain in the *doctrinas.* Smaller *visitas* had no resident missionary.

Surviving documents and archeological excavations disclose a great deal about the layout and construction of these missions.

The assorted buildings—chapel, storehouse, living quarters for the Franciscans, and kitchen—had wattle-and-daub walls and thatched roofs. A wattle-and-daub or perhaps a more substantial wall enclosed the entire complex. Spaniards and Indians both had lived in walled towns before contact, and missions reflected a blending of Mediterranean and aboriginal characteristics. With traditional and European tools, natives built the chapels, living quarters, walls, and large crosses, and they fetched basketloads of red clay, which, mixed with water, was poured to make floors. Perhaps using new iron hoes and shovels, Indian farmers provided Franciscans with food. The labor required to build and sustain a mission was considerable, and, at least to all appearances, the new converts worked voluntarily. Hardly ever was a Spanish soldier brandishing a musket on hand to drive the natives.

There are several explanations of why to a large degree natives built and lived in the missions of their own volition. Foremost was the shock and disruption to Mississippian culture caused by pandemics. Indians recognized that Spaniards did not die off so rapidly. When natives watched their families and friends expire and saw traditional values and practices being questioned, there was the clear implication that maybe the missionaries were right and aboriginal priests in error: Perhaps the European god was more powerful. Without too much difficulty pantheistic Southern Indians could absorb another god into their pantheon, particularly if he could save them from smallpox. At the earliest period the padres reported that Indians fervently came forward to kiss the newly erected cross. The cross itself was an aboriginal motif, identified with the Southeastern Ceremonial Complex, the sun, the sacred fire, and the giver of life. Dismayed natives may have felt that missionaries knew better how to placate this inscrutable giver of life and that their own priests had led them astray.

Another attraction of the missions was that through them natives acquired European manufactures. Although Indians had some knowledge of metal, and the technological gap between them and the Europeans was not as great as is frequently portrayed—English yeomen wielding longbows as late as 1346 won the battle of Crécy, for example—nevertheless Indians held in high esteem European knives, hatchets, hoes, spades, carpentry tools, hardware, textiles, guns, and munitions. Franciscans made it clear that manufactures, except for guns, which were illegal throughout America, were available if natives agreed to take instruction and to work for the mission. Florida Indians soon draped themselves in European blankets and skirts, began tilling their fields with iron hoes, and by the latter part of the seventeenth century, because of the danger on the Atlantic Coast and in Apalachee, even legally acquired guns.[53] Missions also provided a measure of security. A wall enclosed them, and Spanish soldiers, mounted or on foot, usually were not many miles away and occasionally were stationed at the mission itself. Fear of retaliation by Indians and Spaniards combined deterred enemies who threatened Christian Indians.

One must not overlook the pious example set by Franciscans to explain in part why the aborigines were drawn to mission life. The padres left the relative comforts of a Castilian monastery to spread the gospel in an unknown land. Difficulties and hardships confronted them, though recent archaeological finds suggest that on balance mission life was not as primitive as had been thought. But there were challenges enough, not the least of which was the diversity of languages. After Spain abandoned Jacán and the South Carolina back country, the number of languages decreased. Franciscans mastered various tongues of the greater Southeast, especially Timucuan and Apalachee. Knowledge of these extinct tribes survives in part through their languages, which, thanks to the Franciscans, have been preserved.

The most notable linguist was Father Francisco Pareja, who ministered to Timucuans in the late sixteenth and early seventeenth centuries. His dedication and that of his contemporaries gave renewed vigor to Spanish efforts to expand coastal missions north of St. Augustine. Pareja learned Timucuan and, while Englishmen struggled to found Jamestown, published a number of works in Mexico City, including *Cathecismo, en Lengua Castellana, y Timvqvana* (1612), *Confessionario en Lengua Castellana y Timvqvana* (1613), and *Arte y Pronunciacion en Lengua Timvqvana y Castellana* (1614).[54] Aside from their linguistic merits, his writings reveal a good deal about the aborigines and Franciscans alike. The latter were obsessed with sex. An inordinate amount of the *Confessionario* contains admonitions against sodomy, premarital sex, bigamy, and miscegenation. From all that is known about sixteenth-century Mississippians they had other things on their minds as well. Pareja's *Arte de la Lengua Timvqvana*, 152 pages long, included rules for conjugating verbs, grammar, pro-

nunciation, and copious sample phrases in Castilian and Timucuan. This was a remarkable work, and before long Timucuans
and other natives were reading, writing, and singing in choral
groups. Supposedly Timucuans with only two months' instruction began writing each other in their own language.[55] No scholarly Pareja lived among the Apalachee, but after Spain
established missions there, Franciscans became proficient in that
language, which survives in their reports and correspondence.

While countless Indians willingly adopted mission life, others
rejected it. Franciscan successes meant destruction of aboriginal
culture, far more than just marriage customs. From the beginning, the padres censured the medicine man, who was an influential leader and an upholder of traditional culture. Franciscans
treated him as a tool of the devil, their rival to be destroyed.[56]
Missionaries demanded that Indians stop worshiping the new
maize and honor only Christ.[57] The busk and corn mother had
been a vital part of aboriginal religion since the introduction of
agriculture, and they were even harder to stamp out than the
medicine man's influence.

Franciscans never succeeded in prohibiting the ball games.
Their opposition was partly for religious reasons and partly because Indians became so engrossed in the ball games and attending rituals that they neglected crops and failed to protect their
villages. Bestowal of Christian names subtly undermined rituals
or rites of passage whereby Indians received war names or in
some other manner were initiated into adulthood. Disrupting
political life, Spaniards appointed chiefs—miccos or caciques—
irrespective of clan membership or traditional right to rule, and
they relied on local village chiefs rather than a more powerful
tribal one. Ignoring the natives' matrilineal society, at times
Spaniards decreed that sons inherited power. Some Indians
blamed Franciscans for introducing disease and adamantly refused to have anything to do with them.[58]

Missionaries sometimes have been portrayed as meek, unob-
trusive lambs of God. Yet they whipped Indians who missed
Mass, pinched the thumbs of other transgressors in a flintlock,
and forced porters to transport the subsidy 200 miles from St.
Augustine without pay. Franciscans, however, repeatedly urged
the King to send mules so the natives could be spared.[59]

Resentment against the Spaniards led to revolts. In 1571 Don
Luis's kinsmen killed nine Jesuits in Jacán, destroying the mis-

sion. Guale Indians rose in 1597, razing the missions so carefully planted since the Menéndez era and massacring the Franciscans. Survivors were imprisoned and tortured, and, when they could think of little else, Indians forced one wounded missionary to keep the birds away from the maize fields. Seventeenth-century Apalachee was marked by repeated risings as additional Franciscans suffered martyrdom. In most instances, however, Spain put down the rebellions, the padres returned, and missions flourished more than ever. Jacán was an exception. But even here Menéndez captured ringleaders and, after a hasty baptism, hanged them from the yardarm of his ship in Chesapeake Bay.[60] When the bishop of Cuba visited Guale in 1606 the recent rebellion had been crushed, encouraging the bishop to look forward with confidence to a golden age. Spanish military and naval power coupled with the attraction of mission life were enough to make Indians for many decades live with Franciscans and at least nominally adopt Christianity. The real threat to the missions, as will be seen, was not when discontented neophytes periodically rebelled but when they or their Indian neighbors were spurred on by the English or French.

As the result of Spain's presence in *la Florida*, once numerous and powerful kingdoms disappeared. Even before De Soto arrived at Cofitachiqui the process of disintegration was under way. By the end of the following century mighty Cofitachiqui was no more, no titanic struggle having marked its demise. When Menéndez married Carlos's sister in 1566, the Calusas were far less numerous than when Ponce de León visited them. Spain made no permanent settlements among the Calusas, and they did not move elsewhere; they simply disappeared without notice. To an extent Indians survived genetically by mingling with Spaniards, and at the earliest date a mestizo progeny emerged.[61] It was not as important in Florida as elsewhere in Spanish America, because the Spanish population was so small.

During the sixteenth century Spaniards were not the only ones to come in contact with Southern Indians. French, English, and Africans, among others, confronted the aborigines and visited the interior, voluntarily or not. Long after destruction of Fort Caroline in 1565 Frenchmen remained active in Timucua, Guale, and Carolina, and in 1579 some forty lived near Santa Elena.[62] If his account is to be believed, the Englishman David Ingram in 1568–69 walked across much of the South, observing large cities and strange animals in areas traversed previously by De Soto. Ingram had been a member of John Hawkins's expedition, which the Spaniards had routed at San Juan de Ulloa. Put ashore with a few survivors near Tampico on the Mexican coast, Ingram, according to his account, walked 2,000 or more miles to the vicinity of Newfoundland, witnessing en route populous cities, marvelous animals, caches of pearls, and iron tools. An English fishing vessel picked him up and returned him to Europe.[63] Exploits of other Englishmen are better documented. Christopher Newport, who later played a prominent role at Jamestown, in 1591 stopped with his entire fleet somewhere on *la Florida*'s Atlantic Coast;[64] and in 1606 Spaniards at Santa Elena captured an English ship that incautiously came into that harbor.[65]

English and French contacts with Indians in the South, along with the more important Spanish ones, occasionally disclose or hint at how aboriginal culture and patterns of settlement were being modified. For example, there is the tradition that Powhatan, his brother, or a member of his family had lived among the Spaniards, nurturing a great hatred of them, and there are intimations that part of the Powhatan Confederacy were refugees from present-day Florida, Georgia, or South Carolina.[66] Primarily as a result of diseases, the greatest changes in the Southern Indian life-style occurred in the sixteenth century before the founding of Jamestown, one suspects even before Menéndez arrived at St. Augustine. But subsequent relations between Southern Indians and European and African immigrants also are important and must be looked at more closely.

3
Tsenacommacah

Spanish conquistadors, missionaries, merchants, and mariners had profoundly altered aboriginal culture in the decades after Columbus's discoveries. Yet even at that early period one could not ignore the role of England. She claimed generous portions if not all of the South, and during the latter part of the sixteenth century her subjects came to the New World in increasing numbers. No papal bull summoned them to redeem natives from paganism. England had been Catholic before Henry VIII's break with Rome in 1533, but the 1493–1506 bulls applied only to Spain and Portugal. After the break papal edicts carried no force in England. Nevertheless, before 1533 and for centuries thereafter English rulers, making the same assumptions as their Spanish counterparts, acted as if God had decreed that Englishmen alone must bring light to the New World. Indians were pagans having few rights, certainly not to their lands, which must be entrusted to a Christian prince.

England generally ignored or considered inconsequential any aboriginal title. As more and more of her subjects came to the New World the question arose of exactly which Christian prince had a right to precisely what American territory. English jurists made much of the concept of "first discovery": Whichever nation first discovered pagan American lands could claim them. An Anglican minister and colonial promoter, Richard Hakluyt the younger, in his *Discourse on Western Planting*, written in 1584, boldly asserted that the Cabots had sailed from Newfoundland to the southern tip of Florida before the arrival of Ponce de León.[1] If there were any misgivings about this, the resourceful Hakluyt could fall back on the Welsh Prince Madoc, who Hakluyt maintained had planted a colony on the Gulf Coast in the twelfth century.[2] In time England set forth the concept of "effective occupation." It was no longer enough for some European traveler to be the first to spot pagans, as perhaps De Soto and other Spaniards had; lands had to be actually colonized in order to secure valid title. In a vague way England gradually assumed that, because Indians were living in the area, they could at least use the land in question under the concept of usufruct. This meant that the aborigines did not own the soil but were entitled to its use. Whenever they "sold" their lands they were merely relinquishing this secondary right.[3]

What is striking is that at almost no time were English statesmen, theologians, and the public at large particularly concerned with aboriginal claims. Such disputes as arose usually involved England's refuting Spanish and French pretensions. No Las Casas, Montesinos, or Vitoria argued in high moral tones the justification for appropriating native lands. One explanation is that Jamestown was founded more than a century after Columbus's voyage, when Europe had left the medieval world and had entered a more secular and aggressive capitalistic era. Another consideration is the number of Indians. Millions had greeted Las Casas in the West Indies; yet a century later Powhatan lamented that he had seen his people die off three times during his lifetime. On occasion English lawyers and clergy debated aboriginal rights, and this will be dealt with more fully.

At the end of the sixteenth century the Puritan movement had become stronger than ever. Puritans, of course, were those Anglicans who wanted to reform or purify the Anglican church according to the precepts set forth by John Calvin. Many Anglicans associated with the Roanoke colony and especially the subsequent settlement at Jamestown displayed Puritan leanings. Like many reformers, Puritans tended to be aggressive and uncompromising, hence little inclined to tolerate the corn mother and animal deities. Neither Puritans nor the Jesuits who had been in Jacán earlier showed much appreciation for native religion and culture, both assuming they had God's blessing to transform aboriginal life as quickly as possible.

While mentioning De Soto, Ponce de León, and Spain's weak foothold at St. Augustine, English-language histories of colonial North America generally contend that exploration and colonization of the South did not begin in earnest until Raleigh's attempt at Roanoke Island. Dale Van Every, a twentieth-century author of several widely read works concerning the American frontier, describes how bearded whites in enormous winged craft came to Roanoke Island with horses and strange bright metal to impress and intimidate the natives. The aborigines, Van Every continues, were hunters soon forced inland to protect vital hunting lands. Numbering not more than one hundred thousand in the entire Eastern United States, these nomads were doomed from the beginning, he contends. It was inevitable that sturdy European farmers would turn the virgin sod and reap a bountiful harvest from lands touched only occasionally by an Indian moccasin or the hoof of a deer.[4] One gets the same picture in reading Theodore Roosevelt's nineteenth-century *Winning of the West*[5] and from a profusion of other histories and novels.

In almost every respect this traditional viewpoint is distorted, ignoring among other things the fact that for well over half a century before the time of Roanoke Island Europeans had had extensive contacts with Southern natives. Ayllón had come to the Carolina coast with more colonists and horses than Raleigh, and it was Ayllón who had sent out the most caravels to reconnoiter. For generations before the Roanoke undertaking European ships of various nations had been wrecked along the Carolina shore or crews had come ashore for supplies and to barter with the aborigines. For a few years in the 1560s Santa Elena in present-day South Carolina had been the Florida capital, and by land and sea De Soto and Juan Pardo, among others, had explored the Carolina coast and interior. In one or another part of Carolina, Indians had seen Ayllón and De Soto come and go, Pardo's soldiers and Jesuits desert their blockhouses and missions, French Huguenots abandon their wooden fort at Port Royal, and just to the north Jesuits fail in Jacán. By the time of Raleigh's enterprise a precedent had been set that any European colony founded in the Carolina region was doomed to failure.

What is not clear is how much aboriginal culture on the North

Carolina coast had changed from Ayllón's time in the 1520s until Raleigh's day in the 1580s. These Indians—Roanoke, Croatoan, Machapunga, Pamlico, Chowanoc, and others—for the most part were Algonquians, among the southernmost who had drifted south along the coast from Canada. Their culture, a blend of the Mississippian and the Northern hunting tradition, had much in common with that of the Powhatans. When Raleigh's colonists arrived, a loose Secotan confederacy of Algonquians existed in the Pamlico Sound and Pamlico River area; whether at an earlier period they had been subject to a powerful ruler such as the Queen of Cofitachiqui is unknown.[6] Only scattered references hint at sixteenth-century demographic changes. Spanish slavers had seized hundreds of the coastal inhabitants, and Spaniards, Englishmen, and Frenchmen had taken natives away to serve as interpreters or for display in the mother country. Carrying off aborigines in this fashion over half a century cannot have greatly depleted the population, but pandemics introduced by Europeans and Africans could have and in all probability did. Until archeologists and ethnologists come up with new evidence, we shall probably never know if a powerful ruler ever lorded over the coastal North Carolina Indians or exactly how much the population had declined since Ayllón's day.

In English eyes, if not from the aboriginal standpoint, Raleigh's undertaking was the first attempt of any consequence to settle the Atlantic Coast. To Spanish cartographers' dismay, English mapmakers began calling the Atlantic Coast Virginia rather than Florida. Raleigh in 1584 secured a royal patent to this enormous area, stretching from Canada to the Florida peninsula, and sent out Philip Amadas and Arthur Barlowe to explore. Favorably impressed by the Outer Banks and Roanoke Island sheltered behind them, they induced two coastal dwellers, Manteo and Wanchese, to return with them to England for training as interpreters. In secrecy Raleigh established a colony at Roanoke Island in 1585. Despite the interest Manteo and Wanchese had evoked in England, Raleigh gave Indian affairs a low priority. Describing in detail how towns and forts were to be laid out and lands distributed, for all practical purposes his patent did not mention the natives.[7] His colony was a military one, primarily concerned with providing a fortified naval base from which English ships could prey on the Spanish treasure fleet returning to Europe. Sir Francis Drake stopped by Roanoke Island in 1586 after having burned St. Augustine and unsuccessfully attempted to destroy Santa Elena. Distressed soldiers at Roanoke accepted Drake's offer of passage back to England. The following year Raleigh and his associates sent a new expedition to Virginia, and this one, including farmers, women, and children, was designed more to exploit the region itself than just to establish a fortified port.

Indians figured more prominently in plans for this latter colony, the "Lost Colony." Queen Elizabeth, her advisers, and Raleigh gave little thought to aboriginal land claims, but the natives were on the scene and had to be reckoned with. Inspired by a blend of piety and boosterism, Raleigh and his associates resolved to serve both God and Mammon. English promoters and scholars, such as the younger Richard Hakluyt and John Hooker, knew something about the Carolina Indians, but they probably derived more of their notions from Las Casas, Peter Martyr, and others who had written about the Spanish Indies than from Manteo, Wanchese, and the aborigines brought home by Drake and John Hawkins. In any case the Carolina pagans had to be won over and kept out of the Pope's clutches: "For what can be more pleasant to God, than to gain and reduce in all Christianlike manner, a lost people to the knowledge of the gospell . . . and what can be more honorable to princes, than to inlarge the bounds of their kingdoms without iniurie, wrong, and bloudshed."[8] England must not follow the Spanish lead and initiate her own Black Legend. As the younger Hakluyt observed, Indians were idolaters who worshiped the sun, but with proper encouragement an infinite number could be saved. Continuing the tradition of the first great Christian missionary, Paul, Hakluyt urged English missionaries to learn the aboriginal tongue, but of course there was no single Indian tongue, any more than there was a European one. Carolina natives spoke different dialects or mutually unintelligible languages within the same linguistic family. The scholarly Hakluyt must have suspected this but, if so, did not let his readers know.[9]

Manteo returned to Roanoke Island and was christened and invested with the lordship of Roanoke and Dasemunkepeuc.[10] From this beginning Anglicanism was to win more converts and bring the remainder of those simple people into the fold. Authorities at Roanoke Island decreed that aborigines be dealt with fairly and not mistreated. Under threat of severe penalty, soldiers were not to strike natives, appropriate their property, enter their houses without permission, or violate their women. Thomas Hariot, a mathematician and naturalist, who made an invaluable study of the North Carolina flora and fauna, declared that Algonquian sirens did not sexually attract Raleigh's menfolk. From the vantage point of four hundred years later it is uncertain whether Hariot was trying to convince his readers or himself of this verity.[11]

Hariot also described how critically ill local chiefs, despairing of relief from aboriginal medicine men, turned to the English and their god and were miraculously cured. Indians fervently kissed and embraced the Bible, held it to their breasts, and stroked their bodies with it, displaying the same ardor that those to the south had shown when they rushed to kiss newly erected crosses in Spanish missions. Perhaps Hariot, like the Franciscans, exaggerated, but not much, and the reason for such zeal was not hard to find. As Hariot observed, in every town where the inhabitants were at all hostile, the natives, soon after the English departure, "began to die very fast [which had] never happened before, time out of minde."[12] It was not horses, dogs, or strange bright metal that terrified the aborigines—not that they enjoyed fending off mastiffs or being impaled on a lance—but new microparasites, which they could not see and did not understand.

If England looked upon the Roanoke enterprise as a religious crusade, Spain rather than the Indians was the enemy. Raleigh established his colony at Roanoke Island just before a full-fledged Anglo-Spanish war broke out and Spain unleashed her great armada against England. Through force, intrigue, and marriage Philip II tried to coerce England back into the Catholic fold. English invectives against Catholicism were inseparable from anti-Spanish polemics. English hostility against the Catholic Church and Spain spread to the New World, because from the standpoint of patriotic Englishmen it was unthinkable that aborigines in Virginia—or Florida or whatever one called the Atlantic Coast—should become Catholics. They had to be won over to Protestantism to thwart the menacing schemes of the Pope and Philip II.

Raleigh and his associates invested heavily in the Roanoke enterprise, expecting the natives to help make the venture succeed. Whatever their population density, the local inhabitants seemed numerous enough, and their labor could help turn a profit. According to English promoters, Roanoke natives, who would be paid wages, were "of better wittes than those of Mexico and Peru" and readily could be trained to plant and cultivate olives, grow flax, and weave linen.[13] Investors would profit, and England would become more self-sufficient, not having to import olives and linen from foreign Catholics. Writers and artists portrayed the original Virginians as naked, which by Northern European standards was true. Textile manufacturers could serve God and their pocketbooks by clothing the aborigines. They were not entirely nude but wore deerskins; if those pelts could be exchanged for woolens, so much the better.[14]

The Roanoke colony and Raleigh's plans for the greater Virginia came to naught. Although the fate of the Lost Colony is unknown, it seems clear that natives held the key. The 1588 Spanish Armada prevented a relief vessel from being dispatched immediately, and when one finally arived in 1590 Roanoke Island had been abandoned. Neighboring Indians had either killed or absorbed the colonists; odds favor the same treatment for the English at Roanoke as earlier had been inflicted upon Spaniards at Jacán. England made no permanent settlement in America during the sixteenth century, but White's pictures, Hariot's *Briefe and True Report,* miscellaneous publicity associated with the Roanoke enterprise, and the handful of natives brought to England gave potential investors and the clergy a glimpse of the Southern aborigines and their culture.

For years the commodious harbor and fertile lands of Chesapeake Bay had attracted Europeans. Verrazzano had put in there in the 1520s, and if Raleigh had had his way the Lost Colony settlers would have gone to Chesapeake. Even though Raleigh never established a colony there, he learned a good deal about the area. Some information is recorded on John White's detailed map of the Outer Banks and Roanoke Island, which, at its northern extremity, included Chesapeake Bay.[15]

Spaniards had heard about Chesapeake from their mariners and from aborigines, such as Don Luis, who had been picked up around 1560, sent to Spain, and subsequently returned to St. Augustine and eventually to Jacán to help Jesuits found a mission. In the 1580s Spaniards at St. Augustine ordered ships northward to discover where Raleigh's settlers were, and Indians aboard served as interpreters. Spanish sailors, soldiers, and scholars like Father Pareja understood the linguistic diversity existing among aborigines living between St. Augustine and Bahía de Santa María and selected interpreters with care. One was a Christian Indian, María de Miranda, wife of a Spanish soldier stationed at Santa Elena. Sources do not reveal her native tongue or exact tribal identity.[16] She spoke Escamacu, a Muskhogean language, and presumably Siouan dialects as well, allowing her to communicate with Chesapeake Bay Indians or their neighbors. The veteran Francisco Fernández de Écija had marched into the Carolina back country with Pardo and later explored the Outer Banks and Chesapeake Bay to discover what the English were up to. As well as any contemporary, Écija understood the culture and variety of languages existing among the native Southerners. At one point he sent Cape Fear Indians, presumably Sioux or Algonquians, to see what successes, if any, the English were enjoying in Chesapeake Bay.[17]

Whether from coastal inhabitants or personal inspection, both Raleigh and the Spaniards learned about the merits of Chesapeake Bay. As has been discussed, the Powhatan Confederacy (Tsenacommacah) was located in the Tidewater and on the bay's Eastern Shore, and it was in this region that Englishmen with great difficulty finally planted a permanent colony. Much has been written about Jamestown and the Powhatans, how Pocahontas threw her arms about John Smith and saved him from execution, and how Emperor Powhatan alternately fought with and assisted the white newcomers. Yet in many respects the Powhatans remain an enigma. This is so partly because many of the early English documents have not been preserved, and we have to rely on John Smith's writings or none at all. Another reason is that, for all the archaeological work done in the Tidewater, many more sixteenth- and early-seventeenth-century sites need to be discovered and excavated. The Powhatans were Algonquians, but Iroquois, Sioux, and Muskhogeans lived close by if not in the Tidewater itself. When Spaniards sent aborigines to spy on the English, it is not clear whether they were meant to interview Indian strangers or talk with friends and relatives who had moved north to escape the Spaniards and mission life and disorders following in the wake of pandemics.

The size of Tsenacommacah has been and remains the subject of debate, estimates ranging from some nine thousand to well over a hundred thousand. A figure in the higher range seems more likely, especially early in the sixteenth century. From Verrazzano's visit in the 1520s until Menéndez's and Raleigh's time later in the century, new microparasites had been afforded ample opportunity to do their work. Aboriginal life had been profoundly altered in the Chesapeake Bay region in ways that today are still not clear long before Pocahontas and John Smith met. Tenuous as it is, evidence suggests that in a general way the fate of the Powhatans had been the same as that of aborigines in Hispaniola.

If one is inclined to argue that England, in the Las Casas tradition, wrestled with the great moral and legal questions concerning land titles and conduct toward the Indians, Jamestown's early years are the ones to look at, more so than the occasions when in the same century Roger Williams, citing aboriginal rights to the land, questioned the validity of the Massachusetts Bay charter, or when the Quaker William Penn in the 1680s peacefully acquired land in a series of treaties with Pennsylvania Indians. Virginia Company officials, the clergy, laymen, and the King all affirmed the overriding religious motives for settling at Jamestown, occasionally attempting to justify the appropriation of Indian lands. The preface to the Virginia Company charter reminded all concerned that theirs was a noble undertaking to propagate religion among savages living in darkness.[18] Anglican ministers, few of whom ever came to America, at least for a time identified the Virginia experiment with a holy crusade: "Oh how happy were that man which could reduce this people from brutishnes," who upon conversion "will sing for ever of them that did it."[19] A prayer read in the morning and evening by captains of the watch admonished soldiers to set a pious example and "be as Angels of God sent to this people."[20] Middle Temple and Lincoln's Inn barristers in 1613 staged a masque for the royal family: "Virginian princes, ye must now renounce your superstitious worship of the sun, subject to cloudy darknings and descents . . . to this our Britain Phoebus, whose bright skie enlighted with a Christian piety is never subject to black error's night."[21] The Archbishops of York and Canterbury required parishes to subscribe to a fund that would help save the Virginia heathen, and the company's lotteries in part would serve the same ends.[22] A 1615 broadside explained how fortunate subscribers might win the great prize of 4,500 crowns in the pot of gold. The Powhatans Mataban and Eiafintomie stood beside the pot, reminding investors that this was a godly wager: "Deere Britaines, now be you as kinde, bring light and sight to us yet blinde: leade us by doctrine and behaviour, into one Sion, to one Saviour."[23]

Stockholders and Anglican divines sometimes justified appropriating aboriginal lands, but their arguments were not closely reasoned: "We don't intend to disposses the savages but to join them for their own spiritual and temporal good."[24] The Reverend Samuel Purchas contended that Indians were nomads roaming over superfluous fertile lands, and that, as natural men, Englishmen had the right to replenish the earth.[25] The noble savage concept, portraying the native as an untainted child of nature emerging from the virgin forest, did not sweep over Europe until the eighteenth century. In the early years he was more often depicted as a savage, an uncivilized brute.

Writers made much of the barbaric aboriginal practice of sacrificing children. Contemporary authors were describing, quite inaccurately, the huskanaw, a hardening or initiation rite. At the appropriate time children were collected and sent to a designated spot in the woods, where for weeks they subsisted on a limited diet. Part of the time they were probably drugged and, supervised by the priests, underwent a rigorous mental and physical ordeal. But they were not killed, although some of the weaker ones may have succumbed. In the West Indies the Spaniards had branded the Indians cannibals, and probably for religious or political reasons Caribs had occasionally eaten human flesh. But they were no more true cannibals than were the Powhatans sacrificers of young children. In each instance, however, whites insisted that good Christians must take over these barbarous, heathen lands as quickly as possible.[26] War was another legal argument used to justify seizing aboriginal territory. By fighting and rebelling against the English, the Powhatans lost whatever claims they had.

Sometimes the English purchased village lands for copper and other manufactures. It seemed reasonable enough to exchange surplus lands for hardware and woolens, and in the process Indians would become civilized. This policy, pursued by company officials early in the seventeenth century—and by Thomas Jefferson two hundred years later—failed because in each instance the natives did not think and act as whites thought they should.[27] Colonists had a good idea of what a purchase signified, but it is doubtful that the aborigines, with different perceptions of private property, ever did. At one point, in a somewhat ludicrous episode, Christopher Newport crowned Powhatan. Defying centuries of European feudal tradition, the tall emperor refused to kneel, and the shorter Englishman had great difficulty. In time a copper crown perched uneasily atop Powhatan's head. The English, at least some of them, contended that Powhatan was James I's vassal, enjoying his Virginia fief at royal sufferance.[28] When all was said and done, the usual practice in Virginia was to ignore the Indians and not to bother to purchase their lands, "whereby a soveraignity in that heathen infidell was acknowledged."[29] Neither Englishmen nor the Spaniards before them were hypocrites mouthing religious cant while despoiling natives. Investors in the Virginia Company and parishioners who prayed for and contributed to the Jamestown endeavor felt that acquisition of wealth at Indian expense was secondary to the noble mission of saving and civilizing the aborigines.

Attempts to convert Powhatans were inseparable from endeavors to educate them, and from the beginning company authorities and Anglican divines debated how to proceed. They never developed a comprehensive plan, and in the end they failed miserably. Foremost they pinned their hopes on children, endeavoring to wean them from clutches of priests, medicine men, fathers, uncles, or whoever was responsible for rearing them in barbarism and false doctrine. It seemed reasonable to the English that these primitive folk must quickly perceive the advantages of turning over their offspring to white households, where they might imbibe superior moral and material benefits. Language was a problem, and orders were given to make a dictionary. John Smith and William Strachey compiled brief word lists, and the Lord's Prayer was translated into Powhatan. But no scholarly Pareja labored in Virginia. The Emperor's language never completely disappeared, but since Powhatan's and Pocahontas's lips are sealed, modern Virginia Indians and whites alike must rely on these inadequate word lists, for the most part guessing about the language spoken in the seventeenth-century Tidewater.[30]

As time went on it seemed natural, and certainly far easier, for natives to learn English, a Christian language. Instruction, such as it was, would take place in English houses as aboriginal youths inevitably acquired the language of the whites.[31] Anglicans resolved to found a college in Virginia to take the brightest of these English-speaking Indians and further educate and uplift them. Many details concerning the college were never resolved, such as whether the youths had to know English before being admitted or whether whites were to be instructed as well and, if so, would sit in the same room with the Indians.

Whatever the answers, an Indian college, part of a larger colonial university to be erected at Henricus near the fall line of the James River, was to be the capstone of the natives' education. Sermons, broadsides, and entreaties by clergy and company authorities had their effect as wealthy merchants and impecunious parishioners bestowed substantial sums or a widow's mite to redeem the Virginia Tidewater from darkness. Charitable contributions added to those of the company itself were considerable. Ten thousand acres were donated to the college and university, and more than fifty tenants were assigned to work these lands or otherwise labor in support of the college, which initially was to enroll thirty young aborigines. A planter and pious Anglican, Captain George Thorpe, directed affairs. He supervised the workmen laying the college's brick foundations, encouraged local parents to enroll their most promising children, and all the while placated and proselytized neighboring Indians, including the obdurate Opechancanough, who had succeeded Powhatan. The Virginia Company was reorganized in 1619, and critics, frequently with justification, denounced the financial and managerial practices of the new leadership. The administration of the college was no exception. Tenants supposed to labor for the college and its maintenance worked elsewhere for the company in behalf of apprehensive stockholders. Whether the indefatigable Thorpe could have overcome the many obstacles will never be known, because under Opechancanough's leadership the Indians rebelled in 1622, massacring some three hundred whites and burying an ax in Thorpe's skull. The college site was abandoned; underbrush and humus eventually covered the incomplete foundations.[32]

Many years passed before Anglicans in Virginia and in the mother country made another serious attempt to educate and convert the Old Dominion's aborigines. Expectations of Thorpe, Whitaker, the Archbishop of Canterbury, and devout English parishioners came to naught. The obvious cause of failure was the massacre itself. Yet the Spaniards too had experienced reverses: The 1597 destruction of the Guale missions and martyrdom of the Franciscans was a good example. The Spaniards nevertheless overcame this setback, reestablished their missions, and entered upon a golden age in Guale. Despite native hostility, on the surface there was no reason why the English could not have founded schools and missions even after 1622 and have been as successful as Spain was in Guale and Apalachee during the seventeenth century.

The English and Spanish churches, however, manifested certain differences, a salient one being that England had no Franciscans, Dominicans, Jesuits or any other mendicant order. In the aftermath of his split with Rome, Henry VIII in the late 1530s suppressed the monastaries, confiscated and distributed their property, and had the state assume the traditional monastic functions of education and charity. After Columbus's voyage hundreds of Spanish Dominicans, Franciscans, and others eagerly abandoned Castile to seek a new harvest in America. Such groups did not exist in England, and Whitaker and Thorpe, with no intent to belittle their motives and piety, were no substitute.

Other reasons help explain the ineffectual Anglican effort in Virginia. Spanish monarchs and the Inquisition had stifled dissent from orthodoxy emanating from Jews, Moors, and Catholics who flirted with Erasmus's humanism. The Spanish Catholic church had become about as monolithic as conceivably possible. Not so for the English church, as Puritans, High Church Anglicans, and Catholics who expected rehabilitation all struggled and intrigued in the early seventeenth century as the Virginia Company nurtured its settlement. Religious controversy was the key issue in the Puritan Revolution that broke out in 1642. Throughout the seventeenth century and later, dissent and quarrels over the structure of the national church persisted, proving a near fatal weakness in attempts to convert the aborigines. James I in 1606 decreeed that the true Christian faith, as "now professed and established within our realm of England," be planted, preached, and used in Virginia,[33] but Puritans and High Anglicans differed sharply over how it was or should be "now professed" in England. Designed to keep out Catholics, the Oath of Supremacy was required of all coming to Virginia.[34] Nevertheless, there were Catholics at Jamestown, some of them highly placed. Anglican divines, looking upon the Virginia enterprise as a holy mission, wanted to gather the elect from all corners and dispatch them to Jamestown.[35] The Archbishop of Canterbury and Puritan Brownists did not agree at all on whom the Almighty had elected. Despite admonitions that colonists make themsleves of one mind, religious division and diversity of the mother country were transferred to the James River.

There have been attempts to characterize the Reverend Alexander Whitaker, who preached in Virginia for years, presumably baptizing Pocahontas, and Master George Thorpe, who was in charge of the college, as apostles to the Indians in the Las Casas tradition. Surviving documents do not reveal much about their activities. One thing is certain: Neither they nor any of their contemporaries doggedly appeared before the crown to plead the cause of the natives, and none left writings to explain and justify England's mission in America. Like Las Casas, Thorpe did what he could to keep settlers from turning mastiffs loose on the pagans. Virginia's aborigines, however, knew what they were about when they planted a hatchet in Thorpe's skull, perceiving clearly enough the danger posed by alien priests and teachers. In each culture they were the most informed and the strongest defenders of traditional religion and social values. Englishmen, like Spaniards, thought it essential to remove the influence of the priest and medicine man, peacefully if possible, "more sharpely" if necessary, "even to dache . . . these murtherers of souls . . . to the Divill."[36] Thorpe and his fellow colonists complained and were a bit baffled that Indian parents did not readily deliver children to be educated in private homes or at the college. Both races understood the cultural threat, each dealing rigorously with opposing leaders, the Anglican Thorpe and Algonquian priests and medicine men alike.

It was impossible to separate the company's desire to Christianize, educate, and uplift the aborigines from its resolve to reward investors. William Crashaw reminded the faithful in 1609 that those "that seekes only or principally spirituall things, God will reward . . . with those spirituall and temporal things. . . . God will assuredly send us great profit."[37] In each instance the Indians' role was vital. Labor provided by the natives, willingly or not, and traffic with them had much to do with the size of dividends. In the early years company officials did not know how numerous the Powhatans were, and, considering demographic changes of the sixteenth and seventeenth centuries, the confusion is understandable. Sermons might portray natives as brutish nomads, but company authorities usually assumed a sizable and essentially sedentary population, which they resolved to exploit.

They first attempted to follow the Spanish example by instituting a *repartimiento*. Each lord of a province or chief was to pay tribute of so many measures of corn, baskets of dye, and dozens of skins, and a fixed number of able-bodied men from each village in rotation would work for the English. Protection, salvation, and redemption from brutishness were the rewards.[38] The English were never able to impose a *repartimiento* on Virginia's Indians. Considering the colony's weakness—numbers shrank from five hundred to sixty in the 1609–10 winter—failure was not surprising. The company's fortunes revived somewhat after that disastrous winter, and from 1611 to 1616 the exacting Marshal Thomas Dale restored a measure of order and prosperity. He impressed workers from assorted villages and assigned them to essential tasks. The resolute marshal hoped the village elders would approve, not that it made any difference.[39] After the Starving Time English authorities, renouncing any *repartimiento*-style system, emphasized the importance of placing young Indians in Christian households. Religious considerations aside, the company realized that these youths would serve their masters as apprentices for years. By the time they reached their twenties and secured their freedom, they presumably would have become acculturated and could remain among whites, adding to the reservoir of skilled artisans and farmers. Along with adults who could be trusted, some apprentices were to assist colonists in clearing land, planting maize and beating it into flour, fishing, and hunting. Keinps and Tassore, although shackled for a time, were among those Powhatans who taught settlers how to order and plant their fields.[40] Boosters of the Virginia plantation made much of the ability of local Indians to gather great quantities of "silke grasse" (probably of a species of yucca), hemp, and flax and to show more competence than the English in the "exquisite dressing thereof."[41] Surviving early-seventeenth-century Algonquian textiles are almost nonexistent, and it is not clear what promoters had in mind—perhaps little more than prodding investors to dig even deeper into their pockets.

After many tribulations the Virginia Company failed, its charter in 1624 revoked by the crown. Many reasons contributed, but one was confusion over whether the company, in addition to being a trading concern, also had to be a colonizing one. None of the other great English commercial companies founded before 1606, including the East India Company, the Levant Company, and the Guinea Company, had been forced into colonization.

During the early years Virginia Company officials assumed that Powhatans living in the Chesapeake Bay area, like their counterparts in Africa, India, and the eastern Mediterranean, would make their enterprise succeed. It took time before the directors realized that to succeed the Virginia Company had to populate its domain on a massive scale. It was not until 1619 that immigrants arrived in significant numbers, a thousand or so a year. After 1619, and especially after the 1622 massacre, expectations of extensive reliance on a large number of bond or free aboriginal artisans and of the establishment of a large-scale forced-labor tribute system for the most part were abandoned.

Before and after the massacre, trade with the natives was important. For a century before 1607 Chesapeake Bay Indians had bartered skins, furs, and foodstuffs to mariners in exchange for knives, fishhooks, shirts, and blankets, and commerce expanded after 1607. Plying the James River and Chesapeake Bay, English sailors continued this trade, much of which was unregulated. Food stored in Algonquian granaries was essential—literally a matter of life and death to colonists. In the early years Indians brought maize, beans, squash, and fresh or smoked meat to Jamestown of their own volition.[42] Experienced and shrewd bargainers, they repeatedly increased prices to hard-pressed whites. Colonists, seeking out Indian villages and "forcing a trade," provoked innumerable hostilities.[43]

Commerce with settlers altered aboriginal culture in the Chesapeake Bay region, which is not to imply that it would have remained static if Europeans had stayed away. Not long before the founding of Jamestown, elements of the Mississippian tradition had filtered into the Tidewater. The Europeans' arrival merely directed cultural changes along different lines. For a century before 1607 and for years afterward the local inhabitants obtained European manufactures. One item was copper. This metal was not a novelty, it was merely scarce, and copper pots, beads, and knives had a high premium. Glass beads also were traded. The aborigines regarded them highly, as they did their own shell beads of roanoke and peake, which their craftsmen laboriously fashioned. English glass beads served well enough, because they were abundant and relatively cheap. Powhatans also acquired iron hardware, including pots, nails, hoes, and shovels. Whites built an English-style house for Opechanca-nough in order to conciliate him; reportedly the incredulous Chickahominy spent hours locking and unlocking the front door, observing with marvel his new lock and key.[44] Native craftsmen obtained European metal and glass, reworking it to suit their needs. The English willingly traded small hoes to the Indians but not ones with large blades. White and aboriginal craftsmen both calculated that a large iron hoe would equal a dozen or so iron knife blades.[45] Through trade and warfare natives acquired fire-arms, even though colonists who engaged in this traffic risked the death penalty. At an early date the aborigines began stalking game and also colonists with firearms, causing settlers soon to complain that the Indians were as good shots as themselves.[46] Millennia ago the bow and arrow had replaced the atlatl, and in the seventeenth century the musket was beginning to replace the bow. Neither the white man's law nor Governor Yeardley's spies, sent among the Powhatans to steal the feathers of their guns (part of a matchlock's firing mechanism), in the long run made any difference.[47]

Before 1607 the aborigines had bartered skins and furs with the whites, and this commerce accelerated in the seventeenth century. Stimulated by hoards of pelts in nearby villages—Pow-hatan reportedly had four thousand deerskins in a single pri-vate wardrobe—colonists at first centered their attention on the James River.[48] Gradually interest shifted to the Potomac River, the Eastern Shore, and the upper reaches of Chesapeake Bay. Potomac River Indians captured young Henry Fleet, who lived among them for years, learning their language and customs be-fore his redemption in 1627. Once free he put his knowledge to good use and prospered as a trader.[49] The controversial William Claiborne, a member of the Virginia council, an Indian fighter, and a plague to governors of both Virginia and Maryland, estab-lished a fur trading post on Kent Island in Chesapeake Bay and enjoyed a lucrative business for some years.[50] Fleet and Clai-borne were among the first to make their fortunes in the Indian trade, to invest profits in land, and to found dynasties. William Byrd I and other shrewd merchants continued this tradition.

Furs and skins were of obvious value, but it gradually dawned on the English that the aborigines had something else of worth

—themselves. A search for slaves initially had brought Spaniards to the South, yet it took the English a while, sometimes with the natives' encouragement, to appreciate the slave trade's potential. Opechancanough in 1619 suggested a joint Anglo-Indian expedition against his enemies living beyond the fall line. The English would provide soldiers with firearms and armor; Powhatans would serve as porters and furnish moccasins for the soldiers; and booty would be equally divided. The potential spoils included not only furs and foodstuffs but also captives, especially children.[51] This particular small expedition never took place, but it nevertheless suggested there were profits to be made from the slave trade. There is a strong suspicion that aboriginal "apprentices" living in English houses and scholars destined for the college were obtained not from willing parents but along the lines suggested by Opechancanough. Company directors in England were never particularly interested in the slave trade; in Jamestown itself, however, the seed had been planted.

A sharp contrast existed between the humanitarian and evangelical sermons preached by Anglican ministers in London and the directives and policies of John Smith, Marshal Dale, George Percy, and others wielding authority in Virginia. The latter were soldiers, and for years Virginia was little more than a military outpost. Smith and his contemporaries did not deal with Indians in the abstract. They regarded them as enemies, which more often than not was an accurate judgment. Despite the ravages of disease, the Powhatans were still a numerous and powerful foe. It is easy to forget how small the English population was during the first decade, ranging from fewer than a hundred to just over one thousand. Scattered up and down the James River, colonists invariably were sickly and short of food. Modern writers frequently contend that, once the English arrived at Jamestown, the Powhatans were doomed. Without debating the merits of this argument, what is important for the moment is that there is little indication the aborigines realized this. Even though disease had reduced their numbers, they outnumbered English settlers many times, perhaps as much as twenty to one. Looking over the wooden stockade at James Fort, or making expeditions into the countryside, white military commanders had other concerns than saving souls of "savages creeping upon all fours . . . with their bows in their mouths, [charging] us very desperately."[52] Mariners plying the James River did not think it appropriate to explain the Trinity to angry natives furiously paddling two hundred canoes and brandishing bows, arrows, and muskets.[53] Even the Reverend Alexander Whitaker, who diligently labored for years in Virginia, deemed it essential that the Indians first "stoode in feare of us" before they could be won over from the "diuell."[54] Englishmen made much of the point that they, unlike Spaniards, were going to convert the aborigines by reason, love, and example; yet they were conscious that they were beginning an empire and identified more with Roman soldiers than Christ's disciples. Citing St. Augustine and other Christian philosophers, Anglicans justified their wars against the natives: If Christianity must be spread by *"ferro, et flammis,"* so be it.[55]

Nothing in the course of early English relations with the Powhatans has received more attention than the Pocahontas episode. She is firmly enshrined in the American pantheon; Virginia governors and presidents of the United States have proudly claimed descent from Powhatan's daughter; her dramatic rescue of John Smith from execution appears in standard histories; and her statue dominates modern Jamestown. Books have been written about her, three scholarly ones within the last decade,[56] and artists from her time to the present have engraved or painted her portrait. Try as one might, it is hard, if not impossible, to separate myth from reality. As Pocahontas, or to use her Christian name Rebecca, gazes out from the canvas it is not possible to guess her thoughts accurately.

But we must try and perhaps can come a little closer to reality. In many respects writing Pocahontas's biography is more difficult than recapturing the lives of other nonliterate Indians. She left not a single line revealing her innermost feelings, forcing us to rely on the perceptions of John Smith, John Rolfe, and other whites. Her entire life spanned only some twenty years. She first appeared quite naked as a young eleven-year-old doing cartwheels with the boys at Jamestown. Vanishing among her people for a time, she did not reappear until 1613, when Samuel Argall captured her by trickery and used her to influence Powhatan to make peace. She married John Rolfe in 1614, visited England, and died there in 1617, though her son Thomas survived. Her continuous association with John Smith, her marriage to Rolfe, who was so influential in starting Virginia on the road to being a tobacco colony, and the fact that she was Emperor Powhatan's daughter all have made her better remembered than other eleven-year-olds turning cartwheels in the buff.

It can be instructive to examine more closely the few facts of her life that are known. She was Powhatan's daughter, according to tradition his favorite, a nonpareil. She was not Powhatan's only daughter, however, but one of perhaps twenty of his children. On occasion Powhatan swore that "he delighted in none so much" as in another daughter, and he negotiated about marrying her to Thomas Dale.[57] Apparently Pocahontas had been married to an Indian before she became Rolfe's wife.[58] Divorce came relatively easy to the Indians, and it was not unusual for females to have a series of husbands. Pocahontas understood that the bonds of clan membership were as strong as or stronger than those of marriage, but there is no indication that this ever occurred to Rolfe. Whites amiably translated the Algonquian name Pocahontas as "little wanton," as perhaps she was; a more literal translation probably is "penis."[59]

John Rolfe initiated a controversy when he, a commoner, married Pocahontas, a royal princess, without James I's approval. By Algonquian matrilineal standards she was not of royal blood or even of Powhatan's lineage, and it is foolhardy to assume that after Powhatan's death she and her husband might have ruled jointly over the Tidewater. Menéndez had a far better grasp of aboriginal society when he married Chief Carlos's sister. Yet Englishmen made a good deal out of Rolfe's marriage to a princess, debating whether he should be censured, at the same time guffawing at Don Quixote for jousting with windmills.

The Puritan Rolfe wrote a long letter explaining and justifying his marriage, and his letter reveals far more about the author than about Pocahontas. Taking a high moral and statesmanlike tone, he professed he was marrying this "little wanton" for the good of the plantation and the honor of his country: She loves me and it is God's will that I convert her; "shall I be so unnaturall, as not to give bread to the hungrie?" Not quite thirty, Rolfe contended that he easily could have found a more suitable mate in England. But his marriage to Pocahontas served the colony, ensuring peace with the intractable Powhatan.[60] Powhatan may have made peace with the English on behalf of his favorite daughter or merely to win assistance against enemy Indian neighbors. We would like to know his and his daughter's innermost thoughts, but she reveals nothing as she silently stares at us from her portrait.

Pocahontas visited England in 1616, renewed her friendship with John Smith, had an audience at court, and throughout her

stay attracted attention. Devout Anglicans contributed new sums
to build the college and spread the gospel. Pocahontas was not
the only Tidewater Algonquian to arrive in London. At least one
of her brothers had preceded her by several years. Before and
after her visit others came, and, like Pocahontas, most of them
succumbed to disease.[61] Rolfe returned to Virginia, where he
died just before the 1622 massacre. His infant mestizo son,
Thomas Rolfe, remained in England after his mother's death, not
returning to Virginia until 1635. Like many American mestizos
he was part of two worlds, not belonging completely to either.

Despite admonitions of the Reverend William Symonds to follow the example of Abraham and not to marry the heathen,[62]
there were more unions than the Rolfe–Pocahontas marriage,
which is not to say all were sanctioned by the church. But some
were. One of Pocahontas's attendants in London, presumably
her sister, was sent to Bermuda by the company after Pocahontas's death. She married a white settler there, and the company's
intention was to send the mixed Christian couple on to Virginia
to help convert the Indians.[63] Whether they ever arrived is not
known. A number of English colonists, with or without permission, lived with families in assorted Powhatan villages. A few
were young white apprentices placed in wigwams by the company to learn the aboriginal tongue. Others were adults who,
with the company's approval, moved in with nearby Indians to
keep from starving. An undetermined number of discontented
settlers ran away to the natives, at times carrying their arms and
driving, if not their own, at least their masters' cattle.[64] Indians
were attracted by superior white technology and manufactures;
not as well publicized is the fact that from the beginning whites
were drawn to the less demanding, albeit less sophisticated, aboriginal culture. How many mestizos were born out of all this
mingling is unclear, but we can be certain that Thomas Rolfe was
not the only one.

Innumerable vicissitudes confronted the Virginia Company,
and after a decade the white population on the James River still
numbered approximately only seven hundred. Sir Edwin Sandys
assumed leadership in 1619 and reorganized the company, re-
solving to make it succeed. The thousand or more colonists he
sent over annually were scattered along the James from its mouth
to the fall line. Mismanagement accompanied Sandys's frenzied
undertakings: Settlers arrived without enough food to tide them

over until the first harvest, housing was insufficient or nonexistent, and the death rate was appalling. In 1622 Opechancanough led his warriors against the exposed colonists, killing some three hundred, dooming Sandys's hopes, and contributing to the company charter's revocation two years later.

The broad outline and gruesome details of the massacre, of how Indians surprised vulnerable settlers sparing neither sex and no age, is generally clear. But the fundamental causes of this attack are, and probably always will remain, obscure or at least controversial. Opechancanough, perhaps Powhatan's biological brother but more likely just of the same lineage, had carefully laid his plans. His ability to organize and execute simultaneous attacks over a large area discloses the extent of his power. But why did the Indians unleash such a major onslaught against the whites fifteen years after initial settlement rather than in the early years, when chances for success were infinitely better?

A number of considerations help explain this enigma. Until the stepped-up immigration beginning in 1619, the natives probably had not been overly alarmed by English settlers. Other Europeans—the Jesuits, Menéndez, and Roanoke Island colonists—had come to the area but soon departed. There are many indications that Powhatan and Opechancanough before 1619 regarded their more numerous Siouan neighbors as more dangerous. A few hundred starving English colonists were one thing; a few thousand quite another.

As, relatively speaking, the Virginia colony grew dramatically after 1619, it became more difficult for the company to control settlers scattered along the James and on the Eastern Shore. It had always been a problem for London authorities to issue orders and to have them obeyed in Virginia. Troubles intensified after 1619, and colonists at nearly autonomous settlements on the James without permission traded with and cheated the natives, bartering firearms if necessary to secure pelts. More oceangoing vessels than ever plied the James River, some of them sailing more than 100 miles upstream to the fall line. Sailors went ashore in increasing numbers, initiating saturnalia in Powhatan wigwams.[65] New settlers required provisons, and magistrates renewed efforts to "force a trade" and secure foodstuffs, all of which produced recriminations and incidents.[66] The college was one of Sandys's many projects, and the English intensified pressure to get Opechancanough to turn over his children for education. Resenting English endeavors, he defiantly refused.[67] Delivering children of his enemies for a consideration was another matter, however. There is no question that the English were cruel to the Indians and vice versa. Each side killed women and children. Aborigines scalped, burned, and mutilated whites, and the English in turn broke natives on the wheel or executed them in more orthodox fashions. Indians never got over their fear of being ripped to pieces by English dogs of quality. Though torture and barbaric punishments were traditional in both cultures, atrocities committed by each side contributed to the 1622 uprising. One specific murder, that in 1622 of Nemattanew, Jack of the Feathers, an influential subordinate chief of Powhatan and Opechancanough, more than any single incident triggered the ensuing massacre.

There was one other point to consider. Opechancanough and the Chickahominies are something of an enigma, enjoying a measure of independence, even autonomy, within the Powhatan Confederation. There are suggestions that at least part of the Chickahominies were new arrivals, exiles from the South, where presumably they had fought against the Spaniards and lost. Another possibility is that Opechancanough was none other than the Don Luis, who had served Menéndez in St. Augustine and subsequently turned against the Jesuits in Jacán. In any case Opechancanough may have nurtured animosity against whites for years, and after Powhatan's death he got his chance.[68]

It was clear after the massacre that the hopes of Anglicans to win over the Powhatans through love, piety, and Christian example had failed. For years after 1622 settlers waged a relentless war against the Indians, burning and pillaging their villages and cutting down or carrying off their crops. With the exception of John Donne, Dean of St. Paul's, who contended that if Anglicans did not hold fast in Virginia the papists would be glad to have it, few sermons were still preached in London urging unselfish martyrs to take up the white man's burden and go forth to Virginia.[69] The aborigines no longer seemed brutish and uncivilized, essentially loving pagans; rather "consider what those creatures are (I cannot call them men) no character of God in them . . . rooted in evil . . . the very dregs, garbage, and spawne of Earth . . . sprung up like vermine of an earthly slime . . . father'd by Sathan and the sonnes of hell."[70]

Fire and sword were the answer, possibly a profitable one at that. After razing Indian towns and driving villagers off, English farmers could plant tobacco and corn in abandoned fields. No haggling was necessary over food stored in deserted granaries or what must be given in exchange for skins. The destruction of villages and the uprooting of natives presented opportunities for capturing slaves. They might be put to work rebuilding the colony or sold elsewhere, probably in the Somers Islands (Bermuda) or in Barbados, which the English settled in 1624. England began colonizing islands and developing markets for aboriginal slaves, as Spain had done from the beginning.

Once the English recovered from the massacre and began their relentless military campaigns, the Powhatans could no longer ignore or underestimate the danger. From the vantage point of 1624 it can be seen that both sides had suffered heavily. Of the 7,500 settlers who had come to Virginia, barely a thousand remained alive, though disease rather than Indian hatchets was primarily responsible.[71] Those of Tsenacommacah had reason to despair also. The drastic population decline was continuing, and there is every reason to believe contemporary reports that the aborigines were dying off far more rapidly than whites.[72] The picture emerging after the massacre is that the Indians, reduced in numbers, abandoned or were driven out of part of the Tidewater, and the two races for the most part lived in separate areas. Eventually defeated and cowed, independent tribes came to terms with the whites and accepted tributary status. As will be seen, this is part, but not all, of the story.

4

The Indomitable Old Dominion

For good reason Virginia, a military outpost during the early decades, had many governors who were soldiers. Hostilities persisted throughout the seventeenth century. With few exceptions, it was not the Spaniards in Florida, the French in Canada, or the Dutch navy but the New World's original inhabitants who were the enemy. Intervals of peace were infrequent. Occasionally full-scale Indian wars erupted: the 1622 and 1644 massacres, Colonel Edward Hill's expedition against the Ricahecrians in 1656, and Nathaniel Bacon's campaigns in 1676. More often than not conflicts were limited and hardly, if at all, noticed by posterity. For the first seven years intermittent fighting occurred. Arrows had greeted the Jamestown colonists when they first arrived in Chesapeake Bay; not until Pocahontas's marriage to Rolfe was there a semblance of peace. Even afterward, small parties of English soldiers continued to go out against Powhatan's enemies, if not his subjects.

After the 1622 massacre settlers waged relentless campaigns against the natives. General Sherman may have exaggerated in characterizing war as hell, but this assertion was no overstatement in regard to the Virginia Tidewater. Abandoning whatever notions they had about converting the aborigines, the English tried to drive the natives out of as much of the Tidewater as possible, assuming that the only lasting peace was that of the grave. Colonists made no pretense of respecting the traditional rules of warfare. Agreements made with the Indians were not to be honored but were used as a means of retrieving white prisoners or lulling savages into a false sense of security. The English in 1623 negotiated a treaty with rebellious tribes in the Potomac River area. After a toast was drunk symbolizing eternal friendship, the Chiskiack chief and his sons, advisers, and followers, totaling two hundred, abruptly dropped dead from poisoned sack, and soldiers put the remainder out of their misery.[1]

During periods of "peace" Indians sometimes made the mistake of visiting the colonists. If natives were not killed outright they were imprisoned and used for forced labor.[2] William Claiborne, a veteran Indian trader and fighter, invented a device to control or restrain the recalcitrant New World enemy. Without describing it, he explained how it could force natives, who retained freedom of movement, to do whatever their masters desired, including directing them to villages. Claiborne patented his invention (probably the first patent awarded in American history), and the council granted him exclusive control over his device, which seemed to have potential. Furthermore the council —and Claiborne was a member of that body—assigned him a captive with whom to experiment.[3] Indians were just as brutal and retaliated in kind, ambushing and killing men, women, and children indiscriminately, knocking out their brains with clubs and tomahawks, and dismembering and desecrating corpses. Each side took a few prisoners. The treatment of captives is not well documented; it is unlikely, however, that whites among the aborigines suffered any worse than their Indian counterparts.

After 1622 colonists perfected an effective and what over the long term proved to be the standard method of waging warfare against Eastern native Americans. Tactics used in seventeenth-century Virginia had much in common with those later employed by Anthony Wayne and Andrew Jackson against Great Lakes Indians and the Creeks. White commanders clearly understood that the Eastern aborigines, concentrated in villages and dependent on agriculture, were vulnerable. Until armed in the European manner, with few exceptions Indians refused to meet whites in pitched battles. As a result they took refuge in towns, many of which were well known and located on the detailed map made by John Smith; Claiborne's device helped ferret out those Smith missed. Whenever Virginia militiamen came upon an enemy town the strategy was essentially the same: cut down corn in easily accessible main fields and, if possible, in garden plots close to the wigwams; pull up and destroy the stone and basket fish weirs; burn houses, granaries, and ceremonial buildings; and kill or drive off the inhabitants regardless of age or sex. Villages without stockades lay most exposed. For a decade after 1622 the Virginians relentlessly harried the Indians, and occasional details have survived. On July 4, 1627, the council ordered a concerted attack to begin on August 1. Militia throughout the colony were to assemble at different locations and simultaneously move against the enemy. Soldiers mustered at Jones Neck and the College Lands were to go after the Tanx (Little) Powhatans; at Shirley Hundred and Percy Hundred, Jordan's Point, and Chaplain's Choice, against the Weanocs and Appomattocs; at Jamestown against the Chickahominies and Tappahannocks; and at Warrisquoiacke and Newport News against the Nansemonds and Chesapeakes.[4]

Soon after the 1622 massacre at least a few Indians, dismayed to see their houses burned and granaries and weirs destroyed, implored whites to leave them alone and allow them time to plant a crop of corn. They could not turn back the clock a millenium or two and live by hunting and gathering. Instead they starved, or nearly so. Later in the century, during Bacon's Rebellion, the Queen of the Pamunkeys and her attendants were run out of town, for many days forced to live in the woods off roots, nuts, and an occasional terrapin. It was a harrowing experience that nearly killed this ruler, who was somewhat "plump of body."[5] Most Indians evicted in this fashion survived after great difficulty, at least for a time. But their resistance was lowered, and local and imported microparasites lurked. As always they were the real killers. This, more than the colonists' military campaigns or anything else, best explains why they were able to appropriate Powhatan villages and take over their fields on the peninsula between the lower James and York rivers and nearby areas.

Over the years each side modified its tactics, especially the Indians. Powhatan's predecessors in all probability had battled their enemies in open fields before the whites arrived. But the aborigines simply were no match for Europeans, with their superior armaments, in this style of fighting, and natives began relying on surprise and ambush and on improving existing village fortifications. Carefully laying ambushes and patiently waiting for unsuspecting colonists to pass, Powhatans contrived innumerable ruses to lure whites into the woods where they could easily be dispatched. Warriors stealthily approached forts and plantations, stalking settlers much as they crept up on deer.

Major ambushes, such as the massacres of 1622 and 1644, involved hundreds of warriors and required considerable planning. Despite the fact the English did not trust the Powhatans and realized hostilities were possible at any time, settlers in 1622 were truly surprised when Indians, who were eating with them, had spent the night in their houses, or had arrived to sell corn and venison, simultaneously and without warning seized whatever weapons were at hand to butcher the dispersed and isolated colonists. A problem for the Indians was communications. Having no Julian calendar, they could not decree, as the council at Jamestown had, that on August 1 (or whenever) soldiers were to march against the closest enemy. Aboriginal priests understood a great deal about astronomy, summer and winter solstices, and lunar months. In theory Powhatan might order an attack at the next full moon. The danger was that at the critical time it might be cloudy or perhaps raining at Kecoughtan at the mouth of the James and clear at Henricus near the fall line. The Powhatans had no Aztec-type calendar and instead relied on a knotted cord or a bundle of sticks distributed in advance. One day was allotted to each knot or stick. The time to strike was when there were no more knots or all the sticks had been broken. Even without clocks, church bells, and a printed calendar, the Powhatans' system of keeping time was accurate enough, as colonists in 1622 and 1644 could attest.[6]

A dilemma for the native Virginians, one that they never satisfactorily resolved, was that living in villages left them concentrated and exposed. When militia approached, Indians had the options of fleeing into the forest while their granaries, fields, and houses were razed or remaining to fight, risking encirclement and annihilation. Traditional palisades had provided protection against an enemy armed with bows and arrows, and they still served well enough against musket balls. But soldiers with firearms, crossbows, and body armor approached much closer and were better able to set thatch, bark, and wooden structures afire, trapping the inhabitants within or cutting them down as they fled outside. In English Virginia, and to a lesser extent in Spanish Florida, a trend developed among the natives of living in a less compact fashion. Villages built during the seventeenth century and later tended to be spread out over 1, 2, or 3 miles and not enclosed by a palisade, and the percentage of Indians living in isolated houses increased. It took time for this pattern of settlement to emerge, and several reasons explain why. One was strictly military, because the aborigines grew tired of being trapped behind palisades, then burned to death within or shot as they fled.

An alternative to dispersing, one which Indians at times employed with effect, was to modify and strengthen the town's fortifications, employing aspects of European technology. Natives quickly learned much about the white science of military construction. They visited and helped build forts at Jamestown, Kecoughtan, and the falls of the James River, and observant Indians did not spend all their time doing cartwheels like the young Pocahontas. The aborigines had seen at first hand Raleigh's fort at Roanoke Island, the Spanish—and French—ones at Santa Elena, and Pardo's blockhouses in the back country, among others. Either as captives or of their own volition, whites lived in Indian towns and, under duress or voluntarily, instructed natives in techniques of European military construction. With memories of European forts on the African coast and in the West Indies, blacks at an early date appeared in aboriginal villages, at times employing their knowledge to good effect.

All of this means that Indians, if war and disease had not taken too heavy a toll, if they did not disperse, and if time permitted, fortified at least a few villages utilizing a combination of their own technology and certain European features. At the outset of Bacon's Rebellion, Susquehannocks entrenched themselves on the Potomac River, and a joint Virginia–Maryland force of one thousand men never took by assault this rectangular palisaded stronghold, with bastions at each corner, counterscarps, sally ports, and embrasures for both bows and arrows and muskets.[7] After a seven-week siege the starving Susquehannocks abandoned their fort, escaping to safety through enemy lines. With the advantage of surprise or trickery Bacon in 1676 did capture

THE ONLY LAND THEY KNEW

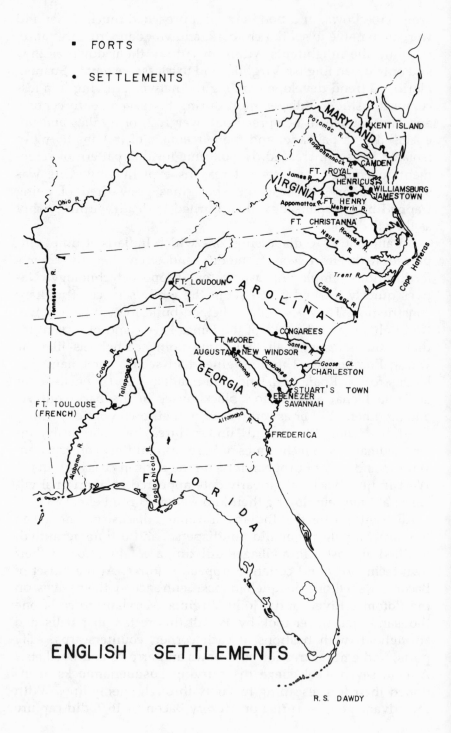

ENGLISH SETTLEMENTS

R. S. DAWDY

the Occaneechee fort on Occaneechee Island in the Roanoke River near present-day Clarksville, Virginia.[8] In the early eighteenth century Carolina militia were never able to take Hancock's stronghold on the Neuse by force because of its deep ditch, double tier of portholes in the stockade, and bastions at each corner.[9] The long-term trend, however, was for Indians not to reside in precontact palisaded villages or in more compact palisaded forts but to live in a dispersed fashion.

Whites as well as the aborigines modified their tactics. Since there were few pitched battles or sieges, razing Indian towns and destroying crops became the principal objective rather than a sideline. Colonial militia adopted more and more of the aboriginal dress for campaigning in the woods, including moccasins and deerskin mantles or jackets. Although effective against arrows, armor and breastplates were cumbersome and uncomfortable, and the Virginia militia gradually abandoned their use. During the first part of the seventeenth century they followed the Spanish example of substituting light quilted coats, which could stop an arrow, for breastplates.[10] Spaniards had gotten this idea from the Indians. Legally or not, Powhatans acquired firearms, and the quilted jackets, affording little protection against musket balls, in time also disappeared from the Tidewater. Natives had scalped victims before the whites arrived, and English colonists followed suit. Returning from a successful foray against Potomac River Indians in 1623, Captain William Tucker and his men proudly displayed parts of fifty Indian "heads," presumably scalps, though somewhat more may have been included.[11]

Following the precedent set by Roman soldiers in Britain, colonists relied on frontier forts for protection. In many respects these forts served a different purpose from that of Pardo's blockhouses or of those later built by Frenchmen in New France. The latter, usually deep in the Indian country, were surrounded by natives on all sides. In Virginia, especially after the 1622 massacre, the tendency was to have the aborigines on one side and whites on the other. The location of the line of frontier forts varied. At first they were at Jamestown, Middle Plantation (Williamsburg), and Chiskiack on the lower peninsula between the James and York rivers. As the white population grew, forts were moved westward to the fall line of the James, Appomattox, Mattaponi, Rappahannock, and Potomac. This string of forts dividing the two races signified that seventeenth-century colonists had lost most of their zeal for converting and assimilating the natives. Militia usually manned these forts, a source of weakness, because historically militiamen did not adjust well to garrison duty. Sometimes friendly Indians were hired to help protect the forts and patrol between them.[12] There was never much doubt that parties of enemy warriors, if they had a mind to, could slip through the gaps. Despite weaknesses and imperfections, the concept of white civilization on one side of the line and aboriginal culture on the other had many merits from a military standpoint, and Virginians employed this tactic as long as Indians posed a threat.

Any number of causes contributed to hostilities convulsing the Tidewater during the first half of the seventeenth century. Despite an inordinate white mortality and the fact that hundreds of colonists perished in the 1622 massacre, the Virginia population dramatically expanded from just over a thousand in 1624 to some twenty-five thousand in 1660. This burgeoning white populace created new tensions, and the number of white–Indian confrontations mounted. For whatever reason, unruly settlers capriciously killed Indians, sometimes influential priests and chiefs. Opechancanough himself, after his capture in the winter of 1644–45, waited in Jamestown before being shipped to England. Without orders a soldier walked up behind the wizened chief and shot him. Murders of this kind were common, and one does not have to know much about clan vengeance, even when chiefs were not involved, to understand why hostilities persisted in the Tidewater. To prevent mischief the assembly in 1641 decreed that if an Indian stole anything from whites or committed any type of felony, the next one along could be imprisoned and must pay—if necessary with his life.[13]

Whites gradually displaced Indians living on the lower peninsula between the James and the York and on the Eastern Shore. These colonists were farmers growing tobacco and corn and raising livestock. Cattle and hogs, branded by their owners, roamed at will until periodic roundups. On occasion they rooted in aboriginal cornfields, or the natives hunted them like deer. As time passed Indians acquired cattle and swine, which hardly ever were fenced in. A constant source of friction, wandering livestock, a new phenomenon, provoked a multitude of incidents.

In seventeenth-century Virginia, and with few exceptions in ensuing years, a fixed policy of the whites was to set Indians against one another, *divide et impera*. John Smith and his contemporaries tried to turn the Potomacs and Monacans against Powhatan; in mid-century authorities prevailed on Pamunkeys and Chickahominies to go against the Ricahecrians. Reviewing the effects of intertribal warfare in 1678, the governor professed: "I never thought it the interest of this colony to hinder them from cutting each others throats."[14] One of the risks of such a policy was that colonists often got drawn into rivalries far more deeply than planned. Closely associated with promoting wars was the kidnapping of native children and their sale into slavery. It was Indians themselves, encouraged by whites to be sure, who surprised neighboring towns and carried off their young. Whenever they could, harassed Indians retaliated against aboriginal aggressors and their white sponsors. Periodically authorities at Jamestown warned against kidnapping children, even passing a law in 1649 to outlaw it.[15] In an earlier day King Canute had commanded the tide in the Thames River not to rise, with the same result.

The second and last major conflict in the Tidewater was the 1644 massacre, plotted by the aged Opechancanough. Even though more than five hundred colonists were surprised and killed, more than in 1622, astoundingly little has been written or is known about this second uprising, in which at least one out of every sixteen Virginians perished. In 1622 the actual percentage of those who lost their lives, one out of four, had been far higher. Never again in Virginia's history after 1644, not even during the 1861–65 Civil War, would such a high proportion of the population be killed. There does not appear to be any deliberate conspiracy to downplay the losses of the 1644 massacre—it was whites, of course, who labeled this and similar conflicts as massacres. Planters hoping to attract more indentured servants and land speculators wanting to dispose of their holdings had no reason to publicize the conflict. Even more significant in explaining this silence is destruction of public and private records by fire, war, and the ravages of time.[16]

It is sometimes argued that the cunning Opechancanough took advantage of confusion caused by the Puritan Revolution in England to launch his surprise attack.[17] There is every reason to assume, however, that Opechancanough did not look beyond the Tidewater, and the disputes already mentioned were serious enough in themselves to provoke hostilities. Whether a specific incident ignited the 1644 attack is unknown. Despite the risks, profits from tobacco culture had encouraged whites to spread out along the James and York rivers. Those farthest from Jamestown, particularly on the western frontier and south of the James River, were most vulnerable, and once again, though separated by great distances, warriors struck simultaneously. They cut down and hacked to pieces colonists in their homes and fields, but details must be left to the imagination.

White militia then employed the same tactics, which had worked so well in the past, against enemy villages. Clad in body armor, William Claiborne and other colonial soldiers led expeditions that drubbed the natives, the Opechancanough himself was captured and killed. Details of the 1646 peace are clearer than the conflict itself. One thing was obvious: Tsenacommacah was shattered. Pressure from settlers, Indian enemies, and disease had taken a heavy toll, and with few exceptions Powhatan survivors were expelled from the peninsula between the York and James rivers, the heartland of the old confederacy. Necotowance, "king of the Indians," signed a peace treaty that recognized the obvious—that the Indians had been defeated. The peace, in every respect satisfactory to the colonists, stipulated that his subjects would stay and hunt on the north side of the York River or the south side of the James. Except for trade and matters of high import, Indians were to have little contact with whites. Whenever it was necessary to communicate with the colonists, native messengers must approach designated forts and fortified plantations on the frontier: Fort Royal on the Pamunkey, Fort Henry on the Appomattox, and Captain John Floud's plantation on the James. Indians found in ceded lands who were not wearing special striped coats picked up at the designated forts were to be killed on sight, and any white illegally entertaining Indians was to be punished severely. Necotowance promised to restore English and Negro prisoners and to hand over all the Indians' firearms. Whatever his color, any servant who had sought refuge among the natives was to be returned. Aboriginal children under twelve years of age could legally remain in ceded lands, all of which was little more than recognition of the slave trade.[18]

In ensuing years the provisions of the 1646 treaty were modified. Indians were permitted to come to Captain Edward Hill's plantation at Westover on the James and to Captain William Taylor's at Chiskiack on the York to pick up the required striped coats, and specific hunting lands in Gloucester and Lancaster counties north of the York River were reserved.[19] The English expected Necotowance, king of all the Powhatan Confederacy Indians, to see that the treaty was scrupulously obeyed. It is doubtful that the natives ever conceded Necotowance as much power as did the whites. Colonists had authority to kill on sight any free Indian they saw in settled areas, and, regardless of what they thought of Necotowance and his treaty, natives understood this well enough.[20]

During the first half of the seventeenth century hostilities occurred largely in the Tidewater, especially on the James and York rivers, and to a lesser extent on the Potomac River and the Eastern Shore. By mid-century the number of aborigines living in the Tidewater had been drastically reduced. Those few who remained continued to lose their lands in one way or another and to see their assigned hunting areas further constricted. After 1650 hostilities shifted to the Piedmont beyond the fall line, where Indians were more numerous and less intimidated by the English.

Expanding European settlements in Maryland, New York, Canada, and Florida created tensions among all the Eastern Indians, which today are still not clearly understood. As they had since De Soto's and Luna's day, Indians continued to move about frequently. "Foreign" warriors appeared on the Virginia frontier in the latter half of the century, creating alarms and incidents. As a result of pressure from colonists in Maryland and New York, the Indians' desire to expand trade and hunting areas, and raids by Iroquois warriors on their southern neighbors, Senecas, Mohawks, and Susquehannocks descended on the Virginia back country.

The enigmatic Ricahecrians also fell into this category, and it is possible that they were Mohawks or Senecas from the north. In all likelihood, however, they had come from the south and were Cherokees, Westos, or Yuchis. Whatever their origin, several thousand of these strangers settled about the fall line of the James River at mid-century. Thoroughly alarmed, the Virginia assembly ordered troops out. At the head of the militia and tributary Powhatans, Colonel Edward Hill marched to Ricahecrian villages, but in this instance it was the colonists who were surprised and defeated. Colonel Hill spent considerable time explaining and justifying his leadership and high casualties.

Without fanfare the Ricahecrians in time moved away, perhaps joining the Iroquois in New York but more likely to the south, where Carolinians may have come to know them as Westos.[21]

The most serious Indian conflict in the latter half of the century, certainly the best publicized, was the fighting associated with Bacon's Rebellion. Much has been written about this struggle, not necessarily because it involved the aborigines but because it represented a colonial challenge to imperial authority. One school contends that hostilities in Virginia in 1676 were a prelude to those at Lexington and Concord a century later.[22] This is not our main concern. It is paradoxical, however, that so much documentation survives about the 1676 Indian hostilities in which at most three hundred colonists perished, whereas so little is left from 1644, when the population was considerably smaller and twice that number died.

Causes of the 1676 conflict in a general way were those basic issues already discussed. Susquehannocks moving into the Potomac River area sparked hostilities, which spread all along the frontier. Whites were killed, including the overseer at the Nathanial Bacon, Jr., plantation in Henrico County near the fall of the James River. Rallying to Bacon as their leader, neighboring farmers demanded an aggressive campaign and denounced Governor Berkeley for depending so much on frontier forts. Bacon and his followers asserted that Berkeley had a secret interest in the Indian trade and was intriguing to monopolize it, which was why he refused to send militia against the hostiles. This is a specious issue. If anyone wanted to monopolize the trade it was Bacon and his adherents, notably William Byrd I.[23] In his study of colonial Virginia, Edmund Morgan contends that the Indians really had little to do with causing Bacon's Rebellion. Instead, he maintains, Bacon contrived to divert the anger and frustrations of unruly, rebellious lower-class whites away from the ruling elite and toward the natives.[24]

Especially in the earlier stages of the rebellion, Indians bore the brunt of the fighting. Pamunkeys and similar tributaries in the Tidewater, along with Occaneechees and other more numerous tribes in the Piedmont, furnished warriors to go against the Susquehannocks. But Bacon's men soon turned against all Indians, friend and foe alike, knocking a female servant of the Queen of Pamunkey on the head because she would not lead them to the Queen's village. The militia found it anyway and managed to carry off skins, trading goods, and forty-five unfortunate Indians.[25] Bacon's major campaign (a few months before his "victory" over the Pamunkeys) was against warriors at Occaneechee Island on the Roanoke River, a great commercial center for trade to the southwest. Initially only Susquehannocks, who had fortified themselves and taken refuge close to the island, were the enemy, and the more numerous Occaneechees were allies. Affairs got out of hand, and Bacon's men, who never even engaged the Susquehannocks, surprised the Occaneechees and laid siege to their fort, which they burned and captured. Inside lay an enormous amount of booty, mostly furs and skins.[26] In accounts of the battle, Bacon's soldiers prided themselves on their restraint: Ignoring potential profits from captive slaves, they instead shot or burned to death almost all the Indians.[27]

During the rebellion Indian fighting became less significant as hostilities more and more concerned Bacon and Berkeley. In June 1676 Bacon's armed followers forced the governor and assembly at Jamestown to authorize a campaign against the natives with Bacon as commander, and at the same time the assembly passed a number of laws, rightly or not, best known to posterity as Bacon's Laws. One can debate at length whether these laws liberalized a colony ruled by the despotic Berkeley, but there can be little argument that they enjoyed widespread popular support, which was not limited to Bacon's followers. These laws treated almost all Indians as the enemy. Lands of tributaries that had been "abandoned" after 1644 were to be confiscated and sold to help pay for the war. Possibilities for fraud and chicanery were unlimited. Militia sent against native towns were to share the plunder, and booty included captives as well as peltry.[28] Friendly Indians who fled at the approach of Bacon's men knew what they were about. In the latter phases of the rebellion most of the fighting occurred in the Tidewater. After Bacon became sick and died, Berkeley was able to regroup and crush resistance even before the reinforcements arrived from the mother country.

In the aftermath, as Bacon's followers were executed and their property confiscated, still another treaty was negotiated with or imposed on the aborigines. This 1677 treaty confirmed provisions of the treaty of 1646, and again one is struck by the debility of the Powhatan Confederacy. When Jesuits had come to Jacán in 1570 and at the time of the 1622 and 1644 massacres this powerful confederacy had displayed the capacity to inflict serious if not mortal blows on Europeans. But no more. They had made their last unsuccessful bid in 1644, paying for it dearly. To a limited extent survivors of the confederacy had been involved in Bacon's Rebellion, but their participation had not counted for much.

In the eyes of Berkeley's ardent royalist supporters the good Queen of Pamunkey had become a victimized heroine. Presumably a collateral descendant of both Powhatan and Opechancanough, she enjoyed the modicum of power and prestige surviving from an earlier day. The Queen had fought with Berkeley against Bacon, or a better way of putting it was that Bacon raided her village, forcing the Queen and a handful of followers to take to the woods and live off roots. Berkeley, and in turn his successor, Colonel Herbert Jeffreys, commended whites and the Queen alike for fighting at great sacrifice against the rebels, at their peril upholding the King's authority. It was pointed out that the Queen had been a loyal subject for years. Her husband had died fighting for the English when he accompanied Colonel Hill in his disastrous campaign against the Ricahecrians in 1656. All but five of the forty-five Pamunkeys whom Bacon had captured and whom he or Berkeley had sold were restored.[29] The Queen was singled out for special consideration. Royal commissioners sent over to quell the rebellion ordered a striped gown, purple robe, necklace, and silver crown adorned with multicolored false stones for her and silver badges and lesser presents for other chiefs.[30] The treaty specified that all chiefs wielded equal authority except the Queen. Scattered tribes of the old confederacy still owed her their ancient loyalty, and the Virginia militia would ensure that the Queen's will was enforced. The treaty also contained provisions relating to all tributaries, specifying where they could hunt, fish, and gather berries, nuts, and bark; how close whites could settle to Indian villages; and the amount of tribute each tribe must pay.[31]

It was ironic that this peace treaty, like many others throughout American history, for the most part was imposed on friends rather than foes. The Susquehannocks and their allies were the villains, but they were dead or out of reach. Whites demanded peace and called upon the closest natives at hand to sign one.

Indian hostilities persisted. Sometimes outbreaks similar to Bacon's Rebellion erupted; more often there were local encounters attracting little attention. Natives were killed visiting frontier forts; whites and Indians raided villages for slaves; and farmers shot aboriginal hunters who they assumed were after hogs rather than deer. The effects of fighting and especially disease proved catastrophic for the natives. The Queen of Pamunkey in 1670 counted as her subjects or neighbors only 725 bowmen scattered over the Tidewater, whereas a century earlier a single village contained that many warriors.[32] Whatever their size before Europeans arrived, by 1677 most towns of the Powhatan Confederacy had disappeared. Yeoman farmers and planters with servants and slaves had appropriated these sites and were busily growing tobacco and maize.

The destruction of aborigines in the Tidewater was obvious, as their population declined from perhaps more than one hundred thousand in 1500 to approximately 1,400 in 1700. Without quibbling about the accuracy of these figures, the broad outline remains clear. The only difference between Virginia and the Greater Antilles was that the percentage of survivors in Virginia was slightly higher. We catch only infrequent glimpses of the disruption of Tidewater villages, whereas two centuries later, when President Andrew Jackson forced Southern Indians to relocate west of the Mississippi River, soldiers, missionaries, government officials, and the uprooted themselves left eyewitness accounts of this Trail of Tears, describing how villages had to be abandoned overnight and how natives marched, bled, and suffered for hundreds of miles before reaching Oklahoma. Almost no such accounts remain of what happened in the Virginia Tidewater.

There is an occasional exception. Virginia and North Carolina long quarreled about their boundary's exact location. In an attempt to uphold her claim and confirm the identity of key landmarks, representatives of Virginia early in the eighteenth century interviewed aged Indians and veteran traders. Great Peter, a Nansemond chief over sixty years of age, recounted how many years before the Weanocs, some of whom eventually merged with the Nansemonds, had lived in a village on the James River. In the aftermath of the 1644 massacre, Weanoc survivors had fled southward to the Roanoke River; soon they moved to Wicocons Creek, building a fort there for protection and for several years planting and harvesting corn. Because of danger from neighboring Indians the Weanocs moved to Ware Keck; when Potkiaks killed their chief, they moved back to the James River seeking English protection. After a short time they retired to Cotchawesk and then to Chowans, where they made a crop of corn one summer. They relocated at Unoonteh, but Tuscaroras attacked them soon after corn was planted. The Weanocs again headed north and solicited protection from the English in Virginia; before long they retired to Musketank. Then, during Bacon's Rebellion, they returned to their old fort near Wicocons.[33] In 1970 Alvin Toffler wrote a best-seller, *Future Shock*, describing the psychological stresses Americans confronted in twentieth-century industrial United States as families frenetically moved about losing their roots. Toffler argued that this hectic twentieth-century mobility was new,[34] but he had overlooked the Weanoc survivors who sought refuge with Great Peter. There is every reason to assume that the Weanoc experience was not exceptional. Most Indians did not live where there was an intercolonial boundary dispute; not often does posterity see smoke rising from aboriginal towns as whites put houses to the torch or as Indians themselves burned them after sickness had killed the occupants.

Relentless white military pressure, constant moving about and the resultant threat of starvation, and the ravages of disease forced survivors in the Tidewater to accept tributary status. Details varied, and some tribes, such as the Weanocs, alternated between areas of effective English control and the more remote Indian country. Statutes and treaties, including those of 1646 and 1677, spelled out the broad outline of tributary status. The aborigines realized they were no longer lords of the Tidewater. As much as anything the annual tribute of so many deerskins, beaver pelts, or arm's lengths of roanoke symbolized the new order. Adding but little to the provincial treasury, this tribute became increasingly burdensome to the Indians as their numbers continued to shrink.[35] On occasion tributaries were not even allowed near white settlements except when wearing striped coats or appropriate medals. Colonists bestowed these silver and copper medals, typically engraved with the bust of the English monarch, on designated chiefs who might or might not have exercised power in their own right. Under the new arrangement, the chief's power stemmed from the English. The Queen of Pamunkey after 1677 appealed to the colonists to make remnant Powhatan tribes show her proper respect and pay her the customary spring and fall tribute.[36] If they had dealings with other tribes, village elders had to negotiate through the whites; that is, the English had to either deliver the belts of wampum personally or first see and approve them.[37]

Dependent Indians at times were required to hand over children as hostages. While guaranteeing the good behavior of their
elders, these youths would be apprenticed to masters who would
teach them a trade or European methods of farming. When they
reached a specified age, usually in the twenties, they might re-
join their families or work as freemen among the whites.[38] The
children the Indians delivered to whites were not necessarily
their own but perhaps their neighbors'. Virginians, bound to
protect their wards, at times had to save them from the wrath of
neighbors whose children they had stolen.

Another aspect of the tributary system was to require warriors
to hunt wolves. These predators had proved a costly nuisance to
settlers, and at an early date natives had been paid to kill them.
As the tributary system took hold, Indians did not necessarily
have a choice, nor were they paid. Annual tribute sometimes
included wolves' heads or ears.[39] It was not a difficult transition
from requiring warriors to deliver animal ears to paying them for
human scalps.

Tributaries constantly traded with the English. White merchants and interpreters (sometimes the same person) visited villages, perhaps living there, exchanging hardware, textiles, guns,
powder, and rum for peltry, lands, captive children, and favors
from native women. Over the long run, however, it was the more
numerous nontributaries who were the most important commercial partners. From the initial settlement at Jamestown until the
eve of nineteenth-century removal, the Indian trade throughout
the South remained important, though in Virginia it was less
significant than tobacco culture. Unlike other colonies, such as
New Jersey, Connecticut, and Rhode Island, Virginia had a large
hinterland to tap; for more than half a century she was England's
southernmost colony, having no competitors except the Spaniards in Florida, and she claimed the Ohio Valley to the west. As
a result, the peltry trade did not die out in early years after settlement.

During the seventeenth and eighteenth centuries the demand
increased in Europe and the colonies for leather and furs used for
clothing, saddlery, and shoes. Surviving customs records suggest
the variety and magnitude of this commerce. Along with the
hogsheads of tobacco are listed the chests or weight of buckskins
and doeskins, beaver, fox, wolf, skunk, moose, raccoon, elk,
muskrat, bear, mink, and otter. As time passed deerskins became more important than furs.[40]

As long as they survived in any numbers, the Powhatans and their neighbors had surplus food to trade. When Indians bartered maize they sometimes included a basket or clay pot in the transaction. Whites kept and used these containers in their households, and some of the finely woven baskets, painted and embroidered with beads, were highly treasured. Wooden Indian bowls, spoons, and platters also appeared in English kitchens.[41] Precontact aborigines had gathered cane and rushes for mats to cover sides of wigwams, to serve as partitions, to sit on, and for a variety of other utilitarian purposes. Colonists had need of these mats, especially as sleeping pads. Indians grew and smoked tobacco and used it for medicinal purposes, but the local tobacco of Powhatan's Virginia, *nicotiana rustica*, was too bitter for white consumption. John Rolfe imported a new variety from the West Indies and perfected a method of curing it. Rolfe's tobacco, grown by English planters rather than by Indians, was exported from Virginia. Natives as well as whites smoked tobacco, and their decorated clay pipes if not their tobacco were exchanged during the early years.[42]

More valuable than wooden spoons, mats, and hundredweights of leather were aboriginal slaves. Colonists acquired them in a variety of ways, sometimes labeling them apprentices. Such unfortunates were bought and sold in Virginia and used locally or shipped to other mainland colonies and the West Indies. Because of incomplete customs records, and because so many captives remained in Virginia, it is not at first apparent how significant this aspect of the Indian trade was.

There were, of course, two sides to commerce. The aborigines received highly prized manufactures, including iron hoes, shovels, and other agricultural implements, carpentry tools and nails, occasionally an entire English-built house, knives, hatchets, woolen clothing from hats to stockings and leggings, rum, brandy, and similar distilled spirits, belts used by English soldiers to hold cartouche boxes, and, most important of all, firearms and munitions. Throughout the seventeenth century the Jamestown government alternately prohibited and sanctioned the sale of firearms. It made little difference, however, because if the Indians did not get them from Virginia they could obtain them from Maryland and New York to the north or, after 1670, from Carolinians to the south.

Much, presumably most, of the Anglo-Indian trade was simple

barter. Several commodities and items of English or aboriginal manufacture served as a medium of exchange to facilitate commerce. Among them were roanoke and peake, different types of wampum or shell beads laboriously fashioned by native craftsmen. Goods, services, and even court fines were valued at so many arm's lengths of roanoke or peake. The English soon imported or manufactured locally their own wampum, blue beads, which became standard trade items and have been uncovered by archaeologists in profuse quantities. An aboriginal canoe in 1624 was worth 10,000 blue beads, a stack of mats, 20,000.[43] Matchcoats also served as a medium of exchange. The term was an English corruption of the Algonquian "matchkore," the common deerskin mantle. The English began manufacturing woolen mantles, distributing them to natives, who gradully discarded matchkores. Indians sold land at one matchcoat per 100 acres, and they also reckoned guns, powder, skins, and days of service in matchcoats.[44]

The center of the Virginia Indian trade changed from time to time. At first there was a northern thrust, as William Claiborne and others exploited commerce on the upper Chesapeake Bay. Competition from Maryland, founded in 1633, and from the Swedes on the Delaware River and the Dutch in New York encouraged Virginians to look elsewhere. Trade on Virginia's northern frontier did not disappear, as conflicts with Maryland competitors on the Eastern Shore and the upper Potomac River testified. Richard Lee, founder of a famous dynasty, was a ruthless trader, for years deeply involved in commerce on the York and Potomac rivers.[45] Until Charleston was founded in 1670, the only permanent European settlements south of Virginia were those of the Spaniards in Florida and a handful of English on Albemarle Sound. Spain exercised control over Florida through the mission system. Franciscans and civil authorities supplied manufactures to the aborigines only in limited quantities. For decades Virginia traders in the Tidewater met little competition in the enormous Indian area to the south and southwest.

By land and sea enterprising merchants invaded the Indian country to the south. In mid-century Francis Yeardley, son of a former governor living at Lynnhaven near the mouth of Chesapeake Bay, sent his agents to Roanoke Island, where ruins of Raleigh's colony were still visible. From this base they traded with coastal Algonquians and more numerous Tuscaroras in the interior. Aboard Yeardley's ships or on their own by land, some of these Indians traveled to Yeardley's plantation, and a few lived with him permanently. Yeardley carried on a brisk trade, acquiring not only skins and furs but, if Yeardley is to be believed, title to most of the future North Carolina.[46]

Other Virginia merchants, indeed most of them, used well-worn aboriginal trails. Planter merchants living at or below the falls of the James River and at the Appomattox River, which empties into the upper James, dominated the southwestern Indian commerce. Packhorses, perhaps a handful or up to fifty or one hundred, set out on journeys that might take them 400 miles into the interior. Months later these animals and their drivers returned from distant villages laden with skins and other valuables. Abraham Wood survived the vicissitudes of the early years, in time becoming one of the wealthier and more powerful figures in the province. The Indian trade helped explain his affluence. He was in charge of Fort Henry on the Appomattox (Petersburg), and in 1650, accompanied by Edward Bland, two other whites, and Indian guides, he explored part of the Carolina back country, learning more about the Occaneechees and their entrepôt at Occaneechee Island.[47] More than two decades later he sent first Robert Fallam and Thomas Batts, and then James Needham and Gabriel Arthur, across the mountains in an attempt to open up a more westerly branch of his trade.[48] Wood had rivals for this lucrative commerce. The Hatchers—Henry, Edward, Joseph, and others—living in Henrico Country on the James River, trafficked with Occaneechees and remnants of the Cofitachiqui.[49] William Byrd I was Wood's most serious competitor, his packhorsemen doing everything possible to ensure that skins came to the James rather than the Appomattox. Reputedly Byrd summarily killed Indians friendly to Wood.[50] In the long run the principal trading routes of colonial Virginia were to the south and southwest, as Byrd, Wood, the Hatchers, and their successors battled for this commerce.

For years controversy flourished as to whether there should be a monopoly or free trade with the Indians. Theoretically a monopoly, ensuring a dependable supply of goods for the natives, brought order to this commerce. It also excluded disgruntled white competitors and allowed Indians to be gouged. This issue was never resolved in seventeenth-century Virginia or anywhere else in the South as long as the trade remained of any consequence.

Virginia Indians could be divided into three broad categories: tributaries settled on reservations in the Tidewater close to or surrounded by whites; foreign or enemy tribes living beyond the frontier having little to do with any colonists other than traders; and slave, bond, and free natives living and working among the settlers. These diverse Indians gave rise to myriad legal problems, which the colonists never completely resolved, partly because they did not try. Foreign Indians legally occasioned the least difficulties. Magistrates regarded them as "sovereign" nations and normally did not try to impose the common or Roman law on them.

It was not so simple for tributaries. In theory they were also considered sovereign, but statutes and treaties had spelled out their subordinate status in detail. Courts at times meted out justice. Indian subjects, for example, did not necessarily approve of the king or ruler picked by the whites: Chickahominies and Rappahannocks refused to show proper respect to the good Queen of Pamunkey; the Potomac chief complained to the English that his great men were trying to poison him; and natives were inclined to shoot puffed-up chiefs living in English-built houses.[51] Depending on circumstances, the courts or militia were called on to restore order.

Whether slave or free, Christian or pagan, Indians living intimately among the whites caused the most problems. Slaves were governed by the slave code. Virginia did not have a rudimentary code until sometime after 1660, and confusion persisted as to whether provisions applied to blacks and Indians alike, or whether the aborigines were special. Stemming from medieval apprenticeship laws, a considerable body of law applied to all servants, but the fact that native apprentices frequently were pagan presented difficulties. County courts heard cases concerning Indian indentured servants, perhaps ruling that the servant had violated his contract in one fashion or another and must serve his master additional time. Occasionally the court freed an Indian held beyond his period of service or ordered a master to furnish better food and clothing.[52] A number of free Christian Indians lived in the Tidewater, owning land and servants, making wills and contracts, and in most ways treated by the courts as any other freeman.[53] No free Indian, however, could own a white indentured servant.[54]

Exactly how an Indian, regardless of his or her condition, was to be treated varied according to circumstances. Sometimes when a native was accused of murder, whites decided the simplest solution was to let clan vengeance take its course;[55] at other times the culprit was tried by a white jury. A Virginia Quaker, thrown into the Jamestown jail in mid-century, complained that he was fastened with a heavy ox chain to an Indian who had been condemned to execution for murder.[56] Natives got into debt and like whites were imprisoned when they could not pay. The Weanoc king, a tributary chief, found himself in this circumstance. Magistrates decided to free him, at least for the time being, to avert still another war.[57] On occasion whites who assaulted or shot Indians were brought to trial, but the penalties, a matchcoat or a few arm's lengths of roanoke, were far less severe than those meted out to the aborigines. Authorities took seriously strictures against fornication and bastardy, as innumerable seventeenth-century Virginia women with stripes on their backs or who had stood penitent in front of a church congregation could testify. When attempts were made to bring female Indians into conformity with Christian precepts and to whip them for fornication, the court frequently ruled that in such matters natives were outside the law.[58] Not so for Priss, a mixed-blood Virginia Indian in the early eighteenth century, who became pregnant. In her case the Indian Edward Bagwell stepped forward, promising to assume all costs the parish might have to bear.[59]

For other infractions, Indians—tributary, slave, free, or "foreign"—were fined, whipped, imprisoned, and hanged, as were whites. The aborigines did not always passively accept the white man's law. When the constable of Accomack County delivered a warrant to John the Bowlmaker, John seized the poor constable by the hair, "drawing blood." The county court imposed a sentence of sixty lashes on John, and the unnerved constable eventually had his day.[60]

Like their counterparts in the mother country, magistrates in Virginia used the threat of transportation to keep the disorderly in line. In England transgressors were threatened with exile to the colonies; in America refractory Indians faced the prospect of being cut off from their families and shipped to the West Indies. There is no record that felons going in opposite directions crossed paths on the high seas, but they easily could have.[61]

The aborigines did not understand the intricacies of English law. Because they did not normally own land outright, bring suit, or enter into contracts, they had little contact with the proceedings of the judicial system. Their names are usually missing from surviving court records. One exception is the lists of tithables compiled annually for tax purposes. Whether the Indians knew it or not—and they probably did not—their names appeared in these records. Indians served whites in various capacities, and masters were obligated to list them along with children and other dependents. Masters were more likely to "forget" to list such Indian servants, however.

More than anything else, land brought the aborigines into contact with English law. Desire for land impelled aristocrats and lowborn alike to come to Virginia; those who survived acquired holdings at Indian expense. Colonists assumed that sovereignty resided with the company and the King. Indians could not or would not see this logic, and during the early years they greatly outnumbered the colonists. Settlers considered it essential to make the natives realize that they had never really owned their lands and that Christians were going to colonize them. Despite an occasional purchase from the Indians and high-flown rhetoric about dealing gently with the natives, force was the usual answer. English forts and military expeditions, immeasurably assisted by epidemics, destroyed and uprooted villages on the lower James. Colonists settled there, appropriating abandoned villages and fields, and the tempo accelerated in the wake of the 1622 and 1644 massacres.

Particularly in the aftermath of the later massacre, colonists purchased native lands, exchanging copper, beads, matchcoats, horses, bridles, saddles, and English-built houses for aboriginal title. A variation was for white merchants to advance goods to Indians on credit and to require the natives, hopelessly in debt, to part with their lands. It was ironic that aboriginal title in one sense was of no consequence and at the same time of overriding importance to prospective settlers. Regardless of whether the crown, general assembly, governor, or anyone else approved, Indian purchases were consummated, for, as ambitious colonists recognized, the first step in winning a handsome tract was to secure a deed signed by one or more chiefs who, according to promoters, had authority to make the sale. The fact that lands in question might belong to the seller's neighbors or enemies was of little consequence. After acquiring a native grant of whatever validity, the next and most important step was to get the crown, governor, general assembly, or county court to confirm it. Once this was done, the owner might develop and sell his tract with some confidence, even though still involved in legal disputes. A basis for such optimism was that many purchasers also were county justices of the peace, assemblymen in the House of Burgesses, and members of the council, having good reason to expect the government to listen sympathetically to their pleas. Giles Brent and George Mason, Westmoreland County magistrates, in the early 1660s attempted—unsuccessfully in this instance—to have the local court condemn Wahanganoche, the Potomac king, to death as the first step in taking over his lands.[62] Samuel Mathews was more fortunate, getting the provincial government to confirm his Wighcocomoco cession in Northumberland County. Mathews was governor.[63] The assembly ruled in 1656 that Indians could not sell or alienate lands without that body's approval, so colonists began "leasing" lands or holding them until gambling debts had been satisfied. Some four decades later the assembly decreed that these practices too were illegal, but by then the bulk of the Tidewater had been disposed of, as had most of the aborigines living there.[64] In seventeenth-century Virginia the precedent was established for colonists, by whatever means, to obtain an Indian purchase and then to intrigue to have the provincial government or the crown confirm it. Virginia's last royal governor, run out of the colony by Patrick Henry in 1775, was busy doing just this on the eve of his expulsion. So was Patrick Henry himself.[65]

The Virginia Company, and after 1624 the crown, disposed of an enormous amount of land according to the system of headrights. As a means of stimulating colonization, each head of a family received a specified amount of land (usually 50 acres or more) for each person he brought into the colonies, including himself, his wife, children, indentured servants, and slaves. It was a twist of irony that Indian headrights were used to secure grants of land in America awarded to European immigrants. Indians involved were not originally from Virginia, or at least they were not supposed to be; instead they came from the West Indies and the mainland colonies, especially Carolina. Throughout the century, from 1625 when Thomas, an Indian boy, was listed on a ship's muster, until 1699, when Robin, a Jamaican Indian, set foot in Virginia, imported natives, usually indentured servants or slaves, arrived in the colony, securing fifty acres for some enterprising white.[66]

Reviewing the seventeenth century, it can be seen that Virginia set the pattern for Anglo-Indian relations in other mainland colonies. Accustomed to trading with Europeans before 1607 and suffering from severe epidemics, the natives had not been startled or overly alarmed by whites who arrived at Jamestown. After 1607 the Indians experienced a love-hate relationship, sometimes crawling on all fours to shoot at unwary colonists, at other times filling baskets with maize and killing deer for venison, which they brought to Jamestown to barter. In time unremitting military campaigns and diseases shattered Powhatan society. The good Queen of Pamunkey toward the end of the century was thoroughly cowed and accepted tributary status. Estimates of the Powhatan Confederacy's population in 1600 vary widely, but there is every reason to accept Mooney's and other traditional figures for the end of that century. The Queen counted at most 725 bowmen as dependents in 1668, and by the end of the century that number had been cut in half.[67] Tributary or not, aboriginal villages repeatedly had been consolidated from two, three, or more into one, leaving innumerable Indian "old fields." Natives might have slowed down this process had they cooperated among themselves, but the white policy of encouraging tribal rivalries, of dividing and conquering, had succeeded. At the end of the century most Indians, certainly those posing a military threat to Virginia, lived some distance beyond the fall line frontier. But commerce and smallpox epidemics made Tuscarora, Cherokee, and even Seneca warriors, though possibly they never saw a white face, aware of the English presence in the Tidewater. With local variations, this pattern was repeated again and again, especially in Carolina.

5

Goose Creek Men

The spacious area south of the English settlements on the James River became known as Carolina. Considering it an integral part of Florida, Ayllón and his Spanish contemporaries had partitioned the region into provinces such as Chicora, Xoxi, and Anoxa. In Raleigh's day the English regarded this territory as part of Virginia, but during the seventeenth century they began referring to it as Carolina. According to limits set forth by the 1665 royal charter, Carolina extended to the 36°30′ parallel on the north and the 29° parallel on the south. This included much of Florida, not only areas that Spain had briefly explored or temporarily occupied but also St. Augustine and the Guale-Orista (Santa Elena) missions on the Atlantic Coast, along with those in Apalachee. The Spanish population in Florida was not large, but through forts, blockhouses, missions, and thousands of Christian Indians she effectively controlled much of "Carolina." Spaniards and Indians either did not know about Charles II's charter or else paid it no mind.

When one journeyed south from the James River in the seventeenth century it was necessary to travel 500 miles before encountering another European settlement—Franciscan missions at Port Royal Sound. Englishmen had made several attempts to settle the intervening area. Raleigh had failed in the 1580s. Around 1630 the English Attorney General, Robert Heath, endeavored to colonize Carolina, primarily with refugee French Huguenots. Although in the end his efforts came to naught, a few hopeful colonists got as far as Virginia. His ships explored the Carolina coast, and a temporary fort may have been built. Dissatisfied with conditions on the James River, other settlers drifted with little fanfare south to Albemarle Sound in the 1650s if not earlier.[1] English ships continued to stop for supplies or be shipwrecked on the Carolina coast. In 1633 a storm drove colonists bound for Virginia ashore above Port Royal. Indians killed and robbed some outright, kept others prisoners, and sent some to St. Augustine.[2] In the 1660s, after Charles II had been restored to the throne, diverse English noblemen, merchants, colonial Indian traders, and adventurers displayed more interest than ever in Carolina. Competition intensified between promoters in New England, Virginia, Barbados, and the mother country, but in the end the eight Lords Proprietors, magnates who had helped restore Charles II to the throne, succeeded. It was they who received a charter in 1663 and a more liberal one in 1665 with boundaries previously mentioned.

There was a flurry of activity in Carolina during the 1660s as expeditions of the proprietors and their competitors arrived on the scene. Among the first was that commanded by the New Englander William Hilton, sailing at the behest of a group of Massachusetts speculators. In 1662 he explored much of the province's coastline. Hilton was attracted to the Cape Fear River area, ascended that river for almost 100 miles, mapped it, and named it the Charles River. Perhaps it was Ayllón's Jordan; in any case the Jordan was not far off. One is struck by the contrast between Hilton's depiction of the Cape Fear River and Ayllón's description of the area a century and a half previously. In his brief report Hilton acclaimed the region, lauding its fertility, flora, and fauna. He had little to say about the aborigines except that they were primitive, friendly, and not very numerous. Hilton exaggerated, and in one sense his report, advising potential settlers that there were neither hostile Indians nor mosquitoes about, was little more than a real estate promotional tract. Without difficulty Ayllón had carried off more than 150 slaves from this populous region; if his report is to be believed, Hilton in three weeks did not even see that many natives.[3]

Hilton made a subsequent voyage to Carolina in 1663, this time under the auspices of Barbadian planters overcrowded on their tiny island. He took a closer look at the southerly part of Carolina and, like Luna, Menéndez, Ribault, and so many others, was attracted by the harbor and fertile lands in the Port Royal region. Hilton Head Island still bears his name. The Spanish presence was in evidence at Port Royal (Santa Elena), *la Florida's* former capital. According to Hilton the Indians were far more numerous there than at the Cape Fear River, many of them speaking Spanish, or at least understanding Spanish words. Sailing about Port Royal Sound he saw Mississippian-style villages with council houses or rotundas, plazas, and fields of maize. A large wooden cross stood before the rotunda, but "it was not apparent that the Indians paid much attention to it." Spaniards, if not immediately at hand, were close by. Hilton had touched the northern extremity of the coastal missions. In fact, though there were no resident Franciscans, he may have seen a *visita* visited periodically by the padres.[4]

As it turned out, maneuverings and intrigues of the powerful Lords Proprietors were responsible for their obtaining a charter in 1663 and making the first significant settlement; it was not until 1670, however, that Charleston was founded. Even before the initial charter, the Duke of Albemarle, one of the proprietors, had sent out his own expedition to explore Carolina. Little is known about this voyage except that a Carolina Indian was seized and taken to London. When the English subsequently returned to Carolina, the native ran off, disappearing from history.[5] The proprietors in 1666 dispatched a large expedition of Barbadians, commanded by Robert Sandford, to the Cape Fear River. This expedition, considerably smaller than Ayllón's, suffered the same fate. Before Sandford abandoned the Cape Fear River he explored the southerly part of Carolina and, like Hilton, was impressed with Port Royal. Young Henry Woodward, a surgeon (of the barber-surgeon type, one suspects), volunteered to remain among the Port Royal aborigines and learn their language and customs. Allotted a maize field and a young female to care for him, Woodward lived among the natives for some months. Exactly what he did is unclear. He may have visited Cofitachiqui, which he described as an astonishing town of one thousand bowmen or four thousand to five thousand inhabitants in all. There is no way to know whether Woodward saw Cofitachiqui or merely heard about it from the Indians. Crosses, Iberian manufactures, peach and fig trees, swine, and broken Castilian phrases made him aware of the Spanish influence, which was brought home even more forcefully when Spanish troops and Christian Indians marched into his village and captured him, sending him off to St. Augustine for interrogation. All the proprietors' endeavors to settle Carolina in the 1660s failed. Sandford abandoned the Cape Fear River, and Doctor Woodward languished in St. Augustine until in 1668 he was fortuitously freed by an English pirate who raided the city.[6]

The proprietors finally succeeded in 1670 when they founded Charleston. In a variety of ways the culture and life-style of the Southern aborigines had changed since original European contact, and one of the most significant was that the Indians had firearms. They obtained guns from Spaniards, from European vessels stopping along the coast to barter, and from Virginians like Abraham Wood, who sent his packhorse trains hundreds of miles to the south. By 1670 some, though not necessarily most, of the Carolina Indians relied more on European weapons than on the bow and arrow. The Westos are a case in point. They were well armed, saluting Henry Woodward in 1674 with "a hollow" and a volley fire by fifty to sixty small arms, and they terrified less well-armed Indian neighbors. Little else is known about this now extinct tribe. The best guess is that they were Yuchis or Ricahecrians, who may or may not have been the same. The Westos in 1670 lived on the Savannah or Westo River near Augusta in part of the kingdom of Cofitachiqui. Whether there was any connection between the Cofitachiqui and the Westos is uncertain. Woodward, who had called Cofitachiqui "a second paradise" containing some four thousand souls, also described the ingeniously fortified Westo headquarters. It is not possible to tell if he was referring to the same or different towns.[7] Spaniards during this era denounced raids by the Chichimecos, but whether they meant the Westos, Yuchis, or Savannahs is still not clear.

At least we can be sure that the Westos were not the Savannahs (the Shawnees), because the latter destroyed the Westos, for a time taking their place on the Savannah River. The Savannahs, who did not become extinct, are less enigmatic than the Westos, and it is possible to follow their subsequent movements westward into Alabama, northward into Kentucky and the Ohio country, and eventually to Oklahoma. Before their victory over the Westos in 1680, however, the history of the Savannahs is obscure. They have left their name to one or possibly two Southern rivers, the Savannah and the Suwannee, but when and how these Algonquians originally arrived in the South—in their native tongue their name means "southerners"—remains a mystery.[8] Considering the Savannahs, Westos, Ricahecrians, Chichimecos, and a variety of other tribes of indefinite backgrounds makes it obvious that the *entradas* of Narváez and De Soto and the ensuring pandemics had created population disruptions and tribal movements that are still not well understood.

In 1670 it was no secret where the Westos, several thousand strong, obtained guns. Setting out from the fall line of the James and Appomattox rivers, the packhorse trains of Abraham Wood, William Byrd I, and the Hatcher clan did a thriving business. After his providential escape from St. Augustine, Henry Woodward joined the English party that founded Charleston and in 1674 visited the Westos, describing their double-palisaded town on the Westo (Savannah) River; their bark-covered houses, some of which were adorned with scalps; their pottery and pipe-making; and at least a hundred canoes drawn up on the river bank.[9] This bastion helped account for why the well-armed and mobile Westos were such a terror to adjoining Indians and why many of the latter turned first to the Spaniards and later to the English for protection. The fortified Westo town on the Savannah River, like that of the Occaneechees on the Roanoke, both of which were commercial entrepôts, partially explained why Abraham Wood was one of the wealthiest Virginians.

From previous experience with the Sandford undertaking, Woodward had learned a good deal about the life-style of coastal tribes in southern Carolina, including the Wimbee, Edisto, Stono, Kiawa, Coosa, Wando, Etiwaw, Sewee, Santee, Wanniah, Elasie, Isaw, Cotachicach, Ashepoo, and Sampa. Most if not all of these were remnants of the Cusabo chiefdom, which had fallen on hard times, and individually none was strong enough to protect itself; they looked to the English, the Spaniards, or the Westos for protection. Not numerous or especially powerful in 1670, the English at Charleston were nevertheless at hand and seemed to offer the best prospects. From the outset Woodward and his colleagues enjoyed friendly relations with, or at least dominance over, the above-listed Indians. Carolinians traded with them, acquiring their lands without great difficulty and employing them as allies against the Spaniards and enemy Indians. Whenever natives grew dissatisfied, such as the Cacique of Stono who in 1674 attempted to confederate tribes and lead a rebellion, Carolinians through force—and epidemics—quashed all opposition.[10]

The Westos and Occaneechees, who were great traders, were destroyed within a few years of each other for essentially the same reason. Bacon in Virginia and Woodward in Carolina assumed it was more profitable to remove these middlemen and make new arrangements. The Westos' principal failing in Woodward's eyes was that they depended too much on Virginia, and this was the main cause of the Westo War of 1680. Details of the origins and conduct of that conflict are as shadowy as are the Westos themselves. Without proprietary approval, Woodward and other Carolinians resolved to exterminate the Westos and install the Savannahs in their stead. Soon after Charleston's founding Savannahs began trading with Carolinians for guns, raiding Spanish Indians in or near the missions, bringing skins and booty to Woodward, and having nothing to do with Wood's and Byrd's packhorsemen.[11] Incomplete and conflicting accounts describe the destruction of the Occaneechee stronghold on the Roanoke River; not a single one depicts the Westos' abrupt collapse. Considering their strength, the battle was likely to have been hard fought and costly, unless by chance smallpox had suddenly enervated the Westos. Whatever the exact cause, it is clear that Indians (Savannahs) rather than Carolinians did most of the fighting and that the Westos were almost annihilated. A few survivors, perhaps no more than fifty, fled westward, seeking refuge among the Creeks; others were sold as slaves. With new guns and shiny hatchets obtained from Charleston, Savannahs for a period replaced Westos on the Westo River in the vicinity of the future Augusta.[12]

Woodward and his fellow Charleston merchants aspired to appropriate the Indian trade of the entire lower South from northern Carolina to the Gulf Coast and from the Atlantic to the Mississippi. Algonquians, Iroquois, Sioux, Yuchis, and especially Muskhogeans lived in this enormous area and, though pandemics had taken their toll, were still numerous. Visions that earlier had fired De Soto, Pardo, and Menéndez now inspired the Carolinians. Within a few decades they came close to success despite the Spanish presence in Florida and, after 1699, the French in Louisiana. Closely identified with the proprietors, Woodward at times was their principal Indian agent. In provoking the Westo conflict, however, he had gone against their wishes and for a time was out of favor. Another group of Indian traders, having few ties with the proprietors and usually at odds with them, emerged and assumed more power in the colony. They were known as Goose Creek men because many of them lived northwest of Charleston on Goose Creek, a tributary of the Cooper. It is unwise to overemphasize the cohesiveness of the Goose Creek faction, because over the years its composition and objectives varied, and it was never a tightly knit party in the modern sense. Besides drawing most of their support from the same region, the Goose Creek men manifested several other traits. They were from Barbados, had fallen on hard times or in any case were not wealthy, were attracted to Carolina with its unlimited lands and economic opportunity, and after arrival in the colony quarreled with the proprietors. They increased their influence in the council and assembly, and at the turn of the century a Goose Creek man became governor. In defiance of the religious toleration established by the proprietors, Goose Creek men endeavored to entrench Anglicanism firmly in the colony. Though frequently bickering with Goose Creek partisans, other Carolinians in fact shared many of their basic beliefs.[13]

Despite strictures from the proprietors and at times from the governor and council, Goose Creek men resolved to take over the Southern Indian trade. Some of the more prominent leaders were Maurice Mathews, Arthur Middleton, and James Moore, all Barbadian immigrants. Mathews lived among the aborigines for a period, learning their language and serving as interpreter. Early involved with the Indian trade, young Middleton in time became a wealthy planter. James Moore personally led expeditions south into Spanish Florida and west toward the Mississippi. A self-made man in the Abraham Wood tradition, after first becoming a leader in the assembly, he served as provisional governor from 1700 to 1703. Goose Creek men were a power in—and frequently dominated—the assembly and council. Middleton became governor in the 1720s.[14]

After the destruction of the Westos in 1680, the dreams of the

Goose Creek men were fulfilled as their influence dramatically expanded in all directions, partly at the expense of Virginians. Carolinians appropriated more and more of the trade of William Byrd I and his neighbors, seizing goods from their packhorsemen, detaining their traders in Charleston, and if not encouraging at least not dissuading warriors from attacking their stores and caravans. At the end of the seventeenth century this Virginia–Carolina rivalry was most intense among the Usherys, a remnant of Cofitachiqui; by the eve of the American Revolution the conflict had shifted westward to the Cherokee country as descendents of William Byrd and the Goose Creek men still maneuvered and intrigued to secure influence.

More remarkable than the takeover of much of Virginia's trade was South Carolina's westward expansion. Both James Moore and Henry Woodward in the 1680s and 1690s visited the Chattahoochee River and beyond. Muskhogean Lower Creeks lived in scattered villages on the Chattahoochee. Their principal towns were Coweta and Kashita near modern Columbus. Upper Creek villages lay farther west on the Coosa and Tallapoosa rivers. Moore and Woodward encouraged the Lower Creeks (Appalachicolas as they were known) to maraud Spanish mission Indians. Alarmed about Apalachee and about losing influence among the Lower Creeks, Spaniards countered as best they could. Spanish detachments at San Luis (Tallahassee), accompanied by Indian warriors, some of whom had guns, intimidated, raided, and sometimes burned Lower Creek towns that were dealing with Carolinians. For a brief period from 1689 to 1691 Spain built and garrisoned a blockhouse in the heart of the Lower Creek country near Columbus. Spanish officers conducted Creek chiefs to San Luis and St. Augustine, impressing on them the importance of retaining the Spanish connection.[15]

Numbering approximately four thousand in 1700, white Carolinians were not much more numerous than the Spaniards in Florida. The Goose Creek men, however, soon brought most of the Southern aborigines into their commercial orbit at the expense of Spain, Virginia, and later France. The key to Carolina's success was that by the end of the seventeenth century England had established herself as a leading, and in many respects *the* leading, European manufacturing country and had refined her banking system and the ability of the nation and private entrepreneurs to extend and obtain credit. This meant that the Indians

—Creeks, Savannahs, Cherokees, Yamasees, or whoever—more often than not could get cheaper guns, hardware, and clothing from Carolinians than from anyone else. For all the brightly colored hats, striped suits, beads, and looking glasses, it is misleading to consider most trading goods as luxury items. Firearms and powder were essential for hunting and defense. Armed by Virginians, the Westos had made neighboring tribesmen fear the footsteps of their warriors. Carolinians furnished guns to the Savannahs, who destroyed the Westos. Spain abandoned her traditional policy of not arming mission Indians, but she refused to give weapons to every warrior. The Goose Creek men had no such scruples. One reason the Englishmen so easily supplied arms and manufactures was that English merchants both in Carolina and the mother country were able to extend and obtain credit. Commerce with the Indians was complex, involving far more than simple barter. It took months, usually years, before English merchants or their Charleston factors received any return on the capital risked.[16]

In most respects the Carolina trade followed the pattern earlier set by Virginia. If the Masons, Lees, Claibornes, Byrds, and Fleets gained their start in part through trafficking with the Indians, the same was true of the Moores, Middletons, Wraggs, and Grimkes in Carolina. As in Virginia, Carolinians bought a variety of furs and skins: beaver, otter, bear, wolf, deer, fox, and raccoon, but deer overshadowed all others. Furs from the Southern beaver were inferior in quality to those of colder regions. Deer abounded throughout the South and proved to be the trade's mainstay. Through hunting, commerce with other Indians, and raids on neighbors, first the Westos and subsequently the Savannahs assembled large quantities of deerskins at their villages on the Savannah River. They were made up into packs and transported by horse trains or water to Charleston. More than Virginia, South Carolina had an enormous hinterland to exploit, and the Indian trade did not die out after rice and indigo plantations became established in the Low Country. The heyday of the peltry trade was between 1730 and 1763; had it not been for the American Revolution, Charleston's dominance would have continued long after 1775.[17]

A result of the southward expansion of Indian commerce was destruction of the Spanish missions. One can argue that Carolina traders, by furnishing cheap goods and by not criticizing pagan

customs, denouncing fornication, or overtly tampering with aboriginal culture, offered a greater appeal than the Franciscans.
This philosophical argument is not likely ever to be resolved; at
the time the important consideration was that mission Indians
were not safe. Small contingents of Spanish soldiers stationed at
St. Catherines Island in Guale and San Luis in Apalachee and
Spain's arming of the most trustworthy Christian converts were
not enough. More and more Southern aborigines, Christian and
non-Christian alike, came to the conclusion that the best way to
preserve their lives and freedom and to obtain trade goods was
through the English. As a result it was the natives themselves, to
be sure incited and at times led by Goose Creek men, who overran the missions, burned chapels and sometimes the padres, and
carried off booty.

Beginning soon after Charleston's founding and continuing for
half a century or more, the depredations were an ugly episode.
First to fall were the Guale missions and some of those in Timucua, whose founding dated back to the Menéndez era. Timucuans, Guales, Yamasees, and others lived in these missions,
which in 1670 stretched north from St. Augustine to the Savannah River. While visiting Florida, which was in his diocese,
Bishop Calderón of Cuba in 1675 inspected and described the
coastal missions, the state of the wattle-and-daub structures, the
padres' effectiveness, and the converts' religious zeal.[18] Numbered among the mission Indians were Yamasees, a Muskhogean
people closely related to the Guales. In time the Yamasees absorbed and became indistinguishable from the Guales. Like
Guales, many Yamasees since the sixteenth century had voluntarily accepted mission life. But that was before English settlers
arrived in Carolina and firearms became common throughout the
Southeast. Yamasees, like so many other Indians, had moved
about in the period after white contact. As far as is known, when
Charleston was founded they were concentrated in the Guale
missions and on the Chattahoochee River. For protection Yamasees from both the coastal missions and the Chattahoochee began
moving in large numbers closer to Charleston, principally occupying a 45-mile coastal stretch between the Savannah and the
Combahee rivers.[19]

Goose Creek men used the Savannahs to destroy the Westos
and at the same time relied on Yamasees to demolish missions
in Guale and Timucua. Missions yielded up silver plate, orna-

ments, peltry, and especially slaves, all of which the Carolinians exchanged for guns, powder, hardware, and textiles. Sometimes joined by Lower Creeks and a few Cherokees, from 1680 on Yamasees raided missions on Sapelo, St. Catherines, and St. Simons islands. One of the larger forays occurred in 1680, when 300 warriors surprised the fortified padres' quarters on St. Catherines Island. Previously a Spanish garrison had sufficed to protect nearby natives, but that day had passed, and troops and a handful of armed Indians were unable to secure the island. Although the Yamasees never overran the desperately defended mission itself, they did not have to. It was exposed Indian settlements that Yamasees were after, and here they succeeded, burning and looting almost at will.[20] In the aftermath Spain made frenzied efforts to stimulate immigration to St. Catherines Island so there would be a reservoir of white militia to shore up defenses. Potential emigrants from the Iberian peninsula and the Canary Islands, some of whom were tempted by opportunities in the New World, for good reason were disinclined to try their luck on the exposed St. Catherines frontier.[21] Raids by Yamasees and West Indian buccaneers who harassed the Sea Islands forced Spain to abandon Guale after a century's occupation. By 1690 her northernmost mission was at Santa María on Amelia Island. Because of religious conviction and Franciscan entreaties or merely out of terror, mission Indians either retired with the Spaniards, moved westward to the Creek country, or moved north toward the English.

Guale had been lost, but Timucua survived, which is not to say that all, or even most, of the aborigines in this province were Timucuans. Pestilence and wars had taken a heavy toll. When Bishop Calderón made his visit in 1675 only a few thousand natives remained in the province, and even at that early date many were refugees from the English. There was no peace in Timucua, and in 1675 Timucuan-speakers were closer to extinction than they realized. Englishmen, or in actuality Scottish immigrants, in 1683 founded a new settlement, Stuart's Town, at Port Royal. Covenanters came to Stuart's Town to escape religious persecution and to make their fortunes. Henry Erskine, Lord Cardross, and his fellow Scots, a bit overawed by hundreds of Yamasees moving into the Port Royal area, resolved to turn them loose on Timucua. As a result chapels, quarters of the Franciscans, and other mission buildings in exposed *doctrinas* and *visitas* were put to the torch, and Timucuans were killed or brought back to Carolina for sale.[22] The fact that Stuart's Town failed provided Timucua little respite. Sickness and mismanagement reduced Cardross's colony to barely thirty able-bodied men, and Spaniards and their Indian allies easily overran the Covenanters, for a time exacting retribution on the Yamasees. England and Spain became allies during the European war raging in the 1690s, which also provided missions in Timucua below the St. Mary's River some relief—but not for long.

Extending southward to the 29° parallel below St. Augustine, Carolina's southern boundary included Timucua and Apalachee. These provinces, especially Apalachee, attracted the Goose Creek men. At least for a while Apalachee fared better than Guale and Timucua, because Apalachee lay more than 300 miles away from Charleston, Spaniards had more Indian allies available there to defend the province, and the missions were inland, relatively safe from buccaneers. The fort of San Luis, with its moat, 550-foot irregular stockade, a stout blockhouse mounting four cannon on top, and at least a fifty-man garrison, was formidable. Since the time of Narváez, De Soto, Pardo, and Luna, aborigines in Apalachee, on the Chattahoochee River, and in adjoining areas had seen few Europeans save Spaniards. The natives had not forgotten that it was Spanish steel and Spanish diseases that over the past century and a half had disrupted Mississippian culture. When Woodward, Moore, and the Goose Creek men came to the Chattahoochee, Indians were cautious and circumspect. But Westo, Guale, and Yamasee fugitives arrived among the Lower Creeks, describing poignantly what to expect should they not cooperate with the English. At the same time Moore and Woodward offered cheap goods. Increasing numbers of Southern Indians—Lower Creeks, Upper Creeks, Mobilians, and Chickasaws, among others—turned to the English and in so doing sealed the fate of the Apalachee missions.

The Guale missions had disintegrated over a period of several decades; those in Apalachee, consisting of some fourteen *doctrinas*, were destroyed in two campaigns during the disastrous winter and summer of 1704. England and Spain were at war, and the Barbadian James Moore and some fifty Goose Creek men led one thousand Creeks, Yamasees, and Apalachicolas against Apalachee. La Concepción de Ayubale, 20 miles from Fort San Luis, was the first to fall. After a bitter struggle the Franciscans and

113

their charges surrendered, the mission buildings were put to the torch, and so were the Franciscans. Indians customarily burned captives, particularly prominent or especially valiant ones. The fiery torment of the Franciscans lasted for hours; periodically charred victims were revived with water, and the agony continued. Their cries could be heard over long distances and have echoed in pages of religious tomes over the centuries. There is no way to determine if Creeks, Yamasees, and Apalachicolas treated these Franciscans just as any other unfortunate prisoners who had put up a stout resistance or whether, remembering De Soto and what had befallen the Mississippian villages of their ancestors, they took special gratification in their prisoners' anguish.[23]

Moore and his warriors raided neighboring missions, taking some by storm, accepting the surrender of still more without a struggle, and easily defeating a relief expedition that had sallied forth from Fort San Luis. He returned in triumph to Carolina with thousands of Apalachees who either were slaves or had agreed to relocate to save their lives. Creeks, Yamasees, and especially Apalachicolas remained about the missions, destroying at least four more in a summer campaign, all the while sending additional Apalachees to Carolina. The attacks of 1704 marked the end of the Apalachee missions. Although threatened on several occasions, Fort San Luis was never captured, and hundreds of terrified Christian Indians had sought sanctuary within the stockade's confines. With one exception all the outlying *doctrinas* and *visitas* lay burned and deserted. Hard pressed throughout all of Florida, Spain destroyed San Luis in 1704, for all practical purposes giving up Apalachee. When Bishop Calderón had visited this province in 1675, ten thousand to fifteen thousand natives lived there; earlier population figures had been considerably higher. After the 1704 campaigns almost none were left. It is not possible to be precise about the fates of all the Apalachees. Most of them, probably 10,000 or more, ended up in Carolina as slaves or tributaries, and the distinction was not always clear. Moore boasted of having brought back 4,000 women and children as slaves, while 1,300 voluntarily returned with him, and in addition he killed or enslaved 325 men. His Indian allies on their own herded an undetermined number of captives over trails back to Carolina. Not since De Soto's day had natives been impressed in such numbers.[24]

Not all of the Apalachees were killed or enslaved. Two hundred or more fled westward to Mobile, where French padres relocated them and looked after them in new missions; approximately the same number remained in Apalachee amid charred, deserted missions and villages; and an undetermined though not large number moved to Timucua, closer to the castillo in St. Augustine, where they made the mistake of assuming they would be safe.[25] The Goose Creek men did not exaggerate much when they asserted that the spacious province of Apalachee was depopulated, and they renewed efforts to settle this more distant but fertile part of Carolina.

Scenes of devastation in Apalachee were repeated throughout Florida. Spurred on by Moore and his friends, Uchizes (Creeks) and Yamasees roamed for hundreds of miles, settling scores with aboriginal enemies. Timucua was ravaged repeatedly, and the natives—Timucuans and diverse Indians who had relocated there—saw their towns burned, livestock plundered, and villagers marched off in captivity. Spanish troops in St. Augustine and outposts provided minimal protection against these small-scale but persistant raids. In Pensacola, almost 500 miles from Charleston, the picture was the same as, huddling for protection in the new fort, the tiny garrison watched aboriginal towns and Spanish houses being destroyed.[26] Even far to the south in the Keys, about as remote from Charleston as one could get and still remain in Florida, there was no sanctuary. Uchizes and Yamasees paddled over to these islands, surprising, terrifying, and killing the Indians.[27] Unable to protect the natives during Queen Anne's War (1702–13), Spain shipped hundreds to Cuba, including remnants of the Calusas and Tequestas who had taken refuge on the Keys, as well as Apalachees, Guales, Timucuans, and others from Timucua.[28] Since the first Spanish discovery a stream, or at least a trickle, of Indians had flowed from the Southeast to the Greater Antilles, and the tempo accelerated during Queen Anne's War.

The fate of the Carolina Indians was not what the proprietors had planned. They had envisioned a feudal-style colony in which everyone from nobles to the humblest tenants, including the aborigines, would have a fixed place in society and be dealt with according to his station. Their prerogatives and influence diminishing, the absentee proprietors watched with dismay as the Goose Creek men assumed power in the provincial council and assembly. Colonists ignored key provisions of the Fundamental Constitutions, a frame of government for the colony drawn up by the Earl of Shaftsbury, one of the most influential proprietors, by his personal secretary John Locke, and perhaps by some of the other proprietors. This document, which reflected the spirit of a more rational era, by seventeenth-century standards provided considerable religious toleration. Indians were expected or encouraged to join with and labor alongside Protestant immigrants, helping to make Carolina and the proprietors prosper. The aborigines would be dealt with justly; in no case would colonists provoke wars or capriciously kill and enslave natives. Oblivious to the fact that many of them had been Christian from before his birth, Shaftsbury assumed all natives were pagans. In any case, through love, reason, and example the Indians, whether pagan or Catholic, gradually would be won over to Protestantism.[29]

Proprietors concerned themselves little with Indian land titles except to assert peremptorily at the outset that the aborigines had no claim. Christian Indians, nowhere to be found when Englishmen had come to Virginia or Spaniards to *la Florida*, were at hand when colonists settled Carolina, and it was just as well that the proprietors did not bother to refute the natives' claims. The English magnates had coerced Charles II to grant them the province in order to make money, and they projected well-regulated, growing agricultural settlements in which they would profit directly or indirectly from quitrents, tenants working their holdings, outright grants to stimulate colonization, and trade developing between Carolina and the mother country. The proprietors conceded, for a time even guaranteed, to the Indians small tracts of land that adjoined or were surrounded by those of white neighbors, and the natives, like newly arriving tenants, would work for the colony, stimulating commerce and agriculture.

The Goose Creek men ignored proprietary attempts to control exclusive distribution of land and began concluding land cessions with the Indians, continuing the Virginia practice of recognizing the aboriginal right of usufruct. Understanding that a good way to found an estate was to begin with an Indian cession, the Goose Creek men were not deterred by the attitudes or prohibitions of authorities in the mother country or anywhere else. During the 1680s they extracted land cessions from coastal Edistos, Ashepoos, Stonos, Combahees, Wimbees, Coosas, and Wit-cheaus, most if not all of whom were survivors of the moribund Cusabo confederation or chiefdom.[30] In time proprietors grudg-ingly approved such treaties, their misgivings assuaged by as-surances that coastal Indians were not numerous and that they would inevitably relinquish large tracts that they could not pos-sibly use. As the Quaker governor of North Carolina, John Arch-dale, later observed: "it . . . pleased Almighty God to send unusual sicknesses amongst them [and his hand] was eminently seen in thining the Indians to make room for the English."[31] Following the Virginia precedent, the proprietors inaugurated the headright system to encourage immigration; thus, as in Vir-ginia, there was the irony of native American servants imported into both the northern and southern parts of Carolina to secure fifty acres each for their European masters.[32]

Two major Indian conflicts convulsed Carolina during the first part of the eighteenth century: The Tuscarora War broke out in the north in 1711, and the Yamasee uprising began four years later in the south. The Tuscaroras, of Iroquoian stock, occupied much of North Carolina's Tidewater. North Carolina's poor har-bors, the relatively sparse settlement of the region in the early colonial period, and the fact that most Tuscaroras lived inland had kept them isolated from whites to a considerable degree. Packhorse trains dispatched from the James and Appomattox riv-ers and shallow-draft coastal trading vessels ascending North Carolina rivers provided the main contacts with Europeans.

There are no records of debates in Tuscarora villages and forts explaining why they suddenly turned on whites, but if one looks closely it is apparent there are parallels between Opechanca-nough's uprising in 1622 and the Tuscarora War a century later. In each instance, by accident or design, white colonists allied them-selves with traditional native enemies. In all likelihood there had been Tuscarora–Algonquian rivalry antedating white contact. When English colonists settled among and sometimes militarily assisted coastal Algonquians, whose numbers had diminished since Ayllón's and Raleigh's time, ancient Indian quarrels were exacerbated.

Incidents between colonists and Tuscaroras multiplied at the outset of the eighteenth century. In 1707 Virginia embargoed trade with the Tuscaroras in an effort to force them to hand over murderers. Virginians were frustrated for several reasons, not the least of which was that the Goose Creek men and North Carolinians continued supplying the Indians.[33] There is little doubt that traders, particularly unlicensed ones, took advantage of the Tuscaroras. Some merchants were blacks, and, as will be dealt with more fully later, Negroes contributed to and participated in various "Indian" wars, including the Tuscarora conflict.[34] During the first part of the eighteenth century, epidemics broke out anew in the Tuscarora country, forcing feverish victims, after sweating in hothouses, to plunge head over heels into cold streams. Traditional cures offered no security against smallpox, as smoke rising from the burning houses of the deceased attested. Epidemics placed new stresses on Tuscarora society, and presumably the Indians, or at least the medicine men, blamed European immigrants, who were coming to North Carolina in increasing numbers.[35] Even more alarming was the fact that whites and their aboriginal allies were enslaving and selling Tuscaroras as never before.

Despite the mounting fear of enslavement, there is no confusion about the immediate cause of the Tuscarora War, and here the parallel with Virginia is close. Until the unprecedented immigration into Virginia beginning in 1619, the Powhatans had not felt overly threatened by the English. The Tuscaroras, who lived inland, had not been unduly disturbed when Ayllón, Raleigh, and later a sprinkling of English colonists had arrived on the North Carolina coast, and they had welcomed Virginia traders bringing munitions, textiles, and hardware. Deep in Indian territory, these merchants more often than not were at the Tuscaroras' mercy. But early in the eighteenth century Baron Cristoph von Graffenried, in collaboration with English partners, organized immigration of German Palatines and Swiss to North Carolina, founding New Bern in 1710. North Carolina's population spurted, and the Tuscarora War was at hand.[36] By 1711 the colony had already experienced minor hostilities as, discontented with the new governor, Edward Hyde, Thomas Cary led a rebellion that was soon crushed. Cary's detractors contended that it was he who stirred up the aborigines and turned them on Hyde's supporters.[37] There is little reason to believe this and every reason to assume that the Tuscaroras would have risen even if Cary had never existed.

Like Opechancanough previously, Tuscarora chiefs carefully laid their plans, as the naturalist and land speculator John Lawson discovered to his dismay. Accompanied by von Graffenried and Negro servants, he unsuspectingly explored the upper Neuse River, where Indians siezed the party, apparently burning Lawson in slow torment and threatening poor von Graffenried with the same fate. Although he was spared, he remained a prisoner unable to give warning, and soon he witnessed triumphant war parties returning with booty, prisoners, and scalps of some of the 120 Swiss and English colonists killed in the first onslaught. Within days more settlers died, and plantations on the Neuse, Trent, and Pamlico rivers lay smoking and abandoned.

For the next two years a full-scale Indian war raged, each side suffering heavily. In fact two wars were being fought simultaneously: one between Tuscaroras and whites and the other between Tuscaroras and their aboriginal enemies. In this latter conflict large numbers of Indians fought on both sides, and in many respects the Tuscarora War represented more of an Indian war than one between natives and whites. Arrayed against the Tuscaroras were some of the Algonquian tribes, including the Chowanocs and the peripatetic Savannahs; the Muskhogean Creeks, Yamasees, and Apalachees; and Cofitachiqui remnants such as the Esaws, Waterees, Sugerees, Catawbas, Waxhaws, Congarees, and Santees. Spurring Indians on against the Tuscaroras, beyond the chance to settle old scores, were prospects of plunder, glory, and European manufactures. Authorities in North Carolina, Virginia, and especially South Carolina equipped natives who agreed to march against the Tuscaroras with weapons and clothing. Warriors were also promised a liberal share of the booty, including trade goods captured in forts, cattle, and especially Tuscaroras themselves, who could readily be sold to the Goose Creek men.

After two years the Tuscaroras were finally defeated. It was not easy: North Carolina was poor and weak, and suffered heavily from the war, and the Tuscaroras, not usually living in large exposed towns, were dispersed and difficult to destroy, besides which they had built strong forts in the interior, which they resolutely defended.[38]

South Carolina played a leading role in the war, and some one thousand captive Tuscaroras and their allies were sold, in one sense making it possible to consider this conflict merely a phase of the expansion of Carolina's Indian trade. The Irishman John Barnwell, "Tuscarora Jack," led thirty-three South Carolinians

119

and five hundred warriors into North Carolina, destroying towns and scattered cabins and razing crops, but he was unable to take by force Chief Hancock's fort on the Neuse. During the assault his men dropped their fascines (bundles of sticks to be placed in the moat) when the Indians opened fire, and several were "deservedly shot . . . in their arses."[39] Once they had captured slaves, Tuscaroras or not, many of Barnwell's native allies set out for Charleston.

According to his critics, Barnwell killed and enslaved more friendly Indians than enemy Tuscaroras. Throughout American history this kind of treatment meted out to Indian allies was not unusual, and for other examples one only has to look at the fates of Bacon's confederates at the Occaneechee fort or Andrew Jackson's Lower Creek supporters during the Creek War of 1814. Barnwell concluded a truce or treaty with the Indians, and Tuscarora Jack and his warriors returned home in 1712, reporting on his "successes" and extolling the Tuscarora country, a land as fertile as Apalachee. Barnwell boasted that during the early years of the eighteenth century Carolina arms had been victorious from Pensacola to Apalachee to the Florida Keys and, most recently, to the lands of the Tuscaroras. Although Tuscarora Jack did not dwell on this point, the Tuscarora country was not deserted like Apalachee, and hostile warriors with guns and powder were still entrenched in their old forts or were building new ones.[40]

James Moore, Jr., son of the vanquisher of Apalachee, late in 1712 headed a second South Carolina expedition, leading some thirty whites and a thousand warriors back into North Carolina. This time the South Carolinians were more successful. Their main objective was Fort Nohoroco on Contentnea Creek. After a furious assault in which twenty-two whites and a larger number of Indians died, this stronghold fell. Losses of four hundred killed and even more captured broke the core of Tuscarora resistance.[41] As a result, even more slaves and booty were forwarded to Charleston, and Tom Blount, a chief of the once proud and powerful Tuscarora, was forced to sign a treaty accepting tributary status.[42] Blount, however, had never been enthusiastic about the war and did not object strenuously to handing over hostages who were his political rivals. Blount became a dependant and a tributary, but his personal influence over the surviving Tuscaroras was enhanced as a result of the war. A majority of the Tuscaroras had been marched off to Charleston as slaves, had been killed, or had drifted northward, most of them joining their Iroquois brethren in the Mohawk Valley.

Two years after James Moore, Jr., returned to Charleston with news of his North Carolina victories another far more destructive war erupted. It has somewhat inaccurately been labeled the Yamasee War, for in fact there was a widespread Indian confederation or conspiracy, which included many natives other than Yamasees. Engaged in this "Yamasee" War were Lower Creeks, Guales, Apalachees, Savannahs, Cherokees, Yuchis, Cheraws, Catawbas, Waterees, and Waccamaws. Some played a more active role than others, and in time the Cherokees broke away from the confederacy. Looking closely at the participants, one is struck by the fact that so many components of the old Chiefdom of Cofitachiqui were involved. Accepting the premise that the Queen of Cofitachiqui spoke a Muskhogean rather than a Siouan, Yuchian, or some other tongue makes it easier to explain such widespread collaboration and to speculate that possibly the Yamasee revolt was Cofitachiqui's dying gasp.[43] Without further debating Cofitachiqui's influence, one thing is clear: Nowhere —in Virginia, New York, or New England—had whites been confronted by such an array of hostile Indians.

In a general way the Yamasee War was the aboriginal response to the commercial empire established by the Goose Creek men. The English system, which did not include resident Franciscans constantly moralizing in native villages, had both its appeal and its drawbacks. In London at the time, William Byrd II with perverse gusto enumerated Indian grievances before royal officials. He recounted how Carolina traders got the natives drunk; forced them hopelessly into debt; sent warriors off to hunt or fight and then debauched their wives and daughters; arbitrarily appropriated native dugouts; required men to serve as beasts of burden, carrying heavy loads many miles on their backs; and beat Indians unmercifully, regardless of age or sex, sometimes killing the victim.[44] Yamasees were vexed when traders took it upon themselves to proclaim that the English pound contained only eight ounces. After they fled to Florida, Yamasees reiterated all of these complaints to the Spaniards. As far as whipping was concerned, this was a common punishment for Indians, blacks, and whites during the colonial era. In some respects it was more risky to whip Indians. A black slave or a white indentured servant, particularly if the latter had been illegally spirited away by a press gang or was a convict, frequently was alone in the New World. Although the Europeans' arrival had been traumatic for Mississippians, many aspects of their culture had survived, including the importance of clan membership. At times whipped and beaten Indians had someone to turn to, as the Carolinians found out in 1715.

The Virginian William Byrd II, who related Carolinian misdeeds, was not an impartial witness, but even so his charges were essentially correct. In turn the Carolinians may not have exaggerated when they accused Byrd's agents of trading with and abetting the Indians, notably the Cheraws.[45] Spain and France have been charged with instigating the Yamasee War, but these allegations must be discounted. Spanish Florida and French Louisiana were feeble, their governors even during the War of the Spanish Succession having failed to stir up the Indians. They did not redouble or, for the most part, even continue their efforts after the general peace in 1713. Anglican ministers in South Carolina explained the war as God's wrath against the sins of colonists, especially non-Anglicans.[46]

Overriding all concerns was fear of enslavement. Despite opposition from the proprietors, the crown, and provincial authorities, for years the Goose Creek men had captured thousands of aborigines throughout the Lower South. With few Tuscaroras, Apalachees, Timucuans, and similar enemies left, Yamasees and other Goose Creek allies began to worry. They knew well that Carolinians were as likely to enslave friends as enemies. The Goose Creek men had provoked many a war to secure prisoners, and somewhat belatedly the Southern Indians may have realized they had been duped. One was chief of the Yamasee village of Tama, a leader of the uprising who had arrived in the Port Royal area only a short time after 1700. Previously he had been in Apalachee, but complaints against Franciscan missionaries and Spanish soldiers and lack of security had prompted him and his followers to relocate. After the outbreak of hostilities in 1715, he went as a spokesman for 161 villages to St. Augustine, professing that he and fifty thousand or more Indians were anxious to put themselves again under Spanish control: Whatever grievances they formerly had against Spaniards, the possibility that at any moment, for whatever spurious pretext, their women and children might be enslaved by their white protectors was not one.

Yamasees initiated the hostilities, and as a result the war bears their name. Many, but not all, of these Indians had settled in ten villages on the mainland in the vicinity of Port Royal Sound. After the Stuart's Town fiasco, Carolinians began moving back into this region, grazing herds of cattle and appropriating aboriginal lands, all of which gave rise to numerous incidents. Three veteran Indian traders and agents, Thomas Nairne, John Wright, and John Cochran, met with the Yamasees to calm them. The Scot Nairne had come to Carolina and had become a planter, land speculator and Indian fighter, enthusiastically joining the Goose Creek men in disseminating Carolina's influence over the Lower South.[48] Wright, who for a time succeeded Nairne as provincial Indian agent, was more Nairne's rival than colleague.[49] The trader Cochran had lived for long periods in native villages, protesting when Wright, Nairne, or any other provincial agent had tried to license and regulate his relations with the Indians.[50]

Despite their differences, these three and other Carolina traders met with head men in a town near Port Royal, drank black drink in the customary ritual, and, after apparently having conciliated them, retired for the night reassured. Painted red and black, symbolizing war and death, at daybreak the Yamasees surprised these whites, killing Wright and other traders outright, getting even with Cochran for having defrauded them of booty previously seized from Spaniards, and burning Nairne for three days before he expired. Up to a hundred traders and planters, both men and women, suffered similar fates, while with only the briefest of warnings, four hundred from nearby Port Royal, some of them wounded, fled in panic, swimming or paddling pirogues to an English smuggler fortuitously anchored nearby. The war was on, and at the outset the Port Royal area was destroyed.[51] Hostilities soon shifted to the vicinity of Charleston, as smoke rose from plantations at Goose Creek, Stono, and other outlying areas. Indians—slaves, indentured servants, or freemen—lived among the colonists on plantations and in Charleston, and despite precautions these natives communicated with the enemy. At one point Captain Barker with a hundred mounted men, including a few Indians and Negroes, marched out beyond Goose Creek to meet the enemy. He was surprised and cut down, his command routed, betrayed by one of the accompanying Indians. The elder James Moore had captured or bought this Indian, who subsequently had won his trust and had been freed. Carolinians were bewildered by such ingratitude.[52]

In time the hostile confederation was broken and the aborigines defeated. Men and supplies arrived from North Carolina, Virginia, New England, and the mother country, and joining the whites, the Cherokees turned against the Yamasee partisans. Small parties of Tuscaroras and Corees from North Carolina, who earlier had suffered so much from South Carolina Indians during the Tuscarora War, also assisted. The result was the shattering of the remarkable Indian unity of 1715 and the destruction and humiliation of the belligerents. Yamasees and Guales living among them retreated into Florida, rejoining Spain and resuming mission life. Whereas before 1715 they had been the most feared and implacable foe of Spain and of the Florida Indians, after the war they became Spain's most dependable allies until their virtual extinction in the latter part of the eighteenth century, never renouncing their hatred of the Goose Creek men. The Ocheses (Lower Creeks) retired from the Upper Ocmulgee River, returning to their old home on the Chattahoochee. The Palachacolas (Lower Creeks living near the Savannah's mouth) also moved to the Chattahoochee.[53] The Congarees, Santees, Sewees, Pedees, Waxhaws, and Cusabos continued their rapid march toward extinction, some incorporating with the Catawbas, helping that tribe to sustain its population.[54] A few Yamasees, Lower Creeks, and Yuchis moved into deserted Apalachee and founded six villages.[55] Aborigines living among Carolina settlers were more than ever cut off from their kinsmen in the Indian country. Carolinians built frontier forts and laid out townships, many of which were near the headwaters of navigable rivers and eventually became population centers; all served further to isolate the coastal Indians from those beyond the frontier.

By many standards the Yamasee War was an exceptional conflict. Losses on both sides were high, four hundred colonists perished, some 6 percent of the white population.[56] Indian losses are impossible to assess, and it is perhaps enough to say that in the aftermath many of the tribes became extinct. The war had considerable effect on South Carolina's development. Port Royal remained deserted for years. The conflict exacerbated discontent with proprietary rule, and in 1719 colonists revolted and proclaimed South Carolina a royal colony. Because Carolinians were so weakened by the war and a recent epidemic, a rejuvenated Spain in this same year outfitted a powerful expedition in Havana, planning to redeem the more northerly part of Florida.

Whether she could have done so will never been known, because, for reasons having nothing to do with Carolina, the expedition was sent elsewhere. For a while, however, it seemed remotely possible that the Spanish flag would fly over Charleston and that the coastal missions would be reestablished.[57] As will be seen, before 1715 the Anglicans had made an earnest effort to convert the aborigines, but after the outbreak of the war, as ministers fled their parishes and huddled in Charleston for safety, neither they nor any other Carolinians displayed much eagerness for converting the savages.

The parallel with the aftermath of the 1622 massacre in Virginia was close. Carolina followed the Virginia example in other respects by augmenting her tributary system over weakened nearby tribes, appointing and unseating chiefs, and collecting tribute. In Carolina after 1715, as earlier in Virginia, the debate intensified as to whether free trade or a provincial monopoly provided the best regulation of the Indians. Samuel Wilson, secretary to the Earl of Craven, one of the proprietors, had published a tract in 1682 recounting how the Carolina Indians, decreasing in number and constantly at war with one another, could never unite against the English.[58] The thousands of angry warriors who in 1715 roamed the countryside and threatened Charleston had been a shock to the terrified whites who had sought refuge inside. Authorities resolved never to allow such a confederacy to emerge again. As in Virginia, they kept alive intertribal differences, determined that in the future when the Indians did "a little mischief . . . they should do it upon their own tawny race."[59]

It is not possible to comprehend fully the Yamasee and similar wars, conflicts among the aborigines themselves, the far-reaching influence of Carolina and Virginia traders, and indeed much of the history of the Southern Indians since first discovery, without considering Indian slavery. From time to time this has been touched upon, but now it must be looked at more closely.

6
Brands and
Slave Cords

Throughout history slavery, or something similar to it, has been the norm, while freedom has been the exception; it was natural and perhaps inevitable that when Europeans arrived in the South they began seizing the aborigines. In this regard two distinct periods stand out: the sixteenth century in Spanish *la Florida*, and the late seventeenth–early eighteenth centuries in English Virginia and Carolina. Books dealing with Spanish Florida, the English colonies, and French Louisiana mention that colonists captured Indians, but readers usually get the impression that this was a transitory and not a particularly significant phenomenon. The aboriginal perspective was quite different. From the time of European contact in the early sixteenth century until well into the nineteenth century, whites enslaved natives so long as it was profitable and sufficient numbers remained to be captured. Europeans brought over to the New World the institutions of chattel slavery and the slave trade, both of which became an integral part of the Southern Indians' life-style.

This is not to contend that Mississippians knew nothing of slavery before 1492. The earliest European explorers observed that Timucuans in Florida and Powhatans in Virginia held slaves. Just before the American Revolution the naturalist William Bartram described how Lower Creeks, who had moved from Georgia into Florida, were served by Yamasee slaves, who, according to Bartram, stood in greatest awe of their masters.[1] Garcilaso de la Vega, writing about De Soto in the sixteenth century, and John Lawson, describing North Carolina natives more than a hundred years later, both related how aboriginal owners dealt with runaways. After sending out a party to recapture them, they severed their Achilles tendons or cut off their toes and half their feet, carefully folding the skin over the stumps so the wound would heal. These slaves could still get about and till maize fields but would not stray a second time.[2] There is evidence that slavery at first was of slight consequence for Mississippians but that, as Southern Indians were caught up in dynamics of Europe's commercial expansion, the institution assumed new dimensions.

Far more is known about slavery's antecedents in Europe during Greco-Roman times and the medieval era than its practice among the precontact Mississippians. It had flourished in Greek city-states and under the Romans; finding new sources of slaves had been one reason for the empire's expansion. In Northern Europe during the medieval period, serfdom tended to supplant chattel slavery. The process took time and was never completed, and large numbers of slaves still were on hand in 1066 when William the Conquerer subdued England. Slavery continued, one might say thrived, on the Iberian peninsula and in the entire Mediterranean world throughout the medieval era, as Moors, Africans, Hungarians, Serbians, and others were enslaved from one end of the Mediterranean to the other. Eventually the tradition evolved that Christians should not own fellow Christians— but they did, even though over the years this became more difficult.[3]

Important developments during the High and Late Middle Ages were efforts by the papacy to extend its authority and the revival of trade and commercial expansion. In the thirteenth century Henry of Susa, Cardinal Archbishop of Ostia, wrote a treatise asserting that before the birth of Christ all men had a natural right to their property. If they remained pagan after the advent of Christ, however, they forfeited these rights, which now were vested in God's vicar the Pope. Those who refused to accept the new religion were threatened with the loss of not only their lands but also their freedom.[4] As Europeans expanded eastward during the crusades, southward on the Iberian Peninsula during the *reconquista,* and in time down the African coast, pagan captives were brought back to Christian Europe. The numbers increased as Iberians conquered the Canary Islands, sailed around Africa to India and China, and arrived in the New World. When Columbus shipped several boatloads of aborigines from Hispaniola to Spain, he assumed his prisoners were Japanese, Chinese, or their close neighbors. With a better grasp of geography, European cartographers realized that these slaves were not Orientals. What is important is that long before Columbus's voyage a tradition was established that European progress, commercial expansion, Christianity, and slavery went hand in hand. The Protestant revolt did not alter this, and it is unlikely that Southern Indians perceived much difference between the Catholic De Soto and the Anglican Goose Creek men. Although Isabella eventually freed those slaves Columbus sent home, Europe witnessed a revival of chattel slavery. More than 7 percent of the population of sixteenth-century Seville, which was prospering as never before, was slave. Black Africans, white Moriscos and Moors from Granada and North Africa, and Indians from America all could be seen in the bustling streets.[5]

When Spain came to the New World, without fanfare she enslaved natives there as previously she had Moriscos, Moors, Canary Islanders, Turks, Hungarians, and black Africans. A decree promulgated in 1512 sanctioned what already had occurred in the West Indies since 1492 and reiterated arguments of the Cardinal Archbishop of Ostia: Natives in the Greater Antilles were to labor for the Spaniards in their mines and on their ranches and farms. These Indians might be outright slaves, prisoners seized in a just war, or prisoners bought from other Indians who had captured them. Natives also were allocated to Spaniards under the *repartimiento* system, which, at least in theory, was closer to serfdom than outright slavery. A similar pattern developed in New Spain after Cortez's triumphs. Whatever their status, the aborigines died at a startling rate. Because the native American labor supply was being so rapidly depleted and because of the reformist arguments of Las Casas, the crown in 1530 said no more slaves were to be taken, soon relented, and then in the 1542 New Laws again decreed that Indians should no longer be enslaved. Considering previous European experience, in many respects this type of emancipation was remarkable. Indian slavery never completely disappeared in Spanish America. Thousands who had been enslaved legally or clandestinely before 1542 remained so after that date, and aborigines occasionally still were taken in just wars. In Portuguese Brazil, for an interval under Spanish control, Indian slavery long flourished regardless of its legality or the identity of the mother country. Nevertheless, Indian slavery became of less significance throughout much of Latin America in the latter half of the sixteenth century, partly because the Spanish monarch, if he did not abolish, at least circumscribed this institution, and especially because invading microparasites wreaked such havoc.[6] Ayllón and De Soto in the first part of the century counted their captives in the hundreds; Menéndez after 1565 unsuccessfully petitioned Philip II to let him wage a just war against *la Florida*'s recalcitrant Indians, but there is no conclusive proof he ever took a single slave.

Wherever Spaniards went—to the West Indies or the Valley of Mexico—a labor shortage quickly developed as the aboriginal population dwindled, and in time Portuguese Brazil suffered the same fate.[7] Each European power responded by importing slaves from the Iberian peninsula and Africa. By the end of the sixteenth century blacks and whites, along with Indians imported from elsewhere in the New World, had replaced the aboriginal populace of the Greater Antilles. Less well known is the fact that a similar pattern existed in Mexico, where toward the end of the sixteenth century blacks made up a sizable percentage of the population, having become the backbone of the labor force. In time, African importations subsided; the aboriginal population stabilized and eventually recovered. To a large degree Mexican blacks died off or were absorbed, leaving few traces of their earlier prominence.[8]

It is essential to keep in mind the labor scarcity developing in the West Indies. From Columbus's time until well into the nineteenth century an insatiable demand for workers persisted. Africans, European indentured servants, convicts and political exiles, and aborigines from the American mainland all helped fill this shortage. The Southern Indian slave trade was part of a worldwide phenomenon, and captives from the era of Ponce de León to Henry Woodward's day had much in common with black Africans and European convicts, political prisoners, and children kidnapped from the streets of London, all of whom were sent to the islands.

A principal and at times the primary force behind early Spanish expansion in the Indies was the desire for new sources of Indian slaves; as much as anything else this quest brought Ponce de León, Ayllón, and Narváez to *la Florida*. We must assume that mainland Indians who were sent to the islands underwent an experience similar to that of black emigrants. Coming from different parts of Africa, speaking different languages, perhaps having different religions, after the Middle Passage Negroes suddenly found themselves jumbled together in the West Indies. Drawing on various African heritages, the ways of their white masters, and West Indian influences, they forged a new culture in many respects more than the sum of the parts.[9] Like blacks, Indians from the American mainland came from different geographic regions, including the greater Florida, Mexico, and central and northern South America. They frequently could not understand one another and at times worshiped different gods. Their Middle Passage differed only in that their ships sailed in opposite directions and that their journey was shorter, though not appreciably so for the Lesser Antilles. Once arriving in the islands, mainland Indians mixed with such local natives as still survived and with black newcomers. Creek, Yuchi, Cusabo, Powhatan, and Timucuan languages served little purpose in the West Indies. Presumably Indians learned and helped develop a pidgin, drawing on native West Indian, African, Spanish, and their own linguistic backgrounds to communicate with fellow workers and white masters. Aboriginal bonds of kinship and the clan system were totally disrupted, and what evolved in their place is unknown.

So far emphasis has been—and logically so— on the Spanish West Indies, because England and other European countries did not establish West Indian colonies until the first part of the seventeenth century. Then Barbados, Guadeloupe, and other islands in the Lesser Antilles bypassed by Spain, along with Jamaica and Saint Domingue, became sugar islands with large plantations, cane fields, and sugar mills worked by nonwhite slave labor. Demands for workers in the Spanish West Indies diminished as Spaniards turned their attention and energies to Mexico and Peru, leaving the islands in the backwater on the fringe of their American empire. But in the seventeenth century non-Spanish sugar islands emerged, continuing the great need for labor in the islands. As a result both Ponce de León in the first part of the sixteenth century and the Goose Creek men a hundred years later had a ready market. Indians from Florida and Meso and South America helped sustain the "Indian" population of the islands. The twentieth-century national motto of independent Jamaica is "Out of Many, One People," of which Africans, Englishmen, and Indians are major components. Any Indian genes in present-day Jamaicans, however, are likely to have come from aborigines imported into the island from the mainland rather than indigenous Arawaks, who for all practical purposes had disappeared long before England seized the island from Spain.[10]

Ponce de León or some unrecorded Spanish contemporary initiated traffic in slaves between the South and the islands. Ponce was not very fortunate, returning to Puerto Rico with only a handful of captives in his two voyages. Ayllón and his lieutenants were more successful and shipped hundreds to the islands. Narváez had little chance, for there was scarcely enough room in his makeshift vessels for his own men, much less slaves. De Soto employed Indians extensively, using them as porters, guides, and body servants. On infrequent occasions relief ships sailed over to the Gulf Coast from Havana; whether after delivering their cargoes they returned with slaves is uncertain. In any case De Soto and his men put their iron manacles to good use while in *la Florida*.

During the sixteenth century the Spanish crown had some success in limiting or curtailing Indian slavery. Luna and Pardo in the latter half of the century had opportunities to wage many a just war, to march captives to the coast, and to ship them off to the islands. There is little indication that they did so, certainly not in appreciable numbers. De Soto and Narvéz earlier in the century, had their ventures succeeded, would have taken full advantage of such opportunities. The crown did not allow Menéndez to sell Indians who ambushed his men or refused conversion. Menéndez circumvented other royal commands affecting his purse; whether he did in these instances is unknown.[11] There is no way to measure accurately the number of Indian slaves Spain transported from the South to the West Indies. The broad pattern, however, is clear: This was a sixteenth-century phenomenon, most pronounced in the first half of that century. An estimate of the number carried off during the entire century is in the 2,000–5,000 range, and this reckoning may be understated. In any case, the traffic was extensive enough, helping explain why the aborigines were so hostile to the Spaniards and why, if they did not bitterly contest the conquistadors' arrival, they abandoned their villages and fled.

When Englishmen came to Roanoke Island and Jamestown they manifested little interest in Indian slavery. Anglican propagandists, the crown, and business promoters all insisted that the Church of England and hardy Englishmen were superior to Catholicism and Philip II's minions. England should not treat the natives the way, according to Las Casas, Spain had. At least until the 1622 massacre, Indians were to serve as free or bond labor but not as slaves. Before 1622 England had no West Indian colonies and no large market for aboriginal slaves. The demand for slave labor was in the Spanish islands and on the mainland, and English slavers, such as John Hawkins and his father William, had helped satisfy that market with Africans rather than native Americans.

In time Negro and Indian slavery assumed more importance in Virginia. During the latter half of the seventeenth century the institution of chattel slavery and an inchoate slave code evolved more clearly. Statutes adopted after the 1660s reflected earlier practices. John Smith, for example, had been captured in Hungary and enslaved by the Turks and, despite Anglican rhetoric, saw no reason why he could not deal rigorously with Indians, enslaving them if necessary to make them work and accept the Thirty-nine Articles.[12] Before 1622 Smith and his contemporaries enslaved Powhatans captured in just wars and apprenticed others for a fixed term or until they reached manhood. If young Indian apprentices did not expire, in many instances neither did their terms of servitude. Natives from the West Indies and elsewhere in America, along with Africans, began arriving at Jamestown, more often than not as indentured servants rather than slaves. Indian—and African—slavery was of limited import during the early decades of Jamestown's development. It must be kept in mind how fragile the colony was under the Virginia Company's rule, and there was good reason to worry about depending so extensively on Indian prisoners of war. Claiborne's restraining device might not suffice to keep surly captives in line.

The feebleness of the English colony in Virginia, the dangers of relying on a disaffected labor force, and the fact that at first England had no market for slaves in West Indian sugar islands all restricted Indian slavery. But this began to change. Colonists weathered the 1622 massacre, the white population grew rapidly, and tobacco culture and the Indian trade expanded. England also began to found colonies in the islands, including Bermuda in 1612, Barbados in 1627, Old Providence Island off the Nicaraguan coast in 1631, and Jamaica in 1655. With the exception of Old Providence Island, which Spain recaptured in 1642, the other West Indian islands became sugar colonies. Pandemics had carried off most of the aborigines, and survivors, notably the Caribs, were militantly hostile and difficult to subdue. It was dangerous for English masters to use them as slaves, even assuming that it were possible. Demands for labor in the islands mounted and were fulfilled by imported Africans and mainland Indians. As a result Virginia, New England, and other English colonies began to find a convenient market for their captives.

With a growing demand in the islands for slaves and the proliferation of tobacco plantations in Virginia, Indian slavery became of more consequence in the colony's commercial life. This is not always apparent. Authorities in 1679 estimated the colony's population as some 70,000 to 80,000 souls, including 15,000 servants and 3,000 blacks; the remainder were free. Except for a few tributaries, Indians were not even mentioned.[13] Yet nontributary Indians were very much part of Virginia's population, and it is necessary to look closely at statutes, wills, bills of sale, and miscellaneous court records to find them. Laws enacted by the general assembly, in time spelling out details of the colony's slave code, applied to Indians and blacks alike. The earliest ones of the 1640s and 1650s concerned abuses of "apprenticing" aboriginal youths. The assembly in 1649 decreed that settlers must purchase children from Indian rather than English owners. Colonists who took young Indians into their households naturally were entitled to their labor for the usual term. But, according to the assembly, the real reason was to educate, civilize, and convert these youths. The assembly prohibited colonists from capriciously selling children among themselves.[14] According to a 1658 statute, by the time an Indian servant reached twenty-five years of age, a higher age than for white servants, the native, presumably acculturated, had to be set free.[15] Although ambiguously phrased, the first mention in the statutes of Indian slaves was in 1660. Natives who refused to pay damages assessed by the court were to be seized, sold at auction, and sent off to the West Indies or elsewhere.[16] Subsequent statutes, in 1676 during Bacon's Rebellion, in 1682, and later, clearly specified that prisoners taken in just wars might be enslaved.[17] According to a 1669 law, foreign—that is, non-Virginia—Indians captured in war and those imported into the colony by sea and sold were to remain slaves for life. Those coming into the colony by land were to be considered indentured servants. Children would serve until the age of thirty and adults for a twelve-year term. Considering these long terms and the short life expectancy, the distinction between such a fixed period of service and perpetual slavery was blurred.[18] Runaway slaves, both Negroes and Indians, had to be dealt with. Freemen were entitled, indeed required, to stop fugitives by any means possible, and they would be subject to no liability should the fugitive be wounded or killed. In case of death the assembly agreed to reimburse the owner to the extent of 4,500 pounds of tobacco for a Negro and 3,000 pounds for an Indian.[19]

Beyond provincial statutes there are other indications illustrating the extent of Indian slavery. During his first and second terms Governor Berkeley owned natives. He bought two, presumably children, for 600 pounds of tobacco in 1645;[20] he sold one good Indian man, formerly belonging to a Bacon supporter, in 1677 for 2,000 pounds of tobacco;[21] and when planning an expedition against the Indians in 1666, he contended that the prospect of captive women and children surely must entice sufficient militia volunteers.[22] Occasionally a bill of sale has survived. The Weanoc king in 1659 exchanged young Weetoppen with a colonist for a foal. Weetoppen was not a Weanoc voluntarily apprenticed by his elders but a young Powhatan illegally spirited away. The controversy reached the county court explaining why this particular bill of sale has been preserved.[23] Inventories from the 1670s and 1680s of Indian fighters and traders such as Bacon, the Hatchers, Wood, and Berkeley all reveal that Indians were bequeathed to their heirs. In some cases natives might have technically been indentured servants.

A number of Indian slaves—not large but greater than generally has been recognized—came into the colony by sea from other mainland colonies and from the West Indies. Extant Virginia customs records from the second decade of the eighteenth century disclose that a ship arrived with 166 Negroes and 66 Indians aboard, the latter picked up in Carolina.[24] This vessel carried an unusually high percentage of aboriginal slaves, reflecting the large numbers of captives taken during the Tuscarora and

Yamasee wars. A century earlier, when natives greatly outnumbered colonists, an enterprising captain tried to dispose of a few Caribs in the colony. He had picked them up in the West Indies, where both Ponce de León and English settlers could testify to Carib belligerence. Their reputation followed them to the James River, terrifying the assembly that these "cannibals" would incite local Algonquians to revolt. Caribs, of course, could no more communicate with Powhatan's subjects than a Basque, suddenly finding himself in Eastern Europe, incite the Poles. This logic did not influence the Burgesses, who after debate resolved that the only recourse was to hang all Carib immigrants as expeditiously as possible.[25] For many reasons, including the fact that customs duties were one-fifth less, most Indians imported into Virginia came by land rather than by sea.[26]

Trafficking with the natives traditionally evokes images of white traders arriving in aboriginal villages and—after talks, distribution of a judicious number of kegs of rum, and detailed bargaining—exchanging manufactures for peltry. Slaves are seldom considered. Yet when William Byrd, Abraham Wood, and the Hatchers sent their packhorses deep into Carolina, they returned not only with peltry but also with slaves. Customs records indicate that while furs and deerskins were exported, slaves seldom were, at least according to surviving documents, and the tendency has been to assume that Byrd and his fellow Virginians dealt almost exclusively in peltry. But other sources, especially local court records, reveal that Byrd's employees had brought back more than deerskins. Scattered throughout these records are payments for slave catchers, whom Virginia counties reimbursed for securing Indian runaways. At times Indian slaves appear in records by virtue of being listed as tithables; as chattels they were subject to litigation and were included in wills and inventories of estates. This kind of evidence, scattered as it is, signifies that throughout the seventeenth century, particularly in the latter half, Indian slaves in increasing numbers helped meet Virginia's rising demand for labor.

Slaves worked for white masters throughout the colony, from the James to the Potomac and from the Eastern Shore to the fall line. Surviving evidence suggests that slaves were most numerous in frontier counties such as Westmoreland on the upper Potomac and Henrico on the upper James, but one cannot be sure, because in general local records from frontier counties have sur-

135

vived and those from the earlier, more populous counties have not. During the 1660–1700 period Indian slaves or servants are mentioned almost as frequently as Negroes in Henrico County records, and a similar pattern emerges in Westmoreland and other frontier counties.[27] It must be kept in mind that throughout the seventeenth century Virginia's primary source of labor was white, typically indentured servants, and that slaves, whatever their complexion, constituted a small minority.

Some of Virginia's Indian slaves were exported by sea, and the threat of transportation to the islands was not an idle one. Authorities were quick to ship off defiant aborigines in the same way whites in the West Indies tried to dispose of refractory Caribs in Virginia. Virginia statutes specified automatic transportation for certain crimes. Tributaries caught ranging too far westward and communicating with foreign Indians could expect to be sent out of the colony, as could foreign Indians who ventured onto tributary reservations without permission. During Queen Anne's War the government required rangers to patrol between frontier forts and to sell and export for their own benefit any Indian caught in the area without permission.[28] When whites bought and exported slaves, the authorities did not normally intervene or complain unless it threatened the peace. Daniel Pugh got into trouble in 1690 when he kidnapped Tuscaroras, sending them off to the islands, and their kinsmen living in the North Carolina Tidewater threatened to retaliate on the closest Carolinians. To prevent any altercation between Indians and white North Carolinians, Virginia magistrates took Pugh to task.[29] From Ponce de León's time until well after the American revolution Southern Indians helped sustain the population in the West Indies, and in a small way Virginia made her contribution.

Opposition to enslaving the New World aborigines was manifest in England, and at the outset Anglican propagandists made much of the point that England was not going to be responsible for any *leyenda negra*. For a time a tradition persisted in England, albeit an illogical one, that it was permissible to enslave Africans but not Indians. This distinction or tradition largely disappeared during the seventeenth century. Nathaniel Bacon and Governor Berkeley disagreed on many things, but the seizure of native Americans was not one. A frequent reason for hostilities with Indian enemies and allies alike was the opportunity to capture slaves. Rather than peltry, they were the real plunder. Bacon and his followers made much of the point that in the bitter fighting at Occaneechee Island they killed the colony's implacable enemies, making no attempt to capture and sell them for private gain. In passing they mentioned that it was necessary to commandeer the Occaneechee king's daughter and her companions. What happened to them is not known, but one can assume that their fate was that of the Queen of Pamunkey's subjects, whom first Bacon and then Berkeley sold.[30]

During neither his first nor his second term was Governor Berkeley opposed to enslaving natives, and he had employed them on his Green Spring plantation at least since the 1640s. His brother, Lord George Berkeley, was a member of the Royal African Company, and the Berkeley brothers had few qualms about enslaving any nonwhites.[31] Bacon's followers always maintained that the governor had a secret interest in the peltry trade, which explained why he wanted merely to garrison frontier forts and not wage an aggressive campaign into the heart of the Indian country. The governor's real involvement in Indian commerce, however, was the slave traffic.

Carolina's geographic position and the fact that this colony was founded in the second half of the seventeenth century ensured that her role in the Indian slave trade overshadowed that of other mainland colonies. By coincidence the first settlers arrived at Charleston just as England's participation in the slave trade was accelerating. In addition to Carolina, Englishmen were capturing slaves on an unprecedented scale in Virginia, Central America, northern South America, and Africa, and regardless of their color the majority of these chattels were destined for the West Indies. A striking parallel existed between the situation in Carolina and that in West Africa. Since the sixteenth century English slavers had descended on the West African coast, seized coastal Africans or bought them from Negro dealers, and, after rigors of the Middle Passage, disposed of survivors in America.

Chartered in 1672, the Royal African Company involved English entrepreneurs more deeply in the Negro slave trade than ever. After that date typically Africans themselves, directly or through intermediaries in the interior, captured other Africans, perhaps hereditary enemies speaking a strange language and worshiping a different god. Drawn from an enormous hinterland, these captives were marched hundreds of miles to the coast, where English ship captains purchased them at company

137

factories or castles. From the beginning interlopers, trading on their own and making no financial contribution toward maintaining company forts, plagued the Royal African Company.[32] A similar pattern evolved in North America. Since the sixteenth century Englishmen had picked up coastal Carolina Indians, who were sold elsewhere or trained as interpreters. After the 1670s, however, slaves normally came from the interior, as native captors marched large numbers of prisoners to the coast for sale to English purchasers.

The Lords Proprietors, several of whom were members of the Royal African Company, were not opposed to slavery in principle. They hoped, however, to outlaw or restrict it in Carolina, envisioning a brisk peltry trade with independent tribes and the founding of manors where both whites and aborigines would labor as tenants. Their aspirations came to naught, their prohibitions ignored. During the early decades Indian slavery became a mainstay of the colony's economy.[33] Both the Goose Creek men and coastal Indians, such as the Sewees, captured local natives. After the coastal supply was exhausted, the Goose Creek men tapped the interior, acquiring slaves from 50, 100 and in time more than 600 miles inland, whom they exported or used themselves. Like their English counterparts in West Africa, the Goose Creek men over the long run usually did not personally capture slaves. In Africa more often than not it was blacks who attacked villages and ambushed small parties, capturing the unwary and taking them on the long journey to the coast. In South Carolina Westos, Savannahs, Lower Creeks, and Yamasees among others raided remote towns and brought their prisoners to Charleston.

It is impossible to comprehend the remarkable expansion of the Indian trade without taking slavery into account. The penetration of the interior was a no more enticing enterprise in Carolina than in Africa. Coastal inhabitants, principally Cusabos, were the first to suffer as Woodward and the Goose Creek men picked up where Ayllón had left off a century and a half previously. Promotional tracts by Hilton, Sandford, and the Lords Proprietors disguised the fact that the aborigines frequently did not welcome English colonists, and numerous small wars or encounters ensued. In 1671 the governor and council ordered troops out against nearby Cusabos; those who refused peace on English terms were to be sold and transported.[34] Similar expeditions were sent against Stonos and other tribes; Carolinians pitted one group against another; and friendly tribes were required to pay tribute or be sold and exported. Having other plans for coastal Indians, the Lords Proprietors attempted in a feeble way to protect them, decreeing in 1680 that no peaceful natives within 200 miles of Charleston might be captured; a decade later they extended the limit to 400 miles. Recognizing or acquiescing in the existence of the slave trade and hoping to control and profit from it, the proprietors agreed that prisoners might be transported—but the purchase of a license was first necessary.[35] These restrictions counted for little, and enslavement, disease, and flight to the interior resulted in the desertion of numerous coastal villages.

By developing a network of shifting native alliances, encouraging aboriginal rivalries, and offering cheap goods, the Goose Creek men extended their net of slave catching deep into the interior. Chichimecos in 1675 sold a Chisca woman from the Apalachicola River area to the English; the Chiscas complained but took out their grievances on unsuspecting Apalachees and in turn sold them to the Carolinians.[36] Before 1680 militant Westos disposed of captives in Virginia and to the Goose Creek men. When the Westo war broke out, these hard-pressed Indians sent emissaries to the Savannahs asking them to use their good offices with the whites. Keeping and selling these messengers, the Savannahs went on to defeat the Westos, assuming their lands and their role on the Savannah River. Westos were auctioned in Charleston in appreciable numbers.[37] When Scots founded Stuart's Town in 1684, they sent Yamasees against Spanish missions, and before long warriors returned with captives and manuscripts of prayers used by the Timucuan padres.[38] Far to the west, near the Mississippi, Chickasaws surprised a Choctaw village in the middle of the night, capturing more than 150 slaves, whom they bound, marched away, and sold to the English.[39]

Carolina's records for the early decades are fragmentary. Considering the amount of smuggling and the sympathetic treatment accorded to pirates, there is reason to question such customs and treasury records as do exist. Nevertheless, export licenses and a miscellany of other documents make it apparent that, beginning in the early 1670s and increasing in tempo for the rest of the century, Indians were exported to other mainland colonies and especially to the West Indies. At first slaves usually came from such local tribes as Stonos and Winyaws. Later they were joined by Yamasees, Guales, and Timucuans to the south; Westos and Savannahs from the Savannah River; Cherokees and Usherys from the northwest; and Appalachicolas, Choctaws, and Chatots from the far west. Whenever the Goose Creek men justified their conduct, which was not often, they reiterated the venerable dictum that they were redeeming captives to spare them a cruel death and that at heart Carolinians were humanitarians.[40]

The Goose Creek men knew, as did Bacon, Berkeley, the West African slavers, and the Brazilian *bandeirantes,* that the best way to procure captives was through war. Both whites and Indians fought many an engagement in quest of slaves. In northern Carolina the Machapungas made up with their traditional rivals, the Corees. During the peace-making celebrations and feast the Machapungas fell on the unsuspecting Corees, killing some, selling the remainder.[41] When white militiamen marched against natives, the usual bonus was a share of all captives. Moore attacked St. Augustine in 1702. Part of his force made a relatively easy sea voyage, and the remainder undertook an arduous journey by land, scouring remaining Timucuan missions for prisoners. This same inducement prompted fifty whites to accompany a thousand warriors on a trek of more than 400 miles overland to the Apalachee missions. These Carolinians, most of whom were experienced Indian traders and fighters, bore the brunt of the attack in the bitter fighting at Ayubale, the first mission to fall. But they knew the rewards and pressed the attack.

Long before the great slave raids of Queen Anne's War (1702–13) Carolinians had provoked hostilities in order to secure captives. Savannahs fought Westos, Lower Creeks descended on Apalachees, Machapungas surprised Corees, Yamasees hounded Timucuans, and so on. Pitting England against Spain, Queen Anne's War dramatically increased the tempo of slave raids. Finally in control of the provincial government, the Goose Creek men had a field day, causing the Spanish governor at St. Augustine to lament that twenty thousand of his Indians had been carried off.[42] He sent out patrols to reconnoiter villages that had been raided, and again and again soldiers returned reporting that only a few houses were left standing and only a handful of stunned natives, somehow eluding the enemy, had survived. With some basis Governor Moore's critics charged that he failed to take St. Augustine because he was too busy sending off slaves to the West Indies.[43] Denounced because of the siege's failure, Moore did not boast about his Timucuan captives. His subsequent expedition against Apalachee, of course, proved a great success, and thousands of slaves either returned with him or soon followed, as the Lower Creeks and the Yamasees completed the mission system's destruction. Apalachee's devastation marked the greatest slave raid ever to occur in the South or probably in the United States, with the possible exception of De Soto's *entrada*. French soldiers waged a pitiless war against the rebellious Natchez Indians in the 1720s, nearly destroying that nation and the Mississippian culture of the Natchez Sun. In the aftermath French commanders disposed of a thousand captives in the West Indies, far fewer than the actual number of Apalachees enslaved.[44]

The heyday of the Southern slave trade was in the 1680–1730 era, and after the founding of Louisiana Frenchmen participated. James Moore, Maurice Mathews, Tuscarora Jack Barnwell, and Thomas Nairne, for the most part Goose Creek men, extended their sway over the interior. Proprietors in 1692 decreed that slaves from within a 400-mile radius of Charleston were not to be exported without permission. This prohibition had little effect, partly because the Carolinians ignored it and especially because Indians in Apalachee, on the Mississippi River, in North Carolina, and deep in the Florida peninsula lived beyond that range.

Nairne emerged as a dominant figure in Indian affairs, sometimes *the* dominant figure. Staunch Anglican, land speculator, Indian fighter and trader, he expected to make his fortune in Carolina. He wanted strict regulation of the Indian trade and took seriously the charge to convert the aborigines. Joining dissident Anglicans, Nairne broke with the Goose Creek men and as a result for a period was imprisoned, accused of being a Jacobite. His attempt to reform and regulate trade, his endeavor to bring the natives into the Anglican fold, and his quarrel with, and for a time imprisonment by, the Goose Creek men have led historians to portray him as a reformer, martyr, and true friend of the natives.[45] If one leaves aside his imprisonment on trumped-up charges of treason and closely examines his actions, it becomes obvious that his attitudes toward the Indians were essentially those of James Moore and Henry Woodward. An aggressive imperialist, Nairne wanted to extend the dominion of the Union Jack, the Anglican Church, and Carolina over the entire lower South, which, according to the provincial charter, rightfully belonged to Carolina anyway. His effort to oversee all commerce and to curb traders' abuses by no means implies that he wanted to constrict the trade in slaves and peltry.

Nairne was as quick as any Goose Creek man to reward Indian friends and punish any native who stood in his way. When an Apalachee slave killed his Yamasee master, Nairne at once got the provincial government to make a five-pound donation to the owner's brother.[46] One could almost picture Nairne as a sixteenth-century Spanish conquistador reading the requirement to the natives and taking fire and sword to those who did not submit. Indians who refused to come into Carolina's commercial orbit or to receive Anglican instruction whenever it was offered, and who continued to ally themselves with France and Spain, as Nairne saw it, had to be dealt with rigorously: Our subjects the Tallapoosas [Upper Creeks] have burnt Pensacola town; native Floridians have been driven to the Keys; we are capturing many slaves and have brought over to our side or destroyed all Indians within 700 miles of Charleston.[47] Although Nairne and his warriors were successful enough, he was disappointed that the Spaniards and Frenchmen were able to hang onto newly founded Pensacola and Mobile. As far as the Florida Keys were concerned, they did not prove to be a safe asylum, because Creeks and Yamasees extended their raids to these islands, returning to Charleston with unfortunate refugees.

It was the aborigines who captured most of the slaves. Spaniards in St. Augustine complained again and again that the Yamasees and other pro-Carolina Indians surprised nearby villages, striking without warning in the middle of the night like experienced house robbers, moving swiftly from one dwelling to another, selecting only the healthiest and most able-bodied women and children, then disappearing into the forest before menfolk and troops could organize any resistance. One reason attackers were so successful was that their wives or kinsmen frequently lived in these villages, giving information and serving as guides.[48] Trying to take advantage of this strategy when he besieged St. Augustine in 1702, Governor Moore sent Yamasees posing as mission Indians into the Castillo de San Marcos. They were to incite refugees to rise from within when Moore struck from without, but in this instance the "fifth column" strategy failed.[49] The force impelling Yamasees and Creeks to intrigue with kinfolk living under Spanish rule or to plunge into the wilderness was knowledge that a brisk market waited in Carolina for any captives. This was the best way to obtain essential guns, powder, knives, and hatchets; for many Indians, rum also was in the same vital category.

Queen Anne's War finally wound down, and after protracted European negotiations the Treaty of Utrecht was signed in 1713. Natives who had taken refuge under the shadow of cannons at forts in St. Augustine, Pensacola, and Mobile secured a respite, which is not to suggest that the Southern slave trade ceased or necessarily diminished. This traffic merely assumed new dimensions, and the Tuscarora and Yamasee wars were primarily responsible. The seemingly insatiable demand for slaves in Carolina, the West Indies, Virginia, Pennsylvania, and New England was partly if not primarily responsible for the outbreak of both conflicts.

More than five thousand strong, the Tuscaroras were the most powerful nation in the North Carolina Tidewater, and for years before 1711 they had fallen on their weaker neighbors—Meherrins, Tawasas, Corees, and assorted others—and sold captives to Virginians and North Carolinians. This proved to be a two-edged sword, because as time passed Tuscaroras themselves were captured in increasing numbers by neighbors striking back in retaliation and by whites themselves. The pressure became so intense that in 1710, even before the outbreak of hostilities, the Tuscaroras petitioned Pennsylvania to allow them to move to that province.[50] This was partly because of the Quakers' benevolent Indian policy, and especially because Tuscaroras would be closer to the Senecas and other Iroquois kinsmen who could help protect them. At a much earlier period, probably before white contact, the Tuscaroras, an Iroquoian group, had drifted southward into North Carolina. By moving to Pennsylvania and New York, which many of them eventually did, they were returning to their earlier homeland. During the war itself the Tuscaroras were enslaved as never before. James Moore, Jr., and Tuscarora Jack Barnwell repeatedly complained that their Indian armies melted away after arriving in North Carolina. As soon as auxiliaries captured a Tuscarora or any Indian who might be passed off as hostile, they returned to South Carolina and sought out Goose Creek purchasers. Governor Hyde of North Carolina asserted that his forces had seized up to four hundred captives,[51] and some one thousand Tuscarora slaves, perhaps more, were taken during the war.

Before and after the Tuscarora and Yamasee uprisings North and South Carolina traders had a tradition of enslaving friendly natives whenever enemies were not at hand. There are many examples; the incident in 1713 at Chestowe, a Yuchi town among the Cherokees, was one of the more flagrant. For a considerable period Alexander Long had lived with and taken advantage of these Yuchis. At one point an exasperated Yuchi warrior took offense and "puled of[f] sum of his hair." The furious Long fled straight to nearby Cherokee towns, telling what "a brave parcel of slaves" awaited in Chestowe. Biding his time, Long eventually got his revenge. With Long's collaboration, the Cherokees surprised Chestowe, destroyed the town, and divided up women and children survivors. Long received one woman and five children as his share.[52] Mounting Indian resentment at such conduct, coupled with traders' excesses, brought on the Yamasee War. There were no Yamasees at Chestowe, but many who confederated with them, if not there, were close by.

After the Yamasee War Tuscarora Jack Barnwell led an expedition in 1719 against Yamasees who had retired into Florida. That Britain and Spain again were at war gave him all the excuse he needed. His army, essentially a Creek one, headed for missions on the St. Johns River and those near St. Augustine. The wife of one of his scouts living in Pocotaligo Town, a relocated Yamasee village, was to help. But suspicious of her conduct, the Spaniards were on guard, and Barnwell lost the advantage of surprise.[53] A decade later the two countries again were at war, and once more Carolinians and their Indian allies, this time led by John Palmer, were back in Timucua threatening the missions and St. Augustine. After 1719 captives, including Yamasees, Guales, and Timucuans, trickled back to Carolina for sale.[54] Barnwell and Palmer were not as successful in seizing Indians as the Goose Creek men had been earlier, because so little remained of the Spanish missions.

Slave raids, wars, and especially diseases had swept away almost all Timucuans, Apalachees, Tequestas, and others who had confronted Ponce de León and De Soto. Yamasee refugees helped fill the population void in the provinces of Timucua and Apalachee, but unfortunately this tribe, like its predecessors, continued on its path toward virtual extinction. Some Lower Creeks accompanying Barnwell, Palmer, and later James Oglethorpe remained in Florida, destroying and mixing with aboriginal remnants. By the latter third of the eighteenth century these Indians became known as Seminoles. The Creek Chief Cowkeeper, who settled in the Alachua (Gainesville) region, according to some, is considered the progenitor of the Seminole nation. On the eve of the American Revolution, the naturalist William Bartram visited Cowkeeper, marveling at his flock of cattle, a bit puzzled by the Yamasee slave who stood in such awe of the chief.[55]

The tempo of the slave trade decreased after 1730. This is not to say that no more aborigines were captured, but the supply had been reduced, and it was far more dangerous and difficult to capture those who survived. North Carolina remnants occasionally were still seized, and Tuscaroras—Senecas according to the Tuscaroras—sallied into South Carolina, carrying off a few unfortunates.[56] At the outset of the French and Indian War in mid-century, Carolinians built Fort Loudoun on the Little Tennessee River in the heart of the Cherokee country. Whenever hostilities spread to the frontier, Governor Arthur Dobbs planned to reinforce the fort and raid native villages, enslaving and transporting any women and children not killed.[57] As it turned out, the Cherokees captured the isolated Fort Loudoun, massacring most of the garrison.

After 1720 or thereabouts, Britain's largest supply of American Indian slaves came not from the South but from Central America, primarily the Gulf of Honduras, the Mosquito Coast, and Panama. Prodded by Jamaican merchants, Mosquito Indians, and to a lesser extent warriors from Darien in Panama, raided Spanish settlements and Catholic Indian villages in the interior, returning to the coast with slaves. In the decade after 1712 Mosquito Indians sold more than two thousand such captives, and these, like others from different parts of Central America, were shipped to Jamaica and other islands.[58] West Indian slavers used the same argument as the Goose Creek men—that it was a humanitarian act to redeem captives who otherwise would be put to a cruel death.[59] Whenever Mosquito and Darien Indians did not bring in enough prisoners, British traders began seizing these allies in turn. All the while Spaniards complained that their Christian dependents were being spirited away.[60] In short, conditions in Central America differed little from those in the South. Jamaica plantation records of the early eighteenth century disclose Indian slaves in the labor force.[61] They were not descendants of the Arawaks who had greeted Columbus but probably had been sent to the West Indies by Goose Creek men or Mosquito Indians.

Unlike Africa, the South did not have a seemingly unlimited supply of slaves. It has been estimated that the Congo and Angola needed a population of almost 19 million to sustain an annual exportation of thirty thousand;[62] over the long term the South could not match or even approach those numbers. But in the period from 1670 to 1730 Guales, Timucuans, and Apalachees in the missions, Yuchis at Chestowe, Choctaws near the Mississippi, and Occaneechees and Pamunkeys in Virginia had much in common with the Ibos, Bantus, Yorubas, and Mandingos who were snatched from West African villages. American Indians were illiterate, although Father Pareja had taught many how to read and write, and natives living in English and French households sometimes learned their masters' languages. Africans, or at least some of them, were literate even before European slavers appeared, and a few accounts have survived describing their trauma of being captured, separated from family and friends, taken to the coast, and eventually sent to the New World.

As far as is known not a single such narrative written by an Indian has survived, but the broad outline of the slave trade is clear enough. Whereas white captors—Spanish, English, and French—relied on iron manacles, leg shackles, Claiborne's patented "device," and an arm and neck collar, restraining the captive but allowing him to eat and attend to bodily functions, Indians themselves used a leather cord. Whether accompanying Tuscarora Jack in his North Carolina campaigns, venturing to the southern tip of Florida, or ranging west to the Mississippi, warriors invariably carried such a convenient cord. These rawhide strings were not as effective as iron shackles, because sometimes prisoners cut them and escaped—but not often. The pain of being tightly bound for weeks by a slave cord and making long forced marches was intense, far more so than with shackles. In later life captives still bore marks of where they had been tied. Twenty-six-year-old Lamhatty, a Tawasa captured by the Tuscaroras, after many tribulations made his escape in 1707, crying when he showed white protectors where the Tuscaroras had bound him.[63]

Europeans customarily branded slaves whatever their origins. Spaniards and Portuguese branded Moorish slaves; Europeans

marked Africans; and Spaniards branded Indians in the West
Indies and on the mainland. Spanish officials were vexed when
Florida Indians sometimes retaliated by branding Spanish captives.[64] It is not certain whether Bacon, Berkeley, and their
contemporaries branded Virginia Indians, but it would be
surprising if they had not. A century later Thomas Jefferson's
contemporaries did as had the Goose Creek men done in South
Carolina. In 1716 commissioners in charge of the Carolina Indian
trade sent branding irons to agents in the back country to mark
deerskins and captives alike. Whether belonging to Spaniards or
Englishmen, slaves were marked on the face, shoulder, or arm.
In time Carolinians began marking captives by burning them
with gunpowder, sparing them "the torture of a brand."[65] Marks
for skins and slaves usually were owners' initials. Robert Temple's Indian slave, who in 1775 ran away from his master in
Virginia, had an "R" on his right cheek and a "T" on the left, the
brands being "fresh and not cured."[66]

The slave trade became a notable part of the life-style of nonwhites as they were caught up in Europe's commercial expansion. The numbers of slaves taken, whether Indians or Africans,
vary widely. For the most part demographers have concentrated
on Africa and are not really sure if fewer than 10 million or up to
50 million or more blacks were transported to America over a
period of four centuries. A recent, and presumably the best, reckoning is that a total of almost 10 million reached the Western
Hemisphere, with only about 5 percent coming to what became
the United States.[67] Data to estimate the number of Southern
Indians enslaved are far more fragmentary, though some exist.
Legal disputes in Hispaniola disclose that Ayllón brought back
150 Indians from *la Florida*, and Spanish chronicles, not always
in agreement, make known that De Soto impressed many thousands as he moved from one chiefdom to another. Based on an
examination of South Carolina wills and court records, a recent
study discovers mention of 5,500 slave names;[68] and in 1708 the
Spanish governor in St. Augustine complained that the English
had carried off ten thousand to twelve thousand Indians after the
outbreak of war in 1702 and even more beforehand.[69] In the
aftermath of the Natchez Rebellion, the French shipped off a
thousand survivors to the islands.[70] The difficulty in estimating
the number of enslaved Indians is the fact that most slave sales
went unrecorded, or, if records were made, they have not sur-

vived. When a Yamasee brought a Tequesta from southern Florida back to the Goose Creek men or when William Byrd's men returned to the James River with captives from the Carolina back country, normally the bill of sale, assuming there was one, does not remain to disclose the matchcoats, guns, powder, ball, wampum, and rum exchanged for prisoners. Between the sixteenth and eighteenth centuries tens of thousands of Southern Indians were enslaved, but at this stage it is too risky to estimate how many tens of thousands.

Documents, such as customs records, export licenses, and West Indian plantation records—the same type used to estimate dimensions of the African trade—indicate that aborigines were shipped to the islands and other mainland colonies. Many, perhaps most, were not exported and were employed locally. As best can be told Indians were marketed the same way as blacks. In the early eighteenth century slavers appeared in the upper James with both Africans and Indians in the ships' holds. As captains made their way from plantation to plantation we must assume they made no distinction in the way they disposed of their cargo and that Indians were inspected, probed, and gawked at in the same way as blacks. Colonial cities, notably Charleston, had slave markets where both Indians and blacks were auctioned. Slavers in Africa sailed along the coast, stopping at forts or makeshift prisons on the beach until their holds were filled with human cargo. To an extent ship captains in America did the same thing, though normally their vessels were not especially outfitted for the slave trade. Their primary cargoes were tobacco, rice, naval stores, and peltry, but they also carried a few and sometimes a considerable number of Indians.

The typical and most highly valued African slave was a young adult male, a prime field hand, which is not to suggest that women and children did not make the Middle Passage but that an imbalance existed in favor of young men. In contrast, Indian women and children were more likely to serve as slaves in mainland colonies. Many warriors died in hostilities, and some of those captured proved insubordinate. Virginia and Carolina masters dealt with such slaves the same way West Indian planters treated Africans who were "bad niggers": They sent them away as quickly as possible. Usually blacks went to the mainland and Indians to the islands. Wills, inventories, and assorted other records all disclose a preponderance of Indian females and children on the mainland. The Goose Creek men often made good their boast that they would put to fire and sword all but women and children. When in 1704 Moore returned from Apalachee he had four thousand women and children but fewer than three hundred men. For every male in smaller gangs of captives brought out of Apalachee, Timucua, and similar provinces there were likely to be three to five or more females.[71] Of two thousand known Indian slaves in South Carolina in 1724, nine hundred were women, six hundred men, and five hundred children.[72] The South Carolina commissioners of the Indian trade at one point even ordered their agents to buy no Indian male slave over fourteen years of age.[73] Women were preferred partly because they were considered more manageable, sometimes a grave error. Children, including "apprentices," presumably were more likely to forget their families and kin, having little choice but to accept their fate in the white man's world.

At this point we might digress and mention the debate over whether the enslavement of Africans was more onerous in the Old South than elsewhere in Spanish America. Scholars taking the Spanish-American point of view contend that the Catholic Church and a sympathetic powerful monarch, both emphasizing that slaves were men with souls, mitigated the evils of slavery. Critics respond by mentioning that, although royal edicts and church policy seemed to make slavery less harsh in Spanish America, in reality chattels were better off in the Old South. To prove this they point out that even though only about 5 percent of the Africans arriving in the New World came to the United States, because of natural increase today the republic contains approximately one-third of all Negroes living anywhere in the Western Hemisphere. Obviously conditions in the Old South could not have been all that bad.

Not that we will settle the argument—but all of this brings us back to the Indians. In the heat of argument one factor has been overlooked: The sexual ratio of chattel slaves in the South was more normal than elsewhere in Spanish America because a considerable number of female Indian slaves were already in the quarters when male Africans arrived. This was one, but not the only, reason why the Southern "Negro" population on its own increased so much in contrast to almost everywhere else in the New World. Taking this into consideration in many respects makes it harder, though certainly not impossible, to contend that enslavement of Africans in the United States was more benevolent.

Occasionally evidence has survived giving a more intimate view of the slave traffic. Early in the eighteenth century the Virginian John Evans traded in the Carolina back country, and fragments of his barely legible account book have been preserved. Routine entries disclose the amounts of powder, shot, ball, vermillion, flaps or breechclouts, molasses, duffels, strouds, and petticoats exchanged for raccoon, bear, fox, and deer skins. On February 15, 1704, Evans purchased Merrak, a ten-year-old Indian girl, for £20. His most valuable skin, a buckskin, was worth two shillings. With fifty skins per pack and two packs per horse, each horseload, assuming it contained nothing but the most expensive buckskins, was valued at £10. Evans understood that Merrak was worth more than two horseloads of peltry, which represented the annual labor of one or two warriors. Whether or not the diminutive Merrak realized that as she silently made her way toward the James is unrecorded in the journal.[74]

A Hitchiti war story has been handed down in Southeastern Indian folklore. Early in the eighteenth century Hitchitis (Lower Creeks) were at war with the Yamasees. A Hitchiti woman of the Tcikote clan lived with her two children outside the village. Sending her older boy for aid when Yamasees attacked her cabin, she took up her gun and defended herself and her young son. Driven from her cabin, she hid her child beside a log, but the Yamasees found and scalped him. The distraught mother, shrieking and firing her weapon, killed one warrior and drove the rest off. Astounded at her bravery, villagers displayed the Yamasee scalp in the square ground and, had she not been a woman, would have made her a *tastanagi*, a war chief. The mother, however, confided that though "while I was fighting, I was whooping, [in fact I] was only crying. This is how the story goes."[75]

Hitchiti-speakers survive among Creeks and Seminoles, and their folk tales divulge something of their past. Unfortunately the Timucuans, Apalachees, Cusabos, Occaneechees, and so many others with their oral history are extinct. The frequency of slave raids dropped off sharply after the 1730s, and there has been a tendency to downplay or ignore how important slave wars and the slave trade had been for more than two centuries. The Hitchiti mother of the Tcikote clan, however, never forgot.

7

Exploiting This 'Virgin Land'

Relatively few Indians live in the South today. Unless one visits the reservations of Cherokees in North Carolina, Seminoles and Miccosukees in Florida, and Choctaws in Mississippi, it is easy to assume that all the natives have died out or moved west of the Mississippi River. The general public, and until recently many officials in the Bureau of Indian Affairs, are little aware that some seventy-four thousand Indians reside in that portion of the Old Confederacy east of the Mississippi.[1] Living on farms and in towns and cities, and working in factories, most are indistinguishable from their white and black neighbors. The ordeal of the "Trail of Tears," when approximately sixty thousand Indians were relocated west of the Mississippi River during Andrew Jackson's administration, is better known. But even arbitrarily adding the two figures together, one from the nineteenth century and the other from the twentieth, the total is only 134,000, an almost insignificant number to be scattered over the entire South. However one juggles the figures, a widely held belief is that few Indians inhabit the South today and that it has always been that way.

151

This, of course, is erroneous, making it harder to explain the importance of Indian labor during the colonial era. Despite severe population losses, for many decades after contact the Southern Indians remained relatively numerous, certainly far more so than their brethren north of the Ohio River. A sampling and careful reading of assorted statistics reveals a considerable number of natives living among or near the colonists. The county court at Westover on the upper James River in the last quarter of the seventeenth century for tax purposes adjudged the ages of many Indian servants residing in white households.[2] During the same period, except for the very end, Negroes are seldom mentioned. In Saint Paul's Parish, South Carolina, a 1708 enumeration lists a total of 1,400 heathen and infidel adults, including one thousand Negro and Indian slaves and four hundred free Indians.[3] It is likely that Indians constituted an absolute majority in this parish. In 1720 one-tenth of the slaves in St. Thomas Parish, South Carolina, were Indians; the number of additional free and bond Indians was unrecorded. In any case, well over 10 percent of the nonwhite labor force in this parish was Indian.[4] Before 1711 South Carolina seldom imported more than a hundred blacks annually;[5] yet in 1704 alone the Goose Creek men and their allies returned with thousands of Apalachees, only some of whom were exported. Reporting on the province in 1710, Thomas Nairne asserted that 12 percent of South Carolina's population was white, 22 percent Negro, and 66 percent Indian.[6] The last figure included both natives who resided among whites in the Low Country and those in the west who did not. Out of a total of 194 slaves in French Mobile during its first decade, 183 were Indian and only eleven African.[7] Selected at random, none of these figures are definitive, but collectively they indicate that, despite wars and a string of forts guarding the frontier separating the two races, many Indians lived among whites and worked for them.

Having read about exploits of conquistadors or marveled at American treasures sent to Europe, the Spaniards at an earlier period had assumed that the New World must be thickly populated. Through *repartimiento*, slavery, and wage labor, Spain employed aborigines to pan for gold and silver, tend cattle, till fields, and serve as domestics. Had Ayllón, Narváez, and De Soto succeeded in colonizing Florida, they would have utilized the Southern Indians more effectively. Their *capitulaciónes* empowered them to distribute Indians in *repartimiento* or to enslave them. During their four-year sojourn in *la Florida* De Soto's men relied extensively on native porters, body servants, and guides. It was not until the end of the sixteenth century and later, when Franciscan missions flourished, that Spain systematically organized native workers. For the most part Indians constructed the missions and tilled adjoining fields for themselves and the padres. Spanish governors requisitioned natives to build roads and public structures and levied tribute, usually foodstuffs, on Christian villages.

When Englishmen settled at Roanoke Island and subsequently at Jamestown, they were confused about the Indians' role, because initially they were unsure about the colony's mission and the necessary steps to make it a financial success. In time emphasis shifted from creating a fortified naval base toward promoting agriculture and a more permanent type of settlement. Indians then assumed far more importance. The younger Richard Hakluyt, closely associated with both the Roanoke and the Jamestown enterprises, had read and published innumerable accounts of voyages to America and was aware that the Spaniards had killed many Indians. Like most Europeans he did not perceive the extent of the inordinate population decline. He and his contemporaries assumed that Indians were numerous enough in Virginia and intended to employ them. Their ideas were not well thought out, but Virginia was England's first colony, so ignorance and misconceptions about America were widespread. Letters from colonists, writings by Hariot and John Smith, and John White's drawings helped authorities in London to plan the natives' role. For the most part they expected Indians, paid by whites, to continue working as always by clearing fields, planting, weeding, harvesting, hunting, fishing, and rowing, and they anticipated tribute in foodstuffs, peltry, and service. In return the natives, retaining their freedom, would receive manufactures and spiritual manna.

The Virginia or London Company was financially strapped, and stockholders never even recouped their investments, much less made a profit. Aggressive efforts were made to produce commodities that could be profitably exported, and officials prepared to direct Indian labor along new lines. Natives should plant olive trees; tend silkworms feeding on local or imported mulberry trees and learn the art of sericulture; grow domestic or imported hemp, flax, and similar fibers; and learn how to manufacture linen. All the while they were to render tribute of corn, vegetables, meat, and fish in order to help make the colony self-sufficient. Except for the annual tribute, authorities envisioned Indians as wage laborers.

John Smith's ideas were essentially the same, except that he was not sanguine about paying the natives who were supposed to apply for the new job openings. As Smith saw it, once they were "pacified" they should be compelled to serve, just as Spain had forced them to work in her colonies. The dream of enlisting large numbers of Powhatans as wage laborers failed because of the high death rate and because they were more inclined to shoot and hack away at colonists than to work for them.

The dangers of relying on Indians were exemplified during the 1622 and 1644 massacres. As a result a trend developed of Virginians' depending more and more on Indian women and children and killing off or transporting recalcitrant males. This tendency was manifest even before the 1622 massacre. When the company was reorganized and presumably revitalized in 1619, as has been seen, one of the many projects was to procure children to be brought up and work among the colonists.[8] Even in the months after the 1622 massacre, when settlers waged ruthless war against the natives, soldiers were instructed to spare the young, whose labor was potentially valuable.[9]

Whatever their age and sex, Indians worked for the colonists as slaves, indentured servants, and freemen. The great influx of Africans into Virginia did not begin until the last quarter of the seventeenth century, and for much of that century Indian slaves and indentured servants were at least as numerous as blacks. When in personal correspondence and legal proceedings settlers referred to slaves there was no way, without additional information, to tell whether they meant Africans or Indians.

Nonwhite apprentices in seventeenth-century Virginia were likely to be Indians. In theory all servants, black, Indian, and white, were governed equally by apprenticeship laws. If the natives' lot was a hard one, it does not follow that their white counterparts fared much better. Masters whipped white servants unmercifully and worked them excessively, exacting as much labor as possible during their fixed period of service with little regard for their health and well-being. Indian apprentices complained about the same ill treatment, but there is little indication they suffered more physical abuse.

During the first decades of the seventeenth century not much legal distinction existed between Indian and white servants. Both were regulated by medieval apprenticeship laws and the local "custom of the country." Children of each race were bound out to "sober" Christians, serving their masters while learning a trade, and upon reaching eighteen or twenty-one years of age presumably receiving their freedom.[10] Parental approval was necessary. In 1655 the Virginia general assembly confirmed details by statute: With parents' consent Indian children might become servants, and the indenture had to be approved by all three interested parties—child, parent, and master—before a local justice of the peace.[11] Despite similarities, Indian servants differed in a number of respects from their white counterparts. Although the contract was supposed to be written in proper legal form with copies given to all parties, in fact agreements were commonly oral, perhaps sealed by passing around a bowl of brandy. Unsuspecting illiterate whites also made such contracts, but not to the same extent. Another distinction was length of service. Four years in the case of an adult or until reaching eighteen or twenty-one was the servant's usual term, but for Indians it was considerably longer, extending more than four years for adults and until the age of twenty-four, twenty-five, thirty, thirty-one, or older for children. Promising to teach him a trade and raise him as a Christian, John Barnwell apprenticed a young boy from the Cherokee country for nineteen years, presumably meaning that the Indian would be at least thirty before receiving his freedom.[12] According to an eighteenth-century Virginia statute, apprenticed bastard Indian children had to serve until thirty-one.[13] Alexander, an Indian imported into and sold in North Carolina, agreed to serve his master eighty years, but Alexander was a special case, having previously run away and torn up his original indenture.[14]

In a variety of ways courts arbitrarily apprenticed Indians or extended their periods of servitude. Planters sat on and controlled the courts, and natives seemed to have been discriminated against even more than whites, making Indian servitude close, if not tantamount, to outright slavery. An Indian imprisoned for whatever reason had to pay off by service all the legal expenses incurred. Whenever Virginia magistrates were not sure what to do with a particular native, they bound him out to a local planter. One Indian who strolled into Jamestown at an inappropriate moment in 1628 suddenly found himself appren-

THE ONLY LAND THEY KNEW

ticed to Thomas Willoughby for four years.[15] In the aftermath of a fracas with Nansiaticos, members of the Virginia council drew lots and distributed the children of the culprits. Having first choice of the children, whose ages ranged from one to eleven, the governor received Simon, Little Jack, Betty, and Little Betty; Robert Carter got Ben; John Custis got Kate; John Lightfoot got Nanny, and so on. None of the councilors was left out.[16] Hagar, about twenty-five years old, in 1688 petitioned for her freedom, insisting that she was "Virginia born" and not imported from another colony. Magistrates felt this was a specious argument and ordered her to serve until the age of thirty.[17] When Indian slaves or servants, particularly the younger ones, appeared in court, often they were arbitrarily given surnames, usually those of their masters, all of which was a far cry from receiving war names at the busk or similar rituals.

Bastardy was a perennial social, moral, and economic problem. Masters were annoyed because they lost their servant's labor while she was bearing her child and because they had to feed and support a nonproductive infant. At times Indian mothers who gave birth to bastards were treated like any other misbehaving servant. One punishment was whipping. Masters had the option of turning the miscreant over to the court, where a sentence of thirty or so lashes might be imposed. Such punishment on occasion was inflicted on an Indian servant, though at times the court ruled that because the mother was heathen she could not be convicted. Not every sentence of whipping, regardless of whether a white or an Indian was involved, was necessarily carried out. In some instances the father stepped forward, acknowledging his culpability and assuming financial responsibility for whatever losses the master and the county incurred. A harsh sentence of so many lashes well laid on or some other excessive penalty in part was intended to make the guilty male step forward. Sue, an Indian servant, had a child out of wedlock, and the court decreed that she work for her master two more years or pay him 2,000 pounds of tobacco. Benjamin Elam, apparently a free white, acknowledged he was the father and consented to serve Sue's master a year and pay him 400 pounds of tobacco. At the end of Elam's year the master agreed that Sue and Benjamin might marry and could keep and provide for their child, who would remain free and not be bound out to Sue's master.[18]

Whatever their ethnic background, mothers delivering illegitimate children might escape punishment by killing the infant. From the European standpoint this was murder. For Indians the issue was not as clear-cut. Mississippians sometimes had killed their children, perhaps because they could not stand the cold and other rigors they had been deliberately exposed to or perhaps in an act of ritual murder for burial with a deceased chief, as occurred upon the death of the Natchez Sun. Considering the early age at which many Indians females were apprenticed, one must always wonder how much knowledge they retained about their Mississippian heritage. In any case, after contact female Indian servants, perhaps suffering pangs of conscience, sometimes murdered their offspring, possibly to escape a whipping and an increased period of service, or perhaps to keep their children from growing up in an alien world.

In a variety of ways courts took measures to extend the period of Indian servitude, and as a result many, but not all, became perpetual servants. Some completed their terms and won their freedom. By 1688 Mary, a Virginia Indian, had finished her term and was angry because her daughter, who also had served many years, was not freed.[19] The Pamunkey Robin had been apprenticed as a youth, had learned a trade, and had been set free in 1709. The court agreed that he could remain as an artisan among the whites, because his trade, whatever it might have been, was of no value to the Indians.[20] Through custom, which in time acquired the force of law, servants upon completion of their service received freedom dues, typically clothes and corn or a monetary equivalent of perhaps fifty shillings. Masters sometimes "forgot" to pay freedom dues, and servants, including Indians, turned to the courts for relief. Despite all the impediments, an undisclosed number of Indians completed their terms, possibly acquired a new skill, and remained among the whites and to an extent were assimilated by them.

Whether former servants or not, Indians worked for whites as wage laborers. Colonists employed them to till fields, round up cattle, and serve as domestics, hunters, and artisans. Tributaries hired themselves out to neighboring colonists. After Bacon's Rebellion Pamunkey women worked as maids and the men as hunters.[21] Natives commonly agreed to hunt and fish for pay. Peter struck a bargain with a planter on Virginia's Eastern Shore to kill five deer and deliver two dressed doeskins.[22] Other Indians, also on the Eastern Shore, for a proper consideration

157

promised to catch a certain number of sheepshead, drum, and similar fish.[23] Indians were not usually paid in specie but in roanoke, tobacco, and trading goods. For building a house and related services, South Carolinians gave twelve hatchets to Okala and his men, while a Virginia Indian agreed to construct a weir in exchange for breeches, shoes, and stockings.[24] Any native accepting payment in advance had to be on his guard, because not fulfilling the contract was a sure route to servitude or slavery. Risks to colonists who violated provisions of the bargain were less, but natives who had performed work and had not been paid turned to the courts for relief, sometimes successfully. The white colonist involved might be ordered to pay so many pounds of tobacco or arm's lengths of roanoke; even so, he was not likely to find himself in jail or bound out as a servant.

Free Indians occasionally became sharecroppers. The Potomac king in 1655 sold land to Gerrard Fowke for a horse, bridle, and saddle. Intending to grow corn and tobacco and to graze cattle, Fowke agreed that Potomacs, working on the land alongside whites, might have their proper share of the profits.[25] Another Virginia Indian, young Dick, after producing three barrels of maize and 200 pounds of tobacco for the landowner, was entitled to whatever else he grew, along with his food and lodging.[26]

Slaves and indentured servants were hired out, and most if not all of their earnings went to the master rather than to the Indian. Slave oarsmen in South Carolina were paid three pounds per month,[27] while in Virginia an Indian boy was hired out at one shilling per day.[28] Although Indian slaves and servants might be hired out at any time, this was especially common at the owner's death, to ensure that Indians would not be idle while the estate was being settled. Whenever owners rented out natives, courts were careful to ensure that masters were responsible for whatever damages their absentee servants might incur.[29]

Infrequently chiefs served as labor contractors, promising to deliver so many workers—their subjects or captives—for a fixed term. Chief Altamaha, a powerful Yamasee head man, agreed to furnish three hundred hands for seven years. They were to produce silk and cotton, to make the fortunes of white plantation owners, and to provide the chief with an ample supply of trading goods. This particular arrangement fell through, exactly why is not known.[30]

Since both natives and colonists were typically farmers, it was inevitable that Indian males and females continued tilling household vegetable gardens and fields of maize, tobacco, and beans. Instead of fire-hardened pointed sticks and bone or conch-shell hoes, they began using iron hoes, shovels, and plows. Most appropriately, a seventeenth-century Virginia Indian was known as the "Grubbing Hoe Indian."[31] In South Carolina John Musgrove threatened to beat relocated Apalachees who would not hoe his corn.[32] In Florida both Franciscans and soldiers forced Indians to grow maize and newly introduced wheat, also requiring natives to grind the grain. Sometimes Indians had to spend so much time tilling Spanish fields that they did not have enough to work their own. At almost any period, but especially in earlier years, Spaniards and Englishmen were dependent on Indian foodstuffs. The maize tribute, partially responsible for periodic revolts in Franciscan missions, was constantly readjusted and reduced but never abolished, because Spaniards were so dependent on it. Rice seeds were imported from the Mediterranean or Africa, becoming a staple of the South Carolina economy. It was not long after rice culture took hold in the Tidewater that Indians could be seen working in paddies and flooding and draining fields.[33]

Aboriginal clothing, particularly of those living among the English, was modified, in time differing little from the traditional coarse slave or "nigger" garb; and Indians slept on mats in masters' cabins and in the slave quarters rather than in native villages. Any visitor examining the landscape while sailing up the James River in Virginia or the Cooper in South Carolina would have seen open fields, perhaps originally cleared by the natives, in which the Mississippian staples of maize, beans, tobacco, and squash were still cultivated. If the visitor looked more closely he might discover that in some instances Mississippian descendants still tilled these fields and tended household vegetable gardens.

Despite disruption of their villages, Indians never forgot or abandoned their earlier knowledge of hunting and fishing. In some respects these pursuits were more difficult after colonization, and techniques had to be modified. The gun began to replace the bow and arrow, and with a few exceptions only whites could furnish firearms, powder, and ball and make necessary repairs. Indians eagerly bought or stole guns from colonists, and planters sometimes loaned firearms to trusted servants so they could hunt. Because colonists appropriated so many native village sites, the Indians' fishing practices had to be altered. Mississippians had placed their stone weirs and basket traps in or close to these village sites, but often they had been destroyed or abandoned. Even so, with hook, line, spear, and poison and by maintaining weirs on remote streams, Indians still fished, using their catch for themselves or to trade with whites.

Mississippians had perfected a number of skills. Despite the shock of foreign diseases and wars, artisans retained and continued to practice their crafts. They were competent builders, and in postcontact times one encounters such personages as the "Carpenter" or the "Little Carpenter." Assisted by iron and steel tools, they became even more adept. For the most part Indians constructed the Guale, Timucua, and Apalachee missions. They erected the palisade, assuming there was one, and constructed the chapel and other buildings with their thatched roofs, wattle-and-daub walls, and poured-clay floors. One suspects that natives with European tools fashioned the large hewn crosses conspicuously displayed in *doctrinas* and *visitas*. Employing both European and aboriginal techniques, Indians built houses for Spaniards and Englishmen. With few exceptions, Mississippians had lived near rivers, lakes, and the ocean and, having no horses, relied on the dugout for transportation. Whites took over native villages and, with few or nonexistent roads, quickly appreciated the importance of water transportation and the dugout's utility. They seized and bought them or hired Indians to make them. During Virginia's early years Henry Fleet used an Indian-built shallop, which he subsequently armed and manned with ten Englishmen,[34] while a Nanticoke on Virginia's Eastern Shore agreed to construct a 25-foot dugout, 2 feet wide, 15½ inches deep. These details have survived because the Nanticoke did not live up to his contract, and legal proceedings ensued.[35]

In addition to employing dugouts, Mississippians had regularly transported burdens on their backs. Distances might have been short, merely from a borrow pit to a temple mound several hundred yards away, or many miles as they carried maize and peltry to the village or delivered tribute to a distant chief. In any case Indians were accustomed to bearing heavy loads long before European arrival, and during the sixteenth, seventeenth, and eighteenth centuries files of burdeners still could be seen wending their way throughout various parts of the South. De Soto and his contemporaries used them extensively in the sixteenth century, and the Franciscans, after establishing their missions, especially those in Apalachee, required natives to transport foodstuffs and supplies to and from St. Augustine. If one were patient enough, eventually he could have seen a line of burdeners comprising fifty to two hundred Indians laden with flour or supplies for the missions, making its way over the 200-mile road connecting Apalachee with St. Augustine. Other Indians living closer to the Florida capital brought in logs and timbers from 15 to 20 miles away.[36] Porters serving De Soto, the Franciscans, and the Spanish garrison usually were impressed and had no choice.

They were more likely to have had an option after the English arrived in Virginia and the Carolinas, which is not to suggest that William Claiborne did not have ways to force Virginia Indians to carry loads or that the Goose Creek men did not beat natives who balked at such service. More than Spaniards, Englishmen were able to offer trading goods, and one way natives could pay for them was to serve as porters. When discussing the Indian trade of William Byrd and other Virginians, so far it has been implied that they used only packhorses. This was not so, because at times burdeners rather than horses brought peltry to the fall line of the James and Appomattox rivers.[37] Carolinians used Indian porters in the back country. Either because they did not have enough horses or because they were afraid to risk them among the natives, the Goose Creek men long hired burdeners to carry peltry as much as 200 or even 500 miles.

Packs of skins weighed up to 100 pounds or even more. Payment for transporting such loads varied. One hundred fifteen porters coming into Charleston from the Catawbas and Cherokees were given two yards of blue duffel each, enough to make a matchcoat.[38] At other times payment was only one and one-half yards of duffel and one-fourth yard of coarse woolen stroud, the latter just the amount needed for a flap.[39] Cotton stockings, rum, munitions, and similar trading goods were also used as payment. When burdeners had a load for the return trip, such as powder, ball, and woolens for factors in the Indian country, they could earn more. The agent at Savannah Town on the Savannah River in 1717 reported that he had a serious problem with rats. To the porters' inordinate relief, the Charleston superiors decided to send up ratsbane rather than cats.[40]

With white encouragement native artisans continued to ply some of their crafts. Matchkores and moccasins attested to the abilities of aboriginal tanners. English tanners in Virginia employed Indian servants, and we can only assume that artisans of each race exchanged information and techniques.[41] Another native skill was pipe-making, and Indians continued to make and sell pipes, which were usually clay rather than stone effigy ones. Both in the colonies and in Europe whites began manufacturing clay pipes, eventually nearly monopolizing the market. This took time, because even in 1687 native Virginians were reportedly making clay pipes equal in quality to those manufactured by Germans.[42] The demand for other types of Indian pottery, such as pots, bowls, and imitations of European ware, persisted much longer. John the Bowlmaker, an Algonquian from the Eastern Shore of Virginia, did not forget the knowledge of his ancestors.[43] He and his fellow potters found a market for their wares in Indian, white, and Negro households. Male and female native basketmakers retained their skills and easily marketed their wares. The mistress of a white household might buy a small, tightly woven, decorated basket for her sewing, while her husband purchased a large one in which his servant could transport corn, flour, and other bulky items. Natives worked in the households of medical doctors, but whether they were domestics or disclosed mysteries of aboriginal herbs and cures is unknown.[44]

Mississippians had been weavers, but unfortunately not enough examples remain for a fair assessment of their ability. European contemporaries, however, impressed by aboriginal capabilities, attempted to put local weavers to work. A project of the Virginia Company during the early years was to get Powhatans to weave hemp and flax, but these endeavors fared no better than the making of iron, wine, and glass. The prospect of producing silk like that made by Orientals, Italians, and Frenchmen long excited promoters, including those associated with the Jamestown enterprise early in the seventeenth century and Thomas Jefferson 150 years later. Sericulture and silk reeling were labor-intensive, and the Jamestown investors, as well as others, more often than not expected to draw on the reservoir of native workers: "To the good hopes that the Indians seeing and finding that there is neither art, skill, or pains in the thing: they will readily set upon it. . . . No imployment in the World so likely to make so soon your lasie savage wealthy."[45] Experience in Mexico and Peru gave Spaniards greater knowledge of aboriginal weaving, and they realized that the abilities of Florida Indians were inferior to those in Meso-America. From as early as the 1670s Spaniards hoped to transfer experienced weavers from Campeche to serve as instructors in Apalachee and Guale. Unfortunately the missions in these provinces were being harassed unmercifully and destroyed, and no significant weaving industry was established on the banks of the St. Marks and Altamaha any more than on the James.[46]

Whether founded by the ocean or inland, colonial settlements lay exposed, requiring fortifications against Indians and European enemies. Natives themselves furnished much of the labor to build the various forts, which were usually made of wood though sometimes of stone. Typically a wooden palisade, laid out in rough rectangular form, enclosed the fort, storehouses, and barracks. Having palisaded their villages for centuries, Mississippians needed little instruction, although iron tools speeded the work. Indians helped dig moats, construct bastions, and erect log forts dotting the frontier. Dispossessed Apalachees cut and dressed timber for the new French fort and settlement at Mobile.[47] After the Yamasee War Carolinians erected a fortified trading house, including a barracks for the garrison, at the Congarees (near Columbia). Eighty natives agreed to assist—forty to carry up supplies and the remainder to help build the structures.[48] These and similar wooden buildings have long since disappeared. Not so the stone Castillo de San Marcos in St. Augustine, begun in 1672, essentially completed early in the following century, and still standing today. The technical knowledge required to construct this castillo was clearly of European origin, but for decades, under Spanish supervision, hundreds of Indians labored to complete the project, quarrying coquina shellstone, mixing mortar and stucco, transporting timbers, and digging the well. Workers from all over *la Florida* annually were impressed and brought to St. Augustine, causing women and children left behind in Timucua, Apalachee, and Guale to complain that they could not support themselves and were starving.[49] Of two hundred Apalachees sent in mid-century to work on an earlier fort, only ten returned, and hundreds of natives, their remains sometimes uncovered by archaeologists, are buried in or near the Florida capital.[50] A constant grievance of the mission Indians was that able-bodied men were impressed in the villages and taken away, never to be seen again.

Indians served as mariners aboard vessels navigating interior rivers and the high seas, and often operated ferries as well. Natives were at home on inland waterways, frequently more so than whites, and, as in the case of the Calusa, were no strangers to the ocean. They not only built dugout canoes for whites but manned them for John Smith in Virginia and the Spaniards in Florida. When colonists went to war with each other, warriors frequently hired themselves and their canoes out. Either as freemen or as slaves, the latter let out by their white owners, Indians probably paddled most of the dugouts transporting peltry. Jonathan Dickinson and his party were shipwrecked on the Florida peninsula in the 1690s, and the Spanish governor in St. Augustine assisted them, sending them through the surviving Guale missions on their way toward South Carolina. One of the first indications that he had left the Spanish area of influence was when Dickinson saw a Yamasee from Port Royal, showing no concern about being seen, nonchalantly paddling his dugout laden with skins toward Charleston.[51]

Slave and free Indians routinely served aboard oceangoing vessels, but there is no way to reckon their numbers. Incidental references to a Cherokee as an "experienced sailor," to natives belonging to pirate ships' crews visiting or preying on the Carolinas, and to a small sailing vessel and an Indian man as the principal assets in a Charleston mariner's estate all make the point.[52] In the first part of the eighteenth century the Virginian Harry Beverley outfitted a ship to go in search of a wrecked Spanish treasure galleon. Spaniards, however, captured Beverley, who was furious when an Indian slave in his crew babbled details of his plans.[53] Both England and Spain constructed guard boats or row galleys, powered by oars and sail and armed with small cannon. Particularly effective in navigating shallow inland waterways, they rarely went out of sight of land. Indians such as the Yamasees, who understood the labyrinthine waterways, more often than not formed part of the crew.

Natives attended whites as body servants, which, considering Powhatan's retainers in Virginia and Outina's in Florida, was not a new vocation. Colonial wills disclose that a husband might assign a female Indian slave to care for his widow until her death. One father stipulated that "Jack my Indian boy to keep my son Edward until he comes of age of 19." The latter will further provided that Edward was also to enjoy Indian Rosse's labor until he took a wife.[54] Natives, perhaps personal attendants, served as messengers. Little skill was required when a South Carolina planter sent his boy to town with a letter. There was another class of Indian messenger requiring a great deal of training. They were runners, not those who jogged a few miles to town but those who carried important messages over great distances. Before the introduction of horses, the ability of Mississippians to run long distances was a prized and necessary asset, and one suspects that they became less proficient in this regard after the whites arrived. Even so, colonists were impressed by the natives' speed as they raced for a prize or kept up with a man on horseback for 10 or 20 miles apparently without tiring. Traders and military commanders commonly used runners. During the early disastrous years of the French and Indian War Carolinians paid a warrior four yards of stroud to make a hasty 200-mile round trip to carry a dispatch to an important Creek chief.[55]

After whites arrived, Indians, voluntarily or not, mastered new occupations. One was raising and tending horses, cattle, poultry, and swine. Other than dogs, Mississippians had had no domestic animals until they were introduced by Spaniards. Advocates of the black legend recount how De Soto's cavalry galloped across savannahs, methodically lancing natives careless enough to be caught in the open. Less dramatic but more odoriferous was the tale that De Soto's men steadfastly drove swine with them as they marched about the South. A glance at seventeenth-century Virginia wills reveals that swine and cattle were among the colonists' most precious possessions. From Florida to Virginia Indians were exposed to and acquired these animals at an early date, and because of necessity or the white man's law they began fencing in maize fields to protect crops and avoid disputes. Branded on the ear, cattle and swine usually ran wild and were only periodically fed and rounded up. Throughout the South Indian "cattle hunters" appeared who, either on horseback or afoot, assisted in these roundups, among other things making it awkward for aboriginal children to play cowboys and Indians. There may have been substance to accounts by early Spanish chroniclers that Indians were awestruck and terrified by mounted cavalry, considering man and beast as one. It was not long before natives, frequently with white encouragement, acquired horses and learned about their care. A good inducement for a land cession or to encourage chiefs to lead their young men in war was to present horses, bridles, and saddles. Indians also seized horses from colonists without bothering to pay. Mississippians previously had relied on dugout canoes and their feet for transportation; after whites arrived it became common for them to make long journeys by horseback.

Before whites appeared the Mississippians had not been overly bothered by wolves. It was a different matter after contact; wolves presented a threat to their cattle, swine, and poultry. Whites hired natives to hunt these predators, gave bounties for wolves' heads, and, as has been mentioned, at times demanded wolves' ears as tribute.

Wars, whether between Indians and whites or involving colonial powers, were common, and Indians almost always participated, either serving with colonists or fighting against them. Natives modified their methods of warfare, as did colonists, and frequently there was little distinction between them in the way they were armed and dressed. Sometimes warriors accompanying whites remained together as a unit, retaining a certain cohesiveness and autonomy; at other times natives were an integral part of the white force, serving not only as scouts but also as drummers, trumpeters, pioneers, and crewmen aboard scout boats and gunboats. Warriors helped man frontier forts stretching from Virginia to the Carolinas and were deployed as mounted rangers patrolling the countryside. Whites paid money, clothes, silver gorgets, munitions, and rum for Indian services and offered a bonus for enemy scalps: six blankets, ten pounds, or ten dollars per scalp or head, depending on the time and place.[56] During the American Revolution Benjamin Franklin made much of the fact that Britain paid Indians for patriot scalps, but this was a long-standing practice. It was unfortunate for the patriots' heads, however, that most warriors sided with Britain during that struggle.

Colonists introduced new crafts and technologies, which natives soon mastered. Whether Indian apprentices were ever freed does not alter the fact that they learned new skills, including those of the bricklayer, brickmaker, cooper, wheelwright, blacksmith, boatswain, sawyer, seamstress, and cordwainer. Some of these crafts were more foreign than others. Before the white arrival Mississippians already were competent moccasin makers, tailors, and seamstresses, and after European colonization began native artisans adapted. Rather than making matchkores with bone needles out of deerskin and fiber or sinew thread, they began to use steel needles, imported thread, and duffel. The name of a seventeenth-century Virginia Indian, Edward Gunstocker, suggests another new occupation. It is not difficult to imagine Indian woodcarvers, adept in making handles for war clubs, axes, and celts, learning how to carve stocks for firearms.[57] Whites attempted to establish a silk industry by planting mulberry trees, importing silkworms, and training workers to tend cocoons and spin and weave silk. In Virginia, Carolina, and Georgia, it was expected that Indians would be part of the industry's labor force, and a few mastered some aspects of sericulture. With minor exceptions no silk industry was established anywhere in America, primarily because of the difficulties of instituting a labor-intensive undertaking in a frontier region characterized by a shortage of workers. Few Indians mastered the mysteries of silk production, but neither did many colonists.

Throughout the colonial era Indians lived intimately among and worked for the settlers, customarily as slaves or indentured servants and sometimes as freemen. Unlike whites, natives usually had not voluntarily become apprentices or willingly signed articles of indenture. Instead they were captives sold as indentured servants, children apprenticed by real or spurious parents, or delinquents sentenced to a term of servitude for some crime or debt. In any case many and presumably most Indian apprentices and slaves working for colonists did not do so by choice, though it is not clear how discontented they were. No concerted uprising occurred, which is not surprising considering tribal and linguistic differences, their small numbers relative to whites and blacks (except in South Carolina), and the fact that so many were women and children. Enough Indians poisoned masters or ran away, however, to indicate dissatisfaction. Women and children servants were not necessarily weak and easily intimidated. Mrs. John Wall, a seventeenth-century Virginian of Charles City County, doubtless would have concurred. Young Elizabeth, an Indian servant, at one point struck her mistress violently, on another occasion bit her "by the breast," and still later unnerved Mrs. Wall by trying to thrust her head into the oven, "then red hott and ready for bread."[58] It is not known if Mrs. Wall and her husband, the Captain, ever tamed the impetuous Elizabeth. Another Indian, George Casquescough, assaulted John Cammell "with a battoon," killing him, and George was sentenced to be hanged.[59]

Servants sometimes vented their resentment by killing their

masters, poisoning them, burning down their houses, or, in the case of Elizabeth, attempting to bake them along with the corn-bread. Others ran away. One of the myths in American history is that Indians did not make good slaves because it was so simple for them to escape to kinsmen in the nearby forest. In reality it was not much easier for an Indian than for a black to run away. One reason was that many servants were young children who were not experienced woodsmen and on their own could not make the long, dangerous trip to their home villages. Certainly a two- or five-year-old could not, and one suspects that ten-year-old Merrak, who accompanied John Evans to the James River, could not have found her way to her home in the Carolina back country. For children and adults alike there was another di-lemma: Many had been taken in war; their villages had been razed; and they had no families or homes. It was not possible for an Apalachee, Occaneechee, or Westo to return to nonexistent homes and families. Servants, particularly men who seemed in-clined to escape, were likely to be transported out of the colony, usually to the islands. Or they might be shackled, chained, or maimed in the foot or leg.

Indian servants did not risk slipping away and joining their brethren nearby, because frequently neighboring Indians had captured and sold them in the first place. Yamasees had roamed throughout the Florida peninsula, even to the Keys, capturing Apalachees, Timucuans, and Tequestas and disposing of them to Goose Creek men. Before 1715 the principal Yamasee villages were located south of Charleston. It was unthinkable that a Te-questa slave, perhaps still freshly marked by the slave cord, would run away and seek refuge among the Yamasees, because they had a well-deserved reputation for capturing and selling other Indians, hounding fugitives, and not treating them gently. Yamasees were not unique in returning Indian runaways. Trib-utaries living above Charleston hunted down slaves fleeing northward, and in Virginia Pamunkeys captured fugitives mak-ing their way westward in search of freedom.[60] Usually Pamun-keys, Yamasees, and others who restored runaways did so voluntarily because they were after their enemies and because the colonists paid them. Sometimes Indians set out after fugitives because they had no choice. If a slave was reported to have fled to a tributary village, whites summoned the chief in question to appear before the county court. Magistrates, who repeatedly had bent Indians to their will, demanded that the runaway be returned or the chief and his followers face the consequences.[61] Natives sometimes escaped from plantations and coastal towns, made their way through lands of neighboring tributaries, and turned up in strange villages deep in the Indian country. Yet even here they were not safe. White traders lived in or periodically visited these remote villages, and through their influence, enhanced by a judicious distribution of trading goods, fugitives were secured and returned. In 1723 a trader among the Lower Creeks 250 miles from Charleston saw to it that two Indian runaways who had gotten that far went no farther.[62]

On occasion Indians legally freed themselves through purchase. In 1718 Virginia Indians offered—and as it turned out were unable—to pay for the return of a female Saponi slave. In South Carolina John Wright suggested letting a slave, who already had one-half his freedom, go to war so he could purchase the remainder.[63]

From the earliest times owners and local governments had offered rewards for the return of Indian, Negro, and white slaves and indentured servants, and a group or class of bounty hunters emerged in the English colonies. Tracking down fugitives usually was not a full-time occupation. White "bounty hunters" might be constables merely doing their jobs or small farmers happy enough to earn extra money by going after fugitives. Twenty shillings per returned slave was a typical fee. Natives themselves were among the bounty hunters. Magistrates in 1684 paid a Virginia Indian a matchcoat, tobacco, rum, and sugar for taking almost two weeks to recapture the Indians Jack and Will; and in 1675 they awarded Dick Shoes twenty arm's lengths of roanoke for bringing back an escaped servant.[64] To avoid bother and recovery expenses, planters sometimes published notices that promised forgiveness if the culprit quickly returned of his own volition.[65]

One of the concerns of the fugitives was their dress. An eighteenth-century advertisement pointed out that, although certain Indians were trying to pass themselves off as free, their garb must give them away. To a degree difficult to appreciate in the twentieth century, clothes signified one's place in society. Indian and Negro slaves and indentured servants usually wore similar clothes: shirts and knee-length trousers of the coarsest duffels, kerseys, linens, and calicos. Indian or Negro shoes might

169

or might not be provided. Any native so dressed, traveling alone on a road or crossing at a ferry, came under suspicion. English colonists, particularly in the seventeenth century, insisted that Indians having business in white settlements wear silver, copper, or pewter badges or striped coats. Runaways understood full well that their slave attire threatened to expose them, and whenever possible they took their master's shirt, coat, hat, shoes, and sometimes his arms and horses.[66]

When Indian indentured servants were returned, according to law they were to serve two additional days for every day absent. They also had to reimburse their masters for recovery expenses, and in fact they were likely to serve five or more days for each one absent. In 1709 "Indian Billey" of Westmoreland County, Virginia, who ran away from his master for 222 days, had two years, seven and one-half months added to his term.[67] Runaway slaves' terms of service, of course, could not be extended, so they were whipped, shackled, transported, and maimed.

When slave, bond, or free Indians living among the colonists tilled crops, built canoes, tended cattle, and prepared food, they usually did so under white supervision, or in any case colonists were not far off. Other natives, most of them having little to do with whites, nevertheless labored mightily in their behalf. These were hunters and trappers, who, residing in their own villages, perhaps never saw a European except the local factor and the packhorsemen arriving every year or so with merchandise. Sometimes warrior-hunters attended white talks in major councils, and on occasion young Indians agreed to fight for, perhaps alongside, colonial forces. But most of the time they went their own way, infrequently if at all seeing whites and not understanding their language. No colonist stood whip in hand over a warrior commanding him to hunt. But hunt he did, and to a degree not seen for more than a thousand years. Powerful but unseen economic forces inexorably impelled natives to take up the chase as Europe's commercial expansion reached deep into the Indian country.

At first natives had regarded many of the white man's goods as curiosities or luxuries. A mirror, a musical instrument, a needle, or beads had an obvious attraction, as did the more significant woolen clothing, copper pots, and iron knives. But deerskin mantles, clay pottery, and flint knives had sufficed and still could. It was European firearms and powder and the whites' ability to repair guns that became so essential. Indians were caught up in and never escaped from a deepening cycle: Guns allowed them to hunt more effectively, and it was necessary to hunt more efficiently in order to purchase firearms and trading goods. Of even more consequence was the fact that if warriors did not have guns they were likely to be killed or enslaved by neighbors who did. In time woolen textiles, iron knives and pots, and a multitude of other trade goods, because of their extensive use and because many of the Mississippian skills were being lost, became almost necessities. Periodically Indian reformers talked about returning to the old ways, but for better or worse natives were entrapped by European technology. Reflecting changes that had occurred since Raleigh's day, a Poteskeet Indian from eastern North Carolina merely confirmed a basic truth in 1715 when he declared he and his kinsmen could not subsist without hunting.[68]

In addition to guns, textiles, and hardware it is necessary to include distilled spirits. It is not fair to assert that Mississippians, who before 1492 produced no distilled spirits, had been teetotalers and then after white contact became drunks, any more than it is correct to imply that colonists were abstainers. One should not be misled by Governor Francis Wyatt's criticism that the Virginia Company made an "inexcusable error" in trying to "plant a colony by water drinkers."[69] English colonists were prodigious drinkers; even in Oglethorpe's Georgia, which prohibited distilled spirits, whites kept falling out of boats or off the dock into the Savannah River. Yet after taking all this into consideration the fact remains that Indians, for reasons still confusing to doctors and psychologists, were powerfully attracted to alcohol, and alcoholism among Indians today, as in the colonial period, is acute. Europeans introduced the natives to brandy, wine, whisky, and rum, the last becoming the common American drink. Few packhorse trains wended their way into the Indian country without "kaggs" of rum, and major treaties and individual contracts commonly were sealed by copious drafts of rum punch. Only teetotalers or native reformers aware of the hazards of strong drink treated rum as a luxury. White threats to cut off trade in munitions, rum, and clothing were not taken lightly and frequently were effective. When a Cherokee Indian murdered a white trader, Cherokees hunted down and killed the culprit to avert a trade embargo.[70]

After the Europeans appeared, Indians relied less on agriculture and hunted more. Winter remained the primary hunting season. Before contact sometimes entire villages, including women and children, had moved relatively short distances to makeshift camps, from which males hunted for a month or more. After the white arrival these fall-winter hunts became more common and lasted longer. Women and children often were left behind, and young hunters ranged hundreds of miles, some even crossing the Mississippi River and covering more than 1,000 miles before returning home. During the hunting season, lasting from September until December or later, young men were away and their villages lay exposed. Savannahs understood this clearly when, seeking slaves and booty, they descended on a Cherokee village in the latter part of 1692.[71] Colonists also realized how vulnerable the Indians were during hunting season. A North Carolina planter–land speculator, claiming territory of the nearby Meherrins, went to their village in the fall, demanding that the old men and women gather up the children and depart immediately or face the consequences.[72]

Traffic in "furs" or peltry increasingly was referred to as the skin or leather trade, because, as has been seen, deerskins became the mainstay. The conduct of this trade during the eighteenth century has been treated at some length from the white perspective, but the full story remains to be told. The high point in South Carolina, the most important colony, was the 1730–50 period; the peak for Virginia had been earlier; and it was the period just before the Revolution for Georgia. Companies in London and Glasgow either manufactured themselves, or more likely bought elsewhere in Britain, necessary textiles, munitions, and hardware, then shipped these goods to representatives in Southern ports. Kegs of rum were normally purchased in the New World. Colonial merchants hired packhorses or Indian porters, broke up the imported chests, redistributing trading goods and making up smaller packs, and then from Charleston or the fall line of the James sent them into the Indian country. By the eighteenth century each major village was likely to have a resident factor, perhaps an Englishman, but more likely a Scot. Some factors were Indians, probably mestizos, and occasionally one finds "black" or Negro factors. White traders lived in the villages for much of the year, marrying the chief's daughter or sister, rearing Indian families, and allying themselves with prominent clans and political leaders. Mestizo children frequently assumed their fathers' roles when parents died or were absent. The Indian hunters' contact with whites and their civilization took place through the resident traders more than in any other way. From the founding of Jamestown until the American Revolution Englishmen were never sure how to manage Indian commerce and regulate the factors' conduct: Should there be a free trade, or should the colonies or the mother country strictly regulate it, perhaps even conceding a monopoly? [73]

Looking beyond these resident factors and the principal town miccos, it is necessary to focus on Algonquian, Iroquoian, and Muskhogean hunters themselves, and their conduct and life-style are less well understood. The take from the fall-winter hunt might be one hundred to two hundred deerskins, each weighing 2 pounds, along with a few furs, all of which could be supplemented by peltry obtained from shorter summer hunts. An average hunter had to kill one or more deer every day for four months or longer to produce 300 or 400 pounds of leather. Sample mid-eighteenth-century prices were three buckskins or six doeskins for a blanket; one doeskin for a knife, sixty bullets, or three-fourths pound of powder; seven buckskins or fourteen doeskins for a gun; one buckskin for a quart of rum; and twenty buckskins for a woman's side saddle. [74] Markups for manufactures were high. Assuming nothing disrupted trade, the whites involved—in Britain, colonial cities and towns, and Indian villages—made handsome profits. The total markup from Britain to the Indian villages was several hundred percent. Prices in the Indian country fluctuated widely, depending on whether there was a well-regulated commerce—that is, a monopoly—or whether swarms of traders traveled about undercutting prices of authorized resident factors.

The natives' appetite for trading goods exceeded their ability to pay, and they frequently were in debt. Compounding the predicament was the fact that they commonly "drinked all their skinns." [75] To make up the difference they sold lands, went to war, served as burdeners, or captured slaves. An adult male slave might fetch more than a hundred deerskins, the equivalent of an entire hunting season's kill, and hunter-warriors had good reason to roam 400 or more miles in search of captives. At irregular intervals whites met with Indians in council to negotiate a land cession or to secure their military aid. Distribution of presents was a strong inducement for warriors to consider and accept the colonists' proposals. Invariably natives made the point that if they went to war they could not hunt and plant: Whites would have to meet their needs and those of their families.

Whether hunters in the interior seldom coming into contact with colonists, "grubbing hoe Indians" tilling maize fields and rice paddies in the Tidewater, or craftsmen making pottery, building canoes, and constructing houses, throughout the South Indians worked for Europeans, in no small way assisting them in exploiting this "virgin" land.

8
Jehovah and the Corn Mother

"There is but one God and he is a jealous God." Europeans might disagree about the Petrine theory and about justification by faith and good works or by faith alone, but all believers accepted Christian fundamentals. They were the chosen, the elect, assured of salvation through God's mercy, the sacraments, and personal faith. Unfortunate as it was, others were doomed to hell or purgatory. As set forth in the Bible, it was the duty of the sanctified to spread the news of Christ to all corners of the globe so pagans who had been denied the glad tidings might be saved. Neither steadfast Franciscans nor sanguine Anglicans doubted that as quickly as possible Indians, for their well-being on this earth and the tranquility of their souls in the hereafter, must become Christians. They only differed over which Christian sect was the most suitable and what were the most appropriate means to win over the natives—exhortation, instruction, pious example, or force.

Whether Catholic or Protestant, the church dominated, if not monopolized, Indian education. It was deemed essential that natives receive a rudimentary schooling so they could recite and in a general way explain the Catechism. Directly or indirectly the church founded missions, elementary writing schools, and colleges, and Catholic priests or Protestant ministers more often than not were the teachers. Francisco Pareja, who worked among the Timucuan missions and compiled dictionaries and grammars for the instruction of the Indians, was a Franciscan. One reason William Strachey, though a layman, prepared his Powhatan word list in Virginia was so that local Algonquians might more readily be brought into the Anglican Church.

By insisting that Indians adopt Christianity, whites were asking natives to give up their traditional value systems, to become acculturated, and to live and worship like civilized colonists. Indian religions differed substantially from Christianity. Natives were polytheistic, and it was difficult, though not necessarily impossible, to reconcile their views of the cosmos—the Upper World, Earth, and Under World—with the Christian heaven and hell. With a good deal of justification, colonists characterized the Indians as sun worshipers, because to the aborigines the sun, busk fire, corn goddess, sun circles, and similar symbols were all related to the mystical powers of that fiery orb. Europeans hardly ever attempted to comprehend native religions on their own merits. They regarded the venerated priests and medicine men as sorcerers and considered native dances obscene, as a few were. But many had deep religious and ritualistic significance, and Europeans made little distinction. In 1613 the Reverend Alexander Whitaker sent a painted wooden idol from Jamestown to friends in England. Whitaker looked upon it as a curiosity, a clear manifestation of the New World's paganism.[1] There is no indication that Whitaker made any serious attempt to discover why the Powhatans venerated it so.

Despite differences between the religions and cultures of the two races, whites attempted to discover what and how the natives worshiped. This was not so much to understand their culture *per se* as to discover if there were common beliefs that could be emphasized and used as tools in conversion. The master of breath in some ways resembled the Christian god, and Uktena, lord of the underworld, though not a fallen angel, in time might pass for Lucifer. Wherever colonists came into contact with the natives throughout the South they reported accounts of a flood in the Indians' folklore and ancient traditions, reinforcing the conviction that at some point in the past Europeans or Near Eastern Semites had come to America and transmitted such concepts. Perhaps the Welsh Prince Madoc in the twelfth century was responsible, or at a much earlier date the wandering virgins of Cologne, the Phoenicians, or one of the lost tribes of Israel. During the medieval period Europeans took for granted the existence of a powerful Christian kingdom in Africa or the Near East ruled by Prester John, who, after the collapse of the Roman Empire in the west, had been cut off from fellow Christians in Europe. As increasing knowledge about Africa and the Levant dissipated European credence in Prester John,[2] reports of a lost Jewish or Christian kingdom in America began reaching Europe in the aftermath of Columbus's voyage. Colonists coming to the New World became convinced that a modern-day version of Prester John's domain was to be found in the South. Accounts that Cherokees used Hebrew or Phoenician words, that others, "only a day's journey distant," were Welsh speakers, and that a chief's house was built and painted like an ark, giving visible proof to knowledge of Noah and the flood, all strengthened this conviction.[3]

With the possible exception of Prince Madoc and his Welsh exiles, no tradition was more persistent than the one holding that one of the lost tribes of Israel had come to America. Perhaps the best-known advocate of such an ancient Jewish colony was James Adair, a mid-eighteenth-century Carolina trader who published a valuable history of the Southern Indians. Throughout his work Adair emphasized similarities between Jewish and Indian beliefs. In this regard he had little original to say, merely repeating concepts that already had been widely discussed: Some Indians were supposed to be circumcised, the busk or green corn festival was the Jewish offering of first fruits, and the deer periodically sacrificed by the aborigines was the Jewish sacrificial ram.[4] English colonists during Jamestown's early years and those in Carolina a century later repeatedly commented on such similarities. Convinced of the Jewish influence, the Anglican minister Francis Le Jau, a friend and contemporary of the Goose Creek men a generation earlier than Adair, excitedly reported in 1710 to superiors in London that Brother Robert Maule of St. John's Parish "has an Indian Ladd which he thinks to be circumsised."[5] Ever since she had emigrated from Barbados, Le Jau's confidant, Mrs. Bird, "an ancient woman of a lively spirit," had inquired with some success to find out exactly which Carolina Indians were circumcised.[6]

It hardly ever occurred to Europeans that the Indians might

not be indebted to whites for similarities in religious beliefs. The notion of a flood, "the deluge myth," is common to almost all people of every age, as is the concept of first fruits.[7] Indians told Le Jau and Adair that their earliest ancestor was a man and that God had taken a rib from him to create woman.[8] One suspects that Spanish Franciscans planted the notion of an Indian Adam and Eve and at a much later date natives passed this idea on to Carolinians.

From the outset Englishmen vowed they were going to treat natives more humanely than the Spaniards had, and, more important, England was determined to be more effective in converting them. As Englishmen saw it, by almost any standard Spain had failed, and taking the broad view this conclusion is correct. No Catholic Indian or mestizo population endures in the modern South. Spanish converts were killed, enslaved, swept away by disease, and in some instances transported to Cuba or Mexico. A few converts remained in *la Florida* when Spain relinquished the province in 1763, but when it was restored to her two decades later she made almost no effort to reestablish the missions. During the Second Spanish Period (1783–1821) a Catholic Indian was a rarity. Yet taking all this into consideration it must be remembered that for almost a century and a half Spain had maintained numerous missions throughout the greater Florida, her converts numbering in the tens of thousands. Despite denunciations of Spanish cruelty and decrepitude, Englishmen, though they tried, never approached Spanish successes.

Promotional literature and official correspondence associated with the Roanoke and Jamestown colonies make one aware of English expectations. There seemed to be no conflict between amassing wealth and proselytizing the natives: "as the light accompanieth the sunne and the heate the fire, so lasting riches do wait upon them that are jealous for the . . . enlargement of his glorious gospell."[9] In the aftermath of the 1622 massacre it was apparent that such a policy had failed. For the balance of the century the emphasis was on waging merciless war against the heathen, forcing captives into servitude, selling some slaves off in the islands, and building a line of forts to separate the two races.

In spite of all this the Anglican dream of spreading the gospel among American pagans never completely dissipated. Such successes as the church enjoyed were small. During the early decades of the seventeenth century Powhatan villages were destroyed and abandoned. Bereft of family, relations, local chiefs, and medicine men, survivors were cast adrift in a chaotic world and, because they had been captured or through choice, moved into white households. Masters often looked down on and distrusted such Indians, not without reason, because without warning in 1622 and 1644 they had turned on the colonists, splitting open their skulls and dismembering their bodies. Nevertheless, Indians continued to live with the English, perhaps eating at their masters' tables, and in some instances bonds of affection and trust developed. The church continued to win a few converts. Even in 1622 a Christian Indian had given notice about the impending attack, saving hundreds of colonists. After the massacre Chanco, another Christian Indian, tried to bring about a reconciliation between whites and natives,[10] while the Christian Indian William Crawshaw was still employed and instructed by his white master and perhaps was baptized then. A young Powhatan boy, presumably an orphan placed in a white household, by 1640 having learned how to read, write, and understand Christian fundamentals, was taken into the Anglican Church.[11]

It should be kept in mind that the 1622 and 1644 massacres occurred during the first half-century of Virginia's development and that after 1622 the general feeling was that the only good Indian, if not dead, at least lived beyond the frontier away from colonists. This was brought home to Francis Yeardley of Lynnhaven, Virginia, in 1654. Yeardley and his wife seemed a godly enough couple, although land speculation may have had a higher priority than spreading the faith as far as Francis was concerned. Interested in developing the southern part of Virginia (the future North Carolina), Yeardley was delighted when his agents brought him a chief's son, a young Roanoke Island Indian. After a short period Mrs. Yeardley took the Indian, who had been living in her house, to church. He sat through the service without incident, but once outside the local justices of the peace, threatening a whipping, told him never to come back.

Yeardley persisted. Somewhat later his traders brought forty-five Tuscaroras, including a chief, his wife, and his young son, to Yeardley's house, and this time the justices of the peace did not intervene. If not intimidated by the Tuscaroras, justices at least appreciated the necessity of courting the friendship of this

179

powerful tribe. The chief's son was presented to the minister and baptized in the presence of the congregation and visiting Indians, after which he remained with Yeardley.[12] A few other Indians were brought up in Christian households. Weanocs had captured and sold to Mrs. Short one Metappin, a young Powhatan. Raised in her home and learning how to speak "perfect English," he petitioned for his freedom in 1662, at the same time requesting baptism. Metappin claimed the Weanocs had had no right to sell him. There is no way to tell what connection he or anyone else made between conversion and freedom.[13]

Criticizing failures in Virginia, at the end of the seventeenth century Anglican reformers lamented the fact that, despite the high expectations of 1607, no converts had been made. This was an exaggeration, particularly in the case of children who, like Metappin, had been cut off from their families and looked to English culture and religion for reassurance in a disorganized world.

There was no denying that a century after England attempted to plant a colony at Roanoke Island the Anglican Church had made little headway, in contrast to Spain, which a century after St. Augustine's founding counted numerous Indians in her missions. Rather than a day of Christian worship and meditation, in Virginia Sunday was probably the worst day for the Indians' morals. On their day off white indentured servants visited the closest native settlements, where drunkenness, whoring, and all types of licentiousness were rampant.[14] Aware of the church's failures, the Anglicans hoped to do something about it, and toward the end of the seventeenth century missionary fervor, the likes of which had not been seen since the days of Roanoke Island and Jamestown, returned. Reports that the king of the Pamunkeys and prominent subchiefs wanted to become Christians quickened interest.[15]

A number of causes explain this rejuvenation beyond the fact that crusading enthusiasm tends to run in cycles. The Anglican Church was more unified, and for the first time in many years a measure of religious peace and harmony existed in the mother country. Puritan enthusiasm had burned itself out under Cromwell's military dictatorship, and the restored English monarchs made little progress in efforts to tolerate or possibly even restore Catholicism. Such endeavors by James II were one of the reasons he lost his crown in the Glorious Revolution of 1688. After that

Ancient Life at Ocmulgee, Georgia. Painting. *Courtesy National Park Service, Southeast Archeological Center, neg. 02-035-3396.*

Eagle Dancer, Spiro Mound, Oklahoma. *Courtesy Museum of the American Indian, Heye Foundation, neg. 21,090.*

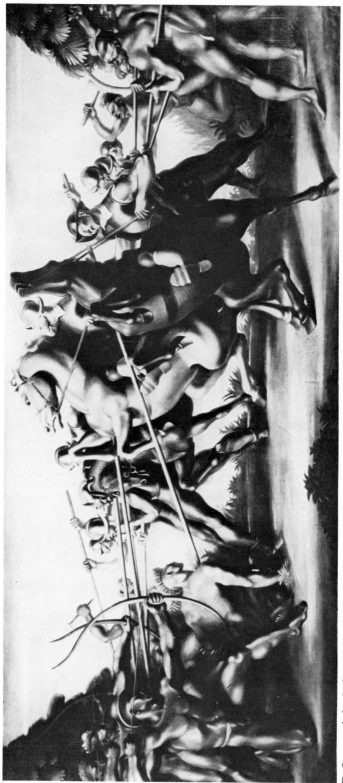

DeSoto and the Indians. Charles Hardman artist. *Courtesy National Archives and Records Service, neg. 121-PS-5996.*

Outina Defeats Potanou. Jacques le Moyne artist. *Courtesy State Photograph Archives, Florida State University Library.*

How They Till the Soil and Plant. Jacques le Moyne artist. *Courtesy State Photographic Archives, Florida State University Library.*

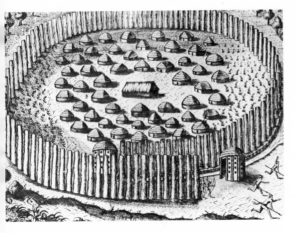

A Fortified Village. Jacques le Moyne artist. *Courtesy State Photographic Archives, Florida State University Library.*

Indian of Virginia. John White artist. *Courtesy Trustees of the British Museum.*

The Town of Secota. John White artist. *Courtesy State Photographic Archives, Florida State University Library.*

Above: Conjectural reconstruction of the "Church" structure, Apalachee Mission of San Juan de Aspalaga, Jefferson Co., Fla. *Courtesy Florida Division of Archives, History and Records Management.* Below: Title page, Francisco Pareja, *Confessionario en lengua Castellana y Timuquana,* Mexico, 1613. *Courtesy Florida Division of Archives, History and Records Management.*

CONFESSIONARIO

En lengua Castella-
na, y Timuquana Con algunos con‑
sejos para animar al penitente.

(✱)

❡ Y assi mismo van declarados algunos effectos y prerrogatiuas deste sancto sacramento de la confes‑
sion. Todo muy vtil y prouechoso, assi para que los padres confessores sepan instruyr al peni‑
tente como para que ellos aprendan à
saberse confessar.

❡ Ordenado por el Padre Fr. Fran‑
cisco Pareja, Padre de la Custo‑
dia de santa Elena de
la Florida.

❡ Religioso de la Orden de nuestro Seraphico
Padre san Francisco.

❡ Impresso con licencia en Mexico, en la Im
prenta de la Viuda de Diego Lopez
Daualos. Año de 1613.

Pocahontas in her twenty-first year. Engraved by Simon van de Passe. *Courtesy Trustees of the British Museum.*

"Powhatan's Mantle," early seventeenth century? *Courtesy Ashmolean Museum, Oxford.*

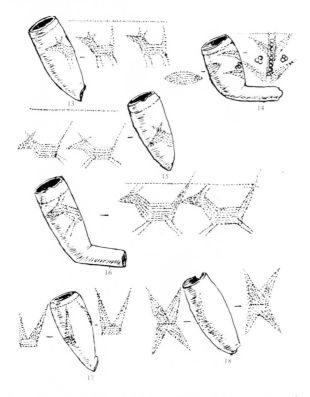

Above: Clay pipebowls from Nominy Plantation, Westmoreland County, Virginia, after 1650. Designs of Indian origin; artisans unknown. *Courtesy Archaeological Society of Virginia, Quarterly Bulletin, 31(1976).* Below: Clay pipes made by Indians, Richmond County Virginia, pre-1650? *Courtesy Archeological Society of Virginia, Quarterly Bulletin, 5(1950).*

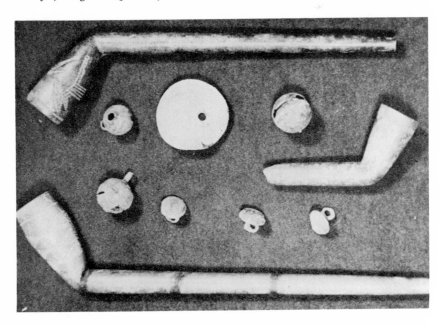

Top: Drum from Virginia, seventeenth century? Sloane Collection, British Museum. *Courtesy American Anthropological Association, American Anthropologist, 8(1906).* Bottom: Medal presented to King of Potomac after Treaty of 1677. *Courtesy Virginia Historical Society.* Opposite page: Susquehannock Fort on Potomac River, second half of seventeenth century. *Courtesy Public Record Office, C.O.5/1371.*

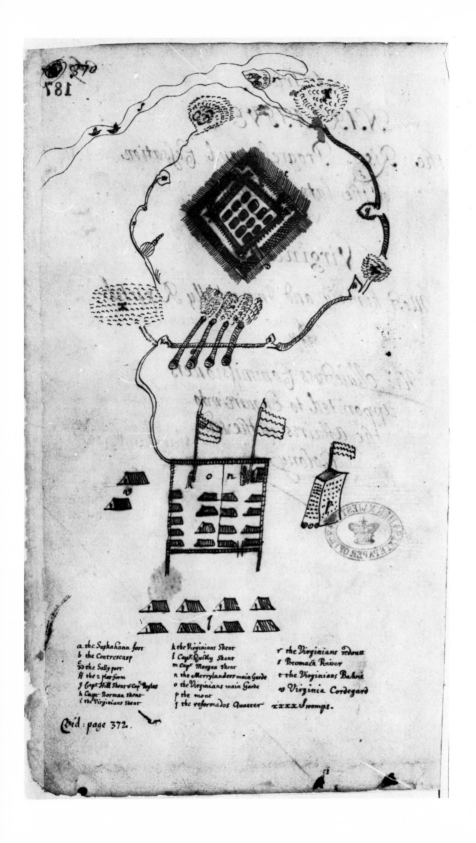

a the Sushahana fort
b the Contrescarp
c the Sally port
ff the 2 platform
g Capt. Hill Skent & Capt. Byglas
h Capt. Dornaa skene
i the Virginians Skent

k the Virginians Skent
l Capt. Quiddy Skent
m Capt. Morgan Skene
n the Merrylanders main Garde
o the Virginians main Garde
p the mout
q the reformados Quaerer

r the Virginians redout
s Potomack River
t the Virginians Bakue
w Virginia Cordegard
xxxx Swomps.

Vid: page 372.

Seal, Society for the Propagation of the Gospel in Foreign Parts. *Courtesy United Society for the Propagation of the Gospel.*

Above: William and Mary College. Indian school (Brafferton Hall) at left. *Courtesy Colonial Williamsburg Foundation:* Below: Moore's Raid: James Moore, Goose Creek Men, and Indians marching across Georgia to attack Apalachee missions. *Courtesy National Park Service, Southeast Archaeological Center, neg. 02-035-3399.*

Tomochichi and Tooanahowi, eighteenth century. Willem Verelst artist. *Courtesy Bureau of American Ethnology Collection, Smithsonian Institution, neg. 1129-b-1.*

Colono-Indian cup excavated on the site of the Brick House Tavern, Williamsburg. *Courtesy Colonial Williamsburg Archeological Collection.*

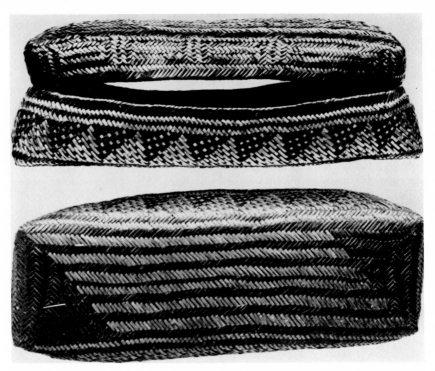

Basket (side and bottom) brought to England from South Carolina by Governor Francis Nicholson, 1720's? Sloane Collection, British Museum. *Courtesy American Anthropological Association, American Anthropologist, 8(1906).*

Creek House in 1791. J.C. Tidball artist. *Courtesy Bureau of American Ethnology Collection, Smithsonian Institution, neg. 1169-A.*

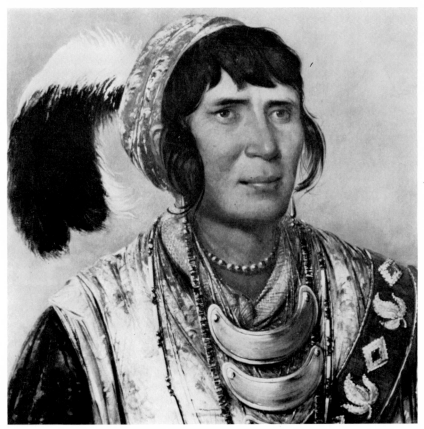

Osceola. George Catlin artist. *Courtesy National Portrait Gallery, Smithsonian Institution.*

Choctaw ball play, nineteenth century. Copied from George Catlin. *Courtesy National Anthropological Archives, Smithsonian Institution, neg. 1101-B-1.*

Above: Ho-tul-ko-mi-ko (Silas Jefferson). Of African and Creek parentage, born in Alabama in early eighteenth century, official interpreter for Creeks in Oklahoma. *Courtesy Bureau of American Ethnology Collection, Smithsonian Institution, neg. 1117.*

Chickahominy family group, near Chickahominy River, Virginia, 1900. James Mooney photographer. *Courtesy Bureau of American Ethnology Collection, Smithsonian Institution, neg. 858.*

Above: Felix MacNeil. Grandson of the Seminole Scipio Bowleg, who fled from Florida to the Bahamas. *Courtesy Society for American Archeology, American Antiquity, 5(1939).* Below: Grades 1 and 2, Catawba Indian Elementary School, 1964. *Courtesy University of Florida Indian Oral History Collection.*

Above: Chief Cook and Pamunkey Indians rendering tribute to Governor of Virginia, 1971. *Courtesy Richmond Newspapers, Inc.* Below: Seminole Indian cattle ranchers, Brighton Reservation, Florida, 1950. *Courtesy State Photographic Archives, Florida State University Library.*

the Protestant succession was ensured, and Englishmen, who earlier might have been Catholics or Puritans, found a reasonably comfortable place in the Anglican Church. When at the end of the century the crown exhorted Englishmen to redeem pagan souls in the New World, the summons was heeded.

During the seventeenth century large numbers of blacks had been imported into the West Indies and to a far lesser extent into the mainland colonies, altering the New World racial complexion. In his 1680 tract Morgan Godwin, who had spent some time in the West Indies, urged the church to concentrate not only on the original inhabitants of the New World but also on newly arriving Africans.[16] Anglicans in the mother country became increasingly aware that both blacks and Indians inhabited Virginia and Carolina. While not forgetting Africans, the church still concentrated on Indians. This was partly out of habit, because Anglicans repeatedly had asserted that their mission was to spread the faith among the aborigines in a milder and more effective way than Spain had done. Some scholars have explained England's concentration on Indians rather than blacks in racial terms. Evidence to support such a point of view is not lacking. The Virginia assembly in 1699 pronounced that imported Africans were barbarians with shallow minds; little progress had been made in converting them, and the result was not worth the effort. But the Indians were another matter.[17] Blacks were not forgotten, but their souls had a lower priority. At the turn of the century Anglicans redoubled their efforts to send missionaries among the Indians to learn their languages and establish schools. The argument that this was done because of racial antipathy toward Africans, however, remains to be proved.[18]

Before proceeding it will be worthwhile to look more closely at the structure of the Anglican Church. Overseeing affairs at home and abroad, the Archbishop of Canterbury was the highest ecclesiastical official. At the end of the century archbishops became more directly involved in saving aboriginal souls. In contrast to those of Spain and France, English colonies had no resident bishop. In an illogical but typically English fashion, colonies had become part of the Bishop of London's diocese. Although London bishops had many non-American responsibilities, they too became more concerned with the Indians. The closest person to a resident colonial bishop was the commissary, who looked after Anglican affairs in a particular colony. In the eighteenth century the Commissaries James Blair in Virginia and Gideon Johnston in South Carolina displayed a lively interest in the natives, hoping that self-supporting parishes might be established everywhere in the colonies and that parishioners—dissenters, blacks, and Indians—all might be brought into the fold.

Even in the Southern colonies where it was most firmly established, the church was not necessarily self-supporting. Parishioners in the colony of South Carolina, which was founded more than sixty years after Virginia, could not simultaneously build a new church, pay the minister's salary, and sustain missionaries in aborginal villages. To meet this kind of challenge, in 1701 a new organization, the Society for the Propagation of the Gospel in Foreign Parts (SPG), was founded. More than the Bishop of London, provincial commissaries, or anyone else, it looked to the Indians. They were the SPG's primary mission. The Archbishop of Canterbury was a founder, and colonial governors and commissaries were members, as were laymen on both sides of the Atlantic. Very much alive today, the society never restricted its activities to America: "Jesus Christ is an universal saviour, and hung on the cross not only for Englishmen, wherever they may be found, but also for the whole world." [19] In the eighteenth century the society was involved primarily in Africa and the West Indies, as well as on the American mainland.

A close association existed between English imperialism and the SPG. Many of that nation's most ardent expansionists were members of the society. Anxious to plant the Union Jack in the Indian country at France's and Spain's expense, Alexander Spotswood, Virginia's colonial governor (1710–22), was a member; and James Oglethorpe, founder of Georgia, as much an imperialist as philanthropist, also belonged. Goose Creek men who led expeditions into Florida and to the Mississippi River or encouraged Indian allies to make such forays actively supported the society. The SPG, and also the Bishop of London and the Archbishop of Canterbury, made little distinction between extending the flag and spreading the faith.

There were two approaches to converting the aborigines: to send conscientious missionaries to work among them, learning their language and something of their culture, or to bring the Indians together among the whites and win them over by godly example and instruction in English. Anglicans tried both methods and in the long run were not very successful with either. At the beginning of the eighteenth century the SPG endeavored to find young men willing to abandon worldly comforts and go to live among the natives, sharing their privations and mastering their language. It quickly became apparent that there was no single Indian language and that, despite the catastrophic depopulation, numerous languages and dialects still flourished throughout the South. Missionaries tried to overcome this obstacle by discovering a lingua franca comprehended by many, if not all, Southern Indians; they believed that any of the several such languages might suffice. One was that spoken by Savannahs, an Algonquian tongue, "fine, smoth, and easy to be got."[20] The movements of this tribe are not well understood, but it is clear that at one time or another Savannahs lived in many parts of the South. By the eighteenth century their numbers had diminished, and some had moved north of the Ohio River. Scattered groups remained, residing among the Creeks, Cherokees, and other Southern tribes. Traders brought word of the Savannahs to SPG missionaries, who eagerly listened to reports that Indians from the South to Canada comprehended Savannah, although it was not usually their first language.

The Savannahs were dispersed, residing some distance from whites. Not so the Yamasees, thousands of whom before 1715 occupied Carolina's southern border. They were Muskhogean speakers, as were most of the Southern Indians. This is not to say that Yamasees necessarily understood Choctaws, or that Hitchiti-speaking Lower Creeks comprehended non-Hitchiti-speaking Upper Creeks, all of whom were in the same Muskhogean linguistic family. But Muskhogean Yamasee could be understood throughout much of the South as a second if not a first language, and SPG missionaries were particularly interested in the Yamasees.[21]

In 1714 Governor Spotswood of Virginia founded a school at Christanna on the western frontier for remnants of the Saponi, Occaneechee, Stenkenocks, Meipontski, Tutelo, and others. Most understood one another, but it is still not clear whether they were Iroquoian-, Alongquian-, or Siouan-speakers. One suspects that they were survivors of a once extensive chiefdom or that their language, at least for some of them, was a second one, a trade jargon. Whatever it might have been, their tongue was comprehended over a large area, and the resident Anglican schoolmaster had great hopes for it.[22] A century before Christanna's founding Anglicans had compiled Powhatan word lists and translated the Lord's Prayer into Powhatan. It was not possible to build on this foundation, because, though some of them were still about in the eighteenth century, Powhatans were on the verge of extinction.

In the long run the SPG was most successful with Mohawks in upper New York. Fairly numerous in the eighteenth century, they remained in the same general location, and missionaries conducted services in the Mohawk language. Anglican Mohawks today are still using the same silver communion service given them by Queen Anne in the first part of the eighteenth century.[23] During her reign the church also had great hopes for the Yamasees, Savannahs, and natives congregated at Fort Christanna. But in the 1720s and 1730s those at Fort Christanna dispersed and became extinct; most surviving Savannahs moved out of the South during the latter half of the eighteenth century; and after Queen Anne's death the Yamasees revolted, remaining implacable enemies of the British as long as any warriors survived.

We have gotten ahead of our narrative, because at the beginning of the eighteenth century Anglicans were optimistic, unaware of the scanty harvest of aboriginal souls awaiting them in the South. The impetus for converting the natives, and such funds as were raised, usually came from England. Having little or no direct contact with the Indians, those in the mother country manifested slight interest in aboriginal culture and religion, assuming that such pagans should abandon their heathenish ways and devil worship as quickly as possible. Thomas Wilson, Bishop of Man and Sodor, one of the earliest members of the SPG, a prolific writer long interested in spreading the faith, exemplified this spirit. He never came to America, and the only Indians he saw were a few who visited England. In 1740 he published his influential *Essay towards an Instruction for the Indians; Explaining the Most Essential Doctrines of Christianity. Which May be of Use to Such Christians, as Have Not Well Considered the Meaning of the Religion They Profess.* . . . Going through innumerable editions, this *Essay* typified the thinking of many eighteenth-century Englishmen.

Wilsons' tract contained a series of dialogues between an American Indian and an Anglican missionary. The missionary patiently and cogently reasoned with the idolatrous Indian, explaining Christian fundamentals, including accounts of Adam

184

and Eve, original sin, Noah and the flood, and how Christians became God's chosen people. The pagan was admonished to memorize the Creed, the Ten Commandments, and the Lord's Prayer. Such dialogues and instruction were the way to "oppose the Devil in his own territories, where he has exercised an uncontroulable tyranny for so many ages."[24] His missionary expounded on how one should not store up treasures on this earth and how it was as difficult for a wealthy man to get into heaven as for a camel to get through the eye of a needle, apparently unaware that Mississippians had a better grasp of all this than had their capitalistic European contemporaries.

Only in one instance did Wilson come to grips in a small way with a peculiarly American problem. Indians in their villages had more contact with resident factors, traders, and packhorsemen than with any other whites, many of whom, while professing Christianity, led dissolute lives. Wilson's missionary warned that these so-called white Christians would burn in hell along with the natives if they did not accept the true word and follow the missionary's example.[25]

The widespread assumption was that when Christianity was rationally explained to the aborigines, in either their own or the English tongue, they must see the deficiencies in their religion and culture and become civilized. This thinking motivated the English scientist Robert Boyle, who bequeathed a legacy to propagate the gospel. Striving to establish a college in Virginia, Commissary Blair seized his opportunity, obtaining part of the Boyle legacy to fund an Indian school in his new university. In 1701 this school, part of William and Mary College, was ready to receive Indian scholars. Blair, who was also the college's president, expected to enroll native children, typically seven or eight years of age. The legacy provided for the purchase of food, clothing, and books for about ten Indians and for a master who would instruct them in reading, writing, "vulgar" arithmetic, the Catechism and church rituals, and by 1723 funds were sufficient to construct Brafferton Hall, a brick structure opposite the president's home. Blair assumed, as had founders of the college at Henricus a century earlier, that chiefs would be happy to send their sons to receive a superior (and free) education. Blair and Governor Nicholson wanted a sober, well-disposed adult Indian to accompany and live with the children, continuing to converse with them in their own tongue, not letting them forget about their village and kinsmen, and periodically reporting to the head men how happy and well treated their children were. Upon receiving a thorough basic education and acquiring a perfect knowledge of Christian fundamentals, it was expected that children would go back to their villages and by example extend Anglicanism and civility into the wilderness. Those displaying the greatest aptitude might be sent on to England for further instruction before receiving holy orders, after which they would return to America and minister to their people. All of this reflected the dreams of Brafferton Hall's founders, few of which were ever realized.[36]

Village life and clan structure had been disrupted, but the tradition that the mother and her family (the child's uncle) were primarily responsible for education would not die out. Despite the reasonableness of arguments like those presented in Bishop Wilson's *Essay*, Indians were not convinced that the Christian religion was superior. To prod tributary chiefs, the Virginia governor agreed to remit the annual tribute so long as their children remained at William and Mary.[27] A few Chickahominies, Pamunkeys, Nansemonds, and Meherrins were enrolled in this fashion. Even so, chiefs complained that after a few years they, or at least some of them, were sold as slaves.[28] Upon completing their studies some Indians remained among the colonists as indentured servants and perhaps, as the chiefs contended, became slaves. Probably most Brafferton Hall pupils attended school not by their own or their parents' wishes. Pressured to furnish children, tributaries sometimes sent those of their enemies. Other students were obtained through purchase and warfare, and perhaps the largest number in the Indian school were hostages. When the Tuscarora War broke out, Governor Spotswood of Virginia, to ensure the neutrality of wavering Tuscarora villages on the frontier, demanded hostages. Young Tuscaroras handed over were abruptly transformed into scholars at William and Mary.[29]

Up until the American Revolution, when the college fell on hard times, a few Indians always attended William and Mary: fourteen in 1712, twenty a few years later (apparently the highest total ever), and by 1754 the number had shrunk to eight. Housed in Brafferton Hall after 1723, as far as is known they received instruction separately from the whites. By 1715 the master reported that his charges were able to read and write, repeat the Catechism, and respond in church.[30] How effective this instruction was in unclear. After leaving Brafferton Hall Hickory, a Nottoway alumnus, first shot and wounded a Totero, another graduate, before knocking his victim down with a tomahawk and killing him. When Hickory returned to Williamsburg all he could see of William and Mary College was what his jail cell window afforded.[31]

Not all graduates were murdered or transferred their domicile from the college to the jailhouse. Yet despite certain successes, persistent efforts, and the expenditure of considerable sums of money, the Indian school did not prosper. Masters complained that they never had enough pupils and petitioned to be allowed to take in local town children on the side who would be instructed separately and whose tuition would supplement the masters' scanty salary.[32] A more fundamental problem was that so many Indians did not like the school, refused to apply themselves, and ran off and returned to "barbarism." Exactly why they did so is not clear. Perhaps they were homesick and ill at ease in the white man's world; perhaps, though young, they understood well enough what a hostage was. It was far easier for students to run away than for slaves, because erstwhile scholars had villages nearby to return to, and neighboring Indians were likely to welcome them rather than track them down.

A few years after the Indian school at William and Mary was opened, Anglicans established another one in Virginia, Christanna on the southwestern frontier near present-day Lawrenceville. Founded in 1714, Christanna was to serve several purposes. One was religious, and the resident missionary was to instruct as many children as could be assembled. Christanna also was a frontier fort. A palisade, containing five bastions each mounting a cannon, enclosed various buildings, including quarters for a small garrison and a log warehouse. In another light Christanna was nothing more than a trading post. Chartered in 1714, the Virginia Indian Company had a twenty-year commercial monopoly and hoped to funnel most of its trade through Christanna. Profits were to support the garrison and missionary.

Governor Spotswood, an active member of the SPG and personally interested in the Indian trade, was enthusiastic about Christanna. Through force, bribery, and cajolery he induced Saponis, Stenkenocks, Occaneeches, Catawbas, Nottoways, Enos, Meherrins, and Meipontskis, among others, to move to Christanna. By 1716 at least seventy children and more than three hundred adults lived in a new village erected on a 6-mile-square township outside the fort. Charles Griffin, formerly an SPG missionary in the West Indies and North Carolina, became the schoolmaster and in a short time taught his pupils to recite the Lord's Prayer and Creed in English. Few adults, however, could understand the white man's language.[33] Regardless of their background—Siouan, Iroquoian, or Algonquian—Christanna Indians were known as Saponis. In a formal ceremony with Spotswood attending, it was planned that the ten-year-old Saponi Queen was to be christened, but unfortunately her ultimely death prevented this.[34] In 1717 Senecas or Tuscaroras attacked the village outside the fort, killing, wounding, or capturing a dozen or so. Worse was that the Virginia assembly the same year, unhappy with the commercial monopoly, dissolved the Virginia Indian Company. Funds for the garrison and missionaries were not forthcoming from other sources, and soon all were withdrawn. Griffin departed, becoming master of the Indian school in Williamsburg. By 1740 the fort, schoolhouse, warehouse, and Indian village at Christanna lay deserted, and the missionary endeavor there had proved even less fruitful than efforts at Brafferton Hall.[35]

At one time or another in the eighteenth century Anglicans founded schools in or near Virginia, enjoying temporary modest successes. Schoolmasters at Sarve on the North Carolina–Virginia border instructed a few children from neighboring Indian towns how to read and write and something about the church.[36] Alternating between Virginia and North Carolina, the SPG missionary Giles Rainsford lived for five months among the Algonquian Chowans in the North Carolina Tidewater, almost learning their language.[37] The church had few lasting conquests in either of these colonies, because disease and warfare had taken such a heavy toll in the Tidewater and Piedmont. The powerful Cherokees lived to the west close to the mountains, but, having failed at Christanna, the church made little effort to win over these Indians, who were even farther away.

Thousands of natives resided in South Carolina either near the coast or in the interior. More Indians lived in this province than in any other eighteenth-century British colony, and there was no dearth of lost souls. The 1663 charter had reminded all concerned that this new colony could serve materially to gain converts, and, with the possible exception of New York, the SPG manifested greater enthusiasm for South Carolina than anywhere else.[38]

Thomas Nairne—trader, Indian agent, resolute expansionist, and outspoken Anglican—expected to spread the gospel and Britain's commercial and political influence throughout the South. Because of his knowledge of Indian affairs, the SPG listened to and frequently agreed with his recommendations. He urged the society to attempt what it essentially already was committed to doing: conserve its limited resources among whites, blacks, and Indians living in populous, presumably self-sustaining coastal parishes and instead concentrate on the frontier, where the church was weakest and the potential harvest greatest. Nairne was willing to use force, to have whites and their native allies go among the Indians "kniving" them if necessary. But once the pagans had been brought into proper political and commercial subjugation to Charleston, the goodly work of conversion could proceed. Disinterested missionaries, Nairne insisted, must settle among these simple folk, master their language, and by instruction and example and with support from the SPG and the state, methodically win them over. Those who could not be brought into the fold should be enslaved, for, as Nairne contended, slavery and the slave trade could be far more productive in converting unbelievers than the efforts of French and Spanish missionaries combined.[39]

As an Indian trader and border captain, Nairne had firsthand knowledge of the Indian country and did not hold a high opinion of the resident factors' and packhorsemen's morals. His judgment, often based on fact, was that these whites were unprincipled rogues who cheated the natives with faulty weights and watered rum, and who debauched the women. Traders, most of whom were unequivocally opposed to missionaries' establishing themselves in native villages, according to Nairne should be effectively regulated, and this included taxing them. Such "sparks" who thought little of spending fifteen pounds in one drinking bout would never miss a few shillings to support missionaries.[40]

One of the problems, recognized by both Nairne and the SPG, was procuring enough missionaries to counteract examples set by these "sparks." Committed to reviving and reforming Anglicanism and unselfishly spreading the word, some clergymen were as conscientious as one could ask. Others did not set a much better example than the traders, lying in the road drunk, wandering about sober but mentally deranged, or coming to the New World to make their way merely because they could not find a living at home. For years South Carolina ministers reiterated to all within earshot that the Reverend Atkin Williamson really had not been in his cups and had not, as accused, baptized a bear—which may have been true, and no such unregenerate quadruped was running amuck.[41] It is clear, however, that the caliber of the missionaries varied from one extreme to another.

Dr. Francis Le Jau was one of the more creditable types. A French Huguenot forced to leave France after the repeal of the Edict of Nantes, he moved to England, made an easy transition to Anglicanism, and, supported by the SPG, came to Carolina. As minister for St. James, Goose Creek Parish, and a friend of James Moore and other leading parishioners, Le Jau encountered many natives who had business in Goose Creek or who had been brought there as slaves, and he interviewed traders who had knowledge of Indian affairs. From every source he tried to find out about their religious beliefs, customs, and languages. His primary contacts were with slave and free natives in his parish, which, though by the standards of the time was a populous one, nevertheless was still on and very much part of the frontier. Requesting free Indians to let their children live with him, Le Jau received the customary rebuff that parents usually did not want to give up their children so they could be civilized. Regardless of their ages, slaves, at least in theory, had little choice as to whether or not they would receive instruction, and with some effect Le Jau impressed on masters the necessity of attending to the spiritual well-being of their slaves, both Indian and Negro. Some of each race attended church, remaining after completion of services so Le Jau could instruct them. He baptized a few, but planter indifference and a fear that baptism would lead to freedom restricted his progress. In the case of the Indian marriages the church agreed that it was not necessary to publish customary marriage banns beforehand or to notify parish authorities that such a ceremony had occurred, but it never really came to grips with the different concepts of matrimony held by the two cultures.[42]

Despite the numerous slave and free Indians in Goose Creek, Le Jau realized that most of them lived beyond the frontier and had relatively few contacts with whites. He was particularly interested in the Savannahs, Apalachees, and Yamasees, because, with the possible exception of the Savannahs, each was numerous, spoke a tongue that might serve as a lingua franca, had lived in Spanish missions, and was already partially Christianized.

Having been baptized with Christian names and having learned much about the gospel, these Indians with little difficulty should make the transition from Catholicism to Anglicanism. The Apalachees, who had relocated on the Savannah River after Moore's 1704 campaigns, still rang a bell in their new village to regulate their daily routine; they told Le Jau how they had supported Franciscan missionaries in the past and that they would now willingly help sustain Anglican ones.[43]

Although they had differences, Le Jau and Thomas Nairne both perceived that these three tribes represented the church's real challenge. With proper encouragement, a century and a half after St. Augustine's founding, it was possible to hope that SPG missionaries might supplant the Franciscans. At times Le Jau thought of undertaking this work personally, but, busy with his charges in Goose Creek, he endeavored to send others, younger and in better health, to live among the Indians. Some of the widely scattered Savannahs lived on the Savannah River near the future Augusta. Le Jau obtained a copy of the Lord's Prayer in the Savannah language, apparently written by a trader but perhaps by a Spanish Franciscan. Because many of them sided with Britain's enemies in Queen Anne's War, the society began to lose interest in these "dull and mean savages."[44]

During that conflict and up until 1715, Yamasees remained steadfast British allies, and the society displayed more interest in them than in any other Southern tribe. In many respects their position in the South was similar to that of Mohawks in the north: Both proved formidable warriors in behalf of Britain and seemed ready, if not eager, to embrace Anglicanism. Having lived for a century or more in Guale *doctrinas* and *visitas*, Yamasees were already Christian or in any case understood a good deal about the white man's religion.

Samuel Thomas was one of the first missionaries sent by the society anywhere in America, and the Yamasees were his principal concern. Arriving in South Carolina in 1701 on the eve of Queen Anne's War, he was dismayed to discover that so many warriors were accompanying Governor Moore in his Florida campaign. Thomas contended that, since the Yamasees were at war, little purpose could be served by going among them. Yamasees ranged all over Florida and westward toward the Mississippi, but they never abandoned their villages concentrated in the coastal area 100 miles below Charleston. Women, children, and some of the menfolk were always there, and warriors were at home as often as not. In reality Yamasee villages were almost as populous and as safe during Queen Anne's War as ever, though considering all the wartime rumors Thomas may not have believed this. Possibly the dangers and rigors of the New World dampened his enthusiasm, or perhaps he simply lost his nerve. Remaining in Goose Creek, he decided against moving to the southern frontier, contending that suddenly forcing Anglicanism on the Yamasees might make them revolt. He and Commissary Johnston summoned Yamasee chiefs to discuss the best course, but for the time being—which proved to be forever—Thomas stayed in Goose Creek ministering to the "ignorant and profane" of all races. The cloth that the society had given to him to distribute to Yamasees for matchcoats began to rot, and Thomas sold it at auction in Charleston.[45]

Prodded by Le Jau, Commissary Johnston, Nairne, and others, the society did not give up. To the best of his ability, a trader translated the Lord's Prayer from English into Yamasee: "Our Father which art atop [in heaven] . . . Thy Great Town [kingdom] come."[46] The society was not happy with the result. Traders were most concerned with the prices of skins and slaves and not overly interested in such abstractions as heaven and God's kingdom. At times they did the best they could for the society, and perhaps the aboriginal vocabulary allowed little improvement. The society hoped other missionaries would take up Thomas's work. The classical scholar Henry Gerrard arrived in the province in 1707. Although well educated he had a "weak delivery" and South Carolinians thought him the ideal person to establish a school among the Yamasees. But they were mistaken, and Gerrard had no success.[47]

On his own John Norris went with some of his family among the Yamasees to learn their language. Norris subsequently returned to England, where he was thrown into prison for debt, all the while insisting he was just the man to establish a Yamasee school—if only the society would get him out of prison.[48] Assorted Anglican laymen opened schools in various parts of Carolina, primarily for whites, though a few Yamasees, usually mestizos whose fathers were white traders, were enrolled. At one point Edward Marston, a clergyman and SPG missionary, having traveled through the Indian country, resolved to take up the Yamasee challenge. Unfortunately Marston remained the "same unhappy and irreconcilable man" and made no progress.[49] Primarily with the Yamasees in mind, the society sent over two boxes of New Testaments written in Spanish, which Commissary Johnston distributed to parish priests and schoolmasters supported by the SPG. Considering the turnover and failures of the schoolmasters and the fact that Port Royal Parish, closest to the Yamasees, had no minister, Johnston was not surprised that the Testaments gathered dust.[50] Finally in 1714 Port Royal Parish got a minister, William Guy, who began working with neighboring Yamasees, but within a year these Indians laid waste the region.

The society was no more successful with the Apalachees. As tributaries in villages on the Savannah River or as slaves on plantations from Goose Creek to Port Royal, many of this tribe already were Christian. After Moore's destruction of their missions in 1704, some refugees had fled westward to Mobile, where Catholic French missionaries established them in new villages. Far more Apalachees had moved to Carolina, and the SPG expected to outdo the French and to put the Spanish New Testaments to good use. On occasion ministers purchased a few Apalachee slaves and, after teaching them to read and write, christened them; missionaries debated whether Indians whom perhaps Spaniards had already christened should not be conditionally baptized by Anglicans. Such modest accomplishments were all the society had to show for its efforts by 1715. In that year the Apalachees joined the Yamasees in taking up the hatchet.[51]

Two years before the Yamasee uprising, the SPG held great hopes for George, a Yamasee prince who had been invited to London. Just what made George a "prince" and his father (or uncle) the Yamasee king is unclear; in any case the society did not dwell on this point, which was just as well. During the eighteenth century the society also brought Mohawk chiefs and the West African Philip Quaque, who was ordained in 1765, to the mother country, and the Mohawk Valley, the Carolina frontier, and West Africa, along with the West Indies, represented the society's chief interests as far as nonwhites were concerned. Publicity attended Prince George's visit. The Bishop of London baptized him at Somerset House, and the new Hanoverian King, George I, officially received him. The society expected that Prince George, like the Mohawks and Philip Quaque, would rally support for further missionary endeavors. George spent almost two years in England being civilized, living proof of what with proper backing the church might accomplish. He was outfitted with a copybook, primer, ciphering book, and slate, and his mentors furnished him proper clothes: shoes, buckles, gloves, shirts, stockings, cravats, and a better than average, though not too stylish, suit. Eventually he learned to read and cipher, but Prince George was homesick for his Carolina village, unhappy as an English schoolboy. He was taught by a series of schoolteachers and seemed uneasy or dissatisfied with them all—or vice versa.[52] Finally in 1715 he returned to Carolina, where the "whole province sees with admiration the improvement of the Yammousea Prince."[53]

When he stepped ashore, news of the Yamasee revolt greeted him, and his first concern was his family's fate. Rumor had it they were safe in St. Augustine, yet before long his father and kinsmen arrived in Charleston as slaves, having been surprised and captured while building a new village on a coastal island nearer the Spaniards. Commissary Johnston hoped that the repentant chief would lead whites against the rebels. The chief refused, assuming he had been given the opportunity, and he and his villagers were sold and presumably shipped off to the West Indies.[54] We can only assume that in his new suit Prince George visited his shackled father in Charleston, and one can only speculate about the youth's emotions. There is no way to know what George might have done had he been at Port Royal at the outbreak of the rebellion. Yamasees had captured the aggressive Anglican Thomas Nairne, slowly burning him for three days. Would the prince have stepped to Nairne's defense, or would he have piled on more faggots?

Prince George lived in Commissary Johnston's house for a time and eventually disappeared from history. The Yamasee rebellion had shocked the SPG, dashing expectations of making wholesale converts among the Yamasees, Apalachees, and Savannahs. All had joined the uprising, and after 1715 few remained near Carolinians. Planters lost most of whatever zeal they had for converting slaves, whether Indian or Negro. Anglican ministers did not completely forget the aborigines' spiritual life but were skeptical about making much headway among local natives, who were addicted to barbarous customs, were wild and stupid, and strayed about not even wearing decent clothes or talking intelligibly.[55]

After 1715 the two largest Indian tribes adjacent to South Carolina were the Creeks and Cherokees, and the SPG turned its attention to them, hoping to counteract failures among the Yamasees, Apalachees, and Savannahs. In 1723 a new missionary, Francis Varnod, arrived in the province and began conversing with traders, visiting the back country, talking to the Indians, and learning as much as possible about these tribes. He envisioned cooperation between Anglican missionaries and traders in spreading the faith. The French and Spaniards had not found this type of collaboration particularly fruitful, nor in time did Varnod. However, he made some progress. On a visit to Savannah Town (near the future Augusta) he baptized five mestizos, children of white traders and Creek, Cherokee, and other Indian women who had located there, and on occasion he baptized mixed-blood natives deep in the Indian country. A Cherokee chief made a promise—which he did not fulfill—to send his son to Varnod to be educated.[56]

From the 1720s until the end of the colonial period the Anglicans enjoyed only modest successes. Both beyond the white frontier and in settled parishes, a few natives were baptized and perhaps taught to read, write, and cipher. At her earnest request a free Indian woman was baptized in South Carolina's St. Bartholomew Parish.[57] Most of these natives, like the ones Varnod christened at Savannah Town, were mestizo offspring of white traders. One such mixed-blood in Perquiman's Precinct, North Carolina, first repeated the catechism by memory in front of a large congregation before she and her three children were baptized and admitted to membership.[58] Ministers insisted that converted aborigines would be a bulwark against rebellions and poisonings, but planters were not convinced.

Taking the broad view, it became obvious that the church made the least inroads among natives in the South, where Anglicanism was strongest and the Indians most numerous. In Northern colonies, primarily among the Mohawks, the missionaries' efforts were longer lasting. The Apalachees and Yamasees in whom the SPG had placed such high hopes during Queen Anne's reign have disappeared. Had Yamasees, like Mohawks, remained fast friends of the British, it is conceivable that today they also would be in the Anglican communion, perhaps using some of the church plate Governor Moore had seized in the 1702 sack of St. Augustine.

195

Besides such obvious problems as the Yamasee rebellion, the Anglican church suffered from fundamental weaknesses. Although it was more firmly established in the South than elsewhere in America, by no means did all Anglicans see eye to eye. Le Jau and Nairne both were devout churchmen anxious to proselytize the heathen. This did not prevent them from quarreling bitterly in a dispute probably more political than religious in nature. Nairne wanted SPG missionaries to go among the Indians; not opposed to the idea, Le Jau at the same time advocated ministering to native slaves in coastal parishes. He and other Goose Creek men were galled that Nairne, eager to convert remote aborigines, treated his slaves at home so badly.[59] Another deficiency of the church was the proliferation of dissenters, including Presbyterians, Lutherans, Baptists, Quakers, and Menonites. Thomas Bray, a founder of the SPG, regarded the Quakers "as almost . . . heathens,"[60] and SPG missionaries showed little tolerance for the increasing number of itinerant "Baptist exhorters."[61] The SPG eventually shifted its attention from converting Native Americans to working with white dissenters, who were more accessible and at least spoke English.

Presbyterians posed a unique challenge. In 1607 Anglicanism was established in England and was brought over to Virginia without controversy. After the Act of Union in 1707, joining England and Scotland, Presbyterianism remained the official Scottish religion. Great Britain had two established churches: Anglican in England and Presbyterian in Scotland. Numerous Scotch-Irish Presbyterian colonists came to America in the eighteenth century, alarming Commissary Johnston when they suggested that since there were two established churches in the mother country there should be two in Carolina.[62] The Anglican Church's resources, which could have been devoted to winning over the aborigines, instead were used increasingly to combat dissenters. Just before the American Revolution the Anglican missionary Charles Woodmason roamed about the Carolina back country simultaneously cajoling and denouncing dissenters, but paying little attention to the Indians.

A further weakness of the Anglican Church was that it had no American bishop. For many reasons, including the fact that some colonial Anglican laymen did not want one, no bishop ever took up residence in colonial America. The colonies were in the Bishop of London's diocese, and he never came to the New

World or apparently even thought of doing so. An absentee bishop in London was not as effective as the Catholic one in Cuba, such as Gabriel Calderón, who at least occasionally visited Florida, or as the resident bishop in New France.

Through Christian example and occasionally active missionary work, dissenters tried to convert the Southern Indians. Germans —Lutherans, Calvinists, and members of pietistic sects—came to the Southern colonies in large numbers in the eighteenth century. Filling up the Virginia frontier, Lutherans hoped to treat the Indians more kindly than had the English and Spaniards, in vain as it turned out, and to bring over their own missionary.[63] Bishop August Spangenberg in North Carolina proclaimed that his Moravian flock would "confer a blessing on the Catawba and Cherokee Indians,"[64] and on the eve of the Revolution the Moravians rejoiced when they finally baptized a Cherokee man and wife, their first converts.[65]

Another German, Christian Priber, eccentric or in any case different from the staid Moravians at Salem, more than anyone else attempted to proselytize the Cherokees. A versatile scholar and lawyer conversant in several languages, he went to live among them, cut his hair and dressed as a native, learned their language, and tried to establish a utopian socialist community on the frontier. Like most Southern Indians, the Cherokees were socialistic to a considerable degree already. Priber remained among them from 1736 until 1743, welcoming runaway blacks and indentured servants to his "kingdom of paradise," all the while educating and enlightening the natives, among other things explaining exactly how the traders' scales, weights, and measures worked. British colonists assumed Priber was a French agent, a Jesuit priest sent to turn Indians against their true father, King George. British traders and Creeks eventually captured Priber and handed him over to James Oglethorpe, who imprisoned him at Frederica. Since Priber soon died and his papers were lost, exactly who he was and what he expected to achieve is unclear. But in the tradition of Spanish Franciscans who had lived among the natives and shared their privations, Priber served conscientiously among the Cherokees. Probably more than any other white missionary, Spanish or British, he understood and appreciated aboriginal culture.[66]

Non-Anglicans besides Priber made desultory attempts to convert Indians. The Society for the Propagation of Christian Knowledge, the Scottish Presbyterian counterpart of the SPG, along with Lutherans, sent missionaries among the Cherokees on the eve of the Revolution, but with little effect. The nonsectarian Charleston Library Society had as one objective the overcoming of the "gross ignorance of the naked *Indian*," but there is no sign that it ever did.[67] At one time or another Quakers worked with a few natives.

Except for the effects of epidemics, the most important single reason Britain failed to convert and civilize the Southern Indians was that in reality she did not have an established American church; instead a variety of Protestant sects competed with one another. Time, persistence, an effective ecclesiastical organization, and at least some knowledge of aboriginal culture were necessary. No church in the British colonies, including the Anglican, had the resources, organization, and stamina for the task. With her monolithic Catholicism, Spain did, and it was not surprising she numbered her converts in the tens of thousands.

This is not to say that British Anglicans and dissenters failed completely. Some slave and free Indians living among the colonists became Christians, a few receiving a rudimentary education at William and Mary or a rural schoolhouse. In the long run Indians accepted more of the whites' vices than of their religion. Seventeenth-century ministers bemoaned the fact that natives, having learned nothing of the true faith, were drunkenly dancing in a circle at Jamestown.[68] A century later SPG missionaries echoed similar complaints. One had gone into the new province of West Florida after Britain acquired it in 1763. A chief visiting Mobile, taking the missionary's hand in one hand and filling a glass of rum with the other, confided: " 'Beloved man, I will always think well of this friend of ours, God Almighty, whom you tell me so much of, and so let us drink his health'—and then drank off his glass of rum."[69]

9
Indians in Utopia

In comparison with other mainland colonies Georgia was an inconsiderable province. Except for the Floridas, which Britain acquired in 1763, Georgia was Britain's last Southern colony, founded in 1733, more than sixty years after Charleston. The colony's Trustees, Anglican reformers and idealists, secured a royal charter that included territory between the Savannah and Altamaha rivers. Within a decade, long before the twenty-one-year charter expired, it was obvious that expectations for their utopian undertaking had come to naught. Under Trustee rule Georgia's population at most was three thousand; in the decade before 1775, however, at least by past standards, the colony experienced a remarkable growth. On the eve of the Revolution Georgia contained eighteen thousand free whites and almost as many slaves. Despite the fact that under Trustee rule the province was small and struggling, the Trustees devoted an inordinate amount of time to Indian affairs, tackled the same questions that had confronted their predecessors in Virginia and Carolina, and frequently made the same mistakes.

Because Georgia was established so late, less than a half-century before the Revolution, in certain respects it naturally differed from older colonies. Regarding the Indians, one point stood out: Few were on hand to greet James Oglethorpe's party in 1733 when it sailed into the Savannah River. This is not to say that the lower Savannah was deserted. Oglethorpe acquired land for the city of Savannah from the Yamacraw Tomochichi and his followers, who agreed to relinquish the bluff and move 6 miles upstream. Assorted other Indians, such as Yuchis and Chickasaws, had villages on the Savannah between its mouth and the fall line at Augusta. On one or the other side of the river the area about Augusta had long been a commercial center for the Indian trade, and a number of full-blooded and mixed-blood natives and white traders lived or rendezvoused there. Below Savannah, on the Sea Islands and coastal estuaries, scattered Indians still were to be found. Much of this area was the old Spanish province of Guale, once dotted with missions and numerous converts. By Oglethorpe's day the missions had disappeared. Disease had swept away most Guale Indians; Guale—and some Timucuan—survivors had merged with the Yamasees, almost all of whom after 1715 had moved close to the reassuring cannon of the St. Augustine castillo or the fort in Apalachee. In the sixteenth century it appears that some Indians had moved from the interior maize-growing heartland to coastal missions, and then after the missions were destroyed in the following century natives again retired inland or, in the case of the Yamasees, moved to Florida. John Smith at Jamestown and Henry Woodward at Charleston did not have to travel far to come upon thousands of Indians. Oglethorpe had to go several hundred miles west to the Apalachicola River before encountering populous villages. Coastal remnants informed Oglethorpe that their oral traditions referred to great cities and a remarkable ancient civilization, but by the eighteenth century the accounts had grown dim.[1]

The area that was to become Georgia contained few whites and, after the Yamasee Rebellion, not many Indians. The region between the Savannah and Altamaha rivers—actually the St. Marys almost 50 miles farther south, because Oglethorpe never felt restricted by the Altamaha—represented the largest stretch of Atlantic Coast in the eighteenth century not colonized by Europeans. The Trustees were not the first to try to exploit this area. Attempting to succeed where others had failed, a Scottish knight, Sir Robert Montgomery, in 1717 had obtained a grant to Azilia, the area between the Savannah and the Altamaha. Prospective colonists were to come from Europe and other British colonies and settle in large regular squares, subdivided into one-mile-square units for yeomen farmers and larger tracts for the aristocracy. Hopes for the Margravate of Azilia were dashed when the speculative South Sea Bubble collapsed in 1719. Nothing came of Montgomery's scheme except that promotional efforts publicized the potential of this unoccupied region. Before and after 1719 Montgomery's critics characterized his undertaking as chimerical and impractical. At least in certain respects Montgomery was on a sound footing. He understood clearly enough that few natives lived in Azilia, and they did not figure in his plans. Neither Indians nor "blackamoors," but rather white immigrants were to furnish Azilia's labor supply.[2]

Twenty-one philanthropists and reformers, Georgia's Trustees, took up where Montgomery left off. They obtained a royal charter in 1732 and founded Savannah the following year. Unlike Montgomery, from the beginning they concerned themselves with the Indians, but before looking into this it is necessary first to consider their overall plans. For the most part the Trustees were devout Anglicans strongly desirous of revitalizing the church and encouraging humanitarian measures. In many respects they were out of step with their age, because eighteenth-century Britain was notable for its callousness and the church for its worldliness, lack of ardor, and sterility. The Trustees envisioned their colony as a pious undertaking where upstanding British or continental Protestants, whether debtors, impoverished peasantry, or political refugees, might have the opportunity to start life afresh. By the terms of the charter the Trustees were not to profit from their venture, but through land sales and a growing commerce settlers and the crown alike expected to improve their fortunes.

The British government in granting the charter was motivated more by pragmatism than by idealism. In addition to eventually making money, it wanted to ensure that no unauthorized foreigners would move into this region. During the eighteenth century a three-way rivalry among Britain, Spain, and France emerged in the Southeast. Spain, undergoing an economic, military, and political revival, hoped to reclaim Guale, while France, which was developing Louisiana, was aggressively pushing eastward, building Fort Toulouse near the forks of the Alabama River (near Montgomery), and temporarily occupying Pensacola. Whether the area south of the Savannah River would be called Georgia, Guale, or Louisiana was yet to be decided. The British Parliament understood clearly that the best way to make good its claim was through occupation.

Not visionaries with heads in the clouds, the Trustees were aware of these strategic considerations. James Oglethorpe, the only Trustee who actually came to Georgia, was a veteran soldier, at heart more interested in containing France and Spain than in peopling his colony with debtors. The Trustees did have a dream, and to make sure their plans were carried out they kept control of the colony in their own hands, legislating from London. It was they who enacted three controversial laws or ordinances that more than anything else set Georgia apart from other British colonies. These measures prohibited drinking of distilled spirits, outlawed Negro slavery, and, with few exceptions, restricted landholdings to 50-acre tracts.[3] By design or not, all had an impact on the Indians.

When the Trustees outlawed slavery, for the most part they had in mind Protestant white immigrants (the potential masters) and African rather than Indian slaves. African slavery was prohibited, while only minor restrictions were placed on Indian slavery. The Trustees' point of view was essentially that of Montgomery and West Indian planters, all of whom perceived dangers of an African slave rebellion and advantages of a large white, yeoman labor force. In the South Carolina Low Country and the West Indies, slaves outnumbered whites by as much as ten or more to one. Both Montgomery and the Trustees hoped to avoid this, especially since neighboring Spaniards could be expected to tamper with British slaves. Some of the Trustees and their associates expressed moral or ethical reservations about African slavery. A definite though faint link exists between Oglethorpe's and John Wesley's pronouncements of the 1730s and the inchoate British abolitionist movement, which emerged more clearly in the 1770s and 1780s.[4]

One should not make too much of the Trustees' aversion to the institution of slavery in principle, because they prohibited only African and not Indian chattels. The Trustees were not unaware of the natives, recognizing that previously South Carolina Goose Creek types had hunted down the aborigines. With this in mind, Oglethorpe, as he made preparations to invade Florida in 1740, was careful to point out—and he did so while he was in Charleston—that Indian prisoners belonged to the crown and could not arbitrarily be sold off.[5] The Trustees made it clear that they were opposed, to some extent at least, to all types of slavery in the remote interior, establishing fines for traders who employed Negro or "other"—that is, Indian—slaves.[6]

Many Georgians did not share the Trustees' aversion to slavery in any form and looked with envy across the Savannah River, where Carolinians, employing chattels, amassed fortunes on rice and indigo plantations and in the Indian trade. Despite minor restrictions, whenever possible Georgians used Indian slaves, and it is reasonable to assume that, had some tribe like the Yamasees been at hand to send out on raids and had large numbers of potential captives been available in the interior, Goose Creek slave-trading magnates in time would have emerged. Legally or by subterfuge, Indian and also African slaves and those of mixed blood labored in behalf of the Trusteeship.

The Trustees never decreed that natives themselves could not acquire or keep slaves, which, among other things, raised the question of how to define an Indian. Mixed-bloods (mestizos) lived in the colony and, depending on circumstances, could claim to be white or Indian. Using a similar approach, a white settler might marry an Indian and contend that slaves of whatever ethnic backgrounds seen at their residence belonged to the aboriginal wife and not the white spouse. The mestizo Mary Musgrove had a series of husbands. The first two, John Musgrove and Jacob Matthews, were white Indian traders and also planters. John and Jacob could always insist that slaves working at their plantation were Mary's and that one would not want to alienate the Indians and risk a war by trying to free them.[7] Mary's last husband, the SPG missionary Thomas Bosomworth, whenever necessary could also assert that the Indian Whonny, a slave on the Bosomworth plantation, really belonged to her.[8]

In most instances Georgians legally employed Indian slaves and with little difficulty contrived ways to circumvent prohibitions against Africans. To escape his creditors, the South Carolinian Captain John Hearne came into Georgia with some forty Indian and mulatto slaves but, as he maintained, with "few if any Negroes."[9] One could find African slaves around Frederica in southern Georgia. The Trustees' colony literally was a slice out of South Carolina, because South Carolina bordered the colony to the north of the Savannah and, curiously enough, to the south below the Altamaha. Compounding the ambiguity over the southern boundary was the fact that the Altamaha has several mouths, in places raising a question as to whether one actually was in Georgia or South Carolina. Planters who arrived in the Trusteeship with their slaves—Indian, African, mixed-blood, or whatever—often found it convenient to go to the Altamaha region, where, if pressed, they could argue they really were not in Georgia but in South Carolina. If they went to the Musgroves' new cowpen and trading post at Mount Venture, on the south bank of the Altamaha 60 miles from Frederica, they were once again back in South Carolina. There was no question that slaves of whatever racial background were permitted there.[10] In 1750 the Trustees legalized slavery, and by the eve of the Revolution chattels roughly equaled the white population. Both before and after 1750, a part of colonial Georgia's slaves were Indian.

To a certain extent the Trustees had natives in mind when they prohibited distilled spirits. For years SPG missionaries and civil authorities, working for a well-ordered Indian trade, had complained about rum's deleterious effects. The Trustees, who saw right at hand what cheap gin was doing to London's populace, did not want to allow rum, the New World's inexpensive drink, to play a similar role in their utopia among either whites or Indians.

It was one thing from the vantage point of London to outlaw distilled spirits; it was another to keep rum out of the natives' hands. Through custom this drink had become an essential trade item. Whether in the interior or in settled parts of Georgia, if natives could not get rum from Georgians, it was readily available from Carolinians. To the missionaries' dismay, Indians outside Savannah staggered about carrying bottles of rum, and whenever they had difficulty quenching their thirst in Georgia, it cost them little effort to paddle across the river.[11] Indian traders, both Georgians and Carolinians, did not have the same qualms about rum as did the Trustees. Negotiations with Yamacraws had to be postponed in 1734 because the interpreter John Musgrove was inebriated, was unable to function, and "so confounded the Indians."[12] Oglethorpe understood that from a military standpoint, if no other, cordial relations with tribesmen were vital and that in negotiations and commercial dealings chiefs and warriors expected to drink as many "healths" as possible. When they came to Savannah he regaled them with a pint of wine or a quart of beer per day, but nothing stronger.[13] The Trustees' proscriptions against rum had some effect on the whites but little on the natives.

Recognizing that relatively few Indians lived near the coast, where Savannah, Frederica, and smaller towns were being established, the Trustees, like Montgomery in an earlier period, at first relied on white immigrants for labor. In Georgia as in every other American colony an acute shortage of workers developed, and it was not long before the Trustees were forced to take a closer look at the natives. One of the Trustees' undertakings was sericulture, which they hoped would help make the colony self-supporting. Although the Carolinians and Virginians had failed, the Trustees were optimistic, citing Georgia's milder climate, a strong European demand for silk, and the fact that silk had been successfully produced in Southern Europe for many years. Colonists were to furnish technical and managerial supervision, while Indians, living near whites or in remote villages, were to supply part if not most of the labor.

The Trustees turned to Martha Causton, wife of Thomas Causton, a testy provincial storekeeper. She imported worms, fed them on local mulberry leaves, and at irregular intervals sent a few balls of thread to England. Whenever Indians came to Savannah, she tried to interest them in sericulture. She showed them her tables full of worms insatiably feeding on mulberry leaves and patiently explained how silk was unwound from cocoons. She contended that this was just the occupation for Indians who needed money to pay for trade goods. One chief promised to bring his wife and children down to learn the art, and, according to Mrs. Causton, visiting Chickasaws were fascinated. They said they already had mulberry trees in their nation and, once instructed, promised to return with a flotilla of canoes laden with silk balls. In Georgia, as previously in Carolina and Virginia, enthusiasm abounded over sericulture's potential, but the results were the same: A few pounds of silk were exported, reaching a total that never justified the effort. Like her precedessors, Georgia was unable to establish a labor-intensive undertaking in a thinly peopled colony, particularly one on such an exposed frontier.[14]

The most effective way in which natives contributed to Georgia's economy was by hunting. Years before Georgia came into existence, Goose Creek men, fostering commercial hunting, had transformed the Southern Indian economy. Oglethorpe understood this, although when he tried to divert part of Charleston's peltry trade to Georgia he touched off a controversy. Indian traders licensed by South Carolina already were established in Georgia when Oglethorpe arrived, and for years the two colonies bickered over who should commission traders, whether rum was to be permitted, and exactly where the interior boundary lay. At one point Captain Patrick McKey, commanding an independent Georgia company, tied an offending Carolinian to the chunkey pole in the Okfuskee square ground, hoping a few well-laid lashes would instruct him that Georgia exercised jurisdiction.[15] The prosperity of lawyers waxed over the litigation, and Oglethorpe's popularity in Carolina waned.

The development of Augusta at the head of navigation on the Savannah River testified that Georgians were succeeding in winning a share of the Indian trade. Whether on the Carolina or the Georgia side of the river, the region about Augusta was a natural commercial center. In the first part of the eighteenth century Carolinians had built Fort Moore on the north side of the river, soon afterward founding the township of New Windsor close by; and in the years before the American Revolution an enterprising Georgian, George Galphin, established a trading post at Silver Bluff just below Augusta, which became the base of his far-flung commercial empire. The Trustees themselves founded Augusta proper, erecting a fort and warehouse and laying out a town. Before long six hundred traders and packhorsemen with at least two thousand packhorses were calling there annually.[16] Georgia merchants also looked southward, particularly after the Spaniards ceded Florida in 1763. Frederica merchants established branch warehouses in what is now the state of Florida. After taking all this into consideration, the fact remains that from 1733 until the Revolution South Carolinians dominated and derived most of the profits from the Southern trade. Two thousand fully loaded packhorses might rendezvous at Augusta, but more often than not the packs of skins would be loaded on small craft and would make their way to Charleston by the Savannah River and coastal waterways. Pelts brought to Frederica also were often forwarded to Charleston before being sent to Europe.

Most of the Trustees were devout Anglicans, members of the SPG eager to convert the Indians, and their dream of making

Georgia a Protestant utopia very much included the natives. After the Yamasee War the SPG's enthusiasm for winning over the Southern Indians had abated, but publicity associated with Georgia revived interest. As in the early years of Jamestown, Anglican parishioners in the mother country devoutly contributed sums for converting the Native Americans. Optimism was manifest among laymen like Oglethorpe and among clergymen such as Samuel Wesley, the rector at Epworth. Samuel followed the Georgia venture closely, and when Oglethorpe returned to England in 1734 after laying out Savannah, Samuel eagerly read the reports, because he wanted to leave England and relocate his ministry in Georgia. Oglethorpe gently reminded the elderly Wesley that Georgia was very much a frontier colony, and to be successful missionaries should be in excellent health, preferably young, and willing to live among the Indians in their own villages, to adopt much of their life-style, and to share their common existence and hardships. Deep in the Indian country and on their own, the missionaries' example would have to counteract that of dissolute traders, in time winning over the natives and rooting out polygamy and clan vengeance. Oglethorpe urged missionaries to exert themselves and learn the pagans' language, which for the General meant Creek or Muskogee proper, comprehended by most members of the Creek confederacy at least as a second language. Barbarism, superstition, and strange New World customs still influenced many of the elders, Oglethorpe pointed out, but he was optimistic that children might be saved from the devil.[17]

Having second thoughts, the elderly Wesley, whose health was not robust, remained at Epworth. His interest in Georgia and enthusiasm for the colony infected those in his family circle, however, including his two sons, John and Charles, and his son-in-law, John Whitelamb. All three were or had been students at Oxford and members of the Holy Club, a controversial reformist group known as Methodists. Samuel's daughter, Whitelamb's wife, had just died in childbirth, and the disconsolate Whitelamb wanted to leave England, where he was Samuel's curate, and plunge into the Georgia frontier, undergoing any privation whereby he might assuage his grief and spread the gospel. John Whitelamb professed that his heart glowed with the love of his Savior, but upon reflection either he or his father-in-law decided he should not go to Georgia, at least for the time being.[18]

Bachelors and Oxford graduates, John and Charles Wesley were not encumbered by personal tragedy, and Georgia provided just the opportunity for their zeal. Charles was appointed Oglethorpe's secretary for Indian affairs, and John, who was ordained, became a missionary supported by the SPG. Their fellow student at Oxford and fellow member of the Holy Club, Benjamin Ingham, came over to the colony as an Indian schoolmaster. Much of the Trustees' and the SPG's hopes rested on these three. After arriving in Georgia they often visited Tomochichi's new Yamacraw town relocated above Savannah and Mary Musgrove's cowpen and Indian trading establishment close by. The Wesleys understood that the day had passed when Anglicans might hope to plant missions along the coast where previously those of the Franciscans had flourished.

After consulting with Yamacraws, Mary Musgrove, and visiting Chickasaws, John Wesley resolved to go far into the Indian country, to "live savage" a year among the Chickasaws and learn their language and customs. A tradition was propagated among the Indians that a white man would come and deliver them from darkness: John thought he was that person.[19] It perhaps did not occur to him or the SPG that, from the Indians' point of view, a "white" man, a village elder responsible for civil government rather than a "red" or war leader, could easily be one of their own or at least have dark skin. John never reached the Chickasaw country, as duties and controversies involving white parishioners in Savannah and Frederica more than occupied his time. His Georgia ministry was not successful. In 1737, discouraged and unsure, he returned to England. Not realizing at first that they had such an unorthodox "enthusiast" on their hands, the Trustees were happy enough to be rid of him. As it turned out John had finally found himself, and after his return his great ministry as the Methodist spokesman began. His sermons moved thousands of Britons, who came to hear him preach in open fields and at pit heads, but the Georgia Indians had not been touched.

John Wesley's colleague Benjamin Ingham had somewhat more to show for his endeavors in Georgia. As Oglethorpe had recommended, primary attention was to be given to the Creeks, and Ingham supervised the construction of a schoolhouse for them outside Savannah near Tomochichi's village. It was a three-room wooden structure, 15 by 60 feet, atop an imposing abandoned temple mound. In a nebulous way this truncated Mississippian

mound held some meaning for the Indians; more than two centuries had not obliterated the consciousness that once it had been
a regional center for the Southeastern Ceremonial Complex. Understanding little of this, Ingham reported that the natives
believed fairies consorted there, but for him the mound
represented an appropriate high and dry site for a schoolhouse.
At least in an elementary fashion, Ingham learned how to speak
Muskogee; with misgivings some elders permitted their children
to attend; the Lord's Prayer was translated into Muskogee; and
all the while Ingham prodded his dear Oxford friends to come
over and join him. Yet in the long run he had little more to show
for his stay in Georgia than had John Wesley. The school fell into
disuse, and "for some unknown reason" Ingham in 1737 returned to England.[20] In the twentieth century progress (Savannah's expanding port facilities) destroyed the mound.

Among the largest ethnic groups arriving in Georgia were the
Salzburgers, pietistic Lutherans persecuted in Germany by Catholic rulers. In the beginning they worked closely with the Trustees and the SPG, sharing their enthusiasm for converting the
Indians: "May He bless the Saltsburger branch of emigrants
which has begun to establish its rights in Georgia and allow it to
become a tree so large that many thousands of Indians may dwell
under its shadow, moved by their love for Jesus in Whom they
have come to believe."[21] Located first at Ebenezer and after 1736
at nearby New Ebenezer, some 20 miles above Savannah, the
Salzburgers, along with Moravians, helped Ingham build his
school, learned about the Indians from the Musgroves and the
Yamacraws, and began compiling a Creek–German dictionary,
mostly of nouns. After spending some months in Georgia, the
Salzburgers, like the Wesleys, found their ardor tempered by
reality. At the outset the Germans had hoped to send a missionary among the heathen, but dispatching a minister to the natives
deprived white Germans of spiritual leadership. The Salzburgers
soon contended that it would be simpler if the Indians came to
Ebenezer, learned German or English, and worshiped with the
colonists. The flaw in such a plan was that few Indians were at
hand, and not many of those found any reason to stop by. In the
final analysis the Salzburgers did not go among the natives, and
the natives did not come to the Salzburgers. Despite the expectations of these German pietists, they made almost no impact on
the aborigines.[22]

The career of the wizened Yamacraw chief Tomochichi is intertwined with the early years of Georgia's development, attempts to convert the natives, and most aspects of Indian relations. Of Muskhogean stock, the Yamacraws (a small band of Yamasees) had moved to the Apalachicola River after the 1715 rebellion and did not return to the Savannah until about 1730. Apparently a former slave hunter for Goose Creek men, Tomochichi had been well acquainted with the British before Oglethorpe's arrival, had traded with them for years, and had a clear perception of the advantages and liabilities of a British connection. When Oglethorpe purchased the Yamacraws' right to the bluff on which Savannah was laid out, the Indians, recently depleted by smallpox and having little choice, moved a few miles upstream. The Wesleys, Oglethorpe, and the Salzburgers proclaimed in grandiloquent terms plans for converting all Southern Indians, but more often that not they merely concerned themselves with Tomochichi's band of 150 or so warriors and assorted Indians who from time to time visited the Yamacraws.

Oglethorpe persuaded the venerable chief, his wife, his (grand?) nephew, and a handful of other Yamacraws to return with him to England in 1734. The same kind of publicity attended Tomochichi's delegation as had accompanied Pocahontas and the Yamasee Prince. Taking lodgings in the Trustees' quarters, they toured London, visited the Tower, held an audience with the Archbishop of Canterbury at Lambeth Palace, and presented eagle feathers and other presents to the royal family at Kensington. Londoners viewed the delegation as personifying the "noble savage," but the Earl of Egmont, an influential Trustee, finding Tomochichi's wife "an old, ugly creature who dresses their meat" and who wore a calico petticoat and loose woolen mantle, had reservations.[23] Dr. Hans Sloan, the King's physician and president of the Royal Society, treated Yamacraws who had contracted smallpox, while the Reverend Samuel Smith, a Trustee, regularly visited Toonahowi, Tomochichi's nephew, instructing him in the Creed, the Lord's Prayer, and the Commandments.

Several years after returning to Georgia, Tomochichi died and was buried with great ceremony in 1739 in one of Savannah's squares. In that year war with Spain erupted, which was one reason, but not the only one, why both Trustees and Germans abandoned serious efforts to proselytize the Indians. By then the Wesleys had returned to England, Ingham's schoolhouse lay deserted, and Germans were still waiting for Indians to come to Ebenezer and receive the Gospel under the shadow of their tree. In the early 1750s, as the Trustees were relinquishing power, the Reverend Jonathan Copp, an SPG missionary, established himself at Augusta, ministering to Indians and whites in the vicinity. Reports that local inhabitants were losing their scalps unnerved him, and almost immediately Copp lost interest in Augusta. He petitioned for removal to a safe parish in the South Carolina Low Country.[24]

The career of the Reverend.Thomas Bosomworth, another SPG missionary, further illustrates the frustrations and failures of proselytizing the Indians. Having spent a short time in Georgia, Bosomworth learned something about the natives and, after ordination, in 1743 was appointed missionary to Georgia. For a brief period he served at Frederica and attempted with little success to found a school for nearby Indian children. Bosomworth was careful to point out that he was not an "enthusiast" like John Wesley or George Whitefield and that his ministry would adhere to traditional, staid Anglican tenets. It served no purpose, Bosomworth avowed, to advocate, as Whitefield had, that everyone —whites, Indians, and blacks—was really equal.[25]

Thomas Bosomworth is best remembered not for being a missionary but for his remarkable mestizo wife, Mary Musgrove. As a youth she had been raised with a white South Carolina family at Ponpon, probably as an indentured servant. Whatever her childhood legal status might have been, as a young woman she was free and after the Yamasee War married the Carolinian John Musgrove, a veteran slave trader and planter of the Goose Creek variety. Their store on the Lower Savannah River prospered until John's death in 1735. The next year she married Jacob Matthews, one of her indentured servants, who proved incompetent, contentious, and dissolute, and her fortunes suffered. Mary spoke Hitchiti and Creek proper, along with English. Presumably a niece of the Creek Emperor Brims, she was a person of consequence, at home in white and aboriginal society. When Oglethorpe arrived at Savannah in 1733, Mary was at hand to serve as his interpreter, go-between in negotiations with Tomochichi's Yamacraws, and confidant and adviser on Indian affairs in general.

She had prospered from the Indian trade, from presents bestowed by South Carolina and Georgia in recognition of her services, and from her cowpen, warehouse, and plantation, "a little sort of a settlement" about 6 miles from Savannah.[26] All this aside, Mary's chief asset was her claim to thousands of square miles located primarily in Georgia. Through her kinship to Malatchi and as a result of a series of transactions with Georgians, Carolinians, Tomochichi, and other Indians, she professed to be rightful owner of lands on the Savannah River, the sea islands of Sapelo, Ossabaw, St. Catherines, and much more. One might argue whether she owned these lands outright or merely enjoyed the right to their use, but there was no denying that potentially she was the largest private landowner in Georgia.[27]

Mary's second husband, Jacob Matthews, died in 1742, and the newly arrived Thomas Bosomworth, aware that both her estate and Mary herself were of remarkable size, saw his chance. Two years later he made her his wife, overnight becoming a man of property of far more consequence than his fifty-pound salary from the SPG indicated. Thomas was attempting—and he was not the first, the last, or even the most ingenious—to convert an Indian claim into a title recognized by white authorities. Once any court—at the local, provincial, or imperial level—assented to this, a land speculator was on his way toward a fortune. Many others, George Washington included, tried to do the same thing.[28] Only in detail, that is, his marriage to a mestizo, did Thomas's approach differ. The Trustees contended that they owned and had the right to distribute all lands. Bosomworth answered that Mary was an Indian of royal lineage with valid claims, which passed to him when Mary became his wife, and that the Trustees had no say.

This dispute, which enlivened and convulsed Georgia for nearly two decades, again brought to a head differences and confusion over usufruct, outright Indian ownership, Europeans' justification for owning lands in America, and the white and aboriginal definitions of "sister," "uncle," and similar kinship terms. Drawing on centuries of precedents, the crown, Parliament, and the Trustees all maintained that from at least the time of the Cabot voyages Britain had owned the lands in question and natives only enjoyed the right of occupancy. Indians had negotiated many treaties and land cessions. With their communal-based society it was difficult for natives to think in terms of ownership in fee simple. Experience, however, had given them a fairly clear notion of the white man's ways. When dealing with the colonists, Mary Musgrove and her Creek relations acted as if they possessed the lands in fee simple and were not influenced by references to usufruct or the Cabots.

The Bosomworth claim was complex. If one agreed that the Indians owned the lands outright, the question arose of which natives had valid title. Mary said she did, but her Indian and white detractors contended the Creeks had never ceded any lands to her and that she could not convey them to her husband or sell them to Georgians and South Carolinians. Ignoring the aboriginal title and assuming that Britain owned the lands, the colonists debated about exactly who in the empire had the right to dispose of them. South Carolinians and Georgians bitterly contended over this prerogative, each claiming jurisdiction in the back country and below the Altamaha.

After many years the Bosomworth affair was settled, but basic issues were left unresolved. During the 1750s, in the early stages of the French and Indian War, Georgians became uneasy about French neighbors in Louisiana and Spanish ones in Florida, fearing that they would tamper with the Indians. As much as anything else the foreign threat put the Bosomworth affair to rest. As a result of protracted negotiations, in 1760 Mary and Thomas surrendered to royal authorities their extensive claims in return for undisputed title to St. Catherines Island and a monetary consideration.[29]

The most important reason why the Trustees failed was the infeasibility of establishing a utopian colony on a military frontier. From 1733 on rumors abounded, usually with justification, that Spaniards, Frenchmen, and their Indian allies were preparing to descend on Georgia. Major fighting occurred after hostilities officially were declared in 1739: Oglethorpe unsuccessfully besieged St. Augustine the following year, and Spain retaliated in 1742 by invading St. Simons Island with a four-thousand-man force. In addition there were lesser raids and Indian forays. The Trustees and the SPG had expounded at length about uplifting and trading with the natives, but all that proved subordinate to the Indians' role as military allies.

Oglethorpe courted Tomochichi and the Yamacraws, always keeping the Trustees up to date on how Toonahowi was coming along with the Creed and the Lord's Prayer. The General understood well enough that the Yamacraws were relatively insignificant and the bulk of the Indians were farther in the interior.

When war appeared imminent in 1739 he made a nearly 300-mile-trip westward to the Apalachicola River, where most of the Lower Creeks had resettled after the Yamasee War. Promising blankets, guns, powder, and much more, Oglethorpe, meeting the chiefs at Coweta, persuaded (he thought) hundreds of warriors to join him. At the same time the Carolinians enlisted the support of the Cherokees. Yet when Oglethorpe finally arrived at St. Augustine, only two hundred or so Indians served in his army, and as the siege wore on week after week many of them became discouraged and slipped away without notice. Others, sharing all the hardships, remained until the final British evacuation. Oglethorpe had particular praise for two Creek mestizos: Mary Musgrove's brother, the veteran trader and border fighter Griffin, and Captain Thomas Jones, in charge of a twenty-man company. Both were at the Fort Mosa outpost, where the bitterest fighting occurred. Oglethorpe captured it in the early stages of the campaign, and later Spaniards caught the garrison off guard, stormed the fort, and retook it. Though shot through both legs, Griffin remained at his post firing as long as he could, and Captain Jones, among the last to leave, at the end savagely fought his way through the Spaniards to safety.[30]

When Spain retaliated in 1742 by attacking St. Simons Island, Oglethorpe, outnumbered four to one, frantically turned to the Indians for assistance. To his relief some volunteered, playing a minor role in the successful defense of Frederica. Usually fighting in the South was not as dramatic as the assaults on Frederica and St. Augustine, and border forays and skirmishes were the norm. Oglethorpe employed scout boats to maintain communications along his chain of sea island forts, and, as has been mentioned, natives served in the crews. Usually Creeks, but perhaps Yamacraws, Cherokees, or other Indians raided Florida, spying out the land and killing or capturing unwary Spaniards, Yamasees, and Negroes. On occasion hostilities spread west to Apalachee, which Spain had been reoccupying and developing. Since James Moore's day, Britons had assumed Apalachee was destined for them. Sharing that view, Oglethorpe was delighted when Creeks killed some unwary Spanish colonists and their dependents, retarding but not preventing reoccupation of that province.[31]

Like Moore, Oglethorpe, as a dedicated Anglican, was glad enough to convert the Indians. But as a soldier he was far more concerned with how effectively they wielded a tomahawk than with how fervently they recited the Lord's Prayer. With great effort Toonahowi, Tomochichi's nephew, learned the Lord's Prayer and the Creed. But he got six muskets for doing so, which suited both Toonahowi and Oglethorpe well enough.[32] Toonahowi died fighting valiantly while raiding Florida in 1744.

During the 1730s interest had revived in converting the aborigines and in Britain's taking up in the South where Spanish Franciscans and Carolinians like Le Jau left off. George Whitefield and John Wesley, leaders of the revival known as the Great Awakening in America and Methodism in Britain, were closely identified with the Georgia project. Despite all the publicity, the private funds contributed, and Tomochichi's heralded visit to London, in the end the Trustees and the SPG brought about no significant changes. After the Trustees surrendered their charter in 1752, Georgia in most respects became a miniature version of South Carolina. The Anglicans failed to make much headway among Indians in colonial Georgia as in colonial South Carolina for essentially the same reasons.

In Georgia, as in South Carolina, natives played an important role in the colony's economic development. This became obvious whether one looked at coastal rice and indigo plantations, cowpens, and production of naval stores, or at commercial hunting in the interior. To a limited extent before, and especially after, Georgia became a royal colony, planters brought in gangs of slaves to sea islands and fertile lands near river mouths. As in South Carolina, at any time a percentage of Georgia's Low Country slaves were pure or mixed-blood Indians. In the interior natives continued hunting as usual, the only difference being that after 1733 a minority of the colonial merchants were Georgians.

Throughout the South in the eighteenth century the free Indians' primary function was to hunt and, when called upon, to serve as auxiliaries. Education and salvation had a lower priority. Moving ahead to 1763, when Britain acquired Florida, these trends become even clearer. A handful of SPG missionaries was dispatched to East and West Florida, but one has to look diligently in these provinces to discover if they had any contact at all with Indians. Yet there is little problem discerning how Florida officials negotiated with Indians in promoting the peltry trade and how, whenever there was danger, they summoned warriors to the provinces' defense. Neither the trustees' efforts in the 1730s and 1740s nor those of Floridians in the 1760s altered the fact that, as far as conversion was concerned, no one had enjoyed greater successes than the Franciscans.

Enough has been said about colonial Georgia, whose development under the Trustees and royal control combined spanned less than half a century. It is time to look at the South as a whole, trying to ascertain how over several centuries European and African newcomers affected the aborigines and vice versa.

10
This
'New American'

When Ponce de León stepped ashore in 1513, as far as is known Europeans and Southern Indians confronted one another for the first time, and in the ensuing years the life-style of each was altered. This is not to imply that otherwise their cultures would have remained static, but because of this contact their development moved along different lines. A number of these changes already have been touched upon; however, a brief review is in order. In this regard we must again lament the lack of information about the sixteenth century. Pandemics had so reduced the aborigines that by the time Jamestown was founded entire tribes or chiefdoms for all practical purposes had disappeared. In general, populations exposed to infectious diseases eventually acquire some natural immunity, stabilize, and in time begin to increase. With a few possible exceptions, for most of the colonial era one sees little of such stabilization and recovery among the Southern Indians.

What stands out in the seventeenth century and the first part of the eighteenth is that diseases continued to take a heavy toll, somewhat like aftershocks of an earthquake. In one year alone,

1613, Franciscans reported that epidemics swept away half of their Timucuan charges.[1] In the following century the Catawba chief reported he had three hundred fighting men before small-pox struck. Then the number shrank by four-fifths.[2] The Carolina trader James Adair advised that in 1738 disease had cut the numbers of the powerful Cherokees in half; in the same century others described how nothing could be heard in Carolina villages but cries of women and children mourning their dead and little seen but smoke rising from cabins of the deceased, which had been set on fire deliberately.[3] Apalachees and Yamasees in 1700 still reckoned their populations in the thousands, yet before the century was out both tribes had become extinct. To be sure, some had been killed in battle and others captured and sold. Extant documents sketchily recount Moore's destruction of the Apalachee missions and the Yamasee Prince's reaction when he realized his father was to be shipped away from Charleston into slavery. Few accounts survive to tell of Apalachee and Yamasee women crying for their dead who had been stricken by disease or the number of cabins that had to be set afire by surviving relatives. But we can be sure that, even more than war and enslavement, diseases destroyed these two tribes. When in the eighteenth century the Cherokee population was cut in half or the Catawbas were decreased by four-fifths, the numbers involved were a few thousand or a few hundred; in the sixteenth century comparable victims had to be numbered in the tens of thousands and possibly hundreds of thousands.

European manufactures and superior technology most attracted the surviving Indians. From the first part of the sixteenth century they had hailed passing ships in order to barter and had plundered wrecks washed up on the shore; in the eighteenth century we have seen how influential was the white factor responsible for distribution of trade goods. As natives gradually acquired more and more European manufactures, their life-style began to change, and often alterations in material culture are the easiest to document. Many eighteenth-century Indians did not dress like their sixteenth-century forbears. Deerskin mantles or matchcores and deerskin breechcloths had been the norm for Mississippians, but woolen matchcoats and bright red or blue flaps had replaced them. Natives adopted far more of the white man's dress, including plain, laced, or ruffled white shirts (invariably greasy and dirty, according to disparaging colonists), scarlet or blue broadcloth coats, brass buttons, gold or silver laced hats, garters, stockings, and leather shoes with buckles. Women wore calico jackets, petticoats, and shirts, and bedecked themselves with brightly colored ribbon. Beads for personal adornment and belts of wampum were likely to be made of trade beads rather than shell ones. Cloth turbans, perhaps adorned with imported ostrich feathers, began replacing the traditional headdress. Indians of both sexes wore ear bobs, armbands, and gorgets of silver and, alternately terrifying or amusing the colonists, painted themselves red, black, ocher, and white before going to war or participating in ceremonies. In all probability the paint had not come from local berries and nuts but had been shipped from London. Indian slaves customarily wore the same rough woolens and cottons as did blacks, while native freemen and tributaries in the Tidewater more and more dressed like their white counterparts. Slave or free, living among the whites or warrior-hunters in the interior, natives had adopted and were dependent on much of the white man's clothing, or at least were modifying it to suit their own purposes. In some instances, even in the twentieth century Indians have retained the dress of the precontact period, such as leather moccasins and woven sashes, the latter in modern times made with commercial yarn rather than wild plant fibers.

Like their clothing, Indian houses changed over the years, though not as much. Reflecting the population decline and smaller family units, eighteenth-century houses were not as large as those De Soto and John Smith saw. The Virginia Huguenot traveler John Fontaine in 1715 described an Algonquian cabin in the Tidewater that was square, built with 9-foot posts set side by side in the ground, and covered with a bark roof, having an opening in the top to let out, at least in theory, smoke from a fire in the center of the dirt floor. At Fort Christanna, which Fontaine also visited, native houses in the new town were similarly constructed, except that the 9-foot erect posts were squared and had pointed ends. All houses were arranged in a circle, touching one another, their outer walls forming a traditional circular palisade, while the doors, the cabins' only openings, faced the center. Wattle-and-daub sweathouses stood outside near the river.[4] Farther south Indians still lived in houses of traditional wattle-and-daub construction, but the ones William Bartram saw in northern Florida were considerably different: 30-by-12-foot rectangular houses were divided in the middle, with a kitchen on one side and sleeping quarters on the other. Both walls and roofs were covered with cypress bark, though some structures had notched-log walls.[5] To the north Cherokees also lived in notched-log cabins.

By the end of the eighteenth century Indian towns were not usually palisaded. Time and considerable labor were necessary to construct a palisade, and the high mortality rate of the natives, frequent relocations, and the fact that houses were more dispersed made it difficult to palisade a town. For protection Indians relied even more on stoutly built forts, using a combination of aboriginal and European types of construction. The forts erected by the Susquehannocks on the Potomac River, the Occaneechees in southwest Virginia, and the Tuscaroras in North Carolina were soundly built and proved difficult to capture. Indians sometimes asked whites to erect and garrison a fort near their principal villages. The natives had mixed feelings about such forts, which not only provided security and helped ensure free commerce but also might be used to bend villagers to the white man's will and could mark the first step in a major land cession. There was no question that such forts provided protection. On more than one occasion young men refused to go to war on behalf of the colonists until they built a fort for the security of women, children, and old men left behind.[6] Huddling in or near the Spanish forts in St. Augustine and St. Marks, Indian refugees were thankful for the cannon and sturdy walls. During the 1750s the Cherokees asked Carolinians to build a fort on the Little Tennessee River in the heart of the Cherokee Country. In this instance warriors had a change of heart about having a colonial garrison in their midst and massacred the soldiers.[7]

After the Europeans arrived, particularly the British settlers, Indians became commercial hunters, more dependent on hunting than before. In the years following the American Revolution whites, notably Thomas Jefferson, attempted to wean the natives from hunting, hoping they would sell their excess lands; devote their energies to farming, cattle-raising, and spinning; and become little different from white yeomen farmers tilling the vacated hunting lands. Jefferson's policy failed because commercial hunting had become ingrained in the Indians' life-style, and the whites were largely responsible. Jefferson always insisted he was trying to uplift and civilize the savages, probably unaware that by emphasizing farming he was, in most respects, except for the use of the plow, attempting to turn back the clock.[8]

Commercial hunting helped make the aborigines less self-sufficient in agriculture. In the earlier period, when St. Augustine, Jamestown, and even Mobile were being founded, Europeans often depended on surplus Indian provisions to keep from starving. At a later date—in the eighteenth and nineteenth centuries—accounts of whites' relations with the natives are replete with examples of how, for military, political, or humanitarian purposes, the whites agreed to furnish distressed tribesmen so many bushels of maize.

Indians did not become commercial hunters overnight; it took time to modify aboriginal techniques. At first guns terrified the natives, but they soon overcame this fear, learning their use and buying, stealing, or seizing them in fights with colonists. Even before the bow and arrow were discarded as the principal weapon, one could see the impact of European technology. Warriors began tipping arrows with glass, brass, or iron, making them more durable and deadly than ever.[9] Whether using bows and arrows or firearms, Indians, especially tributaries, began to imitate the colonists by using hunting dogs.[10]

Whites were responsible for the Indians' hunting of fellow Indians as well as deer. The slave trade, in which the natives were either victims or captors, flourished as never before during the seventeenth and early eighteenth centuries. There was nothing new about stalking deer or enslaving neighbors, but the demands of a burgeoning European capitalism vaulted the traffic in slaves and the hunting of animals into a prominence previously unknown. As the supply of aboriginal slaves diminshed, colonists relied more and more on imported Africans, and, as will be seen, so did the surviving Indians.

The typical trade gun employed by natives was a flintlock musket of dubious accuracy and mediocre quality. Indians complained and demanded better firearms or at least a resident gunsmith to repair them. Except for making and mending wooden gunstocks, Indians did not become proficient in repairing guns and depended on whites. In general warriors preferred European-made gun flints, but when necessary local flint knappers shaped flints as well as projectile points. In some instances Indians, perhaps through trade or as a present, obtained the best firearms available. The SPG, for example, before it heard about the Yamasee revolt, gave Prince George a handsome gun to deliver to his father when the young prince completed his studies and returned to South Carolina.[11] By the mid-eighteenth century some warriors had obtained new small-bore long rifles, which conserved powder and lead. Rifled grooves made these weapons more accurate than smoothbores. Indians so armed, no less than Daniel Boone, could hit a squirrel or an enemy between the eyes at 200 yards.[12]

Despite hunting's increasing importance and the multifarious changes in their culture, Indians remained essentially agriculturalists. At any time—while Jamestown was being established, during the American Revolution, or when Andrew Jackson stormed into the Creek country—whenever whites destroyed Indian granaries and cut down their corn the effect was devastating. Survivors fled to the woods, where they starved or nearly so; they were not as at home in the forest as their hunting and gathering ancestors had been. Living off roots for weeks during Bacon's Rebellion, the distraught Pamunkey Queen understood this, as did the Cherokee Chief Vann, driven from his village a century later during the American Revolution and forced to scratch for subsistence in the wild.[13]

Mississippians had gathered nuts and berries to supplement their diet, and their descendants continued to do so after contact, especially in the upper South. When Virginia commissioners visited Nottoway and Nansemond Indians in 1710, the old men were out gathering chinquapins.[14] Sometimes Indians lived far enough from colonists to be able to roam the woods at will; at other times they had to obtain legal permission to go outside reservations in search of tuckahoe, wild oats, puccoons (for red dye), and strawberries, and also to fish and gather oysters, cut rushes for mats, and strip bark for houses.[15]

Thomas Campbell, an agent of the Scottish land speculator Lord Deane Gordon, visited Upper Creek villages in 1764, traversing a region in the interior that De Soto's men had marched through over two centuries previously. In reading his descriptive account one is struck both by the durability of Mississippian agricultural practices and by changes since the European arrival. As before white contact, men and women alike went out into the fields in the spring with hoes and baskets of corn and beans. Hoes in Campbell's day, of course, were iron. Although the Indians grew small amounts of wheat and rice, maize remained the

staple. When harvested a portion was stored in the chief's gra-
nary, and the remainder was distributed to families according to
their size. Maize was prepared as cornbread and hominy, or after
being boiled with oak and hickory ashes was drunk as a kind of
soup, which the Creeks called sofkee. Campbell watched Indians
plant sweet potatoes, and potato houses were almost as conspicuous as corn cribs. Intensive culture of sweet potatoes was a
recent development. If not this tuber, at least similar root or
subterranean fungus-type crops such as tuckahoe had been of
limited importance for Mississippians, though the Spaniards
who first arrived in the West Indies observed that sweet potatoes
or their close kin were grown and consumed extensively by the
islanders. Some time after contact sweet potatoes assumed a far
more important role in the southern Indians' diet, eventually
becoming second in importance to maize, and European colonists with West Indian contacts may have been responsible.[16]
Peach trees, which Campbell saw blossoming in the spring, had
not been present in Mississippian times, but wild strawberries,
growing profusely just outside the villages, had, and as always
Indians eagerly gathered them.

As Campbell watched the Indians plant, he noted that their
fields were fenced, for grazing nearby were cattle, horses, sheep,
and goats; hogs and chickens were not far off. Campbell made
no mention of a cowpen or horsepen, but by the eighteenth
century they were commonplace. Cattle not butchered locally
were driven long distances, by either Indians or whites, to
coastal cities; along with deerskins, Indians marketed cowhides.
Natives living close to white settlements were required to brand
their cattle and swine. They reluctantly complied, though brands
selected frequently bore a remarkable resemblence to those of
white neighbors.[17]

The Upper Creek Chief Wolf owned two hundred head of black
cattle, and Indians in other villages had even larger herds. Somewhat to his amusement, Campbell discovered that the chief already had distributed these cattle among his children. In the
Mississippian culture, upon a chief's death it had been customary to kill his dogs and sometimes his wives, burying them and
other valuables with him. Europeans had introduced not only
cattle but also a greater awareness of materialism. It was one
thing to shoot a few dogs . . . but two hundred cows! To preserve his herd Chief Wolf had given them to his children, pre-

sumably in some sort of oral trust arrangement.[18] Indians living among colonists, like whites, formally bequeathed cattle and other property through wills; if they died without heirs, their property was escheated to the crown.

Horses had become numerous among the Indians. In the latter part of the eighteenth century each warrior did not necessarily own one but in some fashion usually had access to a horse, and this animal had become the main means of transportation for long distances. Some natives became skillful riders; others "rode more awkwardly than sailors." [19] As much as anything the peltry trade introduced horses into the Indian country. In time these animals replaced native porters; trains of packhorses, varying in size from fifteen or twenty animals up to several hundred, crisscrossed the South. Indians served as packhorsemen, and when horse trains arrived at villages the natives provided fodder, pasturage, and replacements, caring for the animals in horsepens and repairing saddles. Indians themselves furnished an increasing number of horses for the peltry trade. A few years after the American Revolution William Augustus Bowles brought over to Florida's east coast from the Bahamas a large supply of munitions and presents for the Creeks; all they had to do was come and get them. With little difficulty Indians deep in the interior assembled more than a hundred packhorses outfitted with saddles and halters and led them nearly 400 miles overland to pick up the trade goods. Natives then returned home, dropping off the appropriate number of fully laden animals at Seminole, Lower Creek, and Upper Creek villages.[20]

Raising, buying, selling—and stealing—horses became increasingly important pursuits. A mounting demand for these animals existed in the Indian country, and they could be readily marketed in such coastal cities as British Charleston, Spanish St. Augustine, and French Mobile. English colonists complained that Indians rustled horses in Carolina and sold them in St. Augustine or Mobile, while Spaniards and Frenchmen insisted that too many of their horses illegally ended up in Carolina. Since whites often encouraged warriors to make horse-stealing forays, there was truth in these charges. But Indians had no monopoly on abducting horses, and in the eighteenth century their outcries were as shrill as those of the colonists, contending that whites had illegally driven off native horses. Relatively speaking the horse trade and the raising and stealing of horses were more important to the Indians. As it became increasingly difficult for them to seize and sell their neighbors, they began to take (or raise) horses as a substitute.

Indians had enthusiastically traded skins, food, pottery, horses, slaves, or whatever to colonists in exchange for hardware, hatchets, hoes, shovels, scissors, carpentry tools, clothing, guns, and munitions. At the outset firearms and powder had been deemed essential, and in time through custom the white man's tools, clothing, and other wares became more like necessities than luxuries. Natives really did not want to give up the white man's ax and saw to fell trees by burning any more than they preferred trimming their hair with live coals instead of scissors and razors. By most standards glass or metal mirrors must be counted luxuries, yet many an Indian, having discovered what he (or she) had been missing, was no longer content to do without one.

Reflecting more than a half-century of contact, artifacts discovered at a late-seventeenth-century site in Virginia afford an intimate glimpse at how Europeans modified aboriginal and material culture. Located in Caroline County on the Rappahannock River, Camden apparently was occupied by free Indians around the 1680s, and artifacts discarded there lay untouched until excavated by archaeologists three centuries later. As with almost any Indian site, aboriginal pottery sherds, clay pipe fragments, flint projectile points, and faunal remains of game animals are scattered about. But in addition gun flints, bullets, glass arrow points, metal knives, files, nails, buckles, miscellaneous hardware, pewter fragments, glass beads, and silver coins, along with pottery sherds, both of European manufacture and made in the colono-Indian tradition, are to be found. Pipe fragments showed a mixture of European and aboriginal origins. Almost no trace of such perishables as European-made clothing, paint, and rum has survived, but it is highly unlikely that they were not present at seventeenth-century Camden.[21]

In time the white man's law made inroads among the Indians, especially those remaining in the Tidewater. Many adopted, or were forced to accept, European notions of land ownership, including acquiring lands in fee simple, making wills which were recorded in the courthouse, and bequeathing holdings to descendants. Tributaries on reservations, such as the Pamunkeys in Virginia or the Catawbas in Carolina, "owned" their land, but it was more appropriate to regard it as a medieval fief. Each warrior might have between 50 and 640 acres, but the provincial government required that all holdings be lumped together. Indians on such reservations had to render tribute, perhaps a token tribute of three arrows annually or a more substantial one of so many skins. As long as tributaries behaved they could continue to enjoy their land, and the colonial government—that is, the lord —furnished protection when necessary. Tributaries could only use their land and could not alienate it without the provincial government's approval.[22]

Farther westward, among the Cherokees or Creeks for example, the same concepts of fiefdom or usufruct (that the Indians really did not own their lands but merely were entitled to their use) in theory still applied. Reality, however, was another matter. Occasionally these Indians presented elaborately decorated deerskins or belts of wampum to the whites and addressed them as "father," which might be considered tribute and homage. If colonists did not reciprocate with suitable trade goods, it was likely to be a long time before they received any such tribute again. Trade goods were essential to the Southern Indians, but Creeks, Cherokees, and their neighbors had the option of turning to Spaniards or Frenchmen if the British did not take care of their needs.

By the eighteenth century, the natives and the whites and mestizos living among them more forcefully asserted that their territory was no fief, that they owned their lands outright, and that in every respect they inhabited a sovereign, independent nation. If territory was to be sold or alienated it must be with the nation's approval. An Indian difficulty was determining who had the authority to speak for their nation. The answer was no one, though perhaps there were a half-dozen claimants. European arrival had shattered the once-powerful chiefdoms. With occasional successes Indians had attempted to reestablish centralized states, yet in the eighteenth century this remained more of a dream than a reality. No chief spoke for a unified Cherokee or Creek nation, and colonists repeatedly took advantage of this to obtain lands. Colonial statutes and treaties are replete with examples of how a chief or the principal men of one or another tribe, for proper consideration, ceded part of their territory. Never losing their sense of humor, Indians, as they were plied with presents, became adept at disposing of their neighbors' or their enemies' lands. Whites were not necessarily gullible. They wanted a signed title; how they obtained it or what all the Indians thought of it was secondary.

Freemen and tributaries in the Tidewater and natives living in "independent" nations in the interior trafficked extensively with the colonists, usually experiencing an unfavorable balance of trade. Satisfying creditors was a growing concern. Rarely were they imprisoned for debt, as they coped with this problem in other fashions, including accepting indentured service or extending existing terms of servitude. Land cession, however, was the most important. As a general rule it is not fair to say that whites tricked natives into debt in order to make off with their lands. Irresistibly attracted by trade goods and caught up in the European commercial expansion, they inevitably sank into debt, a circumstance that colonists exploited. Indians relinquished more and more of their freeholds to white neighbors; with the legislatures' approval tributaries again and again sold off pieces of their reservations to satisfy debts; and independent tribes farther west from time to time parted with their lands.

During the colonial era two systems of justice applied: aboriginal clan vengeance and European common or Roman law. Inexorable pressure was brought to bear on the Indians, primarily those living in the colonized coastal areas, to become civilized and adopt the European legal system. Natives were brought before local justices of the peace, imprisoned, and sentenced to a specific number of lashes and sometimes to death. At one point in the eighteenth century a Saponi was condemned to die, and the Virginia governor required fellow tribesmen to come to Williamsburg and witness the execution. At the same time a colonist was to be executed for an unrelated crime. At least from the white perspective such a double execution proved conclusively that colonial law was color blind.[23] But eighteenth-century statutes make it clear that colonial courts treated Indians and blacks differently from whites. An Indian, for example, as with any other colonist, might sue a white man for debt. If a felony were committed, however, native testimony would be admitted only if the culprit were an Indian.[24]

Tensions between the white man's law and clan vengeance persisted. Indians repeatedly told the colonists they had no reason to meddle when tribesmen killed one another, and sometimes the courts agreed that perhaps it was just as well. SPG missionaries were appalled by such bloodshed and redoubled their efforts to convert the savages. Natives considered it degrading to be brought before a colonial court, tried according to unfamiliar procedures, and perhaps publicly executed. This was a far cry from being cut down by an offended clansman or even being burned to death as a captive. Warriors occasionally poisoned themselves before white justice had time to make much headway.[25]

Even in areas where clan vengeance prevailed, natives had to deal with the effects of rum. Few packhorse trains ventured into the interior without a goodly supply, and enterprising colonists had erected punch houses on the frontier for the natives' benefit. Drunkenness was common, and in general the sentiment was that an inebriated Indian was not in his right mind and not responsible for his actions; therefore clan vengeance was not justified. A problem that natives never resolved was that they were inebriated far too often and committed serious crimes while under alcohol's influence. In serious cases tribal elders sometimes ruled that, even though the offender was drunk, his crime was so flagrant that clan vengeance should take its course.[26]

The arrival of the Europeans forced the Indians to modify their life-style in a number of ways, including how they disposed of their dead. In precontact times mound burials and ossuaries or bone houses were commonplace, especially among coastal Algonquians, but by the eighteenth century they were a rarity. The drastic population decline and the fact that Indians so often had to move their villages from one location to another largely explain why. Benjamin Dennis in South Carolina met with coastal Indians who in effect had a mobile ossuary. Bones of important chiefs were kept in painted, elaborately decorated wooden chests with woven thatch tops, such as the De Soto chroniclers had described two centuries earlier. Natives carried these chests about with them, burying them at the first sign of danger, to dig them up later if circumstances permitted.[27] When Thomas Campbell visited an Upper Creek town shortly before the American Revolution he observed the burial of a chief, along with his shot pouch, gun, and blanket, but in his written account Campbell made no mention of a village ossuary.[28] Converted natives and pagans living among Christians were likely to be buried in the Christian fashion: lying on the back fully extended, with hands folded on the chest, perhaps holding a crucifix. Non-Christians, especially those in the Indian country, were buried in a more traditional fashion, in a flexed position facing the rising sun.

Although details are skimpy, with modifications Mississippian music and dances continued into the postcontact period. It is logical to assume that dances performed at the busk in the interior or at disorderly revels of the Etiwaws in coastal South Carolina, so upsetting to SPG missionaries, were essentially those of their ancestors. Traditional rhythms were still pounded out on skin-covered wooden drums or clay pots partially filled with water. Coastal Indians were probably telling the truth when they remarked that they were not sure what all the dances signified and that elders who understood them either were dead or had moved into the interior away from the colonists.[29]

Natives gradually adopted and learned to play European musical instruments. How accomplished the seventeenth-century Virginia Indian "Jack the Fiddler" was cannot be determined.[30] Songs played on French horns and similar brass and wind instruments might have been heard in native cabins and square grounds far in the interior.[31] Indians took to the jew's-harp probably more than to any other European importation. Years ago their twanging resounded throughout the South, but the echoes have long since dissipated, making it easy to overlook the importance of this humble instrument. But from the earliest period of English colonization in Virginia jew's-harps were traded to the natives, and archaeologists have uncovered a few. The elder William Byrd included a supply of them on his pack trains dispatched into the Indian Country, while at one point during the American Revolution British agents distributed three thousand just among the Choctaws. It is not known what songs Indians played on these jew's-harps; one might surmise traditional ones, but that is only a guess.[32]

Somewhat more is known about tribal movements after contact than about changes in music and dances, though in each instance details are lacking. After contact Indians became more mobile, more nomadic, and hunting became of far more consequence. The case of the Weanocs in Virginia has already been discussed. In the aftermath of the 1644 massacre these Indians moved about frenetically at times, and their experience was not unique. After Europeans arrived the Yamasees migrated between coastal Georgia, the Apalachicola River, lower South Carolina, Apalachee, St. Augustine, and Pensacola; in 1763 a few survivors retired to

Cuba and Mexico when Spain evacuated Florida. Pressure exerted by the Dutch, the English, and hostile Indians forced Susquehannocks into Virginia during the 1670s, helping to precipitate Bacon's Rebellion. Adversity followed them, and they had to abandon their Potomac River fort and move to the Meherrin River in North Carolina. Local colonists and neighboring Indians gave the Susquehannocks little peace, forcing them to relocate again and again at one or another spot on the Meherrin or Chowan River, until finally "a great sickness . . . swept off the most of them," perhaps a relief.[33]

It is not necessary to continue; the broad pattern is clear enough. Once-powerful chiefdoms or empires disintegrated, and natives, if they did not die, were forced to move about repeatedly. As populations shrank, villages were consolidated, perhaps two or three into one, not all of them necessarily having the same language; and in time these new villages might be combined again and still again. As far as is known the Indian practice of adopting rather than killing or otherwise disposing of captives, which helped stem the population decline, spread after white contact. Captives increased the ethnic diversity, as did imported Indians. Caribs brought to Jamestown during the early years have already been mentioned, and in the eighteenth century Mosquito Indians from Central America, or those captured in Meso-America by these Indians, arrived in the South.[34] Even East Indians were to be found. In 1707 one such unfortunate, who had reached Virginia via the Cape of Good Hope and England, protested that he was free and should not be arbitrarily sold like American aborigines, all the while explaining to the whites what Columbus had been up to.[35]

One needs to be circumspect when referring to Indian tribes or nations, particularly in the eighteenth century. So many tribes were ethnic melting pots, and constituent members could not necessarily understand one another. There is nothing unique about this. At an earlier date peoples of different ethnic and linguistic backgrounds had formed the English and Spanish nations. The difference for the Indians was that the mixing had been more recent and intense. The Creek Nation, Muskogee, or Creek Confederation is a case in point. The terms Creek and Muskogee did not even appear until the eighteenth century. Creek or Muskogee, the primary language, in all probability was not a first language or perhaps even understood by a majority of the Creeks. Lower Creeks, a major part of the confederation, themselves composed of different ethnic groups, for the most part spoke Hitchiti, which was unintelligible to those speaking Creek proper. As time passed whites almost surrounded the Creeks and their neighbors: British settlers on the Atlantic Coast, Spaniards in Florida, and Frenchmen in Louisiana and the Ohio Valley. As a result of the many wars with Europeans, non-Creek refugees had repeatedly retired to the interior, settling among the Creeks and being adopted or absorbed by them. Westos not killed or sold into slavery in the 1680 war departed from the Savannah River and joined the Creeks. Natchez Indians on the Mississippi River fought several wars against the French, particularly the great rebellion of 1729, and in the aftermath survivors fled eastward, establishing themselves among the Upper Creeks. Algonquian Savannahs (Shawnees) had migrated from one place to another during the seventeenth and eighteenth centuries, first arriving in the South from New York, then founding assorted villages before retiring northward across the Ohio River. For long periods, and in some cases permanently, Savannahs lived among and became part of the Creek Confederation. The Shawnee Tecumseh was the product of an Algonquian father and a Muskogean mother who joined the migration from Alabama northward to Ohio.[36]

Whether or not they spoke Creek or Hitchiti, numerous other Indians with or without justification were identified as Creeks, including Yuchis, Alabamas, Hitchitis, Koasatis, Apalachees, Yamasees, Apalachicolas, Okmulgees, Sawoklis, Chiahas, Osochis, Tawasas, Pawoktis, Muklasas, Tuskegees, and Chickasaws. Some of them learned to speak Creek or Hitchiti as a second language; others never did. When it suited their purposes whites considered the Creeks a unified nation, making solemn pacts with its emperor, but in fact many natives in this empire did not consider themselves Creeks.[37] At a much later date after the removal to Oklahoma a young Creek was placed in a Yuchi-speaking household. Not understanding a word of Yuchi, he later confided: "When I think back it used to lonesome there." In time Yuchi became his second language.[38] One suspects that at one time or another there had been many lonely members of the Creek Confederation.

The eighteenth-century Creeks constituted one of the largest racially heterogenous tribes, but many other examples, such as the Catawbas, might be cited. Living in the South Carolina Piedmont, these Indians counted their gun men in the thousands in the seventeenth century and in the hundreds during the eighteenth. Survivors today still live in South Carolina on a much-reduced reservation. The Catawba language has been lost, and scholars are debating whether it should be assigned to the Siouan, Algonquian, Iroquoian, or Muskhogean family. Various Catawbas conversed in assorted languages belonging to these families, making it likely that there never was any single Catawba language during the colonial era. If there were one, there are several possibilities as to what it might have been. Of diverse ethnic and geographic backgrounds, these Indians had little more in common than the fact they had congregated in the Carolina Piedmont.[39] The experience of the Saponis, whom Governor Spotswood assembled at Fort Christanna, paralleled that of the Catawbas, except that the Saponis today are extinct. A few snatches of their language were written down and have survived, but it is still uncertain whether Saponis were of the Siouan, Algonquian, or Iroquoian family. Probably the polyglot "Saponis" at one time or another spoke languages in all three families."[40]

It can be instructive to look at the Seminoles. For good reason, little has been said so far about them, because they did not emerge as a nation until well into the eighteenth century. The first recorded mention of the term Seminole was in 1771. The Florida Indians whom Ponce de León and De Soto encountered, with minor exceptions, had become extinct by the eighteenth century. During that century and early in the nineteenth, Lower and then Upper Creeks drifted into Florida, forming the nucleus of the Seminole "nation." Scattered remnants from earlier days, such as the Spanish Indians (presumably Calusas) and Tequestas, merged with these newcomers. Whites contended that a Seminole nation existed, making agreements with its king, principal chiefs, or head men. But there never was any such unified nation, and Seminoles then, as today, did not necessarily understand one another.[41]

As a final example of tribal ethnic diversity, some mention might be made of the Lumbees living in southeastern North Carolina. Numbering some forty thousand today, they constitute one of the largest tribes in the United States. It has been claimed that these Indians are descendants of Cherokees, Tuscaroras, and Croatans who befriended the Roanoke Island colonists, or assorted other tribes who at one time or another lived in the Carolina Tidewater. In fact they are an aggregation of diverse remnant tribes and also blacks and whites, having geography more than anything else in common, and any search to discover a proto-Lumbee language would be a fool's errand.[42] The question of whether or not to regard Lumbees as Indians has resulted in great fluctuations during the twentieth century when the United States Census Bureau has attempted to tabulate the total number of eastern Native Americans.

When one mentions a Creek, Catawba, Saponi, Seminole, or Lumbee, he must be on his guard, though some tribes, such as the Cherokees, at least for a time, were less affected by racial mixing. Both whites and blacks voluntarily moved or fled into the Indian country, being absorbed or adopted by one tribe or another. As a result it was not uncommon to see an Indian dressed in the customary fashion with blue eyes, red hair, or a black skin. The influence of whites and blacks living in the Indian country subsequently will be discussed more fully, but for the time being it should be kept in mind that they made a significant genetic and cultural impact on the aborigines.

Natives attempted to revive the chiefdoms that had been so badly battered or destroyed, and again we shall turn to the Creeks, who, with at least some logic, might claim to be descendants of Cofitachiqui. In the first part of the eighteenth century the Emperor Brims and his nephew (or son) Malatchi of the Lower Creeks professed to speak for the entire unified nation, and immediately after the American Revolution the Upper Creek Alexander McGillivray asserted that he was the true leader. But try as they might, sometimes with white support, no powerful ruler such as the Queen of Cofitachiqui, Carlos, or Powhatan reappeared among Creeks, Cherokees, Seminoles, or any other eighteenth-century tribe. Disruptions caused by disease and war, the ethnic diversity and internal divisions of so many tribes, and the fact that whites did not want a strong native leader unless he was their tool were obstacles too serious to overcome.

One development after contact was the increasing importance of the war leader, the *tastanagi*, as labeled by the Creeks. An early-nineteenth-century example is Osceola, who rose to power not because of election and membership in a traditional governing clan but because of his military prowess.[43] A division existed in Mississippian society between those leaders responsible for war and peace, between red (war) towns and white (peace) towns. This is not to imply that warriors had nothing to do with civil government, that white chiefs in a white town could not lift a scalp, or that military ability was not important in qualifying for any type of leadership. A rough modern analogy would be a soldier who can vote and in various ways help govern the country and a politician who, if required, can serve in the military. In Mississippian times those responsible for civil government and the white towns had the greatest prestige, but constant wars and slave raids after contact made the war leader more powerful.

Tensions increased between red and white chiefs. One way, perhaps the best, for a white chief or medicine man to preserve his influence in civil matters was to become the broker in trade with the Europeans. This commerce was essential to the Indians. If a white chief became the broker, the "gun merchant," it was possible for him to retain or enhance his authority, and increasingly one finds priests, medicine men, and "conjurers" arranging details of trade.[44] In Africa the most important black, with the greatest authority and social prestige, was the slave broker who supervised the distribution of European wares. This African might be an upstart or a traditional ruler who after the Europeans arrived branched out into a new pursuit.[45] A close parallel existed with eighteenth-century Indian chiefs.

One of the greatest myths in American history concerning the Southern Indians is that little intermarriage occurred between them and whites. Governor Spotswood of Virginia asserted in 1717 that he did not know of a single mixed marriage, and William Byrd II and the historian Robert Beverley made similar comments.[46] This contrasted sharply with France's experience in Canada, where, with Gallic abandon, jaunty *coureurs des bois* and *voyageurs* mingled with the natives and lived among them for long periods, learning their language, adopting their dress, and taking up with their women. A sizable mestizo or métis population resulted. The fact that one-third of New France's population was involved in the fur trade makes intermarriage or any type of relations with the Indians stand out prominently, whereas, though a considerable number of British subjects trafficked with the Indians, their percentage of the total British population was much less than for France.

Despite Spotswood's, Byrd's, and Beverley's disclaimers, the same kind of mixing occurred in the South, and considering the smaller territory involved, perhaps on a larger scale than in New France. There being so many more British than French colonists, this phenomenon has attracted less notice. Marriages usually took place in the Indian country with no banns posted on the church door and no Christian minister officiating. The Southern equivalent of *coureurs des bois* and *voyageurs* were packhorsemen and factors living for extended periods if not permanently among the Indians, learning their language, adopting much of their dress, and forming unions with native women. In time such whites were referred to as "Indian countrymen." John Stewart, an aggressive Carolina trader and expansionist who had traveled widely throughout the interior, in 1693 declared that he had escaped from the common vice of cohabiting with the Indians.[47] Whether Stewart was telling the truth or assuaging a guilty conscience is not known; there is no doubt that few other Britons escaped from this "common vice." Far from home for long periods, it was inevitable that "Indian countrymen" had affairs with young Indian girls whose culture in many instances condoned premarital sex. A considerable number of colonists married Indians and reared families. These unions sometimes were permanent, sometimes not, and, of course, divorce, if not simple, was usually possible among the aborigines, where bonds of clan often were stronger than those of marriage. Compelling reasons dictated why whites married Indians with the permission and encouragement of the natives: Such unions were good for trade. Marriages frequently allied a British trader with a powerful clan, usually that of the white tribal chief, and it was in the interest of that civil ruler, whose power might be threatened by an ambitious war leader, to have a close association with colonial merchants.

A large mestizo population emerged. Fostering a mixed-blood progeny, white parents might live and die in the Indian country or eventually return to white society. In any case their offspring customarily remained among the Indians. As a result, in the eighteenth century "Indian" chiefs had such names as McDonald, Perryman, Colbert, Brown, Price, McGillivray, McIntosh, and Galphin, and by 1800, at least according to available documents, it was almost impossible to find a pure-blooded chief of any consequence. After the Creeks relocated in Oklahoma reportedly not one hundred out of twelve thousand could prove they had no mixed blood.[48] The burden of proof today is to establish that an eighteenth- or nineteenth-century chief in question was not a mestizo or did not have African ancestry. Racial mixing between whites and ordinary Indians was also commonplace, though probably not to as great an extent.

Not all miscegenation occurred in the Indian country. Contrary to Spotswood's disclaimer and despite the fact that some statutes made them illegal, unions occasionally were countenanced by ceremonies in a Christian church. A few years after Georgia's founding, Samuel Quincy, an SPG missionary in the province, was criticized by some for marrying a settler to an unbaptized Indian woman.[49] Far more common were informal liasons. William Byrd II with his usual bravado recorded how he had had "good sport" with an Indian girl.[50] A South Carolina planter forced an Indian to be his wife and then, to the neighbors' consternation, because of an altercation had her "scalloped."[51] Yet another Carolinian, Robert Johnson of St. George Parish, was sincerely attached to his Indian wife Catharina, whom first he freed and then married. In his will he left her his house and part of his estate, while the mestizo offspring received their share of the remaining property and slaves.[52] From the time of Menéndez, Christian Indian women had married soldiers and civil servants in Spanish Florida. At one point two of the offspring were captured and taken to Charleston. The British governor characterized one of these "livers" in St. Augustine as being mestizo and "in trueth the other not white."[53] It was male colonists who most often came into contact with the natives, and the ensuing unions usually were between them and Indian women. Exceptions occurred, however. A "sensible, industrious" Creek man, married to a white woman, in the latter part of the eighteenth century rowed William Bartram across the Altamaha River in southern Georgia.[54] The British surveyor David Taitt in West Florida, just before the Revolution, complained that a white female had run away with her Indian husband and was in the Indian country, not to be found.[55]

Differences in patrilineal and matrilineal descent caused disputes over whether the white father or the Indian mother should raise the offspring. At the end of the American Revolution young Alexander McGillivray had the option of returning to Scotland with his father, a Tory Indian trader, or remaining among the Upper Creeks with his mother. The bonds of clan membership and aboriginal culture won out, and Alexander remained with the Indians. Before the American Revolution, however, his father had brought him to Charleston and Savannah and educated him in his counting house.[56] Another well-to-do Creek Indian trader tried to bring his mestizo children to Charleston for an education, but, as Bartram noted, the Indian mother, to the distress of her spouse, adamantly refused.[57] If mothers were slaves, they had little or no say in the matter. A Carolina trader, Richard Prize, stipulated in his will that upon his death his Indian wife should be free, that she should have two Indian slaves, but that white friends should raise and educate the mestizo children, who would inherit most of his estate.[58] In their wills other Carolinians emancipated slave wives and children, providing them with property and a fixed income. In many instances, such as among the Cherokees, the growing mestizo class encouraged adopting features of the white man's patrilineal society.[59]

Among the Cherokees and the Indians in general, as a result of mixed marriages, tensions developed over property ownership. The Mississippian practice had been for the wife to own or control the house, its contents, and adjoining fields, whereas in Europe the husband generally assumed control of his wife's property upon marriage. Indian wives in the Tidewater fairly soon had to adjust to the white man's law, but remnant tributaries on reservations and especially more powerful tribes on the frontier for many years resisted this innovation, which was undermining the clan system. The Cherokee Council in 1819 even specifically prohibited white men from disposing of their Indian wives' property.[60] The long-term trend, however, was the weakening of the importance of matrilineal descent and the clan system, as Indian males who remained in the East or removed to Oklahoma began to own their houses and lands like their white male counterparts.

Language is another area where one can observe the inroads of white culture. Even when aboriginal languages did not become extinct they often were modified. Because of the disruption of aboriginal culture after contact, the relocation and mixing of ethnic groups, and the increasing importance of trade and hunting, as best as can be discerned it was whites rather than Indians who were primarily responsible for the development of Mobilian, Occaneechee, and similar kinds of lingua franca or trade jargon. Even Tuscarora, Catawba, Creek, and other "tribal" languages, if not in part trade jargons, at least began to serve as languages understood over large regions.[61] In connection with the evolution of trade jargons and for a variety of other reasons, Indians borrowed a number of words from Europeans, particularly those for which there was no aboriginal equivalent. First on the scene, Spaniards made the greatest impact. *Vaca* (cow in Spanish) became *waka* among the Cherokees, *wak* among the Choctaws, and *waga* among the Creeks. Other Spanish loanwords in Creek are *tosina* from *tocino* (bacon), *kapitani* from *capitán* (captain or boss), *kapa* from *capa* (coat or hunting shirt), *askolá* from *azúcar* (sugar), *alóso* (*haloshi* in Chickasaw) from *arroz* (rice), and *simanóli* from *cimarrón* (wild). The last apparently is the origin of "Seminole," which in the eighteenth century referred to certain Florida Indians. As one might expect, a high percentage of Timucuan loan-words from Spanish deal with technical aspects of Christianity, such as angel, purgatory, mass, indulgence, and priest.[62] One reason so many aboriginal languages of the precontact period have been lost is that the natives began speaking English or, to a lesser extent, Spanish, in time forgetting almost all traces of their own tongue. In 1734 authorities in Virginia discharged the Nottoway interpreters, because members of that tribe spoke English as either a first or a second language.[63] Even more than Savannah, Occaneechee, or Mobilian, English became the lingua franca.

Indians doggedly held on to as much of their culture as possible. Foremost was the clan system, which, despite the shock of European contact and repeated commingling of villages, retained much of its earlier potency. Alexander McGillivray owed his political power at the end of the eighteenth century to his association with merchants furnishing trade goods and also to the fact that his mother belonged to the Wind clan, traditionally associated with leadership. Though modified, clan vengeance remained the basis of justice in the Indian country. Still standing at the end of the eighteenth century, temple mounds, as far as the colonists and many Indians as well were concerned, were little more than curiosities, objects of speculation and awe. Large council houses seating thousands occasionally were still built and used, but their number was less than in earlier days. As populations dwindled, it may well be that the open square ground, enclosed on four sides by sheds or lean-to-like structures, in large measure had replaced the more substantial council houses where in earlier times the busk and similar rituals had been performed. The black drink, ball games, and especially the busk, all of which were better able to withstand population declines and relocations, remained very much part of the aboriginal way of life. Again and again whites had to wait for days before conducting treaty negotiations or undertaking a campaign until natives had completed this annual ritual. Even in the twentieth century the Green Corn festival represents one of the purest survivals of the temple mound culture.[64]

Accompanied by hollow log drums or pottery ones partially filled with water, eighteenth-century natives still performed traditional dances both in the Indian country and in coastal areas where remnant tribes survived. South Carolina missionaries in the Tidewater were both intrigued and dismayed by the ceremonial dances of "wild, disorderly" local Etiwaws.[65] Indian mothers continued to strap children to boards, placing small bags of sand on their heads in order to flatten them.[66] A number of dietary changes had occurred, but maize never lost its preeminence. As in the past, natives supplemented their diet with nuts and berries; the Quaker Bartram blushed as he secretly observed "Cherokee virgins [innocently] disclosing their beauties to the fluttering breeze" as they filled their baskets with strawberries and "wantonly chasing their companions, tantalizing them, staining their lips and cheeks with the rich fruit."[67] Firearms and the seemingly unlimited European demand for peltry had altered methods of hunting. Yet some of the old practices, such as fire hunting, persisted. Colonists complained that natives repeatedly fired the woods, and one reason was that game trapped in the ring of fire sometimes displayed a white brand.[68]

The aboriginal style of fighting changed. If possible natives avoided pitched battles where risks of casualities were high. Certain precontact practices survived, including the taking of enemy scalps. Because of the bounties proffered by colonists, Indians became adept at fashioning two or three out of one. The custom of scalping increased after contact and in all probability was more prevalent around the time of the American Revolution than ever. Contrary to what is sometimes asserted, Mississippians had not been true cannibals, literally subsisting off their fellow man. For ritualistic purposes at times they had and continued to eat human flesh. During the French and Indian War warriors in the Ohio country circulated the flesh of slain French officers. Eating token portions, elders in various villages demonstrated their hostility to the French and their willingness to join a coalition against them.[69]

Indians continued to burn captives after contact as undoubtedly they had in Mississippian times. The Indians had no monopoly on burning. When diseases such as the Black Death, campaigning by unruly feudal armies, and economic disasters had most disrupted society in medieval Europe, the burning of witches reached its apogee; when the plague subsided, prosperity returned, and a measure of political stability appeared, witch hunting abated. In the New World after 1492 Indians sent captives to the stake as often as authorities in medieval Europe had condemned witches. Sixteenth-century pandemics, wars with whites, and frequent relocations had devastated native societies even more than the Black Death had consumed Europe. One might speculate that anxious Indians burned victims more frequently after contact than they had in more stable Mississippian days, just as the Europeans, in the heyday of the Black Death, had blindly and irrationally condemned witches.

European arrival eventually altered or destroyed much of the aboriginal way of life, and a considerable body of literature exists concerning one or another facet of this phenomenon. Ignored for the most part is the way in which Indian cultural patterns modified those of the colonists. Few historical works have credited the natives with much more than bequeathing to posterity melodious names of rivers and the concept of the noble savage. Until the nineteenth-century Indian removal, large numbers of natives associated with whites and affected their style of living, especially in the colonial period, when the Indians were more numerous and the white population relatively small. The South contained not quite one hundred thousand whites in 1700 and some five hundred thousand on the eve of the Revolution.

Archaeological discoveries permit a closer look at modifications in white material culture, particularly its pottery. Perhaps using European plates, cups, pitchers, triple-legged cooking pots, skillets, bowls, chamber pots, and porringers as models, natives continued to produce large amounts of pottery in the usual fashion—coiled and hand-worked, shell-tempered, and stick- or pebble-burnished.[70] This or similar pottery has come to be known as colono-Indian ware. Large amounts have been

240

unearthed at sites throughout the South, sometimes perplexing archaeologists. Since colono-Indian ware was inferior to that manufactured in Europe, planters, wealthy merchants, and the governing elite dined and entertained on delft, majolica, and other imported china. But the middle and lower classes regularly used colono-Indian pottery, and it is not necessary to turn to wandering Indians or Negro slaves to explain its abundance on white-occupied sites. Displaying more than the average curiosity about the Indians, the English minister John Clayton visited Virginia in the seventeenth century and remarked that native ware was suitable enough for common use.[71] When Clayton made this observation in 1687, few Africans were in Virginia. Wills of Virginia colonists in modest circumstances reveal that, although aboriginal pottery was not especially valuable, it was worth enough to be inventoried and passed on to heirs. Indian and colono-Indian ware has been excavated at Charleston, dating from that city's earliest years; as Carolina expanded in the eighteenth century, so too did the use of such pottery.[72]

Archaeologists have discovered more about the role of native and colono-Indian ware in Spanish Florida than anywhere else, making it clear that this was the pottery used by most of St. Augustine's inhabitants, meaning those not of the elite.[73] It served well enough, even though the natives did not use the most advanced firing techniques. While the missions flourished one might see colono-Indian plates, pitchers with painted designs and graceful handles, and candelabra holding five or more candles burning in the *doctrinas*.[74] In Apalachee the Spanish commandant in the mid-eighteenth century urged Indians to locate near his fort so they could supply pottery for the garrison.[75]

Mention should also be made of clay tobacco pipes. Particularly in the early years when a colonist puffed on his long-stemmed pipe it was likely to have been made by the natives.[76] If one also considers aboriginal wooden bowls, trenchers, spoons, and gourd dippers, it was obvious that the average colonist, as he prepared his meal, sat down to eat, and smoked his pipe afterward, was indebted to the natives for more than a handful of euphonious words.

Aboriginal baskets and mats appeared in colonial households. Servants, slaves, children, visitors, and possibly the master slept on such mats, which were in great demand as space-savers in crowded households, and, as has been seen, whites utilized native baskets for assorted purposes. Settling on rivers and streams, colonists at once appreciated the utility of the dugout canoe. Archaeologists in Virginia have excavated one of the earliest, dating from approximately 1630. This particular specimen is noteworthy because one can see how it was first made in the customary aboriginal fashion by burning and scraping with stone implements and then modified and improved with metal tools. Archaeologists have assumed that colonists seized or bought this canoe and then altered it to suit their purposes. Perhaps so, but, considering the fact that at an early date Indians acquired European tools and made canoes for the settlers, it is even more likely that the ones who improved this dugout were natives.[77] Partly because they had no choice, colonists began eating New World foods. The staple maize became the Europeans' mainstay, in time making Southern whites almost forget they had not always relied so heavily on grits, hominy, and cornbread. During the early years colonists ate dogs, "as good meate . . . as English lambe,"[78] but growing herds of swine and cattle allowed colonists to revert to more traditional fare. The Chesapeake Bay colonies became the preeminent tobacco colonies in the British empire, indeed anywhere in the world. Their economies depended on this staple, reflecting the importance that the Indians' tobacco had assumed in the white man's culture. Settlers grew and used tobacco on an unprecedented scale; even so it did not appear odd to the natives to see anyone, white or Indian, smoking tobacco in a long-stemmed clay pipe, its bowl decorated with representations of deer and other familiar animals. Natives may have made this pipe, or European manufacturers copied aboriginal designs.

The standard drink in Mississippian times was the black drink, usually made from parched leaves of the yaupon (*Ilex vomitoria*), a type of holly. Despite its name it did not induce vomiting, any more than did East Indian tea or coffee. Few rituals, whether the busk or preparation for the ball game, took place without the natives' consuming large quantities of this stimulant, which, though dark or black, was called the white drink by the Indians because of its use at ceremonies where men were purified. Tea rather than coffee was the standard nonalcoholic drink of the colonists, and not all of it was imported from the East Indies. Like the Indians, British colonists also drank yaupon tea (Spaniards called it casina). Throughout the eighteenth century—and to a minor extent even today—North Carolinians consumed yaupon tea, and at least up until the era of the American Revolution they regularly exported chests to Britain and France. In 1730 yaupon tea sold for two pounds sterling per barrel in North Carolina, and an enterprising promoter hoped to grow and cure it commercially on a grand scale, capturing a large share of the American market dominated by East Indian tea. Had he succeeded, there would have been no Boston Tea Party, but it is stretching a point to suggest that yaupon tea might have prevented the Revolution and saved the empire.[79]

Europeans manifested keen interest in native medicines and cures, and it was not long before they learned the virtues of, in addition to yaupon tea, snakeroot, sassafras, ginseng, pokeberries, horsemint, wild cherry bark, lady's-slipper, ferns, chestnut leaves, and boneset. The list is long, and though there are varied sources, a considerable portion of Southern white and African folk medicine is of aboriginal origin.[80] At times colonists sought out Indian medicine men, paying them a matchcoat or gallon or two of rum for treatment. Settlers borrowed aboriginal words to describe unfamiliar objects. After colonists arrived at the first permanent English settlement in Virginia, as Strachey's word list discloses, they took over words from the Powhatans such as moccasin, matchcoat, terrapin, opossum, raccoon, chinquapin, chum, hominy, pone, and tomahawk. Apparently because of their earlier visits to Chesapeake Bay in the sixteenth century, Spaniards in Florida and the West Indies added *pemmenaú* to their vocabulary. This was the Powhatan word describing the hemp dogbone plant out of which Indians made thread for clothes and nets.[81] Colonists appropriated part of the Indians' dress, including his moccasins and stockings or leggings, while the buckskin hunting jacket worn by Daniel Boone to some extent had descended from the Indian mantle. Early in the eighteenth century, after Mobile was founded, French soldiers and colonists, partly because they had no choice, began making their clothes out of skins like the Indians.[82]

Frontiersmen copied many aspects of the aboriginal style of fighting, including taking scalps. English colonists adopted this practice soon after Jamestown's founding, continuing the custom in conflicts involving Indians and whites alike. Virginians in 1785 presented scalps to authorities in order to collect the bounty, asserting "they believe the Indians . . . from whom these scalps were taken were enemies"—doubtless a correct assumption.[83] During the French and Indian War George Washington asserted that just one of the French messieurs' scalps was of far more consequence than that of an ordinary enemy warrior and that Virginia's Indian allies who lifted it should be generously rewarded.[84]

Settlers in the colonial period were constantly seeking a satisfactory medium of exchange, turning at times to the Indians. Colonists, primarily in the Chesapeake Bay region, began using tobacco, tobacco certificates, and especially two types of wampum, peake and roanoke, as money. The most valuable, peake (polished shell ends usually strung together), in 1649 was valued by the Virginia assembly—one yard equaled two shillings, sixpence, and one fathom equaled five shillings; if the peake was black its value doubled. Inferior and more common roanoke, customarily used in the Indian trade, was worth only ten pence a yard. Peake, however, served as a medium of exchange throughout the colony.[85] Before long whites began manufacturing large quantities of glass beads, depressing the market in wampum, especially roanoke. With the expansion of the peltry trade, deerskins served the same purpose. In the eighteenth century a buckskin was valued at a dollar (a Spanish piece of eight), and when one asked to borrow a buck he had to make sure it did not have antlers.

It is generally assumed that the typical white dwelling, the log cabin, was of European origin, having been brought to America by the Swedes at their colony on the Delaware River. The possibility of aboriginal origins of the log cabin has been little considered. Natives used logs in their palisades, fortified entrance ways, council houses, private dwellings, and tombs for chiefs, which were subsequently covered over and made into burial mounds. Coastal Indians painted by Le Moyne and John White resided not in log cabins but in houses whose sides were made of wattle and daub, bark, or mats. Even wattle-and-daub structures had a vertical log framework. Mississippians in the interior, however, might have constructed the typical log cabins that are today primarily identified with the colonists; after contact travelers noted that Cherokees lived in notched-log structures, apparently modified from their traditional "summer houses."[86] So much else of the white frontiersman's culture—his food, dress, pipe, tobacco, folk medicine, and sometimes the wattle-and-daub technique—came from the Indians, and perhaps the log cabin did also. Based on such evidence as is available today, a slightly stronger case still can be made that the several hundred Swedes who came to the Delaware were responsible.

Less controversial is that colonists, primarily in the earliest period of settlement, definitely lived in Indian-style houses.Spaniards at sixteenth-century Santa Elena built circular or "D"-shaped wattle-and-daub huts, except for a few features differing little from those of their aboriginal neighbors.

For centuries rectangular or square wooden palisaded forts, usually with corner bastions, a firing platform, and perhaps loopholes, were to be seen on the frontier whether in seventeenth-century Virginia, in Daniel Boone's Kentucky, across the Mississippi at Fort Laramie, or throughout Florida during the Seminole wars. These forts have been popularized by James Fenimore Cooper's novels and innumerable Western movies, and except for being triangular the reconstructed one at Jamestown is of this general type. Our concern is the origin of this frontier institution, and the closer one looks the more obvious it becomes that Indians are as responsible as whites. It was not that Europeans, even after the appearance of gunpowder and cannon, still did not erect wooden forts: When Elizabethans subdued the wild Irish they sometimes built puncheon forts with posts erected at intervals connected by stout boards.

The earliest fort excavated in Virginia—or anywhere else in America permanently colonized by Englishmen—is located at Wolstenholme a few miles below Jamestown and is of this sort. There seems to be little doubt that the nearby triangular Jamestown fort also was of the puncheon type and not, as millions of twentieth-century visitors have been led to believe, made of upright posts joined to one another and firmly planted in the ground. Since the frontiersmen's palisaded forts, except for their regularity, look remarkably like those of fortified Mississippian villages, it seems clear that colonists in America, where trees were abundant and labor to saw them scarce, soon appreciated the advantages of Indian construction and the ability of thick upright logs, side by side, to stop both arrows and musket balls.[87]

The sauna is another institution that may be traced to the Indians. Obese twentieth-century Southerners resort to saunas at health spas built on or near the same sites as hot houses or sweat houses of Mississippian times, and at first glance it appears that modern saunas must be of native origin. But the case is not so clear-cut, and perhaps these saunas originated in Scandinavia and were introduced to the New World before Columbus's voyage. Historically the sauna or water vapor bath has been identified with northwestern Europe and North America, leading to the speculation that in the remote past this institution originated in the New World and then spread to the Old or that as a result of the circumpolar culture area, perhaps it appeared simultaneously in the Old and New Worlds. In any case Native Americans had a good deal to do, if not with the sauna's origin, at least with its subsequent development.[88]

Whites exploited the landscape in much the same way as had the aborigines. They settled on the same rivers and streams, and the colonists' villages, plantations, maize and tobacco fields, roads, and ferries frequently were on native sites. The dugout canoe allowed colonists to move about and transport their foodstuffs and peltry in much the same fashion as had Mississippians.

As has been seen, not all Indians and mestizos resided in the interior or necessarily had that option. Living among the colonists some of them, in time forgetting their language and traditions, merged into the white culture. Their contributions in such areas as food preparation, medicine, folklore, and the education of children cannot be overlooked. Genetically they had considerable impact, far more than is generally realized. After many vicissitudes, more than five hundred Creek survivors congregated in southern Alabama near Atmore, where for decades in the nineteenth and twentieth centuries they lived near whites and Negroes. Each had its own school system, though whites clearly were the dominant group, discriminating against both the Indians and the blacks. In the mid-twentieth century the United States permitted Indian tribes to sue the government and win compensation for lands illegally taken from them or taken without sufficient reimbursement. The Atmore Creeks, the Creek Nation East of the Mississippi, filed suit, thereby requiring all tribal members who expected compensation to enroll. When these Creeks lined up, they discovered to their surprise that their white neighbors did also, clasping their new-found "brothers" by the hand, as they were fully entitled to by ancestry.[89] How many other Indians at one point or another passed unnoticed into white society is unknown, but the numbers are substantial.

Whites and Indians lived side by side, and the culture and

physical characteristics of each were modified, particularly that of the Indians. At the end of the eighteenth century, in a book that had considerable influence, the Frenchman Hector St. John de Crèvecoeur portrayed the American—"this new man"—as something more than a transplanted European; instead he was one who came to the New World, intermarried with colonists of diverse Old World backgrounds, and while tilling the rich soil inevitably acquired virtuous customs and traits.[90] Posterity, like Crèvecoeur, has generally ignored the aboriginal contribution to this "new American."

11
Br'er Rabbit at the Square Ground

In 1920 Carter Woodson, founding editor of the *Journal of Negro History* and a pioneer in promoting the study of black history, observed that "one of the longest unwritten chapters of the history of the United States is that treating of the relations of the Negroes and Indians."[1] His contention remains essentially true today, and the reasons are not difficult to ascertain. Since 1920, especially after World War II, interest in the Afro-American and the Indian heritages has intensified. When Woodson made his observation it was widely assumed that the shock of the Middle Passage and harsh plantation life had caused uprooted African slaves in America to lose their traditional culture; and, whether the aborigines had retained any of their life-style or not, Indians around 1900, like the buffalo, seemed on the verge of extinction. Marcus Garvey's black nationalism and back-to-Africa movement, flourishing in the decade after World War I, and the civil rights campaigns of the 1950s and 1960s made clear that descendants of Africans who had come to America had not become completely acculturated but in diverse ways had retained vestiges of their African background. At the same time in the

248

United States Indian nationalism, associated with a pan-Indian movement, revived, which, if nothing else, reminded the world that Native Americans, as well as the buffalo, were not shrinking but actually growing.

With mounting emphasis on both the African heritage and pan-Indianism, scholars have shown little interest in what effects the two groups, living side by side in the South for centuries, had on one another. Exceptions are studies of Negro slavery among the Indians and Afro-Indian collaboration in maroon communities. They, however, are peripheral to any comprehensive treatment of the relationships between Indians and Africans. Instead, focusing on just one group, studies have been published about those aspects of African culture surviving in Negro music, religion, language, folklore, marriage, and kinship patterns, while modern Southern Indians have attended national conventions of Native Americans, donning war bonnets and performing dances of the Plains Indians, fully aware that their ancestors in the South had never dressed or danced that way. Contemporary Southern Indians, or at least some of them, have readily adopted aspects of the better-known Plains Indians culture as a means of establishing their Indianness, that is, to make the point that Southern Indians are Indians and not Negroes or whites. Because segregationist Jim Crow laws discriminated against blacks, Indians had a special reason to insist they were Native Americans not to be confused with Negroes. As a result, sometimes Indians had their own school system or perhaps, if they were not too dark, attended white ones. Based primarily on color or "race," discrimination against Indians was real. Nevertheless, it was not as oppressive as for Negroes. As one old man with perhaps no more than a trace of Cherokee blood responded: "Tell you the truth . . . we don't know what the hell we is . . . but we know we ain't niggers. We know that!"[2]

Despite the impression one might get from attending a contemporary course in black studies or a national convention of the Congress of American Indians, evidence is overwhelming that over the centuries Africans and Indians did not remain separate but for a long time associated and intermingled, in various ways influencing each other's development. In his old age the venerable former slave Abraham related how when he was young he had watched soldiers in Alabama round up Indians and march them to Oklahoma on their "Trail of Tears." But "Uncle Abe," who stayed behind, himself was part Indian.[3] More dramatic was the experience of Susan, a full-blooded Creek, and her six children, all of whom belonged to Judge Lane in Nashville. A body of displaced Creeks removing to Oklahoma passed by the judge's house and spotted Susan. Realizing she was an Indian, they made signs for her to accompany them. One of her children accepted the offer, and Susan herself was on the verge of joining them. But Judge Lane "pleaded hard with her not to go. He told her the Indians ate raw meat and were often nearly starved." She decided to stay—and thereby remained a "Negro."[4]

Not all Indians were exterminated by disease and warfare or relocated west of the Mississippi, and in part they have remained in the South, surviving through being absorbed by or, more accurately, through helping to create nineteenth-century Negroes like Susan and "Uncle Abe." Frederick Douglass, the runaway slave who became an eloquent abolitionist spokesman before the Civil War, was only one such part-Indian abolitionist whose accounts appeared in the *Liberator*.[5] Alex Haley, author of the twentieth-century *Roots*, which has so stimulated interest in the African background, also has Indian forebears.[6] During the New Deal surviving former slaves were interviewed, and unfortunately more often than not details about their ancestry were neither sought nor volunteered. In those instances where mention was made, the Negroes' forebears were as likely to be Indians as Africans. Some former slaves readily admitted their Indian background; others did not. Because of high cheekbones and a long nose, the South Carolinian Elias Dawkins throughout his life had been accused of being an Indian—but "I ain't no Indian and I does not feel dat way, no sir, not narry bit does I feel like I is a Indian."[7]

In the 1920s the anthropologist Melville Herskovits, who has done so much to illuminate the survivals of Africanisms in the New World, made a random anthropometrical survey of students at Howard University in Washington and of a selected group of Negroes living in Harlem, New York City. Herskovits was surprised to discover that almost one-third of each group displayed physical characteristics of Indian ancestry.[8] There was no reason to be astounded. Although Herskovits did not give the geographical origins of all his subjects, it is logical to assume that they or their ancestors, like so many others, had migrated from the South. Considering the close association and common experiences of Southern Africans and Indians after contact, and the tendency of so many of their mixed-blood progeny in time to become "Negroes," one might wonder why the percentage was not even higher. The historian August Meier in 1947 made a genealogical rather than an anthropometrical survey of Negro college students in the Southern heartland of Mississippi and adjoining states. His results, based on a much larger sample, revealed that approximately 70 percent of the students had Indian ancestors, a figure more than twice as high as Herskovits's.[9]

There was a sharp contrast between the Africans' fate in the Southern United States and in Mexico. Because of severe Indian depopulation during the sixteenth and early seventeenth centuries, more Africans labored in the Valley of Mexico than anywhere else in the New World. The Indian population there in time acquired some immunity to new diseases and began to recover. African slaves stopped being imported in any quantity, and long before formal emancipation in 1827 most of those already in Mexico had died out or had been absorbed by the Indians. As a result relatively few today appreciate the importance of African slave labor in Mexico's colonial history.[10]

In the South, on the other hand, Africans did not even begin arriving in large numbers until the end of the seventeenth century. Virginians in 1679 estimated that Africans accounted for approximately 4 percent of the colony's population.[11] Africans, of course, had come to the New World shortly after 1492, working in the cane fields of the Caribbean sugar islands and on the Latin American mainland. At the end of the seventeenth century they were imported into Virginia and the Carolinas, and by 1730 approximately one-third of the Southerners were Africans. As Herskovits's and Meier's anthropometrical and genealogical studies indicate, Indians in many instances were absorbed by Africans. To phrase it precisely in that fashion is misleading, because in fact a new race had evolved in the South, the American Negro, which was much more than a transplanted African, and the cultural and genetic contribution of Indians partly explains why. If the importance of Africans in Mexico's early development often has been forgotten, the same is true for Indians in the South.

Through no fault of their own, geneticists have not been particularly helpful in determining the extent to which Indians have helped create the American Negro. The reason is that today it is not possible to prick the fingers and draw blood samples from

Timucuans, Stonos, Occaneechees, and other extinct tribes, and it is safe to assume that the genetic composition of those, such as Powhatans and Cherokees, who have survived is not the same as it was at the time of contact. Such genetic studies as have been made are inconclusive and conflicting, suggesting that there are either few or possibly a considerable number of Indian genes in the contemporary Negro. Bentley Glass argues that the American Negro does not have many Indian genes, but his study, as far as the Indians are concerned, is based on the Chippewas, who had little or no contact with the South. Considering the regional differences in blood group frequencies, it is not possible to determine whether his findings or those of his critics are valid.[12]

Before proceeding it is necessary to define more precisely such terms as Negro, mestizo, and mulatto, because confusion about them has helped obscure the Indians. Modern dictionaries characterize the Negro as a member of the Negroid ethnic division of mankind inhabiting the Congo and Sudan regions of Africa or as one of their descendants; a mestizo technically is anyone of mixed blood, though in North America he is generally considered a mixture of white and Indian; and a mulatto is a person having one white and one Negro parent or, loosely, anyone with white and Negro blood. It is possible to continue with similar terms, some of which are especially useful for this study. "Zambo," widely employed in Spanish America, refers to a mixture of Indians and Africans; throughout Latin America, including Brazil, one encounters a bewildering array of similar definitions.

They are serviceable and can be used with some precision in the twentieth century—but not for the colonial era. In earlier centuries many of these terms might have been used as discussed or may have meant something entirely different. Without additional information one can never be sure. The rendering of "Negro" is a case in point. It is no secret that the Negro in the United States is not a pure African. Red-haired Malcolm X considered "this rape-mixed race, which the slavemaster began to call the 'Negro' " a mixture of whites and Africans.[13] But it was not that simple. In 1728 an inventory of the estate of Nathaniel Harrison, a Virginia planter, listed Negroes at the home house, and to our surprise we find that Indian Robin was one such "Negro."[14] Elizabeth Digges's estate, inventoried in 1691, listed Negro slaves divided among several plantations in York County, Virginia. "Kate Indian" was one of her plantation Negroes.[15] *The*

Pennsylvania Journal in 1747 advertised for a runaway, "a very lusty Negro fellow named Sampson," who had an Indian mother, looked like an Indian, talked and dressed like an Indian, as did his son, and presumably was fleeing to Indian relatives in Carolina.[16] Frank Freeman, a former North Carolina slave, recounted how his father, who had Indian blood, "passed for a free nigger."[17] On the eve of the Revolution a fugitive slave notice appeared in the *Virginia Gazette* for Phebe, a remarkable white Indian woman who, dressed like a Negro, had run off with a mulatto.[18] Upon occasion in colonial times one might see references to "a Negro man of the Indian breed" or a "mustee [mestizo] Negro fellow."

At an early period an undetermined number of full-blooded or mixed-blood Indians were characterized as Negroes. The names of Negro slaves occasionally afford a clue as to their ethnic background, yet at times one is left more confused than ever. Except that Indians normally cost less, masters made little distinction between African and Indian slaves. All were indiscriminately thrown together in the quarters, sent out to the fields, and employed as artisans and domestics. Slaves were given Christian names, which, at least in the white man's world, were the only ones Negroes had. A random sampling reveals a predilection for names like Kate, Will, Jenny, Moll, Jack, Robin, Betty, Nanny, Phyllis, and Cupid. Without additional information there is no way to tell whether Jenny and Will were Southern aborigines or unwilling West African immigrants. Another slave name frequently encountered was Prince, and a number of Negroes had been members of a ruling family or clan in the Old or New World. Unless there is an additional clue, such as "the Indian boy Prince" or "Angola Prince," the name by itself discloses little.[19]

Cudjo, Quaco, and Quashees were Negro slave names with a probable African etymology. West Africans often named children after the seven days of the week in either their masculine or feminine forms. Cudjo (Joe) was Monday; Quaco (Jack), Wednesday; Quashees, Sunday; and Mimba, Saturday. This kind of slave name in many instances can be traced to West Africa with some confidence, and they and many other words, expressions, and syntactical constructions, primarily associated with the pidgin Gullah, today figure prominently in the debate over black English.

One has to be careful and not assume that every slave name, if it has any meaning beyond being a common English or classical one, derives from West Africa. March was a Carolina Indian male slave, and we really do not know whether his name had an African or an Indian etymology or a combination thereof. Wally was another Negro name perhaps so common because in Bambara it meant work or act and in Hausa a short walk.[20] It must be remembered, however, that coastal Georgia, that is, the Spanish province of Guale (Wally), for some years had been a prime source of Indian slaves. If the English name Wally has any camouflaged significance, one might do better looking to Spanish Guale rather than to African Nigeria and Mali. A popular American Negro name was Fanny, which can be traced to Europe. It should be kept in mind that "fani" also was the Chickasaw and Choctaw word for squirrel (faní in the Mobilian trade jargon). One also has to be cautious when insisting on the African origins of slave names such as Hagar (Haga, "lazy"), Phoebe (Phibbi, "Friday"), Abby (Abba, "Thursday"), and many others, because Indians also bore these names. In these instances they probably did not have any hidden meaning, and those "Negroes" who were Indians were not trying consciously or subconsciously to perpetuate an African heritage.

Spanish names, including María, Catharina, Whan (Juan), Antonio, and Francisco, appeared among Southern slaves, and without more information it is impossible to tell whether these "Negroes" were Africans or Indians. Considering the role played by Spanish and Portuguese slavers in Africa and by Spaniards in the West Indies and taking into account that so many Florida mission Indians had been captured, the presence of Spanish Christian names was inevitable. In South Carolina a good guess is that more often than not they were Indians, especially, as will be seen, if they were females.

Sometimes Negro slave names fairly clearly indicate Indian ancestry: for example Deer, Buffalo, Mahaw (mayhaw, the hawthorne thriving throughout the South), or Redskin Peter. A geographic or tribal reference is a helpful but not infallible indication of Indian background, as in the instances of Apalatia, Muklasa (an Upper Creek town), Tomassee (a Cherokee town), Saponi, Coloose, Notway, Ocala, Hous Pau (Huspaw, a Yamasee town), Altamaha, Sewee Joe, María Yamasee, and Tuscarora Betty. Other geographic names, for example Angola Phyllis, serve to identify Africans. Geographic references are not as helpful in all instances as one might think. To our surprise it turns out that a seventeenth-century Virginian, Jack of Morocco, was not an African but an Indian, and equally confusing is that Black Jack, Bearded Jack, and Mr. Bones also were Virginia Indians.[21] We must leave this inquiry into Negro names, keeping in mind that many, far beyond the obvious ones like Fuskey, Ocala, Apalatia, and Tuscarora Betty, belonged to Indians rather than Africans.

Confusion over definition of the term "Negro" has its origins in the peculiar way slavery developed in the New World, especially in the South. As an institution slavery dated back to the earliest times; the only unique feature about slavery in the Western Hemisphere was its racial aspects. In ancient Greece or Rome a slave might have been white or black, an unfortunate who for whatever reason had lost his or her freedom. In the New World "slave" eventually became synonymous with "black," "African," "Negro," or "nigger," and the initial West Indian experience had much to do with this. Spaniards who had come to the islands first had relied on Indian labor through the institutions of slavery and *repartimiento*. Indians, however, had not made particularly good workers because they died off so rapidly. Infusions of natives into the islands from *la Florida* and elsewhere on the mainland did not greatly improve matters. At an early period African slaves were brought to the West Indies and permanently replaced the Indians. Sugar islands, such as Barbados, Jamaica, and Saint Domingue, developed by Britain and France in the seventeenth and eighteenth centuries, had ratios of ten or fifteen black slaves to one white, and without thinking planters began to use terms "black," "Negro," and "slave" interchangeably.

In a general way the experience of the mainland South duplicated that of the West Indies, and Southern planters, some of whom, like the Goose Creek men, had migrated from Barbados, inevitably employed the islands' phraseology. The difference between the West Indies and the South was that in the islands virtually all Indians disappeared, whereas in the South a significant minority survived. This has caused all the confusion for posterity, though there was far less at the time. In 1698 it did not seem strange, when North Carolina magistrates set up a hue and cry to apprehend three fugitive Negroes who had broken into their master's house, that two of the culprits were Africans and the other an Indian.[22]

Misconceptions also abound about the term "mulatto." In

modern times mulattos are generally regarded as a combination of whites and Africans, and in the United States the tendency has been to equate mulatto with black, ignoring the racial mixing that has occurred. Strictly speaking "mulatto" derives from "mule," a hybrid between a horse and an ass. When the term was used during the colonial period and applied to humans it still meant hybrid, a mixture, without any particular reference to components. A 1705 Virginia statute limited this more by defining a mulatto as the offspring of whites and nonwhites, that is, the child of an Indian and a white or the child, grandchild, or great-grandchild of a Negro and a white.[23] Sometimes in the early years when a mulatto was mentioned, part of the ancestry was disclosed when reference was made to an "Indian mulatto" or to a mulatto of the "Indian breed." A South Carolina missionary in 1715 baptized a mulatto girl whose mother he reported as an Indian and father as a white trader.[24] At other times it was obvious that mulatto meant a Negro–white or Negro–Indian mixture.

No less ambiguity exists about the term "mestizo," technically, like mulatto, denoting hybrid. In the twentieth century, especially in Latin America, a mestizo has come to be known as the offspring of an Indian and a white. In earlier centuries "mestizo," or "mustee," merely signified mixture, perhaps Indian and white, Indian and African, or African and white. Saunders, a runaway slave in 1759, was described by authorities as "a Carolina born Negro man . . . of the mustee breed." In this instance one might surmise that Saunders had Indian and African parents, that he was a zambo.[25] Priss, an inhabitant of Virginia's Eastern Shore, was characterized as being a "molatta or mustee," whatever that meant.[26]

A closer look at misunderstandings over the definition of these words indicates how much of a melting pot the South was. It is misleading to use "slave" or "Negro" as a synonym for a transplanted African, because both culturally and genetically the Southern Negro was a product of Africans, whites, and Indians. From a cultural standpoint, without question transplanted Europeans have made the greatest contributions, and an increasing number of scholars are demonstrating that Africans did not lose all their heritage as a result of the Middle Passage. When interviewed in Raleigh in the 1930s, the elderly former Negro slave Martha Allen, discussing her life, replied: "I am part Injun, part

white, an' part nigger. . . . I reckon dat we is what yo'call a general mixture."[27] It is to the "part Injun" aspect of the modern
Negro that we must turn.

Contact between Africans and Indians in the New World
began early, possibly predating Columbus's voyage by centuries. Large Indian stone heads discovered in Meso-America displaying pronounced Negroid characteristics, presumably carved
several centuries before Columbus's voyage, lend support to
such a theory—but for now we must include it along with the
legendary voyages of the Irish hero Saint Brendan and the op-
pressed Welsh Prince Madoc or rumors of the lost continent of
Atlantis.[28] After 1492 better documentation, although skimpy,
describes the Africans' arrival in the South. Slave or free, blacks
accompanied Narváez's, Ayllón's, De Soto's, and Luna's expeditions, and Africans helped the *adelantado* Menéndez establish
permanent settlements in *la Florida*. The appearance of Africans
at an early period played a devastating role in unleashing pandemics throughout the South.

More Africans arrived after England began establishing colonies, but the seventeenth-century total for the entire South was
not large. Importations accelerated at the end of that century as
large numbers of slaves came to Virginia, Maryland, and South
Carolina. For most of the eighteenth century the ratio of Africans
to whites in Virginia was one to two, while in South Carolina
Africans constituted an absolute majority. On Carolina rice and
indigo plantations they outnumbered whites many times, in
some sections of the Low Country as much as ten to one. The
problem with these statistics (based on the number of slaves or
Negroes in a colony or particular region) is that one is never sure
how many Indians were being counted. As chattel slaves, freemen, and tributaries, Indians were present in some numbers,
living intimately among or in close proximity to Africans and
whites.

The best place to look for the mingling of Africans and Indians
is on plantations and in slave quarters, although after the passage
of so many years this is not easy. During the colonial era slavery
in America had much in common with that institution as it had
existed in the classical Greco-Roman world, and one's color was
secondary. Whites seldom served as slaves anywhere in the
Western Hemisphere, but sometimes the distinction between indentured service, in which the term of servitude at times was

repeatedly extended, and outright slavery was blurred. The status of the white convicts arriving in Chesapeake Bay in increasing numbers, whose terms might be up to fourteen years or even life, did not differ greatly from that of chattel slaves. In America a slave was a slave regardless of whether he was an African or an Indian, and some whites were almost slaves. All were marketed and employed with little distinction.

The two groups of nonwhites lived together in slave quarters, usually at the insistence of masters anxious to keep their chattels reasonably content. As we have seen, a sexual imbalance existed in both the African and the Indian slave trade. Because of the demand, the typical imported African was a male, a prime field hand. Overall approximately two-thirds of Africans arriving anywhere in the Western Hemisphere were male, and only one-third were female. The typical Indian slave who remained in the South was a female, either an adult or a child. Indian males often had been killed in fighting or, after capture, shipped off to the West Indies. This situation, not planned but evolving out of peculiarities of the Indian and African slave trade, almost mandated that the two races would intermingle as they worked on plantations, produced naval stores, cut timber, and tended livestock. A pamphlet written by John Norris, an early-eighteenth-century Carolina promoter, advised impoverished Englishmen and men of substance how, with little difficulty, they could migrate to Carolina and prosper in the Low Country. Those of modest means merely required one African male slave and one Indian female slave on a 150-acre tract. The more affluent on larger estates needed thirty field workers, fifteen African men and an equal number of Indian women. All colonists must prosper, Norris insisted, from exploiting the land and from the natural increase of their cattle and slaves.[29]

Norris only suggested what should be done, but from surviving court and plantation records, wills, and inventories it is apparent that many slave owners followed his recommendations. Shortly before his death in the Yamasee revolt, the planter–Indian trader John Wright mortgaged his slaves, who included fifteen African men, thirteen Indian women, and four African females.[30] In settling her husband's estate, the Carolinian Ann Rowsham testified that at the time of his death early in the eighteenth century her husband owned seven slaves: the Africans Harry and Titus, an African woman and her two children, and the Indian Peggy and her child.[31] We can only presume that Titus and Harry each had a slave wife, one an African, the other an Indian, and that Peggy's child was a zambo. Of course we really do not know who the husband of Indian Peggy was, but much later the Indian (mestizo) Uncle Moble Hopsan, a former slave interviewed in Virginia, related: "et come time tuh marry," and only a black was available. "Dat make me black, ah' 'spose."[32] In all likelihood Peggy confronted the same kind of choice when looking for a spouse.

Regardless of the partners' ethnic backgrounds, only in rare instances did the clergy sanction slave marriages. Because of planters' fears that conversion to Christianity would lead to emancipation or insurrection, Le Jau and his fellow SPG missionaries could do little more than remonstrate against the "promiscuous cohabiting of slaves of different sexes and nations together; when a man or woman's fancy does alter about his party they throw up one another and take others which they also change when they please."[33] Perhaps Peggy would not have objected to a series of partners and children by various fathers, but for them to be cut off from her clan was another matter.

Afro-Indian unions were not confined to plantations, and an emerging zambo population was to be found on reservations of tributary Indians and living among colonists as freemen. On the eve of the Revolution a Virginia planter advertised for the return of Negro Frank, who once again had run away and presumably was skulking about the Pamunkey Indian reservation, where he had gotten himself an Indian wife. The "Negro" Frank was characterized as having a "yellow complexion," raising suspicion that this Negro was a zambo. In any case, whatever children his Indian wife had would have been.[34] Ben was a thirty-year-old Negro carpenter and shoemaker in western Virginia who once had run away and passed himself off as a freeman. In 1776 Ben made another attempt. At the same time his Indian wife, living on a plantation in a nearby county, suddenly disappeared, presumably to join him. This second time Ben may have been successful in setting himself up as a freeman, and he and his wife may have raised free zambo progeny.[35]

Regardless of where mixed unions occurred, chances are that during the colonial period the husband was an African and the wife an Indian. Male slaves frequently outnumbered females on plantations, and the odds are that an African rather than an Indian male would have more success in competing for the affections of the few available African women. Indian women, if they were to have any partner, frequently had little or no choice but to pick an African. After slave importations from Africa were outlawed in the nineteenth century and Indian slave raiding in the South had become relatively insignificant, the percentages of Africans and Indians in the South who were male changed: The percentage of male Africans decreased, while the percentage of male Indians increased. As a result the sexual composition of Afro-Indian unions changed, and before the Civil War one finds more Indian husbands.

Osceola's spouse, or at least one of them, in all probability was a Negro. Whether his wife was a pure African is unknown. Rather than being a full-blooded Indian, Osceola in all likelihood had a white father, and a physical anthropologist who in the twentieth century exhumed and examined his bones, especially the femora, speculates that Osceola himself had African forebears.[36] Modern Negroes are doubtless correct in claiming direct descent from the great Seminole warrior. Symbol of the noble savage and, because of his seizure under a flag of truce, of the white man's mistreatment of the Indian, Osceola in all probability was in fact not a pure Indian but biologically and culturally a mixture of the three major races present in the South. In addition to former Negro slaves, Seminoles in Florida, Creeks in the South and Oklahoma, and Southern whites can—as in most if not every instance they have—claim kinship with the renowned Seminole warrior.

Other pure-blooded Indians or those like Osceola who considered themselves Indians, took African wives. Born near Tuscaloosa, Alabama, the freed Negro slave Anna Baker related in the 1930s that her grandfather was a pure Indian and her grandmother a full-blooded African. Her grandfather had come to an Alabama plantation and had met and fallen in love with her grandmother. The plantation owner, according to Anna Baker, told the stricken Indian: "If you want to stay wid her I'll give you a home if you'll work for me lak de Niggers do . . . ' he 'greed, 'cause he thought a heap o' his Black Woman."[37]

At times Indians owned African slaves and vice versa. The 1725 census in St. George Parish, South Carolina, discloses that the Indian Nero possessed one Negro slave, and the Indian Sam Pickins owned six. In turn the Negro Robin Johnson in the same parish owned nine slaves, all of whom apparently were

Indians.[38] On white plantations worked by Africans a mulatto progeny commonly emerged, and when Africans and Indians owned one another a zambo offspring was likely.

By the end of the eighteenth century African slavery among the Indians had so developed that it is possible to look more closely at this phenomenon. Alexander McGillivray, a mestizo Upper Creek, died in 1793, leaving a considerable estate including sixty Negro slaves.[39] His mestizo contemporaries, such as the Cherokee James Vann and the Creek William Weatherford (Red Eagle), Andrew Jackson's adversary in 1814, also were large slaveowners, and one might find their counterparts among any of the major Southern tribes.

There are two schools of thought as to how Negro slaves fared at the hands of Indian masters. One is that this peculiar institution was more benign and had less racial prejudice in the Indian country than among whites; the other is that Indian slaveowners were every bit as harsh as whites if not more so. At the time of the Civil War a number of the Southern Indians who had been removed to Oklahoma were slaveowners and fought for the Confederacy. Negro slavery among the Cherokees has probably been studied most of all, and it is argued that both before and after removal, as the Cherokees became increasingly acculturated, they adopted white attitudes toward Negroes, "that slavery in the Cherokee Nation was a microcosm of the 'peculiar institution' existing in the southern United States." These sentiments, so apparent in Oklahoma, it is contended, originated in the Carolinas and Georgia before removal.[40] A different picture emerges when one turns to Negro slaves among the Seminoles in the early nineteenth century. As slaves or freemen, blacks lived in close contact with Seminoles, perhaps residing in Indian villages or in their own autonomous settlements. There seemed to be an easy intercourse, a ready acceptance of Negroes by the Indians, little racial antagonism, and, as in the apparent case of Osceola, intermarriage between the two groups. Except for high cheekbones, it would not be apparent that some of the Seminoles who eventually sought refuge in the Bahamas were not Africans.[41] The story of Negro slavery among Indians throughout the South remains to be told. One suspects that the differing Seminole and Cherokee experiences represented extremes, and that the norm lay somewhere in between, probably closer to that of the Seminoles.

Innumerable details concerning relations between Africans

and Indians in the South remain obscure, in many instances unavoidably so. But one development is clear: Culturally and biologically Native Americans helped to form the modern Negro. When considering the heritage of the American Negro, the Afro-American, the tendency has been to assume that whenever Negro speech, religion, and cultural patterns differed from those of whites, the origins of such distinctions must be found in Africa. There is no denying the logic and in many instances the validity of such explanations. Herskovits and his disciples and the messianic orator Marcus Garvey, who in the twentieth century advocated black nationalism and a back-to-Africa campaign, have pointed this out. Their arguments make sense especially when considering the West Indies. Much of Herskovits's research applied to the islands, and Garvey, though frequently preaching and campaigning in the United States, in fact was a Jamaican.

The problem is that the Negroes' West Indian experience in many respects differed from that of the South. Only 5 percent or so of the Africans transported to the New World came to the Southern mainland; the proportion arriving in the West Indies was many times higher. With minor exceptions Indians in the islands became extinct quickly, whereas in the South, though their numbers shrank, thousands persevered. When Africans began reaching the West Indies in large numbers they frequently were established in almost autonomous villages, and because of sheer numbers and the relative permanence and stability of village life, they retained more of their African ways.[42] In the South, Africans were not as numerous, more often came into intimate contact with whites and Indians, and were likely to be moved about and not live in permanent settlements where African traits might more easily survive.

All of this means that when one considers the background of the contemporary Negro one must look not only at whites and Africans but also at the Indians. This becomes apparent when examining the Southern Negroes' material culture. Splint, and to a lesser extent coiled, baskets were common among Mississippian Indians and were made, used, and sold by antebellum Negroes in the cotton belt. A former Alabama Negro slave, Nathan Beauchamp, recounted how his father, a black, when driving his wagon into Eufala for supplies, spotted Mimi alongside the road selling a load of baskets. Nathan fell in love with and soon mar-

ried pretty Mimi, an Indian with long, straight black hair.
Throughout her marriage and up until her death five years after
emancipation, Mimi, who came to be regarded as a Negro, continued to make and sell her baskets.[43] Whether Mimi passed on
her skills to the next generation of Negroes is unknown, but
countless other Mimis at one time or another did. The historian
Eugene Genovese has pointed out that every black man in South
Carolina made a canoe by burning and scraping, implying this
was an African survival.[44] Many of the Southern Negroes in fact
were Indians or zambos. Documentary and archaeological evidence makes it clear that Indians, some of whom came to be
regarded as Negroes, continued to make dugout canoes as always.

Historians have devoted considerable attention to the origins
and development of rice culture in the Southern Tidewater. One
school of thought, the traditional one, is that white planters first
imported rice, realized its potential, and then brought in large
numbers of African slaves to raise it commercially.[45] The other
view is that, accustomed to growing rice in their African homeland, slaves introduced its culture to the Carolina Low Country.[46]
It is also contended that Africans not only brought over their
knowledge of rice culture but also wooden mortars and pestles to
mill the grain. Lost or ignored in this line of reasoning is the fact
that soon after the introduction of maize culture into the South,
Indians had regularly used wooden mortars and pestles, and
wild rice, though procured in a different fashion, had played a
peripheral role in their diet. Regardless of who introduced intensive rice culture into the Carolina Low Country, because of the
Goose Creek men large numbers of Indian slaves at once were on
hand to help cultivate it. Without further artifactual evidence it
is not possible to establish definitively the provenance of the
mortar and pestle. Since they were already at hand when blacks
arrived, for the time being it makes as much, if not more, sense
to look at Mississippian rather than at West African villages. In
this instance, as in many others, we of course cannot rule out the
possibility of independent invention or parallel development.

With a heightened interest in the African background,
twentieth-century archaeologists have searched for locations of
slave quarters, excavating them in hopes of unearthing artifacts
that demonstrate survivals of African culture. Among the objects
excavated or mentioned in contemporary travel accounts, plan-

tation records, and oral traditions are such items as beads, gourds, pottery, conch shells, and pipes. Some of these objects such as the colono-Indian pottery and certain clay pipes, clearly are of Indian origin. Gourds, shell beads, and conch shell horns frequently are cited as African survivals, and to be sure gourds and large shells were used for ceremonial and utilitarian purposes in West Africa. But it must be remembered that Mississippians cultivated gourds for use in their dances and rituals. In the antebellum period a blast on a conch shell summoned Negros from the fields or announced the arrival of the abolitionist Fanny Kemble to St. Simons Island, its sound reverberating over the same landscape where earlier such a blast had called Indians to the busk.[47]

A blue hexagonal European-made bead was excavated at a slave cabin on Cumberland Island, one of Georgia's Golden Islands. Archaeologists have surmised that it was bartered in Africa and later imported into Georgia by a slave.[48] Perhaps so, yet other archaeologists, carefully sifting dirt from Indian graves in Apalachee, have uncovered just one man-made artifact, a bead, one per grave.[49] For whatever reason, Apalachee Indians apparently wore or at least were buried with only one bead. These Indians were the ones carried off by James Moore and the Goose Creek men, and some of them were relocated not far from Cumberland Island. This also has to be considered when trying to explain why no more than one bead was found in a slave cabin on the Georgia coast.

After Africans arrived in the South in many instances they began to live, or at least to eat, like Indians. Much of contemporary Negro soul food can be traced to Native Americans. Maize was consumed by Negros as grits, cornbread, hoe cake (Johnny cake), ash cake, hush puppies, soup (sofkee), and in a variety of other forms. Africans did not necessarily adopt the Indian diet overnight. Accustomed to rice and similar fare, when he first arrived in Georgia the Gambian-born slave Johnson protested that he simply "could not eat corn-meal."[50] Poke and other greens were of Indian origin, but okra came from Africa. Long wooden bread trays, mortars, and cooking paddles found in Negro cabins bore a remarkable resemblance to those described by De Soto and John Smith.[51] Negro slaves in the Old South gathered the same nuts, berries, and bark as had Mississippians in order to make red, blue, and green dyes.

A great deal of Negro folk medicine was of Indian origin. A former South Carolina slave, Martha Richardson, described how her Indian father had showed fellow slaves the proper way to make medicine.[52] Dogwood, elm, and wild cherry bark; rattle-snake and castor (beaver) decoctions; and sumac, sassafras, pennyroyal, and ginseng were routinely administered in slave cabins, usually by Negroes but sometimes by whites. Negroes became convinced that the "gin root," best known today as an aphrodisiac, would make someone fall in love with the user. Colonel Landon Carter, the wealthy, hard-working Virginia planter, personally went down to his slave quarters and supervised administration of castor and rattlesnake potions, ginseng, and dogwood bark.[53] None of this would have seemed unusual to the Powhatans, who at an earlier period had been lords of the Tidewater. Negroes roamed the fields and forests not only for medicines but also for substances to poison fish, to do away with their masters, or even to commit suicide, and in these endeavors the Indian contribution also was considerable.

In time most Southern Negroes adopted, at least in a modified form, the white man's religion, and as the eighteenth century wore on it became obvious that evangelical sects had won more converts than the staid Anglicans. Emphasizing an emotional approach and employing a clergy that frequently had little formal training, the Baptists especially made inroads among Negroes. Those who stress the persistence of African culture among American Negroes contend that the unstructured evangelical approach allowed—or masked—survival of West African religious features such as the shout, call, and response at praise meetings, emphasis on water and the River Jordan symbolizing the Middle Passage, burial practices, the conversion experience or "possession," incantational preaching, and hymns. Many of these points are well taken.[54]

But the career of Henry Francis exemplifies the complexities and pitfalls of this type of approach, because Francis was a mestizo, having an Indian father and a white mother, one of a number of mestizos to be found at the trading post and commercial center of Augusta. Among the very earliest Southern "Negro" Baptist ministers, this mestizo, neither of whose parents was African, had been a slave in Augusta, Georgia, during his youth and in time had been manumitted. When he preached to his congregation, Francis's references to the Jordan may have evoked memories of capture in Africa and the Atlantic passage, and some members of the congregation may have yearned to return to their African homeland. For Francis and "Negroes" like him, references to the Jordan are not likely to have elicited such sentiments. When alluding to the Jordan, baptism, and water, Francis and other mestizos with his background may have drawn on memories of Mississippian hot houses and the regenerative and therapeutic effects of plunges in clear streams, or possibly no more than the nearly universal notion of water as a cleanser and purifier. Presumably one could have heard the shout, call, and response while Francis preached, and perhaps the African influence was responsible. Yet, as Francis may have realized, they all bore a remarkable resemblence to Indian "shouts." Southern Negroes have long been identified with conjurors, charms, and voodoo, some aspects of which unquestionably can be traced to Africa. Indians also had conjurors and charms and believed in witches, and one wonders how much Francis's Indian father told his son about them.[55]

It has been alleged, perhaps rightly, that pottery fragments scattered over the top of nineteenth- and twentieth-century Negro burials are another manifestation of surviving Africanisms. Indians also sometimes placed pottery atop their graves and made holes in pots and broke clay effigies to let the soul escape or to signify a broken spirit. Whether placed deliberately or by accident above ground or consciously below with the corpse, for millennia pottery sherds had been identified with Indian burials, and in this respect pottery fragments had as much significance for Indians as for Africans, perhaps more.[56]

An enormous amount has been written about Southern Negro folklore, much of it symbolized by Joel Chandler Harris's Uncle Remus. Sitting in his cabin and puffing on his corn cob pipe, periodically stirring up embers in the dying fire, Uncle Remus relates to the master's attentive son marvelous stories of Br'er Rabbit, the Tar Baby, Br'er Fox, and their animal friends. When monkeys, gorillas, and elephants are mentioned, one can assume an African origin. The tiger might have been of the well-known yellow-striped African variety or the North American panther. Br'er Rabbit, of course, is the central character, the protagonist who outwits Br'er Fox and Br'er Bear and then hops off gleefully to the briar patch. In all likelihood Br'er Rabbit had made no Middle Passage and instead was on hand to greet African slaves when they arrived in the South. Taking many forms, a trickster can be found in most cultures. Among the Indians at the time of contact, primarily those east of the Mississippi from Hudson Bay to the Gulf of Mexico, some of whom never saw an African until modern times, he was a rabbit, and accounts of how he tricked his adversaries appear in their folklore. One can find the rabbit in the East African–Mediterranean folklore and the African trickster, the spider, in Mississippian culture. Nevertheless, the evidence strongly identifies Br'er Rabbit with the Mississippians and the spider (*anansi* or Nancy tales) with Africa.[57]

Like Br'er Rabbit, myths surrounding the significance of an owl's hooting did not have to make an Atlantic passage. The former Georgia slave Emmaline Kilpatrick described how, if a screech owl hollered in the night, "pappy ud hop right out er his bed and stick de fire shovel in de coals . . . an' look over 'is lef' shoulder . . . den maybe no nigger gwine die dat week."[58] The hooting of an owl as a harbinger of death was deeply rooted in Indian folklore throughout North and South America. Another Negro superstitition is that to ensure a bountiful crop the planting must be done by a full moon. This tradition can be traced to Africa and to Europe—and also to Indians, who understood a great deal about astronomy, reckoned their months by moons, and, like other peoples, regarded that body as a fertility symbol. Among contemporary Negroes there is the saying, "Mr. Bear has got me," signifying that it is hot and they have been out in the sun too long. This expression probably derives from the Indians, who in their folk tales venerated the bear, identifying him with the sun, fire, and master of breath. Twentieth-century distance runners—Negro, Indian, or white—when they tire also are likely to blame the bear.[59] Only a cursory examination of Indian oral history and legends makes it clear that Br'er Rabbit, the owl's hooting as a portent of death, planting by the moon, Mr. Bear, and much more of the Negro folklore is similar to, if not identical with, that of the Indians. Uncle Remus's pipe and the tobacco he put in it unquestionably were of Indian origin, as was possibly Uncle Remus himself, in part at least.

Intercourse between Africans and Indians was two-sided, and if the modern Negro is indebted to Indians, the reverse is also true. There is hardly any other way to explain how monkeys, gorillas, and elephants appeared in stories related in native villages after contact. Early in the nineteenth century Creek prophets or medicine men contended they had supernatural powers to protect warriors from Andrew Jackson's bullets. Drawing on their African background, similar leaders in Haiti also had maintained that by waving an ox tail and interceding with proper spirits, they could shield warriors from buckra's bullets.[60] Pure and mixed-blood Africans lived among nineteenth-century Creeks, and one must wonder where Indian prophets got the notion they could ward off the bullets of Jackson's frontiersmen —perhaps from Africa, yet it should be kept in mind that the important Powhatan leader, Jack of the Feathers, killed just before the 1622 massacre, contended he had the power to protect natives from European bullets.[61] There is also the possibility that each of these examples reflects a common, independently arrived at magical or supernatural response by "primitive" societies to the jarring intrusions of European culture.

For the most part Southern Indians and Africans forgot their native languages and adopted English, but the process took time, usually generations, and in some instances was never completed. Ann Matthews, a former Tennessee slave, confided to her interviewer: "Mah daddy wuz part Indian en couldn't talk plain."[62] Just before the Revolution an African slave arrived at British Pensacola and soon escaped to the Indian country. Advertising for return of the fugitive, his master characterized the runaway as speaking African and Indian but not English.[63] Intercourse between Africans and Indians, which began before De Soto's time and continued long after the African slave escaped from Pensacola, had many consequences, some of which occasionally surface. Linguists have assembled and studied fragments of the Nanticoke language. Long before the twentieth century these Indians, Algonquians from the Eastern Shore of Chesapeake Bay, had become almost extinct. While analyzing Nanticoke numerals, linguists were surprised to discover that in fact they were not Indian but Mandingo or a closely related language straight from West Africa.[64] This same kind of African influence appears among Yamasees. In talking with SPG missionaries early in the eighteenth century, these Indians described how many "pickaninnies" they had and disclosed to inquiring "backararas" other aspects of Indian life.[65] "Pickaninny," a corruption of the Spanish *pequeño niño* (or its Portuguese equivalent), and "buckra," the Ibibio (Southern Nigeria) for white man, were words commonly used by African slave traders, and African slaves introduced these and similar terms to Yamasees in the Carolina–Georgia Low Country.

This raises a larger question: In what ways did Indians help develop pidgin languages; such as Gullah and Geechee, associated with Negro slaves in coastal South Carolina and Georgia? White slave traders speaking English, Spanish, French and a variety of other European languages; Africans of diverse backgrounds; and Indians of different linguistic groups all were thrown together and had to communicate with each other on plantations in the Southern Tidewater. For that purpose pidgin languages emerged. Such words as "pickaninny" can be traced to European trade contacts in Africa; others, including "toad," "saucy," and "shindig," originated in Africa itself; and aspects of Gullah syntax and inflection also bear a close similarity to West African dialects. Considering the extensive slave trade of the Goose Creek men and the numerous Indian slaves in the Low Country, it is logical to assume that Native Americans also contributed to the development of Gullah and Geechee. At this point we can only raise the question and wonder whether further surprises, such as Mandingo numerals among the Nanticokes, are in store.

Most details of how Africans communicated with Indians are not now and perhaps never will be known. It is clear that from a linguistic standpoint the colonial South had much in common with the Tower of Babel and that as a result both whites and Indians relied heavily on Negro interpreters. Unfortunately surviving evidence reveals little about such interpreters other than that in the eighteenth century the Negro Timboe was an accomplished "linguist" in the Creek Trade;[66] that a runaway Negro served as an interpreter at Coweta,[67] a principal Lower Creek town on the Chattahoochee River; that in the early nineteenth century Negroes had to translate white missionaries' sermons into Cherokee;[68] and that in the same century the Negro Abraham played an important role in negotiations between Seminoles and the United States.[69] Very little else is known about Abraham, Timboe, and similar "Negro" interpreters. One suspects that more often than not they were mestizos, mulattos, or zambos rather than pure Africans. It is not difficult to imagine a zambo, for example, learning an Indian language from his mother and a West African dialect from his father, and in time being forced to learn English in order to communicate with whites. Whatever their ethnic background, Negro linguists were among the most versatile in the South.

Music and dancing had played an important role in Mississippian rituals and amusements. Although the powerful chiefdoms were shattered and in time many of the survivors were removed to Oklahoma, vestiges of native songs and dances still could be heard throughout the South, sometimes among Cherokee, Choctaw, and Seminole remnants, who retained something of their tribal identity and culture, and also among Negro slaves on plantations in the cotton belt of the Old South. Many songs and dances performed in the quarters were of African or European origins. But not all were. After a day's labor in the fields Negroes sometimes danced the pigeon wing by circling, waving their arms like a hawk predator, and clicking their heels together in the air and on the ground, which in an earlier time might have been seen performed, perhaps in a more sedate fashion, in Mississippian square rounds. An even better example of the Indian influence was when Negroes danced the Green Corn dance, though there is little indication that the busk or Green Corn ritual itself had much meaning for nineteenth-century slaves.[70] If one can argue that certain Negro dances were of Indian origin, the reverse is also true. Take the stomp dance so often performed at gatherings of twentieth-century Native Americans. Authorities are still debating whether it was Africans who at an earlier date introduced this into aboriginal American villages.

Negro songs and dances were accompanied by drums, banjos, and jew's-harps. Sometimes characterized as America's only truly national musical instrument, the banjo was popularized by nineteenth-century minstrels, and authorities generally agree that the banjo reached the stage via Southern Negro slave quarters. How the banjo got out of the quarters is not as difficult to guess as how it got in. An earlier version of this instrument was made out of strings and a skin-covered gourd whose origins have been traced, probably rightly so, to the West Indies and Africa. Yet in this instance as in so many others the fundamental perplexing question of cultural diffusion versus parallel independent invention arises. As has been mentioned, Natchez Indians in the eighteenth century were using a banjo-like instrument, raising suspicions that not only does the *banga* belong to West Africa but also in a literal sense it may be proper to refer to the banjo as "American."[71] The jew's-harp was European, but whether it reached the Negro slave quarters directly or indirectly via Indians is uncertain. Africans and Mississippians used a variety of drums, and it is not surprising that their beat, alternately pleasing and terrifying to white listeners, was heard on antebellum plantations. We can be reasonably sure that some drums were made in the West African fashion, but unfortunately few are available on which to base a judgment. One drum has survived among Mississippi Choctaws who escaped removal. It was made out of a section of a black gum tree and an untanned goat's skin. This specimen closely resembles an earlier Algonquian drum that has been preserved in the British Museum and also drums currently in use on the West African coast.[72] One suspects that similar confusion exists concerning Negro drums used on Old South plantations.

Most Africans had been brought up in a patrilineal society. Something that has interested and at times confused scholars is that slaves arriving in the South frequently forgot ths aspect of their heritage and became matrilineal. Many facts help to explain this. A minority of the slaves, including some of those coming from West Africa, had been reared in a matrilineal culture, and the instability of the slave family in America enhanced the role of the mother, who was more likely to "stay at home." In time the white man's law decreed that the child must follow the status of the mother, regardless of her racial background. But the most obvious and probably the most likely reason is the fact that so many Negroes were not Africans but Indians. A matrilineal society was the norm among Mississippians, and it is probable that matrilinealism arrived among Southern Negroes in the same fashion as did Br'er Rabbit, grits, ginseng tea, forebodings associated with an owl's hooting, and the Green Corn dance.

After appreciable numbers of African slaves arrived in the South, whites became alarmed about so many Indians and Africans living in their midst. In eighteenth-century South Carolina Africans themselves outnumbered whites, and with the addition of thousands of local Indians colonists became even more of a minority. Throughout the New World masters had reason to dread that the nonwhite populace might rise and slit their owner's throats, and sometimes, particularly in the West Indies, such fears were confirmed. The vast majority of West Indian slaves were of African origin. Planters were on guard to prevent blacks from running off to inaccessible areas and forming autonomous maroon settlements, and they tried to prohibit slaves working on sugar plantations from having any contact with intractable maroons. Southern planters knew enough about the maroon wars in the Caribbean and South America to be concerned, but, whereas in the West Indies the danger was primarily African, on the mainland it was both African and Indian.

Colonists tended to regard Africans and Indians each as a separate people, and whites made a concerted effort to play off one group against the other. They realized that if the two were pitted against one another, if their differences were inflamed, and if they were kept apart, a weakness might be turned to good advantage. Provincial statutes prohibited Africans from going into the Indian country under any pretext. Packhorsemen, burdeners, interpreters, and village factors had to be whites, Indians, or mestizos lest, far from white courts and the watchful eyes of their masters, Africans in the interior might acquire an unhealthy sense of independence, make common cause with the Indians, and encourage slaves to escape from coastal plantations and found maroon communities. Indians were hired and rewarded for hunting down African slaves and for putting down slave revolts, especially the 1739–40 Stono uprising in Carolina. Treaties with sovereign Indian nations stipulated that Indians must apprehend fugitive Negroes. Magistrates reimbursed Indians for the scalps of African runaways or escaped felons, though to prevent fraud authorities sometimes insisted that both black ears be attached.[73] Partly to play up differences between the two races, Carolinians in 1698 provided for a swift trial and summary justice for any African who killed an Indian, and on occasion Indians were invited to witness the execution of the death sentence or mutiliation.[74] Carolinians relocated tributary Winyaws in nearby cattle ranches and rice plantations to intimidate African slaves and keep them from running away.[75] At times whip-wielding Indian or zambo drivers proved effective in working gangs of African slaves.

Attempts to foster racial animosity had some effect in keeping Africans in line, but the many statutes and newspaper accounts advocating such a policy obscure the fact that it failed as often as it succeeded and that Africans and Indians intermingled, learned each others' languages, intermarried, and at times made common cause against whites. Colonial laws prohibiting Africans from participating in most aspects of the Indian trade and forbidding them to venture among the Indians were evaded. The Carolina trader John Vann had three Africans and one mulatto living with him on the Cherokee frontier, while George Galphin near Augusta on the Georgia frontier regularly employed Africans in his extensive dealings. An enterprising and virile trader, during his career Galphin had assorted African, Indian, and white wives or partners. Of the nine children mentioned in his will, three were mulattos, four mestizos, and two white.[76] From time to time there were reports of African traders or "black factors" operating on their own among the Indians, and in 1752 Charleston magistrates became alarmed because an African was being outfitted under their noses to trade with Catawbas.[77] In so many of these instances one must question whether these "Africans" were in fact not zambos, mulattos, or mestizos.

Indians and Africans labored on plantations as slaves and indentured servants, and at times common problems of enforced servitude outweighed cultural and linguistic differences. Early in the eighteenth century Virginia authorities grew fearful when notorious clandestine meetings took place in the Negro quarters. Fortuitous vigilance and judicious interrogation of the ringleaders prematurely revealed the conspiracy and prevented an insurrection. An aroused legislature reaffirmed that under no circumstances were Negro slaves, whether African, Indian, or mixed-bloods, to be allowed arms or to assemble without whites present.[78]

A few years later, in 1710, another slave conspiracy was detected in the nick of time, and Virginians were relieved that "an intended insurrection of the Negroes . . . had been thwarted." The two ringleaders were brought to Williamsburg for trial and condemned. Scipio was sent to Gloucester for execution. His head and one quarter were displayed there, and the remaining quarters were divided between Middlesex, King and Queen, and Lancaster counties. The other culprit, Salvadore, also was decapitated; his head was set up in Williamsburg, one quarter was exhibited by the cannon at Jamestown, and the remaining quarters were sent to New Kent County and elsewhere. All of this was a gruesome warning to any other Negroes harboring seditious notions. Magistrates did not publicly make much of the fact that the Negro Scipio was an African and the Negro Salvadore an Indian.[79]

If one looks close enough it is not hard to unearth similar

collaboration between Indians and Africans. In North Carolina, James Cole's slaves, two Africans and one Indian, ransacked Cole's house while he was gone, carrying off his trunk, clothes, and other personal belongings. The hue and cry went out, and the "said Negroes" were quickly recaptured and in 1698 turned over to the marshal.[80] During the same year an African and an Indian were among those boarding and looting a royal navy ship that had been driven ashore and abandoned on the treacherous Outer Banks.[81] In the first part of the eighteenth century Captain Teach (Blackbeard) and his crew had encountered little difficulty in disposing of their booty in North Carolina, and one suspects that those "Negroes" who plundered the wrecked ship and stole Cole's belongings planned to sell rather than keep their spoils. In South Carolina the Indian slave Dick broke into the parsonage and helped himself to rings, silverware, and other valuables. In the aftermath Dick, sauntering about the neighborhood, became drunk, "made a great entertainment there for a number of slaves," and in a confused brawl got his head split open. He was captured, and, after the smith clapped on handcuffs and shackles, authorities inspected Dick, finding part of the silver sewn into a false pocket in his breeches. Dick's confederate, the African Philip, was also captured, and as soon as the key turned in his iron mouthpiece, Philip decided to reveal all about the robbery.[82]

One of the reasons the blacksmith had put shackles on Dick so quickly was because he threatened to take up his gun and run off to the Indians as he had done previously. As an individual Dick was not particularly important, but that he might prevail on other African and Indian slaves to flee with him was another matter. Carolinians dreaded the appearance of any maroon community. In retrospect it can be seen that in Carolina and throughout the South white fears were magnified and that, except in a few instances, no maroon settlements, such as those in Jamaica's mountainous cockpit country, among the Bush Negroes of the Guianas, or in the forbidding Darien jungles on the Isthmus of Panama, emerged on the North American mainland. In Jamaica and the Guianas the maroons were essentially Africans, and in Darien the maroons (cimarrones) were an amalgamation of Indians and Africans. Maroon communities developing at one place or another in the South were more like those in Darien.

A relieved governor of Virginia, William Gooch, in 1729 reported that his militia had just recaptured fifteen fugitive Negroes, the work force on a new plantation near the headwaters of the James River. With arms and tools they had slipped off to the west and founded a settlement in the mountains. The militia discovered them and after a few shots recaptured them all, thereby preventing another cockpit-country type of refuge on the Virginia frontier. Gooch's letter and other brief accounts reveal little about these fifteen slaves—whether new Africans, African creoles, mestizos, mulattos, Indians, or what. The headwaters of the James had long been a center for the Indian trade, and few regions in Virginia had a higher percentage of Indians in the labor force on plantations like those of William Byrd and his neighbors. If they were not Indians, the fugitives easily could have talked to slaves who were. It was in the interest of any newly arrived African planning to run off to do so.[83]

South Carolina Negroes endeavoring to establish a maroon settlement fared even worse. They rebelled in 1720, unsuccessfully attempting to take over the countryside, even threatening Charleston. Next they retired to the fall line of the Savannah River, hoping the Lower Creeks there would join. At the same time Waccamaw Indians rose in the Carolina Tidewater. It is possible only to guess that there was coordination among Negroes, Lower Creeks, and Waccamaws. In any case, the Lower Creeks did not join the fugitive Negroes or serve as their guides; the Savannah garrison captured many of the half-starved runaways; and concerned whites summarily burned and hanged up to one hundred of the rebels—Negroes taken on the Savannah River, Waccamaw Indians, and others. By remaining neutral, the Lower Creeks had made a wise decision.[84]

Runaway Negroes sometimes fared better. In 1716 a Carolina slave made good his escape to the Indian country and stayed there; several decades later the Carolina planter Edmund Gray complained that a Cherokee half-breed had seduced six of his Negroes, prompting them to run off. Three had a change of heart and returned to Gray of their own volition; as far as is known the remainder did not, reached the Cherokees, and won their freedom.[85] Uprooted by hostilities, at the end of the American Revolution three hundred Negroes congregated on an isolated stretch of the Savannah River and sustained themselves in an autonomous community until 1786.[86] Christian Priber had known what he was about when in the eighteenth century he had welcomed runaway blacks to his "kingdom of paradise" in the Cherokee back country.

Spanish Florida provided a refuge for runaway slaves. Since Charleston's founding in 1670 they had been fleeing southward, their presence or asylum in Florida contributing to numerous diplomatic quarrels. In the eighteenth century Spanish authorities normally granted freedom to fugitives who professed Catholicism, and as far as is known all of them did. Most were granted land; males were incorporated into the militia and stationed just north of the Castillo de San Marcos at Fort Mosa, an outpost that came to be known as the Negro Fort. On rare occasions documents reveal whether these fugitives were African, Indians, mulattos, mestizos, or zambos. Seven Carolina runaways reached St. Augustine in 1697, at a time when England and Spain were allies in trying to curb the expansionist policies of Louis XIV. Because of the alliance, the St. Augustine governor, after interrogating the fugitives, decided to return them to South Carolina. Questioning revealed that six of the runaways were African and one was an Indian, the latter perhaps originally from Apalachee or Timucua, at an earlier period having been seized by Goose Creek men. He also might have been from Virginia or elsewhere, little more at home in the Carolina Low Country than recently imported Africans but having good reason to make common cause with them.[87] The next year three more Carolina Indian slaves, Titus, Cupitt, and Polaw, ran away, presumably to St. Augustine, but whether they were relocated at Fort Mosa or in a Franciscan mission, or even if they reached Florida, is unclear.[88] The brief period of Anglo-Spanish collaboration came to an end. During the eighteenth century slaves continued to seek refuge in St. Augustine, and few were returned. Such evidence as exists suggests that the former slaves established in a segregated community adjoining the Negro Fort included not only Africans but also Indians and mixed-bloods. Presumably they had lived together in slave quarters at or not far from Goose Creek and once in Florida remained together as freemen. Spaniards did not look upon Fort Mosa as a maroon settlement, but Goose Creek men did.

The inexorable expansion of the English colonies forced Indians westward and also southward. For the most part the Seminoles were Creeks who from the first part of the eighteenth century drifted into Florida, and Africans came with or joined them. It is among the Seminoles, though much later, that we get our best glimpse of maroon communities. As has been seen, the term Seminole itself is a corruption of *cimarron*. Slave and free Africans lived among, and indeed were part of, the Seminoles. Their presence became more conspicuous and controversial during the nineteenth-century Seminole wars. In 1816 American gunboats fired into the "British" or "Negro" Fort on the Apalachicola River, setting off the powder magazine and killing only a few hostile Indians but several hundred Negroes. Two years later Andrew Jackson stormed into Spanish Florida, and one of his major objectives was Bowlegs Town, a sizable Negro settlement on the Suwannee River. In this instance most of the Negro-Seminoles escaped. Before 1821, when Spain ruled Florida, and afterward, when the United States possessed that territory, Indians friendly to the Americans periodically scoured the peninsula for Negroes, taking them back to Georgia and Alabama and selling them to white cotton planters. With some justification abolitionists charged that the Second Seminole War, which broke out in 1835, was really not an Indian but a Negro war, resulting from Southern white determination to capture and enslave Negro-Seminoles.

Sometimes Negroes lived in Seminole villages, scarcely distinguished from any other Indian, and at other times Negroes lived apart in autonomous settlements, such as by the Negro Fort on the Apalachicola River or at Bowlegs Town on the Suwannee. Many parallels exist between the maroon wars in Jamaica and the several Seminole wars fought in Florida, Georgia, and Alabama. An obvious difference, however, was that, with minor exceptions, only Africans were involved in Jamaica, but Africans and Indians combined against whites in the Southeast.[89]

It is possible to discover the same kind of Afro-Indian collaboration in wars against whites variously labeled as Indian conflicts or Negro insurrections. Several years before the Tuscarora revolt two Virginia free Negroes were accused of stirring up the North Carolina Indians, and mention already has been made of the Negro who joined the Tuscaroras and supervised their building of European-style forts. The first thing the colonial militia did after capturing Nohoroco Fort was to cut that enterprising Negro to pieces. In the great Yamasee uprising, Negroes ran away from their masters to join the rebels or, if living among the Indians, helped to foment the conspiracy. While Yamasees and their allies laid waste the countryside, Charleston Negroes plotted to seize the magazine and massacre the whites. Little is known about these Charleston Negroes, but, considering the racial composition of South Carolina's slaves, one can assume that some were Indians or zambos in communication with their confederates outside the city.[90] A significant percentage of the Yamasees themselves were zambos, and during the eighteenth century this tribe became increasingly noted for its Negroid features. In the 1739–40 Stono Rebellion, the most serious Negro revolt of the colonial era, unacculturated African slaves apparently took the initiative, turned against their masters on the Stono River outside Charleston, killed perhaps twenty-five whites, and, with drums beating and flags flying, set off for St. Augustine. In this instance perhaps emphasis is correctly placed on the role played by recently imported Africans, but it should be kept in mind that for decades Indian and African slaves had worked side by side on Carolina plantations and that repeatedly they had fled to Spanish Florida. There is little reason to assume that 1739–40 was any exception. Yamasee, Timucuan, and Apalachee slaves knew the way; newly arrived Africans did not.[91]

During the early months of the American Revolution the hard-pressed royal governor of Virginia, Lord Dunmore, issued a proclamation freeing Negro slaves who would desert rebel masters, seek sanctuary in royal lines, and, if able, fight for George III. This policy infuriated slaveholders in the Chesapeake Bay Tidewater, because hundreds of slaves fled to Dunmore, whom they regarded as a liberator. Some of these fugitive "Negroes" in fact were Indians, or at least mulattos of the "Indian breed,"[92] and winning their freedom in this fashion represented a remarkable change from earlier years. When Jamestown was founded Indians in the Tidewater had not looked upon any English governor as a liberator.

As we know, the Frenchman Crèvecoeur ignored the Indians' contribution in shaping this new American, who, as he saw it, if something more than a transplanted European, in any case was white. Crèvecoeur, who spent most of his time in the North, also disregarded the Negro. An amalgam of Africans, Europeans, and Indians, the Negro also was something more than a transplanted African and, even more than Crèvecoeur's white, was a new American.

12

Conclusion

It can be helpful from the vantage point of the late eighteenth and early nineteenth centuries (the end of the colonial era) to survey changes in the Indians' life-style that had occurred since the Mississippian era. One must be circumspect in setting an exact time for the end of the colonial period. Members of the United States Congress regarded the date as 1776 or at the latest 1783, when Britain signed the peace treaty conceding independence and giving the United States title to lands stretching to the Mississippi River in the west and the thirty-first parallel in the south. Yet it was only Americans who assumed that the United States had clear title to the Old Southwest. Spaniards, Britons, and Frenchmen, many of them on the scene in Indian villages, perhaps wearing their army uniforms, disagreed, as did most of the natives.

For some years after 1783 it was Indians and not whites who occupied and exercised effective control over most of the Old Southwest. For them the elimination of European influence and the end of the colonial era did not come until 1815 or shortly thereafter. By then Andrew Jackson had soundly defeated the

Creeks at Horseshoe Bend (1814) and the following year trounced the British at New Orleans. After 1815 few denied that the United States was master of almost all the Old Southwest, and when she acquired the remainder of Spanish Florida in 1821 all the South was finally incorporated into the Republic. Restless, with a population growing at a prodigious rate, and displaying an aggressive spreadeagle nationalism, the United States had the power to do what it pleased with the Southern Indians. President Andrew Jackson in the 1830s resolved to remove them west of the Mississippi River, and scholarly and polemic accounts have portrayed at length how Creeks, Cherokees, Choctaws, Chickasaws, and Seminoles were uprooted and relocated by land and water in Oklahoma.

When the Southern Indians' way of life in the years just before removal is contrasted with that of an earlier period, one characteristic that stands out is that the battered native population finally had achieved a measure of stability. Descendants of Indians who fought against the young border captain Andy Jackson are very much in evidence today in both Oklahoma and the South. On the eve of removal Southern Indians still suffered from epidemics and assorted diseases, but their mortality rate did not appear to differ much from that of whites. By then time and intermixture with Europeans and Africans had brought about a measure of immunity. Available evidence at best is incomplete. One recent demographic study of the Creeks concludes that in the latter part of the eighteenth century their population was actually increasing.[1] By necessity one must be uneasy about data on which such a finding is based. Even so it may be true, not only for Creeks but also for other Southern tribes, that around 1800 their actual numbers were slowly growing; we really do not know. The significant point is that in Jackson's lifetime (1767–1845) the issue of whether the Indians were increasing or dying out was debatable. This was not the case when De Soto and John Smith were alive, and today one looks in vain for Timucuans, Yamasees, Weanocs, Saponis, and so many others.

During the several decades before removal, Southern Indians were not forced to move about as frantically as in previous centuries, and there was a good chance that children would reach maturity in the village or general region where they had been born. This held true regarding small tributary tribes such as the Pamunkeys in Virginia and the Catawbas in South Carolina, and it was the norm among Cherokees, Choctaws, and other major tribes. Of course, exceptions could be found. Repeatedly defeated in a series of wars with American frontiersmen, groups of Cherokees at one point or another in the latter part of the eighteenth century sought refuge north of the Ohio, farther south closer to the Gulf of Mexico, and even beyond the Mississippi. In eastern North Carolina surviving Tuscaroras continued to drift toward New York and Pennsylvania. After a series of wars and relocations, Upper Creeks, born in middle and northern Alabama around 1800, if they were still alive in the 1840s found themselves in Florida's Everglades. Osceola was part of this group, though disease struck him down in his prime in middle Florida, and he did not have the opportunity to conceal himself in inaccessible hammocks at the peninsula's tip. Living among and adopted by the Creeks, Natchez Indians never lost hope that they might return to the Great Sun's domain on the Mississippi River, and several times they prepared to move back.[2] As it turned out they remained with the Creeks and by so doing participated in the greatest displacement of all—the removal to Oklahoma in the 1830s and 1840s. Nevertheless, after taking all this into consideration, Southern Indians at the beginning of the nineteenth century were far more settled than in earlier times, when pandemics had disrupted village life, warriors had been turned into commercial hunters and slave catchers (or their victims), and hostilities were common with both white settlers and aboriginal neighbors.

By the nineteenth century the Indian slave trade had diminished considerably from the days of the Goose Creek men. But as long as the "peculiar institution" survived in the Old South Indians were still captured and sold. During hostilities associated with the nineteenth-century westward removal, natives were not only killed and relocated but also captured and enslaved. It made little difference whether or not this was legal or whether whites insisted that the Indians in question were Negroes. Small remnant Indian groups, not forced to take the Trail of Tears, living peacefully but precariously in one or another part of the South, were not spared. In the 1920s Eugene P. Southall, a Negro, reported that the "old people [had related] many times" how his great grandmother had been stolen from her Indian parents in Virginia and auctioned off in the Norfolk market.[3] The former slave Emily Mays, born in Georgia in 1861, recounted how her father, a mixed-blood free Virginia Indian, had been captured and shipped away to the Lower South.[4] Julia Woodbury, a South Carolina freed woman, described to interviewers how her mother had told her "a thousand times" that she was "Chee[?] Indian . . . born on de sea beach." Whites in a big covered wagon had spotted her and her brother John. Although her mother was a big girl, they ran her and John down and stuffed them into the back of the wagon. They "cried en cried, but dat never do no good." After the Civil War Julia continued to live near her master's house and remained a Negro, while brother John returned to the sea beach, perhaps resuming life there as an Indian.[5]

Over the long term Indians accepted more and more of the white man's law and government. Given the high aboriginal mortality and an accelerating European immigration, this was probably inevitable. Clan vengeance and in many instances the vitality of the clan itself disintegrated, at first among coastal tributaries. The Spaniards in Florida and later the English in Virginia appointed their own native rulers, giving medals to selected chiefs, great ones to the more important rulers and smaller medals to those of less consequence. Long before the end of the eighteenth century there was little doubt that tributary chiefs were picked by whites and reigned at their pleasure. Even so, though submerged and often not recognized by outsiders, tensions existed between chiefs established by whites or perceived by whites to wield power and traditional Indian leaders. To an extent the confusion and internal controversy have persisted into modern times. One need only look at the struggle between Christian "progressive" Seminoles and tribal medicine men.

Traditional native government, founded on decisions made by elders in council, on clan vengeance, on leadership in peace and war of white and red chiefs, on communal ownership of property, and on the integrity of the clan, survived much longer among larger "independent" tribes. When the mestizo Upper Creek Alexander McGillivray came to New York in 1790 as spokesman for the entire confederacy, President Washington gave him a general's commission in the army, a $1,200 annual pension, and other emoluments; yet after General McGillivray returned home he refused to turn over the Creek lands he had promised. With only limited success Americans attempted to set up another supreme head of the Creek Confederacy who would.[6] In the first part of the nineteenth century, after McGillivray's death, the United States Indian agent Benjamin Hawkins made progress in substituting white criminal justice for clan vengeance among the Creeks and in establishing a national council along the lines of the new American republic. Some Creeks resented and refused to accept these reforms, and the Creek War that broke out in 1813 in part was caused by tensions between those who favored or at least agreed to acculturation and those who did not.[7]

Despite many failures, colonists still endeavored to convert the Indians. After Britain defeated France and Spain in 1763 and won vast territories in America, once again the SPG envisioned a bountiful harvest among the unregenerate. As a start missionaries proposed establishing three frontier Indian schools near British forts—in New York among the Mohawks, at Fort Pitt (Pittsburgh) in Pennsylvania, and in the South Carolina or Georgia back country. Understanding a good deal about the different sexual mores of the two cultures, Edmond Atkin, Britain's Southern Indian superintendent, thought all in all it would be best for the SPG's emissaries not to be so young and virile. A variety of reasons, not the least of which were the disturbances leading to the American Revolution, prevented Anglicanism and the Union Jack from prevailing in the western Indian country.[8] After the Revolution American Protestant sects—Congregationalists and Baptists, among others—as best they could took up where the SPG left off, establishing missions and schools among Cherokees, Choctaws, and some of their neighbors. The Trail of Tears disrupted this work, though in time Indians who escaped removal and remained in the East became Christians as part of the relentless process of acculturation, usually joining one or another fundamentalist evangelical Protestant denomination. Exceptions were some of the Cherokees, Choctaws, and Seminoles who continued to use their native tongues and retain a measure of their cultures, including their religions.

Long before removal the concept of usufruct as applied to the Indians had become firmly established in the white man's law, and, whether they agreed or not, Indians were forced to accept that, in the final analysis, they did not own their land. The notion of usufruct itself had not been foreign to Mississippians, since large agricultural fields in most instances had been owned and administered by the village; individual families had been entitled only to the use of certain portions.

To make the point that in modern times the United States did not regard the Indians as sovereign one merely has to cite the controversial decisions of the Supreme Court headed by Chief Justice John Marshall. Emphatically denying the states' rights argument of Georgia, the Court in the Cherokee Nation *v.* Georgia (1831), and in Worcester *v.* Georgia (1832), ruled that Cherokees were "independent," that they had solemn treaties with the national government, and that Georgia's laws had no validity in the Cherokee nation. But in this and similar cases Marshall, giving the matter little more thought than his colonial predecessors, made it clear that the independent Cherokees really did not own their lands but merely enjoyed their use.[9] The United States Indian Claims Commission, created immediately after World War II and lasting until 1978, adjudicated a multitude of claims from diverse tribes. The natives were to be compensated for lands taken from them improperly or for which they had not been fairly paid, and in time Creeks, Seminoles, and other Southern Indians were compensated. In the scores of cases brought before the commission much was made of "Indian" or "aboriginal" title. The underlying assumption in these twentieth-century cases was that compensation was merely for the unjust loss of their right of occupancy. Henry of Susa, Cardinal Archbishop of Ostia in the thirteenth century, had been prophetic and close to the mark when he maintained that pagans had no real title to their lands. Without lasting success, contemporary Indians occasionally have refuted the concept of usufruct. Soon after Fidel Castro came to power in Cuba, Miccosukee-Seminoles on their own visited Havana, securing Cuban recognition of their independence.[10] Nevertheless, today the principle of usufruct is little questioned for the same reason that the concept of "one nation indivisible" has not been debated much in the years after Appomattox.

Modern times have witnessed a growing trend among Indians toward downplaying cultural and tribal differences and joining together in a pan-Indian movement. For many this phenomenon first became manifest on the Great Plains in the latter part of the nineteenth century, when Indians speaking different languages communicated and collaborated with one another through a universal sign language and especially when the Plains Indians, distraught by the destruction of the buffalo and loss of their lands, regardless of their tribal affiliation eagerly embraced the messianic Ghost Dance revival. There is no denying the importance of this movement for twentieth-century Indian nationalism. We must remember, however, that a number of Plains Indians formerly had been Easterners, making it necessary to go back farther in time than the 1890s to discern all of pan-Indianism's roots.

In no small measure whites themselves were responsible for native attempts at unity. The French had founded Louisiana in the eighteenth century, establishing settlements and isolated posts stretching from the Gulf of Mexico to Canada. For security and in an effort to expand the peltry trade, again and again authorities encouraged Indians to cast aside differences, unite, and put themselves under French protection. Jointly they could deny the British frontiersmens' relentless advance. In the same century Britain's policy varied. When there was no danger from France or Spain, British officials usually found it convenient to pit one tribe against another, yet when an intercolonial war erupted authorities reversed themselves, encouraging Indians to unite under British supervision. During King George's War in the 1740s Oglethorpe worked with New York's governor to align Southern with Northern Indians, and in the French and Indian War in the following decade Southern governors continued collaborating with their Northern counterparts in promoting Indian unity. When fighting ended in 1763, John Stuart, Britain's superintendent for all Southern Indians, reverted to the old policy of *divide et impera*, inciting hostilities between the powerful Creeks and Choctaws. At the outbreak of the next major conflict, the American Revolution, Stuart hastened to patch up the Creek–Choctaw dispute, triumphantly reporting to his London superiors that he had succeeded. During the Revolution, as a result of unforeseen and unplanned circumstances, Britain assumed France's former role on the North American mainland, occupying Canada in the North, the Floridas on the Gulf, and, through Indian allies, most of the intervening territory. Like France beforehand, Britain encouraged Western Indian unity to contain and chastize the expanding Americans, many of whom had become rebels.

Even though Britain lost her thirteen colonies, on and off until Jackson's victory at New Orleans in 1815 she continued to prod Western Indians to combine. The post-1783 careers of British subjects like William Augustus Bowles, Director General of the Creek Nation (Muskogee), and Jackson's adversary, Edward Nicholls, for the most part loyalists or closely identified with them, is sufficient evidence of this. Frenchmen also, whether Bonaparte in France or LeClerc de Milfort, who after 1783 lived among the Creeks, had not forgotten that Louisiana was named for a French king. They solicited the favor of Western Indians in restoring the French ensign to the Mississippi. From 1699, when France first founded Louisiana, until the general peace in 1815, assorted Europeans—Iberville, Milfort, unheralded *coureurs des bois*, Oglethorpe, Bowles, nameless British packhorsemen, and countless others—visited and for lengthy periods lived in native villages, where they pointed out the advantages of collaboration.[11]

Indians frequently thought this a good idea, not that they necessarily accepted the white man's logic. As the eighteenth century progressed, natives became aware for the first time of their Indianness, the fact that despite diverse languages, different customs, and ancient feuds, they were blood brothers, having much more in common with one another than with Europeans and Africans. The sign language did not originate on the plains; from an early date Westos, Shawnees, and other Southern Indians had employed one.[12] And as far as is known, trade jargons such as Occaneechee and Mobilian had developed and flourished after contact. Eighteenth- and early-nineteenth-century attempts at Indian unity, facilitated by sign languages and trade jargons, went far beyond reestablishing defunct chiefdoms existing at the time of contact. As a means of protecting their lands, culture, and identity, reformers cajoled natives to put aside differences and combine.

The 1715 Yamasee Rebellion was a forerunner. A better example is Pontiac's Rebellion, which broke out in 1763 and primarily involved Indians north of the Ohio in the Old Northwest. This was a widespread and for a period successful uprising against scattered British posts, and authorities were frightened that Southern Indians would be brought into the fray. Unfortunately there is little record of contemporary debates in Southern Indian square grounds and council houses, but it appears that British officials in the South had good reason to be edgy.

Sources are better, though still skimpy and incomplete, for the most ambitious attempt at Indian unity, the one led by the Shawnee Tecumseh and his brother the Prophet early in the nineteenth century. Despite their small numbers, it was appropriate for Shawnees to take the lead. During the seventeenth and eighteenth centuries they had ranged from Canada to the Gulf and then northward into Kentucky and across the Ohio. Like many Northern Shawnees, Tecumseh had family and clan ties with Southern Indians. There were assorted other Shawnee chiefs like Tecumseh. The mestizo Shawnee Peter Chartier, whom both British and French Indian agents in the mid-eighteenth century had courted to help unify Western Indians, had an Apalachee wife who had been carried off by James Moore.[13] Tecumseh traveled throughout the West and talked at length with Cherokees and other Southern Indians in the South or when they visited the Old Northwest and Canada. As well as, if not better than, anyone he had witnessed the effects of American expansion. He insisted with fervor that Indians were brothers and that they should unite, repudiate any land cession not approved by all, and, if necessary, fight to protect their domain and culture.

Tecumseh's movement also included a nativistic religious revival, of which his brother the Prophet was the most conspicuous leader. He was by no means the first prophet or medicine man to denounce contamination by whites and to counsel a return to aboriginal ways. The Delaware Prophet in the mid-eighteenth century and Pontiac and his followers in 1763 had advocated the same types of reforms as had Powhatan medicine men of John Smith's day, and one can find similar nativistic movements in societies throughout much of the world in recent centuries threatened by European expansion. In the eighteenth and nineteenth centuries Indian medicine men more often than not were concerned with a greater geographical area and with Native Americans of disparate backgrounds. Early in the nineteenth century medicine men or prophets with this broader vision, disciples of the Shawnee Prophet, emerged in the South, especially among the Creeks.

The Shawnee Prophet and his Southern counterparts were concerned about a number of evils, not the least of which was firewater—rum. Even more than whites, natives recognized the pervasive and debilitating effects of this mainstay of the Indian trade. When prophets exhorted temperance, their entreaties had some effect. Rum was only one commodity of the Indian trade, and the Shawnee Prophet hoped to sever all, or almost all, commercial intercourse with the whites. It was Europeans who had corrupted the natives, and the only way to restore Indian virtues and physical well-being was through separation. The Shawnee

Prophet had this in mind when he advocated a return to the bow and arrow. This would help Indians extricate themselves from the white man's commercial hunting. Furthermore, cutting off trade with whites would reduce or eliminate the importance of resident village factors and enhance the prestige of medicine men.

The problem with this reasoning was that, when Indians in the sixteenth century eagerly had paddled out to barter with passing European ships, they had become addicted to and dependent on European manufactures. No prophet wielded enough power to cut that tie. Theoretically it was possible to return to the bow and arrow and blow gun, to restrict hunting to the smaller scale of Mississippian times. The problem was that in a conflict these primitive weapons were no match for whites and their auxiliaries armed with muskets and rifles.

The mestizo Creek Hillis Hadjo, best known to the whites as the Prophet Francis, was an ardent disciple of Tecumseh's brother and undertook to revive and purify not only Creeks but also other Southern Indians. Yet whether he approved or not, Francis realized that commerce with whites was inevitable; the only question was with which whites. It was unthinkable for him to consider the Americans, because Andrew Jackson, his fellow frontiersmen, and their Creek allies who accepted acculturation were Francis's enemies. He therefore turned to Britain, in 1815 even visiting London, and as a result followed in the footsteps of many another medicine man who became a commercial factor. Francis returned to Florida and in 1818 eagerly boarded an approaching ship flying the Union Jack, presumably laden with British trade goods for the Creeks. Instead it turned out to be one of Jackson's gunboats. Soldiers escorted Francis into Fort St. Marks, hanged him, and then with little ceremony dragged him outside by the heels for burial. The mission of a reforming prophet was neither easy nor safe; in all likelihood, it was not realistic either.[14]

In the early nineteenth century prophets had counseled Indians not to rely so much on hunting, and in fact they did become far less dependent on commercial hunting than previously. However, Jackson and the frontiersmen had far more to do with this than any native reformer. It was they, the Americans, in a series of encounters, notably the 1814 triumph at Horseshoe Bend, who defeated the Indians and opened up enormous tracts for yeoman farmers and slaveowning planters. The loss of hunting lands forced Indians to place more emphasis on growing crops and raising cattle to keep from sinking even further into debt. The removal to Oklahoma followed by two decades the defeat at Horseshoe Bend, and, for the first time since the days of William Byrd I and the Goose Creek men, commercial hunting became of little consequence in the South.

The impression that after the 1830s all Southern Indians had been either killed or removed to Oklahoma is misleading, because Indians, some 74,000 strong, are present in the South today, living in loose, ill-defined clusters such as the Creeks around Poarch, Alabama, and the Lumbees south of Fayetteville, North Carolina, or on reservations, like the Cherokees, Choctaws, Seminoles, and Pamunkeys. Pamunkeys still render annual tribute of deer and turkeys to the Virginia governor, as they have since the seventeenth century. Some modern Indians look remarkably like the earliest pictures of their ancestors; others show the results of intermixture with white and African neighbors. Regardless of their genetic composition these contemporary Indians are debating the same problems that so perplexed their ancestors: What should be the relationship with whites; how much of their culture should be adopted; or should they even try to resist out-and-out acculturation? Contemporary Indians sometimes advocate preserving and blending the best of white and Indian society. This has not yet proved possible, and as Indians lose more and more of their language, religion, clan structure, and communal notions of property holding, it will be harder, if not impossible, even to consider this alternative. The advantages of Indians' absorbing or identifying with aspects of African culture are hardly considered today, though it has not always been that way.

Indian influence is perpetuated in the contemporary South beyond the 74,000 survivors and names such as Tuskegee, Altamaha, and Roanoke. The Mississippian priest, temple, and idol cult for the most part have disappeared, but massive temple mounds have survived the ravages of time, perhaps being incorporated into a historical park or lying unnoticed, overgrown with trees and underbrush. Despite the enormous changes since De Soto's day, one can still stand on top and, ignoring the din and pollution of passing heavy trucks and nearby industry and the cries of children noisily and probably illegally climbing up the sloped sides, envision a Mississippian priest performing rituals; animated natives, drenched with perspiration, playing the ball game or participating in rituals of the busk; and smoke rising from clusters of villages in the distance. And if one looks closely enough, usually in the South but possibly also in Oklahoma, he can still discover survivals of the Mississippian Southeastern Ceremonial Complex, including motifs such as sun circles and hands, the black drink, ball games, square grounds, and occasionally (in Oklahoma) even a mound, albeit a very small, recently constructed one. As late as the end of the nineteenth or early twentieth century, Creeks in Oklahoma still annually displayed at the busk copper plates that they had carefully brought with them from Alabama and whose origin apparently dated back to the Mississippian era. One would be hard pressed to identify the Equal Rights Amendment and the contemporary feminist movement with the Mississippians. There is a paradox, however, that nineteenth- and twentieth-century Southern women have been and are battling for rights, many of which long ago were enjoyed by their Mississippian predecessors in their matrilineal society.

In many respects it is not the modern Southern Indians but whites and Negroes who have perpetuated so many features of Indian culture. One need only mention soul food and Uncle Remus in regard to Negroes or Jimmy Carter, the first President from the Lower South, in respect to whites. President Carter's native state of Georgia lies in the old Mississippian heartland, and it is revealing that a white man rather than an Indian has done so much to popularize grits in the national capital. The eagle, of course, has been there for some time.

Abbreviations

ABBREVIATIONS USED IN NOTES

Add. MSS.	Additional Manuscripts, British Library
Adm.	Admiralty, Public Record Office
AGI	Archivo General de Indias, Seville
AGN	Archivo General de la Nación, Mexico
AGS	Archivo General de Simancas, Spain
BL	British Library
CO	Colonial Office
CSP	*Calendar of State Papers*
DAB	*Dictionary of American Biography*
E.	Exchequer
FHQ	*Florida Historical Quarterly*
GDAH	Georgia Department of Archives and History
JNH	*Journal of Negro History*
LC	Library of Congress
NCA	North Carolina Division of Archives and History
PRO	Public Record Office
RSUS	Records of the States of the United States of America
S.D.	Santo Domingo
SPG	Society for the Propagation of the Gospel in Foreign Parts

SCA	South Carolina Department of Archives and History
SCHGM	*South Carolina Historical and Genealogical Magazine*
SRNC	Spanish Records of the North Carolina Historical Commission
SAC	Southeast Archeological Center, National Park Service
SP	State Paper Office (London)
VCRP	Virginia Colonial Records Project
VHS	Virginia Historical Society
VMHB	*Virginia Magazine of History and Biography*
VSL	Virginia State Library
WMQ	*William and Mary Quarterly*

Notes

For fuller data on works cited in these notes, see the Bibliography, pp. 335–357.

CHAPTER 1: THE ORIGINAL SOUTHERNERS (pp. 1–26)

1. Jesse D. Jennings, *Prehistory of North America*, pp. 50–62. Jennings is skeptical of the forty-thousand-years-ago date, but excavations since 1968 in Florida, on the Pacific Coast, and elsewhere support the earlier period.
2. U.S. Department of the Interior, National Park Service, *Russell Cave National Monument, Alabama*, and Dick Bothwell, "The Earliest Known Americans," pp. 11, 14.
3. Iola B. Parker, "Meadowcroft Dig Continues to Throw Light on Prehistory," pp. 6–8.
4. State of Florida, Division of Archives, History, and Records Management, *Archives and History News*, 5 (July–August 1974): 1, and personal communication, Wilburn A. Cockrell, the division's underwater archaeologist excavating Warm Mineral Springs and other early sites.

5. Charles M. Hudson, *The Southeastern Indians*, pp. 38–97.
6. The most detailed account of this chiefdom is Steven G. Baker's master's thesis, "Cofitachique: Fair Province of Carolina."
7. Ibid., p. 206, and James Mooney, "Myths of the Cherokee," p. 499.
8. A recent study of this controversy is Carol I. Mason, "A Reconsideration of Westo-Yuchi Identification."
9. James M. Crawford, ed., *Studies in Southeastern Indian Languages*, pp. 4, 5, 67.
10. Hudson, *Southeastern Indians*, pp. 62, 292–93, and Walton C. Galinat, "The Evolution of Corn and Culture in North America."
11. Edmund S. Morgan, *American Slavery, American Freedom: The Ordeal of Colonial Virginia*, pp. 44–70.
12. G. Melvin Herndon, "Indian Agriculture in the Southern Colonies," pp. 284–97.
13. Lyman Carrier, *Agriculture in Virginia, 1607–1699*, p. 6.
14. René Laudonnière, *Three Voyages*, ed. and trans. Charles E. Bennett, pp. 15, 62.
15. A convenient reference for Le Moyne's and White's pictures is Stefan Lorant, ed., *The New World: The First Pictures of America, Made by John White and Jacques Le Moyne and Engraved by Theodore De Bry*. For White, however, one should consult Paul H. Hulton and David B. Quinn, *The American Drawings of John White, 1577–1590*.
16. Laudonnière, *Three Voyages*, pp. 15, 121, and "The Description of Virginia by Captaine Smith," in Philip L. Barbour, ed., *The Jamestown Voyages under the First Charter, 1606–1609*, 2: 359–60.
17. Frank G. Speck, "The Ethnic Position of Southeastern Algonkian," pp. 184–200.
18. Mooney, "Myths of the Cherokee," pp. 422.
19. Lewis H. Larson, Jr., "Historic Guale Indians of the Georgia Coast and the Impact of the Spanish Mission Effort," pp. 127, 133.
20. Personal communications, Curtiss E. Peterson, L. Ross Morrell, and their colleagues at the Florida Division of Archives, History, and Records Management; see also John M. Goggin and William C. Sturtevant, "The Calusa: A Stratified Nonagricultural Society (with Notes on Sibling Marriage)," in Ward H. Goodenough, ed., *Explorations in Cultural Anthropology, Essays in Honor of George Peter Murdock*, pp. 179–219.
21. John R. Swanton, *The Indians of the Southeastern United States*, pp. 454–56.
22. A convenient source with illustrations of aboriginal pottery is Emma Lila Fundaburk and Mary Douglass Fundaburk Foreman, eds., *Sun Circles and Human Hands: The Southeastern Indians, Art and Industries*.
23. I am indebted to Mr. Curtiss Peterson for discussions concerning

aboriginal metallurgy, because so little exists on this subject in print.

24. Carl Bridenbaugh, *Cities in Revolt: Urban Life in America, 1743–1776,* pp. 216–17, and John R. Dunkle, "Population Change as an Element in the Historical Geography of St. Augustine," pp. 7–10.
25. John R. Swanton, "Social Organization and Social Usages of the Indians of the Creek Confederacy," pp. 170–296.
26. Henry Timberlake, *Lieut. Henry Timberlake's Memoirs, 1756–1765,* ed. Samuel C. Williams, p. 59; James Adair, *The History of the American Indians,* ed. Samuel C. Williams, p. 451; and William C. Sturtevant, "Notes on the Creek Hothouse."
27. Swanton, "Social Organization of the Creek Confederacy," pp. 467–68, 544–45.
28. Swanton, *Indians of Southeast,* pp. 718–28.
29. "Soto's Further Discoveries in Florida . . . ," Samuel Purchas, ed., *Hakluytus Posthumus or Purchas His Pilgrimes, Contayning a History of the World in Sea Voyages and Lande Travells by Englishmen and Others,* 18: 15.
30. Garcilaso de la Vega, *The Florida of the Inca,* ed. and trans. John G. Varner and Jeanette J. Varner, p. 169.
31. "A Relation of a Voyage on the Coast of the Province of Carolina, 1666, by Robert Sandford," in Alexander S. Salley, Jr., ed., *Narratives of Early Carolina, 1650–1708,* p. 91, and Marcel Giraud, *Histoire de la Louisiane Française,* 1: 68–69.
32. Antonio J. Waring, Jr., and Preston Holder, "A Prehistoric Ceremonial Complex in the Southeastern United States," pp. 1–31, and John W. Griffin, "Historic Artifacts and the 'Buzzard Cult' in Florida," pp. 299–301. The most recent comprehensive study is James H. Howard, *The Southeastern Ceremonial Complex and Its Interpretation.* A decade ago archaeologists excavated a Mississippian site by Lake Jackson, Florida, which indicated an early origin of the Southeastern Ceremonial Complex. For a brief discussion see Frank B. Fryman, Jr., "Tallahassee's Prehistoric Political Center," pp. 2–4.
33. Hudson, *Southeastern Indians,* pp. 185–200.
34. Swanton, "Social Organization of the Creek Confederacy," p. 335.
35. Hudson, *Southeastern Indians,* p. 29.
36. William Strachey, *The Historie of Travell into Virginia Britania* (1612), ed. Louis B. Wright and Virginia Freund, pp. 70–74.
37. John R. Swanton, "Aboriginal Culture of the Southeast," pp. 681–83.
38. Hudson, *Southeastern Indians,* pp. 122–32.
39. John R. Swanton, "Religious Beliefs and Medical Practices of the Creek Indians," pp. 546–615.
40. Swanton, *Indians of the Southeast,* pp. 730–33.

41. John Lawson, *Lawson's History of North Carolina*, pp. 18, 41, 44.
42. Virgil J. Vogel, *American Indian Medicine*, pp. 35, 37–38, 267 ff.
43. Douglas S. Freeman, *George Washington: A Biography*, 7: 637–47.
44. William H. Gilbert, Jr., "The Eastern Cherokees," pp. 257–66.
45. Swanton, *Indians of the Southeast*, pp. 674–84, and Amy Bushnell, " 'That Demonic game': The Campaign to Stop Indian Pelota Playing in Spanish Florida, 1675–1684," pp. 5–6.
46. "Description of Virginia by Captaine Smith," Barbour, ed., *Jamestown Voyages*, 2: 362–63.
47. Swanton, "Social Organization of the Creek Confederacy," p. 628.
48. Gilbert, "Eastern Cherokees," p. 257.
49. James Mooney, "The Aboriginal Population of America North of Mexico," pp. 4–10.
50. Ibid., pp. 5, 7.
51. Sherburne F. Cook and Woodrow Borah, *Essays in Population History, Mexico and the Caribbean*, 1: 401.
52. Ibid., 1: viii.
53. Henry F. Dobyns, "An Appraisal of Techniques with a New Hemispheric Estimate," p. 414, and Dobyns's unpublished paper, "The Historic Demography of Indian North America," delivered at the annual meeting of the Organization of American Historians, Atlanta, 1977. Based on limited data, estimates made by physical anthropologists support an aboriginal population density approximately four times higher than Mooney indicated. Douglas H. Ubelaker, *Reconstruction of Demographic Profiles from Ossuary Skeletal Samples: A Case Study from the Tidewater Potomac*, p. 68.
54. Dobyns, "Historic Demography" and personal communication.
55. Personal communication, B. Calvin Jones.
56. Garcilaso, *Florida of the Inca*, p. 360, and W. W. Ehrmann, "The Timucua Indians of Sixteenth Century Florida," p. 173.
57. Mooney, "Myths of the Cherokee," p. 28.
58. Gonzalo Solís de Merás, *Pedro Menéndez de Avilés, Memorial*, ed. and trans. Jeannette T. Conner, p. 145.
59. Gabriel D. V. Calderón, "A 17th Century Letter of Gabriel Diaz Vara Calderón, Bishop of Cuba, Describing the Indians and Indian Missions of Florida," ed. and trans. Lucy L. Wenhold, p. 13.
60. Baker, "Cofitachique," p. 97, and Garcilaso, *Florida of the Inca*, pp. 122, 343.
61. Juan Rogel to Francis Borgia, Bahía de Santa María, 28 August 1572, in Clifford M. Lewis and Albert J. Loomie, *The Spanish Jesuit Mission in Virginia, 1570–1572*, p. 111.
62. William Symonds, *The Proceedings of the English Colonie in Virginia Since Their First Beginning from England in the Yeare of Our Lord 1606, Till this Present 1612 . . .* , p. 60.

63. Olivia Vlahos, *New World Beginnings: Indian Cultures in the Americas*, p. 156.

CHAPTER 2: THE INTRUDERS (pp. 27–52)

1. John R. Swanton, John R. Fordyce, Walter B. Jones, et al., *Final Report of the United States De Soto Expedition Commission.*
2. Hale G. Smith, *Documentation Concerning the First Christmas in the United States Presented to the United States Postal Service Commemorative Stamp Committee.*
3. James A. Williamson, *The Cabot Voyages and Bristol Discovery Under Henry VII; with the Cartography of the Voyages by R. A. Skelton*, p. 156.
4. Lawrence C. Wroth, ed., *The Voyages of Giovanni da Verrazzano, 1524–1528*, pp. 74–84. Scholars do not agree concerning the site of Verrazzano's landfall and his subsequent course.
5. Morgan, *American Slavery*, p. 44.
6. The four bulls of 1493 and the one of 1506 are in Frances G. Davenport and Charles O. Paullin, eds., *European Treaties Bearing on the History of the United States and Its Dependencies*, 1: 56–83, 107–11.
7. A large body of sixteenth-century Spanish literature—sermons, disputations, tracts, official decrees, and so forth—exists concerning the nature of Spain's title to America. The best single work on this topic is Lewis U. Hanke, *The Spanish Struggle for Justice in the Conquest of America.*
8. John H. Elliott, *Imperial Spain, 1469–1716*, pp. 214–21, 232–37.
9. A convenient summary of these early years in the Greater Antilles is John H. Parry and Philip M. Sherlock, *A Short History of the West Indies*, pp. 1–12.
10. Cook and Borah, *Essays in Population History*, 1: 376–410.
11. Gonzalo de Guzman et al. to crown, Santiago, Cuba, 16 September 1530, in *Colección de documentos inéditos relativos al descubrimiento, conquista y organización de las antiguas posesiones españolas de ultramar*, segunda serie, 4: 147.
12. Rodrigo de Figueroa to crown, Seville, 7 April 1519, in Joaquín Pacheco, Francisco de Cárdenas, Luis Torres de Mendoza et al., eds., *Colección de documentos inéditos relativos al descubrimiento, conquista, y colonización de las posesiones españolas en América y Oceanía, sacados en su mayor parte, del real Archivo de Indias*, 1: 368–69.
13. Cédula dirigida á los padres gerónimos . . . 1517, in ibid., 11: 295–96, and representación hecho al rey por el clérigo Bartolomé de las Casas, n.d., in ibid., 7: 10.

14. Antonio de Herrera y Tordesillas, *The General History of the Vast Continent and Islands of America, Commonly Call'd, The West Indies, from the First Discovery Thereof; with the Best Accounts the People Could Give of Their Antiquities . . .* , trans. John Stevens, 2: 36.

15. Capitulación con Juan Ponce sobre el descubrimiento de la isla Beniny, Burgos, 23 February 1512, in Pacheco et al., eds., *Documentos inéditos*, 22: 26–32. An analysis of Ponce's voyages, landfalls, etc. with supporting documents is T. Frederick Davis, ed., "History of Juan Ponce de Leon's Voyages to Florida, Source Records."

16. El rey con el dicho Juan Ponce sobre la dicha ysla Beniny, Valladolid, 26 September 1512 [1514], in Pacheco et al., eds., *Documentos inéditos*, 22: 33–37.

17. Vicente Murga Sanz, *Juan Ponce de León: fundador y primer gobernador del pueblo puertorriqueño, descubridor de la Florida y del Estrecho de las Bahamas*, p. 238.

18. Hanke, *Spanish Struggle for Justice*, p. 44; Woodbury Lowery, *The Spanish Settlements Within the Present Limits of the United States, 1513–1561*, pp. 153–57; and Paul Quattlebaum, *The Land Called Chicora: The Carolinas Under Spanish Rule, with French Intrusions, 1520–1670*, pp. 7–13.

19. Crown to Lucas Vásquez de Ayllón, Valladolid, 12 June 1523, in Pacheco et al., eds., *Documentos inéditos*, 14: 508–13.

20. Relación del descubrimiento de nueva tierra a la parte del norte de la isla Española, Valladolid, 12 June 1523, in ibid., 22: 79–93, and Quattlebaum, *Chicora*, pp. 3–31.

21. Early instances of silver and occasionally gold among the Southern Indians are in Herrera, *General History*, 3: 119, 122, and Quattlebaum, *Chicora*, p. 17.

22. John H. Parry, *The Establishment of the European Hegemony, 1415–1715: Trade and Exploration in the Age of the Renaissance*, pp. 21–26, and Clarence H. Haring, *Trade and Navigation Between Spain and the Indies in the Time of the Hapsburgs*, pp. 261–62.

23. El rey . . . capitulación que se tomó con Pánfilo de Narváez, Granada, 11 December 1526, in Pacheco et al., eds., *Documentos inéditos*, 22: 224–45.

24. "The Narrative of Cabeza de Vaca," in Frederick W. Hodge and Theodore H. Lewis, eds., *Spanish Explorers in the Southern United States, 1528–1543*, pp. 19–44.

25. El rey . . . capitulación que se tomó con Hernando de Soto, Valladolid, 20 April 1537, in Pacheco et al., eds., *Documentos inéditos*, 22: 534–46.

26. Based on a comparison of original sources, Swanton et al., *Final Report*, is a useful but by no means definitive account of the De Soto expedition.

Notes

27. Herbert I. Priestley, ed. and trans., *The Luna Papers: Documents Relating to the Expedition of Don Tristán de Luna y Arellano for the Conquest of la Florida in 1559–1561*, 1: xxxvii–lxvi.
28. Haring, *Trade and Navigation*, pp. 201–30.
29. Relación del viaje que hizo a las Indias hasta la Virginia . . . Don Diego de Molina, Antonio Pérez, y Francisco Lymbry, in Duke de Lerma to Antonio de Arostegui, el Pardo, 13 November 1611, AGS, estado 1008.
30. "The Narrative of the Englishman," n.d., in Priestley, ed., *Luna Papers*, 2: 177.
31. Luis de Quirós and Juan B. de Segura to Juan de Hinistrosa, Ajacan, 12 September 1570, in ibid., 2: 92.
32. Strachey, *Historie*, pp. 151–52.
33. Hernando de Escalante Fontaneda, *Memoir of Dº d'Escalante Fontaneda respecting Florida, Written in Spain, about the Year 1575*, ed. and trans. Buckingham Smith, p. 19.
34. Eugene Lyon, *The Enterprise of Florida: Pedro Menéndez de Avilés and the Spanish Conquest of 1565–1568*, pp. 29–30.
35. This figure is a rough estimate based on major sixteenth-century expeditions known to have come to Florida. Most of the immigrants were associated with the Luna, Ribault, and Menéndez ventures.
36. The best account of the early settlement of Florida is Lyon, *Enterprise of Florida*, p. 166.
37. Mary Ross, "With Pardo and Boyano on the Fringes of the Georgia Land," pp. 267–85, and Michael V. Gannon, *The Cross in the Sand: The Early Catholic Church in Florida, 1513–1870*, pp. 30–31.
38. Garcilaso, *Florida of the Inca*, p. 333.
39. Escalante, *Memoir*, p. 19.
40. Maynard J. Geiger, *The Franciscan Conquest of Florida, 1573–1618*, p. 178.
41. Francisco Pareja, *Francisco Pareja's 1613 Confessionario: A Documentary Source for Timucuan Ethnography*, ed. Jerald T. Milanich and William C. Sturtevant, trans. Emilo F. Moran, p. 34.
42. "Narrative of Cabeza de Vaca," pp. 50–54.
43. It is possible that for several decades after 1539 a few Indians remained about Crystal River, but the mounds no longer served as a major ceremonial center. See Ripley P. Bullen, "The Famous Crystal River Site," p. 34.
44. Garcilaso, *Florida of the Inca*, pp. 314–25.
45. José A. Saco, *Historia de la esclavitud de los indios en el nuevo mundo seguida de la historia de los repartimientos y encomiendas*,1: xliii.
46. Pedro Menéndez reports damage and murders caused by coast Indians of Florida (1573–74) in Jeannette T. Connor, ed. and trans., *Colonial Records of Spanish Florida*, 1: 33–35, 77–81.

47. Solís de Merás, *Menéndez*, pp. 189–93.
48. Lyon, *Enterprise of Florida*, p. 197, and Garcilaso, *Florida of the Inca*, p. 641.
49. Testimony, Pedro Menéndez Marqués, Madrid, 15 January 1573, in Connor, ed. and trans., *Colonial Records*, 1: 41.
50. Juan Rogel to Francis Borgia, Bahía de la Madre de Díos de la Florida, 28 August 1572, in Lewis and Loomie, *Spanish Mission*, p. 111.
51. Larson, "Historic Guale Indians," p. 133.
52. Much research remains to be done on the Spanish missions. Two standard works are John T. Lanning, *The Spanish Missions of Georgia*, and Robert A. Matter, "The Spanish Missions of Florida: The Friars Versus the Governors in the 'Golden Age,' 1606–1690." See also Gannon, *The Cross in the Sand*, pp. 54–67. Of particular value for the Apalachee missions is archeological work performed under the direction of the State of Florida's Division of Archives, History, and Records Management.
53. Pablo de Hita Salazar to crown, St. Augustine, 14 May 1680, in Manuel Serrano y Sanz, ed., *Documentos históricos de la Florida y la Luisiana, siglos XVI al XVII*, p. 217.
54. Scholars have edited and translated two of Pareja's Florida works: Francisco Pareja, *Arte de la Lengua Timvqvana compvesto en 1614 por le p^e Francisco Pareja . . .* , ed. Lucien Adam and Julien Vinson, and *Pareja's 1613 Confessionario*.
55. Luís Gerónimo Oré, *The Martyrs of Florida (1513–1616)*, ed. and trans. Maynard Geiger, p. 103.
56. Fred L. Pearson, Jr., "The Florencia Investigation of Spanish Timucua," p. 174.
57. Pareja, *Confessionario*, p. 28.
58. Félix Zubillaga, ed., *Monumenta Antiquae Floridae (1566–1572)*, p. 418, and Jerald T. Milanich, "The Western Timucua: Patterns of Acculturation and Change," p. 67.
59. Matter, "Spanish Missions," pp. 129, 154, 279.
60. Relation of Juan Rogel, between 1607 and 1611, in Lewis and Loomie, *Spanish Mission*, p. 121.
61. Though no systematic study has been made of *mestizaje* in sixteenth-century Florida, contemporary accounts frequently mention Spanish–Indian marriages. For example, see Oré, *Relación*, p. 25.
62. Antonio Martínez Carvajal to king, Havana, 3 November 1579, in Connor, ed., *Colonial Records*, 2: 249.
63. David Ingram, *The Land Travels of Davyd Ingram and Others in the Years 1568–9. From the Rio de Minas in the Gulph of Mexico to Cape Breton in Acadia*, in Plowden C. J. Weston, ed., *Documents Connected with the History of South Carolina*, pp. 7–23.

64. "Voyage of Christopher Newport, 1591," in Richard Hakluyt, ed., *The Principal Navigations, Voyages, Traffiques, and Discoveries of the English Nation*, 10: 189–90.
65. Thomas Edmondes to Charles Cornwallis, 22 June 1606, Cotton Vespasian, IX, BL, ab 281, 449–50, microfilm LC.
66. Lewis and Loomie, *Spanish Mission*, pp. 58–62, discuss this tradition and indicate some of the contemporary sources.

CHAPTER 3: TSENACOMMACAH (pp. 53–76)

1. Richard Hakluyt, "Discourse of Western Planting, 1584," in Eva G. R. Taylor, ed., *The Original Writings and Correspondence of the Two Richard Hakluyts*, 2: 293–97.
2. Ibid., p. 290.
3. Max Savelle discusses the doctrine of effective occupation in *The Origins of American Diplomacy: The International History of Angloamerica, 1492–1763*, pp. 199–201, and I elaborate more fully on usufruct in J. Leitch Wright, Jr., *Britain and the American Frontier, 1783–1815*, pp. 38–40.
4. Dale Van Every, *Disinherited: The Lost Birthright of the American Indian*, pp. 6–9.
5. Theodore Roosevelt, *The Winning of the West*, 1: 16–19, 331–35.
6. Two of the more recent works describing the coastal North Carolina Indians are Frank Roy Johnson, *The Algonquians: Indians of that Part of the New World First Visited by the English*, and Stanley A. South, *Indians in North Carolina*.
7. Letters patent to Walter Raleigh, in David B. Quinn, ed., *The Roanoke Voyages, 1584–1590: Documents to Illustrate the English Voyages to North America Under the Patent Granted to Walter Raleigh in 1584*, 1: 82–90. Quinn's introduction and explanatory notes afford a perceptive account of the Roanoke venture.
8. John Hooker on the Virginia Colony, 12 October 1586, in Quinn, ed., *Roanoke Voyages*, 1: 490–91.
9. Hakluyt, "Discourse of Western Planting," 2: 215.
10. "John White's Narrative of his Voyage, 1587," in Quinn, ed., *Roanoke Voyages*, 2: 531.
11. Thomas Hariot, "A Briefe and True Report," February 1588, in ibid., 1: 379.
12. Ibid., 1: 377–78.
13. Dedication by Richard Hakluyt to Raleigh, October 1587, in ibid., 2: 550, and pamphlet for the Virginia enterprise, by Richard Hakluyt, lawyer, 1585, in Taylor, ed., *Writings of Hakluyts*, 2: 334–36.

14. Ralph Lane to Richard Hakluyt the elder and Master H_____., in Quinn, ed., *Roanoke Voyages*, 1: 209.

15. Hulton and Quinn, eds., *American Drawings of John White*, plate 59.

16. Report of Francisco Fernández de Écija, after 24 September 1609, in Barbour, ed., *Jamestown Voyages*, 2: 295.

17. Ibid., pp. 316–17.

18. Letters patent to Sir Thomas Gates, Sir George Somers, and others, 10 April 1606, in ibid., 1: 25.

19. William Crashaw, *A Sermon Preached in London before the Right Honorable the Lord La Warre, Lord Gouernour and Captaine Generall of Virginea, and Others of His Majesties Counsell for that Kingdome, and the Rest of the Aduenturers in that Plantation . . .* , and Robert Gray, *A Good Speed to Virginia, 1609,* ed. Wesley F. Craven, c 2 verso.

20. "A praier duly said morning and euening upon the court of guard, either by the captaine of the watch . . . 1612," in Peter Force, ed., *Tracts and Other Papers, Relating Principally to the Origin, Settlement, and Progress of the Colonies in North America, from the Discovery of the Country to the Year 1776,* 3: 67.

21. "The memorable maske of the two honourable houses or Inns of Court; the Middle Temple and Lyncoln's Inn . . . at White-Hall, 15 February 1613," in Edward D. Neill, *History of the Virginia Company of London, with Letters to and from the First Colony Never Before Printed,* pp. 61–62.

22. Peter Walne, "The Collections for Henrico College, 1616–1618," pp. 260–61.

23. A declaration for the certain time of drawing the great standing lottery, 22 February 1615, Society of Antiquities, London, broadside, VCRP, reel 621.

24. "New Britain," 1609, in Alexander Brown, *The Genesis of the United States*, 1: 266.

25. "Virginias Verger . . . 1625," in Purchas, ed., *Pilgrimes*, 19: 222.

26. Gray, *Good Speed to Virginia,* c 3, and Swanton, *Indians of Southeastern U.S.*, pp. 709–12.

27. "A True Declaration of the Estate of the Colony in Virginia, 1610," in Force, ed., *Tracts*, 3: 6.

28. Ibid.

29. Court held for Virginia, 17 July 1622, in Susan M. Kingsbury, ed., *The Records of the Virginia Company of London*, 2: 95.

30. A good discussion of these Algonquian word lists is John P. Harrington, "The Original Strachey Vocabulary of the Virginia Indian Language," pp. 189–202.

31. "Virginia council instructions . . . to Thomas Gates, May 1609," in Kingsbury, ed., *Records of Virginia Company*, 3: 14–15.

Notes

32. Robert H. Land, "Henrico and Its College," pp. 475–98.
33. Instructions for the government of the colonies, 20 November 1606, in Brown, *Genesis*, 1: 67–68.
34. Virginia Company charter, 23 May 1609, in ibid., 1: 236.
35. "A True and Sincere Declaration," 14 December 1609, in ibid., 1: 339.
36. "Virginia council instructions . . . to Thomas Gates, May 1609," in Kingsbury, ed., *Records of Virginia Company*, 3: 15.
37. Crashaw, *Sermon Preached in London*, G3.
38. "Virginia council instructions . . . to Thomas Gates, May 1609," in Kingsbury, ed., *Records of the Virginia Company*, 3: 18–19.
39. Dale to president and council, Jamestown, 25 May 1611, in Brown, *Genesis*, 1: 492.
40. "The proceedings of the English colony in Virginia," in Purchas, ed., *Pilgrimes*, 18: 524.
41. Hariot, "Briefe and True Report," 1: 325.
42. Edward M. Wingfield, journal, 25 June, 3 July 1607, Lambeth Palace Library, VCRP, reel 607.
43. John Pory, "A Report of the Manner of Proceeding in the General Assembly . . . James City," 30, 31 July, 2, 3, 4 August 1619, in Kingsbury, ed., *Records of Virginia Company*, 3: 157.
44. Edward Waterhouse, "A Declaration of the State of the Colony," in Warren M. Billings, ed., *The Old Dominion in the Seventeenth Century: A Documentary History of Virginia, 1606–1689*, p. 222.
45. Proceedings of the Virginia assembly, 1619, in Lyon G. Tyler, ed., *Narratives of Early Virginia, 1606–1625*, p. 270.
46. Richard Ffrethorne to his father and mother, 3 April 1623, in Kingsbury, ed., *Records of Virginia Company*, 4: 61.
47. Minutes of council and general court, 1 November 1624, *VMHB*, 20 (1912), 157.
48. "A true declaration of the estate of the colony in Virginia . . . 1610," in Force, ed., *Tracts*, 3: 13.
49. Dorothy F. Monroe, "Henry Fleete," typescript, 7: 1, F6248: 1, VHS.
50. Nathanial C. Hale, *Virginia Venturer: A Historical Biography of William Claiborne, 1660–1677*, pp. 148–68.
51. Council in Virginia, "The Putting out of the Tenante . . . ," 11 November 1619, in Kingsbury, ed., *Records of Virginia Company*, 3: 228.
52. George Percy, *Observations Gathered out of a Discourse on the Plantation of the Southern Colony in Virginia by the English, 1606*, ed. David B. Quinn, p. 8.
53. Richard Ffrethorne to his father and mother, 3 April 1623, in Kingsbury, ed., *Records of Virginia Company*, 4: 61.

303

54. Alexander Whitaker, *Good Newes from Virginia. Sent to the Covnsell and Company of Virginia, Resident in England. From Alexander Whitaker, the Minister of Henrico in Virginia*, p. 40.
55. Strachey, *Historie*, p. 28.
56. Philip L. Barbour, *Pocahontas and Her World: A Chronicle of America's First Settlement in Which Is Related the Story of the Indians and the Englishmen—Particularly Captain John Smith, Captain Samuel Argall, and Master John Rolfe;* Grace S. Woodward, *Pocahontas;* and Frances Mossiker, *Pocahontas*.
57. Ralph Hamor, *A True Discourse of the Present Estate of Virginia . . .*, pp. 41–42.
58. Strachey, *Historie*, p. 62.
59. Harrington, "Strachey Vocabulary," p. 196.
60. "Letter of John Rolfe to Sir Thomas Dale, 1615," in Tyler, ed., *Narratives*, pp. 240–42.
61. Francis Magnel's relation, 1 July 1610, in Barbour, ed., *Jamestown Voyages*, 1: 154, and Edward D. Neill, *Virginia Carolorum: The Colony Under the Rule of Charles the First and Second, A.D. 1625–A.D. 1685 . . .*, p. 29.
62. William Symonds, *Virginia: A Sermon Preached at White-Chappel in the Presence of Many Honourable and Worshipfull, the Adventurers and Planters for Virginia, 25 April 1609*, p. 25.
63. Neill, *Virginia Carolorum*, p. 29, and Virginia Company, quarter court minutes, 13 June 1621, in Kingsbury, ed., *Records of Virginia Company*, 1: 496.
64. Gov. Argall, pardons, 20 October 1617, in Kingsbury, ed., *Records of Virginia Company*, 3: 74.
65. Thomas Smyth and Robert Johnson, reply to . . . John Bargrave, November 1621, in ibid., 3: 522.
66. Order of general assembly, 30 July 1619, in ibid., 3: 157.
67. Yeardley to [Edward Sandys], 1619, Ferrar Papers, Magdalen College, box xii, no. 1249, VCRP, reel 6702.
68. Hamor, *True Discourse*, p. 11.
69. "A sermon preached to the Honourable Company of the Virginia Plantation, 13⁰ November 1622," in John Donne, *The Sermons of John Donne*, ed. George R. Potter and Evelyn M. Simpson, 4: 265–73.
70. Christopher Brooke, "A Poem on the Late Massacre in Virginia," p. 285.
71. Wyndham B. Blanton, "Epidemics, Real and Imaginary, and Other Factors Influencing Seventeenth Century Virginia's Population," p. 454.
72. Samuel Argall to Virginia Company, 10 March 1618, in Kingsbury, ed., *Records of Virginia Company*, 3: 92.

CHAPTER 4: THE INDOMITABLE OLD DOMINION
(pp. 77–101)

1. Robert Bennett to Edward Bennett, Bennetes Welcome, 9 June 1623, *WMQ*, 2d ser., 13 (1933): 122.
2. Minutes of council and general court, Jamestown, 4 March 1628, *VMHB* 31 (1923): 148.
3. Ibid., 4 September 1626, 26 (1918): 11.
4. Ibid., 4 July 1627, 28 (1920): 101–2.
5. John Berry and Francis Moryson, "A true narrative of the rise, progresse, and cessation of the late rebellion in Virginia . . . , 1677," PRO, CO 5/1371, VCRP, pp. 197–99.
6. Swanton, *Indians of Southeast*, pp. 610–11.
7. A sketch of the Susquehannock fort is included with Berry and Moryson, "A true narrative," CO 5/1371, VCRP, p. 187.
8. Occaneechee fortifications are described in "A description of the fight between the English and the Indians in Virginia in May 1676. Nathaniel Bacon, Esq. being their Generall and the number of his men being 211." CO 1/36, VCRP, 92: 21–22.
9. John Barnwell to your honor, New Berne, 12 March 1712, *VMHB*, 6 (1899): 45.
10. Minutes of general assembly, 10 January 1644, *VMHB*, 23 (1915): 234.
11. Robert Bennett to Edward Bennett, 9 June 1623 (note 1 above), p. 122.
12. "An act for the safeguard and defence of the country against the Indians, 2 September 1674–7, March 1675–6," in William W. Hening, ed., *The Statutes at Large, Being a Collection of All the Laws of Virginia from the First Session of the Legislature in the Year 1619*, 2: 330–31.
13. Minutes of general assembly, James City, 12 January 1641, *VMHB* 9 (1902): 53–54.
14. Herbert Jeffreys to Sir Joseph Williamson, Virginia, 8 June 1678, *VMHB* 5 (1898): 52.
15. "An act preventing the kidnapping of Indian children, October 1649," in Billings, ed., *Documentary History*, pp. 228–29.
16. A brief description of the 1644 massacre can be found in William L. Shea, "Virginia at War, 1644–1646."
17. Richard L. Morton, *Colonial Virginia*, 1: 153.
18. Peace treaty with Necotowance, 5 October 1646, in Hening, ed., *Statutes*, 1: 323–26.
19. Act, 3 November 1647, ibid., 1: 348, and ibid., 5 July 1653, 1: 382.
20. York County court, 25 July 1648, in Beverley Fleet, ed., *Virginia Colonial Abstracts, York County, 1648–1657*, p. 389, n. 2.

21. Act, 10 March 1655/6, in Hening, ed., *Statutes*, 1: 402–3, and at a meeting of the militia, 25 July 1656, Charles City County records, VSL, 1: 61.
22. Thomas J. Wertenbaker, *Torchbearer of the Revolution: The Story of Bacon's Rebellion and Its Leader*, is the best known advocate of this interpretation, though considerably earlier the nineteenth-century historian George Bancroft in his multivolume history of the United States made the same point.
23. "Proposals of William Byrd touching the Indian trade, 29 September 1683," CO 1/51, VCRP, 96: 149.
24. Morgan, *American Slavery, American Freedom*, p. 257.
25. Berry and Moryson, "A true narrative," pp. 197–99.
26. Wilcomb E. Washburn, *The Governor and the Rebel: A History of Bacon's Rebellion in Virginia*, pp. 40–48.
27. A description of the fight between the English and Indians, May 1677, WMQ, 1st ser., 9 (1900): 4.
28. Acts of assembly, 5 June 1676, in Hening, ed., *Statutes*, 2: 341–52.
29. Berry and Moryson, "A true narrative," p. 199.
30. Berry and Moryson, "Most humble proposals on behalf of the Indian kings and queens . . . [May 29], 1677," CO 5/1371, VCRP.
31. Articles of peace between King Charles II and Indians, Middle Plantation, 29 May 1677, *VMHB* 14 (1907): 289–96.
32. Ibid., p. 289.
33. Henry Brigg's deposition, 3 October [1711], *VMHB* 7 (1900): 349–52, and examination of Great Peter, 23 October [1710], *VMHB* 8 (1901): 5–6.
34. Alvin Toffler, *Future Shock*, pp. 12–13.
35. Tribute, 29 April 1699, CO 5/1310, VCRP.
36. ? to Joseph Williamson, Virginia, 28 June 1678, Lee Family Papers, VHS, mss. 1, L51, f.8.
37. Minutes of Virginia council, James City, 22 February 1700, *CSP, Colonial*, 18: 80.
38. "An act concerning the northern Indians, 2 December 1662," in Hening, ed., *Statutes*, 2: 193–94.
39. "An act for destroying wolves, October 1669," in ibid., 2: 274–76.
40. Samples of Virginia's seventeenth-century peltry exports can be found in Port Book, London, overseas imports, 1633–34, PRO, E 190/38/5, VCRP, and skins imported, 1699–1715, CO 5/1317, VCRP.
41. For examples, see Edward Bestwicke inventory 8 June 1641, Northampton County records, 1640–45, VSL, 2: 82–83, and Robert Partridge inventory, 2 March 1667, York County records, VSL, 2a: 243.
42. Michael Upchurch to Mr. Ferrar, Virginia, 4 May 1652, Ferrar Papers, Cambridge University, box 10, VCRP, 574: 1031.

43. Minutes of council and general court, 8 November 1624, *VMHB* 21 (1913): 46–47.
44. Harrington, "Strachey Vocabulary," sheet 10, and Rappahannock Co. Deed Book No. 2, 9 August 1662, *WMQ*, 2d ser., 18 (1938): 299.
45. Ludwell L. Montague, "Richard Lee, the Emigrant, 1613(?)–1664," pp. 19–34.
46. Francis Yeardley to John Farrar, Linne Haven, 8 May 1654, Rawlingson mss., Bodleian Lib., Oxford, A14, VCRP, 637: 84–87.
47. "The Discovery of New Brittaine . . . 27 August 1650, by Edward Bland, Merchant, Abraham Woode, Captain, Sackford Brewster, Elias Pennant, Gentlemen," in Salley, ed., *Narratives of Carolina*, pp. 16–17.
48. Abraham Wood to John Richards, Ft. Henry, 1674, *CSP, Colonial*, 7: 604–7.
49. Agreement, Edward Hatcher, Thomas Shippey, and John Davis, June 1672, *WMQ*, 2d ser., 16 (1936): 458, and William Byrd, "A Journey to the Land of Eden, Anno 1733," *The Prose Works of William Byrd of Westover: Narratives of a Colonial Virginian*, ed. Louis B. Wright, p. 400.
50. Nicholas Spencer to Lords of Trade, 18 March 1679/80, CO 1/44, VCRP, 94: 131.
51. Accomack County, court, 10 November 1663, Accomack County records, 1663–1671, VSL, 1: 44.
52. A useful published treatment of indentured servitude, including brief but incomplete mention of Indian servants, is in Philip A. Bruce, *Economic History of Virginia in the Seventeenth Century: An Inquiry into the Material Condition of the People, Based upon Original and Contemporary Records*, 2: 52–56.
53. Will of Edward Gunstocker, 20 October 1676, *WMQ*, 2d ser., 16 (1936): 593.
54. Act, October, 1670, in Hening, ed., *Statutes*, 2: 280–81.
55. William Fitzhugh to Nicholas Spencer, 16 February 1687/8, in William Fitzhugh, *William Fitzhugh and His Chesapeake World, 1676–1701; the Fitzhugh Letters and Other Documents*, ed. Richard B. Davis, pp. 237–38.
56. George Wilson, diary, James City, 20 September 1661, writings of George Wilson, Library of Society of Friends, box C, VCRP.
57. Order of assembly, 13 March 1659/60, in Hening, ed., *Statutes*, 1: 547.
58. Charles City County, court, Westover, 4 August 1690, Charles City County records, VSL, 13: 298.
59. Accomack County, court, 7 August 1706, Accomack County records, 1676–1709, VSL, 79: 75.

60. Accomack County, court, 1671, Accomack County Order Book, 1671–1673, in Billings, ed. *The Old Dominion*, p. 232.
61. Grand assembly, 11 October 1660, in Hening, ed., *Statutes*, 2: 16, and Culpeper to ?, Virginia, 25 July 1681, CO 1/47, VCRP, 96: 79–81.
62. C. E. Gilliam, "An English Conspiracy Against Wahanganoche, King of Potomac, *circa* 1660," pp. 8–9.
63. Assembly, confirmation of grant, 13 March 1658/9, in Hening, ed., *Statutes*, 1: 515.
64. Ibid., 10 March 1655/56, 1: 396, and journal, 10 July 1700, in Henry R. McIlwaine, ed., *Executive Journals of the Council of Virginia*, 2: 94.
65. Thomas P. Abernethy, *Western Lands and the American Revolution*, p. 100.
66. Thomas Dunthorne muster, 1625, in Blanche A. Chapman, *Wills and Administrations of Elizabeth City County, and Virginia, and Other Genealogical and Historical Items, 1610–1800*, p. 14. Apparently the Indian Thomas arrived by ship, but documents are vague in this instance. Other Indians after 1625 without question were imported by sea. See also Westmoreland County, court, 29 March 1699, Westmoreland County records, VSL, 53: 30a.
67. Act, 17 September 1668, in Hening, ed., *Statutes*, 1: 274–75, and Edmund Andros to Board of Trade, Virginia, 22 April 1697, *CSP, Colonial*, 15: 456.

CHAPTER 5: GOOSE CREEK MEN (pp. 102–125)

1. William S. Powell, "Carolana and the Incomparable Roanoke: Explorations and Attempted Settlements, 1620–1663," pp. 3–20.
2. Luis Horruytiner to King, St. Augustine, 15 November 1633, AGI, S.D., 54-5-18, John B. Stetson Collection.
3. J. Leitch Wright, Jr., ed., "William Hilton's Voyage to Carolina in 1662," pp. 99–102.
4. "A True Relation of a Voyage, upon Discovery of Part of the Coast of Florida, from the Lat. of 31 Deg. to 33 Deg. 45M North Lat. in the Ship Adventure, William Hilton Commander . . . Aug. 19, 1663," in Salley, ed., *Narratives of Carolina*, pp. 37–45.
5. Robert Harley to Edward Harley, 3 November 1662, Harley Papers, Loan, 29/179, BL, VCRP.
6. "A Relation of a Voyage on the Coast of the Province of Carolina, Formerly called Florida . . . 1666," in Salley, ed., *Narratives of Carolina*, pp. 98–108.
7. Henry Woodward to Earl of Shaftsbury, 31 December 1674, in ibid.,

pp. 132–33, and Thomas Colleton to ?, Carolina, 19 November 1670, in ibid., pp. 620–21.

8. The history of the Savannah Indians before the mid-seventeenth century is little understood, but these Algonquians were of far more consequence in the Lower South than is generally recognized. No comprehensive ethnohistory of them exists, but the best starting point is Jerry E. Clark, *The Shawnee*.

9. Woodward to Shaftsbury, 31 December 1674, in Salley, ed., *Narratives of Carolina*, pp. 132–33.

10. Council journal, 25 July 1674, in *The Shaftsbury Papers, and Other Records relating to Carolina and the First Settlement on Ashley River Prior to the Year 1676*, ed. Langdon Cheves, p. 451.

11. Woodward to Shaftsbury, 31 December 1674, in Salley, ed., *Narratives of Carolina*, pp. 133–34.

12. Verner W. Crane, *The Southern Frontier, 1670–1732*, pp. 18–20.

13. Marion Eugene Sirmans, *Colonial South Carolina: A Political History, 1663–1763*, pp. 17–18, 41–50.

14. Details of Mathews's, Middleton's, and Moore's careers are found in Sirmans, *Colonial South Carolina*, and in Jonathan P. Thomas, Jr., "The Barbadians in Early South Carolina."

15. Herbert E. Bolton, "Spanish Resistance to the Carolina Traders in Western Georgia (1680–1704)," pp. 122–26.

16. Crane, *Southern Frontier*, pp. 108–36.

17. Ibid, p. 112.

18. Gabriel D. V. Calderón, "A 17th Century Letter of Gabriel Diaz Vara Calderón, Bishop of Cuba, Describing the Indians and Indian Missions of Florida," ed. and trans. Lucy L. Wenhold, pp. 7–14.

19. Crane, *Southern Frontier*, pp. 25–26.

20. Hita Salazar to crown, St. Augustine, 14 May 1680, AGI, S.D. 58-1-26, SRNC, reel 4: 72.

21. Juan Marqués Cabrera to crown, 8 December 1680, AGI, S.D., 54-5-11, Stetson Col.

22. Woodward to John Godfrey, 21 March 1685, *CSP, Colonial*, 12: 19.

23. B. Calvin Jones, "Colonel James Moore and the Destruction of the Apalachee Missions in 1704," pp. 25–31.

24. Moore to Lords Proprietors, 26 January 1704, America, British Colonies, 8, LC, and council of war, St. Augustine, 13 July 1704, in Mark F. Boyd, Hale G. Smith and John W. Griffin, *Here They Once Stood: The Tragic End of the Apalachee Missions*, p. 57.

25. Admiral Landeche to the viceroy, Havana, 11 August 1705, in ibid., p. 84.

26. King to viceroy of New Spain, Madrid, 4 December 1709, reales cédulas, originales, AGN, tomo 34, exp. 88.

27. Martínez de la Vega to crown, Havana, 7 July 1732, AGI, S.D., 58-2-10, Stetson Col.

28. Crown to Francisco de Córcoles y Martínez, 18 July 1711, ibid., 58-2-3.

29. Fundamenal constitutions, 21 July 1669, in Mattie E. E. Parker, ed., *North Carolina Charters and Constitutions, 1578–1698*, pp. 148–51.

30. Indians deeds, 13 February 1683, in James H. Easterby, ed., *The Journal of the Commons House of Assembly*, 15 December 1736, 1: 104–6; indenture . . . casique of Ashepoo, 13 February 16(84), SCA, misc. records, 1682–90, pp. 107–8; and indenture . . . casique of Witcheaugh, 13 February 16(85), ibid., pp. 115–16.

31. John Archdale, "A New Description of that Fertile and Pleasant Province of Carolina, 1707," in Salley, ed., *Narratives of Carolina*, p. 285.

32. Records of Perquiman's Precinct court, February 1694, in William L. Saunders, ed., *The Colonial Records of North Carolina*, 1: 394, and Joshua Snell warrant, 14 July 1694, in Alexander S. Salley, Jr., and R. Nicholas Olsberg, *Warrants for Lands in South Carolina, 1672–1711*, p. 468.

33. Council journal, 18 February 1708, in McIlwaine, ed., *Executive Journals, Council*, 3: 207.

34. Ibid., 9 August 1704, 2: 381–82.

35. Edmund Jenings to Board of Trade, Virginia, 20 September 1708, CO 5/1316, VCRP.

36. Hugh T. Lefler and William S. Powell, *Colonial North Carolina: A History*, pp. 66–68.

37. "DeGraffenried's manuscript . . .," in Saunders, ed., *N.C. Colonial Records*, 1: 913.

38. John Barnwell to your honor, Narhantes Fort, 4 February 1712, *SCHGM* 9 (1908): 30–36.

39. Barnwell to your honor, New Berne, 12 March 1712, *VMHB* 6 (1899): 45.

40. John Barnwell to your honor, Narhantes Fort, 4 February 1712, *SCHGM* 9 (1908): 34–36.

41. James Moore, Jr., to Thomas Pollock, 27 March 1713, in Saunders, ed., *N. C. Colonial Records*, 2: 27.

42. Thomas Pollock to ?, Chowan, 25 April 1713, in ibid., 2: 37–39.

43. Baker, "Cofitachique," p. 211.

44. Testimony of William Byrd and Thomas Bannister, 15 July 1715, Great Britain, Board of Trade, *Journal of the Commissioners for Trade and Plantations . . . Preserved in the Public Record Office . . .*, 3: 54–55.

45. Some paragraphs of letters from South Carolina, 15 May 1715, CO 5/1265, VCRP, 889: 44(iii).

Notes

46. Francis Le Jau to secretary, S.C., 10 May 1715, SPG mss. A 10: 114.
47. Córcoles to crown, Florida, 5 July 1715, AGI, S.D., leg. 58-1-30, Stetson Col.
48. Verner W. Crane, "Thomas Nairne," *DAB*, 13: 379.
49. John Wright *v.* John Cochran, 19 April 1714, Court of Common Pleas, judgment rolls, SCA, box 6, 490.
50. Richard Berisford *v.* John Cochran, 19 April 1712, ibid., box 2, 143, 19A, and John Wright *v.* John Cochran, 19 April 1714, ibid., box 6, 490.
51. Charles Rodd to his employer in London, Charleston, 8 May 1715, *CSP, Colonial*, 28: 166–69.
52. Le Jau to secretary, S.C., 21 May 1715, SPG mss. A, 10: 110.
53. John Barnwell, map, 1722, SCA.
54. Robert Johnson to Board of Trade, Charleston, 12 January 1720, *CSP, Colonial*, 31: 301.
55. Diego Peña to Juan de Ayala Escobar, Sante Fe, 8 October 1717, in Mark F. Boyd, ed. and trans., "Documents Describing the Second and Third Expeditions of Lieutenant Diego Peña to Apalachee and Apalachicola in 1717 and 1718," p. 134.
56. Sirmans, *Colonial South Carolina*, pp. 114, 132.
57. J. Leitch Wright, Jr., *Anglo-Spanish Rivalry in North America*, pp. 71–72.
58. Samuel Wilson, "An account of the Province of Carolina in America: Together with an Abstract of the Patent, and Several Other Useful Particulars . . . (London, 1682)," in Salley, ed., *Narratives of Carolina*, p. 173.
59. George Burrington to Alured Popple, N.C., 2 November 1732, *CSP, Colonial*, 39: 243.

CHAPTER 6: BRANDS AND SLAVE CORDS (pp. 126–150)

1. William Bartram, *The Travels of William Bartram, Naturalist's Edition*, ed. Francis Harper, p. 118.
2. Garcilaso, *Florida of the Inca*, p. 330, and Lawson, *History*, pp. 52–53.
3. The best single, though not comprehensive, work on medieval European slavery is Charles Verlinden, *L'esclavage dans l'Europe médiévale*.
4. A. J. R. Russell-Wood, "Iberian Expansion and the Issue of Black Slavery: Changing Portuguese Attitudes, 1440–1770," p. 27.
5. Ruth Pike, *Aristocrats and Traders: Sevillian Society in the Sixteenth Century*, pp. 170–72.

6. Silvio A. Zavala, *Los esclavos indios en Neuva España*, pp. 40, 107, 117–18, and Saco, *Historia de la esclavitud*, 2: 247–356.
7. Stuart B. Schwartz, "Indian Labor and New World Plantations: European Demands and Indian Responses in Northeastern Brazil," p. 58.
8. Colin A. Palmer, *Slaves of the White God: Blacks in Mexico, 1570–1650*, pp. 3–4, 26–30.
9. H. Orlando Patterson, *The Sociology of Slavery: An Analysis of the Origins, Development and Structure of Negro Slave Society in Jamaica*, pp. 113–259.
10. Samuel J. Hurwitz and Edith F. Hurwitz, *Jamaica: A Historical Portrait*, p. 215.
11. Zavala, *Esclavos indios*, pp. 197–98.
12. Edward Arber and Arthur G. Bradley, eds., *Travels and Works of Captain John Smith, President of Virginia, and Admiral of New England, 1580–1631*, 1: xxix–xxx and 2: 956.
13. Culpeper's instructions, 6 December 1679, *CSP, Colonial*, 11: 157.
14. Virginia assembly, acts 17 and 18, 10 October 1649, in Warren M. Billings, ed., "Some Acts Not in Hening's Statutes: The Acts of Assembly, April 1652, November 1652, and July 1653," pp. 64–65.
15. Grand assembly, 13 March 1658, in Hening, ed., *Statutes*, 1: 455–56.
16. Ibid., 11 October 1660, 2: 16. It was possible that some of the earliest Indians shipped out of Virginia technically were indentured servants. If so, all indications are that their terms of service were perpetual.
17. Ibid., 5 June 1676, 2: 346, and 10 November 1682, 2: 491.
18. Ibid., 20 October 1669, 2: 283.
19. Act for apprehension of runaway Negroes and slaves, James City, 24 September 1672, CO 1/29, VCRP.
20. Estate of Thomas Smalcombe, 10 March 1645, *VMHB* 17 (1910): 105.
21. An account of the estate of James Crews, 8 May 1677, CO 5/1371, VCRP.
22. William Berkeley to Robert Smyth, 22 June 1666, in Billings, ed., *Old Dominion*, p. 231.
23. King of Waineoake's deed to Elizabeth Short, 2 July 1659, *WMQ*, 1st ser., 6 (1897): 214–15.
24. List of ships . . . imported slaves . . . District of Upper James River, 1710–1718, CO 5/1320, VCRP.
25. Minutes, 11 October 1627, in Henry R. McIlwaine, ed., *Minutes of the Council and General Court of Colonial Virginia, 1622–1632, 1670–1676*, p. 155.
26. Alexander Spotswood to Board of Trade, Virginia, 6 March 1711, *CSP, Colonial*, 25: 416.

27. Many Henrico County and Westmoreland County records for these years have survived and are in the VSL.
28. "Act for appointing rangers, 25 October 1710," in Hening, ed., *Statutes*, 4: 10.
29. Council minutes, 26 January 1690, in McIlwaine, ed., *Executive Journals, Council*, 1: 147.
30. Berry and Moryson, "A true narrative."
31. Kenneth G. Davies, *The Royal African Company*, p. 65.
32. Ibid., pp. 213–90.
33. Converse D. Clowse, *Economic Beginnings in Colonial South Carolina, 1670–1730*, p. 66.
34. Governor and council, 27 September 1671, in Alexander S. Salley, Jr., ed., *Journal of the Grand Council of South Carolina, August 25, 1671–June 24, 1680*, pp. 8–9, and ibid., 2 October 1671, p. 9.
35. Instructions from the Lords Proprietors, 17 May 1680, *CSP, Colonial*, 10: 526, and journal, 22 June 1692, in Salley, ed., *Journal of the Grand Council of South Carolina, April 11, 1692–September 26, 1692*, pp. 45–46.
36. Hita Salazar to crown, Florida, 15 June 1675, SRNC, reel 4, and ibid., 10 November 1678, in Serrano y Sanz, ed., *Documentos históricos*, pp. 205–9.
37. For example, see export licenses (1681) in records of appellate court, RSUS, S.C., F reel 1.
38. Information on Yamasee Indians, 6 May 1685, *CSP, Colonial*, 12: 40.
39. Jay Higginbotham, *Old Mobile: Fort Louis de la Louisiane, 1702–1711*, p. 242.
40. Lords Proprietors to governor and deputies . . ., 30 September 1683, *CSP, Colonial*, 11: 510.
41. Lawson, *History*, pp. 211–12.
42. Matter, "Spanish Missions," p. 298.
43. "Representation to Lords Proprietors, 26 June 1705," in Saunders, ed., *N. C. Colonial Records*, 2: 904.
44. Jean Bernard Bossu, *Jean Bernard Bossu's Travels in the Interior of North America, 1751–1762*, ed. and trans. Seymour Feiler, p. 47.
45. Crane, *Southern Frontier*, pp. 89–94, 148.
46. Journal, 26 June 1707, in Alexander S. Salley, Jr., ed., *Journals of the Commons House of Assembly of South Carolina, June 5, 1707–July 19, 1707*, p. 63.
47. Thomas Nairne to [?], 10 July 1708, in Alexander S. Salley, Jr., ed., *Records in the British Public Record Office Relating to South Carolina, 1663–1710*, 5: 195–200; Nairne to [Earl of Sunderland?], S.C., 10 July 1709, *CSP, Colonial*, 24: 422–23; and Thomas Nairne, *A Letter from South Carolina; Giving an Account of the Soil, Air, Product, Trade, Government, Laws, Religion, People, Military Strength, etc. of that Province*, p. 34.

48. Córcoles to crown, St. Augustine, 18 April 1708, AGI, S.D., 58-1-28, Stetson Col.
49. Charles W. Arnade, *The Siege of St. Augustine in 1702*, pp. 51–52.
50. Douglas L. Rights, *The American Indian in North Carolina*, p. 46.
51. Edward Hyde to Giles Rainsford, Chowan, in Saunders, ed., *N.C. Colonial Records*, 1: 850.
52. Alexander Long, "A Small Postscript of the Ways and Manners of the Indians Called Charikees," p. 3, and journal, 4 May 1714, in William L. McDowell, Jr., ed., *Journals of the Commissioners of the Indian Trade, September 20, 1710–August 29, 1718*, p. 53.
53. John Barnwell to Robert Johnson, [1720 ?], *CSP, Colonial*, 31: 307–8.
54. John J. TePaske, *The Governorship of Spanish Florida, 1700–1763*, pp. 208–9.
55. Bartram, *Travels*, pp. 118–21.
56. Journal, 22 January 1734/5, in Salley, ed., *Journals of Commons House*, p. 32.
57. Arthur Dobbs to William Pitt, 14 October 1759, in Saunders, ed., *N. C. Colonial Records*, 6: 61.
58. Diego de la Haya Fernández, junta, Cartago, 30 September 1722, in León Fernández, ed., *Colección de documentos para la historia de Costa-Rica*, 9: 154.
59. Remarks on the Spanish ambassador's memorial of 20 October 1734, SP94/120.
60. Charles Wager to Edward Vernon, Admiralty Office, 10 June 1740, in B. McL. Ranft, ed., *The Vernon Papers*, p. 110.
61. Wilbur R. Jacobs, "The Tip of an Iceberg: Pre-Columbian Indian Demography and Some Implications for Revisionism," p. 131.
62. Roger Anstey, *The Atlantic Slave Trade and British Abolition, 1760–1810*, pp. 79–82.
63. Robert Beverly's account of Lamhatty, ca. 1707, Lee Family Papers, VHS, L51, f. 677.
64. Deposition, Juan Ripalta, 1573, in Connor, ed. and trans., *Florida Colonial Records*, 1: 63.
65. Journal, 23 July 1716, in McDowell, ed., *Journals of Indian Trade*, p. 83, and ibid., 29 November 1716, p. 134.
66. *Virginia Gazette*, supplement, 29 April 1775.
67. Philip D. Curtin, *The Atlantic Slave Trade: A Census*, pp. 86–92.
68. William R. Snell, "Indian Slavery in Colonial South Carolina, 1671–1795," p. 3.
69. Córcoles y Martínez to crown, St. Augustine, 14 January 1708, AGI, S.D., SRNC, reel 11.
70. Bossu, *Travels*, p. 47.
71. Many accounts of these slave raids are found in autos sobre la entrada de los enemigos yngleses en las provincias de Timuqua,

Apalachicole, y Caueta, 1685–86, Jeannette T. Connor Collection, LC.
72. Snell, "Indian Slavery," p. 96.
73. Journal, 24 July 1716, in McDowell, ed., *Journals of Indian Trade*, p. 86.
74. John Evans's journal, 1702–1715, South Caroliniana Library, University of South Carolina, p. 2353.
75. John R. Swanton, *Myths and Tales of the Southeastern Indians*, p. 115.

CHAPTER 7: EXPLOITING THIS 'VIRGIN LAND' (pp. 151–174)

1. U.S. Bureau of the Census, *1970 Census of Population, Subject Reports: American Indians*, p. 1. Since 1960 the Census Bureau has considered anybody an Indian who claims to be one, which has increased the number of Southern Indians recorded.
2. Examples of Indians whose ages were adjudged are scattered throughout Henrico County court records during the 1670s, 1680s, and 1690s, reels 53 and 65, VSL.
3. William Dun to secretray, Charleston, 20 September 1708, SPG, mss. A, 4: 385.
4. Notitia parochialis, St. Thomas Parish, S.C., 16 February 1720, ibid., 14: 70.
5. Sirmans, *Colonial South Carolina*, p. 107.
6. Nairne, *Letter from S.C.*, p. 44.
7. Higginbotham, *Old Mobile*, p. 540.
8. John Pory, "A Reporte . . . general assembly, Jamestown, 30, 31 July, 2, 3, 4 August 1619," in Kingsbury, ed., *Records of Virginia Co.*, 3: 165–66.
9. Treasurer and council for Virginia to governor and council in Virginia, 1 August 1622, in ibid., pp. 672–73.
10. ? to Edwin Sandys, 1620, in ibid., 1: 307–8.
11. Grand assembly, 31 March 1655, in Hening, ed., *Statutes*, 1: 410.
12. Journal, 10 July 1717, in McDowell, ed., *Journals of Indian Trade*, pp. 198–99.
13. Act, 5 December 1722, in Hening, ed., *Statutes*, 4: 133.
14. Indenture, Mary Scott and Alexander, 8 April 1690, Perquiman's Precinct court records, 1688–1693, NCA.
15. Minutes of council and general court, Jamestown, 4 March 1628, *VMHB*, 31 (1923): 148.
16. Council, 12 May 1705, in McIlwaine, ed., *Executive Journals, Council*, 3: 5–6.

17. Court, 20 September 1688, Henrico County records, VSL, 53: 280.
18. Ibid., 1 August 1688, 53: 205–6.
19. Ibid., 20 September 1688, 53: 280.
20. Journal, 27 October 1709, in McIlwaine, ed., *Executive Journals, Council*, 3: 226.
21. Curtis C. Davis, "A Long Line of Cupbearers: The Earliest Little-pages in America," p. 438.
22. Court, 8 December 1697, Accomack County records, 1676–1709, VSL, 79: 8.
23. Ibid., 1 August 1704, 79: 33.
24. Journal, 24 January 1702, in Salley, ed., *Journals Commons House*, p. 21, and court, Lower County of Norfolk, 10 January 1637, *VMHB*, 39 (1931): 9.
25. Deed between King of Potomeck and Gerrard Fowke, 14 July 1655, in John F. Dorman ed., *Westmoreland County, Virginia, Records, 1661–64*, p. 1.
26. Court, 16 April 1678, Accomack County records, VSL, 79: 131.
27. Journal, 30 July 1716, in McDowell, ed., *Journals of Indian Trade*, p. 93.
28. Court, Westover, 3 April 1689, Charles City County records, VSL 13: 200.
29. Ibid., 14 September 1661, VSL, 1: 295.
30. John Stewart to William Dunlop, Watbu, S.C., 23 June 1690, *SCHGM*, 32: 94.
31. Court, 1676–1709, 1677 Accomack County records, VSL, 79: 91.
32. Journal, 21 September 1710, in McDowell, ed., *Journals of Indian Trade*, p. 4.
33. For a discussion of the introduction of rice into Carolina see Peter H. Wood, *Black Majority: Negroes in Colonial South Carolina from 1670 through the Stono Rebellion*, pp. 35–62.
34. Dorothy Fleet Monroe, "Henry Fleete Biography," p. 9.
35. Court, 6 June 1705, Accomack County records, VSL, 79: 47a.
36. Matter, "Spanish Missions," p. 252.
37. William Talbot, "The Discoveries of John Lederer, in Three Several Marches from Virginia to the West of Carolina . . ., 1672," in Clarence W. Alvord and Lee Bidgood, eds., *The First Explorations of the Trans-Allegheny Region by the Virginians, 1650–1674*, p. 156.
38. Journal, 28 January 1717, in McDowell, ed., *Journals of Indian Trade*, p. 154.
39. Ibid., 18 July 1716, p. 82, and Theophilus Hastings to Board, Too-goloe, 27 June 1716, in ibid., p. 77.
40. Journal, 1 May 1717, in ibid., p. 177.
41. Surrey County records, 6 May 1671, *WMQ*, 2d ser., 19 (1939): 534.
42. John Clayton to Dr. Grene, 1687, Add. MSS, 4437, VCRP, reel 546.

43. Court, Accomack county, 1671, in Billings, ed., *Old Dominion*, p. 232.

44. John Chisman release to John Adison, 31 December 1647, *WMQ*, 1st ser., 23 (1914–15): 274.

45. *The Reformed Virginian Silk-Worm, or a Rare and New Discovery of a Speedy Way, and Easy Means, Found Out by a Young Lady in England* . . ., *1655*, in Force, ed., *Tracts*, 3: 1, 33.

46. Crown to Hita Salazar, Madrid, 13 February 1676, AGI, S.D., 58-1-21, SRNC, reel 4.

47. Higginbotham, *Old Mobile*, p. 359.

48. Journal, 10 July 1716, in McDowell, ed., *Journals of Indian Trade*, p. 73.

49. Nicholas Ponce de León to crown, St. Augustine, 8 May 1674, AGI, S.D. 54-5-11, SRNC, reel 4.

50. Juan Gomez to reverend father, Havana, 13 March 1657, Historic Letters of Southeast, 16th, 17th, and 18th centuries, SAC.

51. Jonathan Dickinson, *Jonathan Dickinson's Journal, or, God's Protecting Providence. Being the Narrative of a Journey from Port Royal in Jamaica to Philadelphia between August 23, 1696 and April 1, 1697*, eds. E. W. Andrews and C. M. Andrews, p. 74.

52. Arnade, *Siege of St. Augustine*, p. 33; admiralty court, 19 November 1718, court of admiralty, T. 309, RSUS, p. 308; and judgment against Joseph Healis, Charleston, 17 July 1705, judgment rolls, SCA.

53. Harry Beverley to ?, 1716 [?], *VMHB*, 3 (1896): 176.

54. Richard Ward will, 18 April 1682, in Benjamin B. Weisiger, ed., *Colonial Wills of Henrico County. Virginia, Part One, 1654–1737*, p. 9.

55. Lachlan McGillivray to James Glen, Augusta, 17 February 1756, in William L. McDowell, Jr., ed., *Documents Relating to Indian Affairs*, 2: 104.

56. Jour. of Va. Council, 24 October 1711, in Saunders, ed., *N.C. Colonial Records*, 1: 815, and Robert Dinwiddie, *The Official Records of Robert Dinwiddie, Lieutenant-Governor of the Colony of Virginia, 1751–1758, Now First Printed from the Manuscript in the Collections of the Virginia Historical Society*, ed. R. A. Brock, 2: 507.

57. Will of Edward Gunstocker, 20 October 1676, *WMQ*, 2d ser., 16 (1936): 593.

58. Court, 4 February 1663, in Fleet, ed., *Virginia Colonial Abstracts, Charles City County Court Orders, 1661–1664*, p. 365.

59. Court, 6 August 1659, Northumberland County records, *WMQ*, 1st ser., 6 (1897): 118–19.

60. Journal, 13 February 1701, in Salley, ed., *Journals of Commons House*, p. 4, and court, 20 August 1683, Henrico County records, VSL, 53: 63.

61. Council, Edenton, 23 April 1731, in Saunders, ed., *N.C. Colonial Records*, 3: 218.
62. John Woort to John Bee, Ocheese River, 30 July 1723, *CSP, Colonial*, 33: 351.
63. Council, 23 April 1718, in McIlwaine, ed., *Executive Journals, Council*, 3: 465–66, and journal, 18 April 1712, in McDowell, ed., *Journals of Indian Trade*, p. 23.
64. Court, 17 July 1675, Accomack County records, VSL, 2: 296.
65. *South Carolina Gazette*, 24 February 1759.
66. Snell, "Indian Slavery," pp. 174–78.
67. Court, 28 April 1709, Westmoreland County records, VSL, 54: 120a.
68. Council journal, Little River, 10 March 1715, in Saunders, ed., *N. C. Colonial Records*, 2: 172.
69. Francis Wyatt to ?, Virginia, 1623–24? *WMQ*, 2d ser., 6 (1926): 118.
70. Lodvic Grant to James Glen, Cherokees, 8 February 1754, in McDowell, ed., *Documents, Indian Affairs*, 1: 474–76.
71. Journal, 13 January 1693, in Salley, ed., *Journals Commons House*, p. 12.
72. William Baron to Thomas Pollock, 17 October 1706, colonial court records, misc. papers, 1677–1775, NCA, CCR 192.
73. There is no comprehensive account of the Southern Indian trade. Of value are Crane, *Southern Frontier*, pp. 108–36, and references scattered throughout Adair, *History of the American Indians*.
74. List of the prices of goods for the Cherokee trade, 1 November 1751, in McDowell, ed., *Documents, Indian Affairs*, 1: 146.
75. James Beamer to James Glen, Estertoe, 21 February 1756, in ibid., 2: 105.

CHAPTER 8: JEHOVAH AND THE CORN MOTHER
(pp. 175–198)

1. Whitaker, *Good News from Virginia*, p. 24.
2. Parry, *European Hegemony*, p. 30.
3. Le Jau to John Chamberlayne, S.C., 10 January 1712, SPG, mss. A, 7: 394, and Varnod to secretary, Dorchester, S.C., 15 January 1724, ibid., 17: 122.
4. Adair, *History of the American Indians*, pp. 99–126.
5. Le Jau to secretary, Goose Creek, 13 June 1710, SPG, mss. A, 5: 346.
6. Ibid., 19 February 1710, 5: 193.
7. Mooney, "Myths of Cherokee," p. 445.
8. Le Jau to secretary, Goose Creek, 19 February 1710, SPG, mss. A, 5: 205–6.

Notes

9. "Richard Hakluyt's Preface to Divers Voyages, 1582," in Taylor, ed., *Original Writings, Hakluyts*, 1: 178.
10. Minutes of council and general court, 1622–1624, *VMHB*, 19 (1911): 117.
11. Capt. William Tucker, muster, 1624/5, in Chapman, ed., *Wills and Administrations of Elizabeth City County*, p. 6, and minutes of council and general court, 10 June 1640, *VMHB* 11 (1904): 281–82.
12. Francis Yeardley to John Farrar, Virginia, 8 May 1654, Rawlingson Mss., Bodleian Library, Oxford, A 14, 637: 84–87, VCRP.
13. Journal, 23 March 1662, in McIlwaine, ed., *Journals of House of Burgesses*, 2: 16.
14. "Virginia's Cure: or An Avisive Narrative Concerning Virginia . . .," in Force, ed., *Tracts*, 3: 7.
15. Culpeper to Lords of Trade, 20 September 1683, *CSP, Colonial*, 11: 497.
16. Morgan Godwin, *The Negro's and Indian's Advocate, Suing for Their Admission Into the Church . . . to which Is Added a Brief Account of Religion in Virginia*, pp. 9–86, 172–73.
17. Virginia assembly journal, 2 June 1699, *CSP, Colonial*, 17: 261.
18. Winthrop Jordan contends that Negroes were discriminated against primarily because of their blackness; in contrast, he argues that lighter Indians who had rubbed themselves too often with bear grease and in fact seemed almost white fared much better. This line of reasoning, emphasizing color, does not take into account the effects of disease on the Indians and the fact that Englishmen had to justify colonizing America but not Africa. Winthrop D. Jordan, *White over Black: American Attitudes Toward the Negro, 1550–1812*, pp. 89–98, 478–81.
19. Charles F. Pascoe, *Two Hundred Years of the SPG: An Historical Account of the Society for the Propagation of the Gospel in Foreign Parts, 1701–1900*, 1: xv.
20. Le Jau to secretary, St. James, Goose Creek, 2 December 1706, SPG, mss. A., 3: 152.
21. Swanton, *Indian Tribes of North America*, pp. 114–16.
22. The best, though not a definitive, account of the Indian language at Christanna is Edward P. Alexander, "An Indian Vocabulary from Fort Christanna, 1716," pp. 303–13.
23. Mohawks sided with Britain during the American Revolution and moved across the border into Canada after the war, carrying their communion service with them. A photograph of it appears in Charles M. Johnston, ed., *The Valley of the Six Nations: A Collection of Documents on the Indian Lands of the Grand River*, facing p. xlix.
24. Thomas Wilson, *Essay Towards an Instruction for the Indians; Explaining the Most Essential Doctrines of Christianity. Which May Be of*

Use to Such Christians, as Have not Well Considered the Meaning of the Religion they Profess; Or, Who Profess to Know God, but in Works Do Deny Him. In Several Short and Plain Dialogues. Together with Directions and Prayers for the Heathen World, Missionaries, Catechumens, Private Persons, Families, of Parents for Their Children, for Sundays, etc., pp. xxx–xxxi.

25. Ibid., p. 43.
26. Francis Nicholson to Robert Hicks and John Evans, Virginia, 1700, Fulham Palace papers, Magdalen College, no. 181, VCRP.
27. Spotswood to Bishop of London, Virginia, 26 July 1712, in Alexander Spotswood, *The Official Letters of Alexander Spotswood, Lieutenant-Governor of the Colony of Virginia, 1710–1722, Now First Printed from the Manuscript in the Collections of the Virginia Historical Society,* ed. Robert A. Brock, 1: 174–75.
28. W. Stitt Robinson, Jr., "Indian Education and Missions in Colonial Virginia," p. 162.
29. Spotswood to Board of Trade, Virginia, 28 December 1711, in Spotswood, *Letters,* 1: 129–30.
30. Spotswood to Bishop of London, Virginia, 27 January 1715, in ibid., 2: 91.
31. Council, 22 August 1728, in McIlwaine, ed., *Executive Journals, Council,* 4: 186.
32. General meeting of visitors and governors . . . William and Mary College, 26 March 1716, Lee papers, VHS, Mss. 1, L51, pp. 133–34.
33. John Fontaine, *The Journal of John Fontaine, an Irish Huguenot Son in Spain and Virginia, 1710–1719,* ed. Edward P. Alexander, p. 155; journal, 23 February 1715, in McIlwaine, ed., *Executive Journals, Council,* 3: 396; and ? to Richard Beresford, Chowan, 4 July 1716, CPS, *Colonial,* 29: 142.
34. Spotswood to Bishop of London, 26 October 1715, in Spotswood, *Letters,* 2: 138.
35. Spotswood to Board of Trade, Virginia, 29 August 1717, *CSP, Colonial,* 30: 18–19, and journal, 12 November 1717, in McIlwaine, ed., *Executive Journals, Council,* 3: 456.
36. Giles Rainsford to SPG, 2 July 1712, SPG journal, 10 October 1712, 2: 228.
37. Rainsford to secretary, Pasquotant, 19 January 1715, in Saunders, ed., *N. C. Colonial Records,* 2: 152–53.
38. Charles II's charter to Lords Proprietors, 24 March 1663, in ibid., 1: 21.
39. Nairne to [Earl of Sunderland?], S.C., 10 July 1709, *CSP, Colonial,* 24: 422–23.
40. Nairne to Edward Marston, St. Helena, 20 August 1705, Historic Letters of the Southeast, 16th, 17th, and 18th centuries, SAC.

41. Thomas Smith to Robert Steevens, Carolina, 16 January 1708, SPG, mss. A, 4: 54–55.
42. Le Jau to secretary, St. James, 2 December 1706, ibid., 3: 152; ibid., 18 February 1709, 4: 303–4; and act of assembly relating to church in South Carolina, 30 November 1706, ibid., 8: 400.
43. Ibid., 22 April 1708, 4: 227.
44. Ibid., 13 March 1708, 4: 34, and SPG journal, 18 May 1711, 2: 44.
45. Samuel Thomas to Thomas Bray, Carolina, 20 January 1702, SPG, mss. A, 1: 86, and Thomas to SPG, 10 March 1704, *SCHGM*, 4 (1903): 280.
46. Ibid., 1706, 5 (1904): 41.
47. Nicholas Trott to SPG, S.C., 13 September 1707, SPG, mss. A, 3: 389–90.
48. John Norris to SPG, 15 September 1712, ibid., 7: 88–89.
49. Gideon Johnston to secretary, 27 January 1711, in Gideon Johnston, *Carolina Chronicle: The Papers of Commissary Gideon Johnston, 1707–1716*, ed. Frank J. Klingberg, p. 84.
50. Ibid., 5 July 1710, p. 55.
51. Nairne to Marston, St. Helena, 20 August 1705, Historic Letters of Southeast . . ., SAC, and Le Jau to secretary, St. James Parish, 22 April 1708, SPG, mss. A, 4: 227.
52. SPG journal, 19 June 1713, 2: 297, and expenses of yᵉ Indian youth, SPG, mss. A, 8: 26. The best published account of Prince George is Frank J. Klingberg, "The Mystery of the Lost Yamassee Prince," pp. 18–32.
53. SPG journal, 6 July 1716, 3: 159.
54. Johnston to secretary, Charleston, 27 January 1716, SPG, mss. A, 11: 116.
55. The account of St. John's Parish, 25 May 1724, ibid., 18: 82.
56. Francis Varnod to secretary, Dorchester, S.C., 15 January 1724, ibid., 17: 122, and ibid., 21 July 1724, 18: 85–87.
57. SPC journal, 16 January 1741, 8: 209.
58. Ebenezer Taylor to secretary, Perquiman's Precinct, 23 April 1719, in Saunders, ed., *N. C. Colonial Records*, 2: 332–33.
59. Thomas to SPG, 1706, *SCHGM*, 5 (1904): 47.
60. Thomas Bray, *A Memorial, Representing the Present State of Religion, on the Continent of North-America*, p. 11.
61. SPG journal, 18 July 1766, 17: 97.
62. Francis Le Jau, *The Carolina Chronicle of Dr. Francis Le Jau, 1706–1717*, ed. Frank J. Klingberg, pp. 1–2.
63. Councillor Koehler to Theophilus A. Francke, Pommerania, 11 May 1736, *VMHB*, 14 (1906): 145–46.
64. Diary of Bishop Spangenburg, Edenton, 13 September 1752, in Saunders, ed., *N. C. Colonial Records*, 5–6.

65. Salem diary, 11 January 1774, in Adelaide L. Fries, ed., *Records of the Moravians in North Carolina*, 2: 815.
66. Katharine de Baillou, ed., "Oglethorpe's Statement on Christian Pryber," pp. 100–101, and Knox Mellon, Jr., "Christian Priber's Cherokee 'Kingdom of Paradise,' " pp. 319–28.
67. Chapman J. Milling, ed., *Colonial South Carolina: Two Contemporary Descriptions by Governor James Glen and Doctor George Milligen-Johnston*, p. 149.
68. John Clayton to Robert Boyle, Virginia, 1687 ?, in John Clayton, "Another 'Account of Virginia,' " ed. Edmund Berkeley and Dorothy S. Berkeley, *VMHB*, 76 (1968): 436.
69. Charles Woodmason, *TheCarolina Backcountry on the Eve of the Revolution: The Journal and Other Writings of Charles Woodmason, Anglican Itinerant*, ed. Richard J. Hooker, p. 83.

CHAPTER 9: INDIANS IN UTOPIA (pp. 199–216)

1. James Oglethorpe to Samuel Wesley, Old Palace Yard, 19 November 1734, in George F. Jones, ed. and trans., *Henry Newman's Salzburger Letterbooks*, pp. 514–15.
2. Robert Montgomery, *A Discourse Concerning the Design'd Establishment of a New Colony to the South of Carolina, in the Most Delightful Country of the Universe*, ed. J. Max Patrick, pp. 21–22.
3. Two recent perceptive accounts of the background and early development of Georgia are Kenneth Coleman, *Colonial Georgia: A History*, and Phinizy Spalding, *Oglethorpe in America*.
4. J. Leitch Wright, Jr., "Southern Black Loyalists," paper delivered at Conference on American Loyalists, St. Augustine, 1975.
5. Oglethorpe's orders, Charleston, 1 April 1740, in Easterby, ed., *Journal of Commons House*, 2: 297.
6. "Bylaws, Trustees, London, 21 March 1733," in Allen D. Candler, ed., *The Colonial Records of the State of Georgia*, 1: 40.
7. Thomas Jones to Trustees' accountant, 6 May 1742, in ibid., 23: 329.
8. President and assistants, 10 August 1749, in ibid., 6: 259.
9. Ibid., 9 February 1748, 6: 209.
10. John Dobell to Trustees, 30 November 1742, in ibid., 23: 437–38.
11. Deposition of Peter Shepherd, 8 April 1736, in Easterby, ed., *Journal of Commons House*, 1: 151.
12. Earl of Egmont diary, 9 October 1734, in Great Britain, Historical Manuscripts Commission, *Manuscripts of the Earl of Egmont. Diary of the First Earl of Egmont*, 2: 129.

13. Harman Verelst to Thomas Causton, Ga. Office, 11 August 1737, *CSP, Colonial*, 43: 224.
14. Martha Causton to Trustees, Savannah, 16 January 1738, in Candler, ed., *Ga. Colonial Records*, 22 (pt. 1): 66.
15. Journal, 15 December 1736, in Easterby, ed., *Journal of Commons House*, 1: 79–80.
16. *A New Voyage to Georgia. By a Young Gentleman. Giving an Account of His Travels to South Carolina, and Part of North Carolina. To Which is Added, a Curious Account of the Indians, by an Honorable Person, and a Poem to James Oglethorpe, Esq.; on His Arrival from Georgia,* p. 78.
17. Oglethorpe to Samuel Wesley, Old Palace Yard, 19 November 1734, in Jones, ed., *Newman Letterbooks*, pp. 514–15.
18. John Whitelamb to Samuel Wesley, Wroat, 5 December 1734, in ibid., p. 517.
19. Newman to John Wesley, Bartlet's Buildings, 8 June 1736, in ibid., p. 195, and Newman to Oglethorpe, London, 4 June 1736, in ibid., p. 193.
20. Benjamin Ingham to John Phillipps, Savannah, 15 September 1736, in Candler, ed., *Ga. Colonial Records*, 21: 221–23.
21. George F. Jones, ed., Hermann J. Lacher, trans., *Detailed Reports on the Salzburger Emigrants Who Settled in America . . . Edited by Samuel Urlsperger*, 1: xxii.
22. Martin Boltzius and Israel Gronau to Gotthilf Francke, Ebenezer, 8 January 1736, in ibid., 2: 239.
23. Diary, 3 July 1734, Hist. Mss. Comm., *Egmont Diary*, 2: 114.
24. Alexander Garden to SPG, Charleston, 20 November 1751, SPG journal, 12: 117–18.
25. Thomas Bosomworth to Trustees, Savannah, 10 March 1742, in Candler, ed., *Ga. Colonial Records*, 23: 231–50.
26. *New Voyage to Georgia*, p. 36.
27. E. Merton Coulter, "Mary Musgrove, 'Queen of the Creeks:' A Chapter of Early Georgia Troubles," pp. 2–12.
28. James T. Flexner, *George Washington: The Forge of Experience, 1732–1775*, pp. 289–305.
29. Coulter, "Musgrove," pp. 28–29.
30. Oglethorpe's vindication of his conduct, 24 January 1741, Historic Letters of Southeast . . . , SAC.
31. Thomas Causton to Trustees, 24 March 1737, *CSP, Colonial*, 43: 87.
32. Earl of Egmont, *The Journal of the Earl of Egmont: Abstract of the Trustees Proceedings for Establishing the Colony of Georgia, 1732–1738*, ed. Robert G. McPherson, p. 64

CHAPTER 10: THIS 'NEW AMERICAN' (pp. 217–247)

1. William C. Sturtevant, "Spanish–Indian Relations in Southeastern North America," p. 68.
2. Answers to queries sent by Board of Trade, 1761, in Saunders, ed., *N. C. Colonial Records*, 6: 616.
3. Adair, *History of American Indians*, p. 244, and Lawson, *History*, p. 5.
4. Fontaine, *Journal*, pp. 85, 96–97.
5. Bartram, *Travels*, p. 122.
6. Conference with king and warriors of Catawbas, Salisbury, 26 May 1756, in Saunders, ed., *N.C. Colonial Records*, 5: 583.
7. John R. Alden, *John Stuart and the Southern Colonial Frontier: A Study of Indian Relations, War, Trade, and Land Problems in the Southern Wilderness, 1754–1775*, pp. 101–18.
8. Reginald Horsman, *Expansion and American Indian Policy, 1783–1812*, pp. 104–14.
9. Journal, 20 November 1707, in Salley, ed., *Journals Commons House*, p. 45.
10. Richard Nixon deposition, Bath, 1722(?), colonial court records, misc. papers, 1677–1775, NCA, p. 192.
11. Journal, 20 August 1714, SPG journal, 2: 395.
12. Daniel Pepper to William Lyttelton, Ockchoys, 30 November 1756, in McDowell, ed., *Documents, Indian Affairs*, 2: 296.
13. John Stuart to William Howe, Pensacola, 16 June 1777, Sir Guy Carleton papers, PRO, 586, microfilm, Florida State University Library.
14. Journal of the proceedings of Philip Ludwell and Nathaniel Harrison . . . , 22 September, 2 October 1710, *VMHB*, 4 (1896): 35, 39.
15. Act, October 1705, in Hening, ed., *Statutes*, 3: 467.
16. The background of the sweet potato's rise to prominence as an important Southern crop is obscure. Indians (rather than colonists) who had visited or emigrated from the West Indies or Meso-America may have been responsible. For background see Redcliffe N. Salaman, *The History and Social Influence of the Potato*, pp. 130–33.
17. Thomas Campbell to Deane Gordon, Portsmouth Harbor, 14 June 1767, *FHQ*, 8 (1930): 156–63.
18. Ibid., p. 160.
19. Byrd, "The Secret History of the Line," *Prose Works*, p. 146.
20. J. Leitch Wright, Jr., *William Augustus Bowles: Director General of the Creek Nation*, pp. 30–31.
21. Howard A. MacCord, "Camden: A Postcontact Indian Site in Caroline County," pp. 1–37.
22. For a discussion of English land policy as it related to the Indians

in Virginia, see W. Stitt Robinson, Jr., *Mother Earth: Land Grants in Virginia, 1607–1699*, pp. 1–10.

23. William Gooch to Board of Trade, Williamsburg, 29 June 1729, *CSP, Colonial*, 36: 415.

24. Journal, House of Burgesses, 4 October 1734, in McIlwaine, ed., *Journals of House of Burgesses*, 6: 233.

25. Journal, 22 April 1708, in McIlwaine, ed., *Executive Journals, Council*, 3: 173.

26. Treaty, Catawba Indians, 29 August 1754, in Saunders, ed., *N.C. Colonial Records*, 5: 142.

27. Benjamin Dennis to secretary, Goose Creek, 3 July 1711, SPG, mss. A, 6: 143.

28. Thomas Campbell to Deane Gordon, Portsmouth Harbor, 14 June 1767, *FHQ*, 8 (1930): 162.

29. Le Jau to secretary, Goose Creek, 13 June 1710, SPG, mss. A, 5: 342–43.

30. Court, Richmond County, 6 March 1704, *VMHB*, 39 (1931): 170.

31. Alexander McKee to Dragging Canoe, Foot of the Miamis Rapids, 22 July 1791, Claus Papers, Public Archives of Canada, 4.

32. Dorothy F. Monroe, "Henry Fleete," typescript, 7: 1, F6248: 1, VHS, p. 17, and John Stuart to William Knox, Pensacola, 9 October 1778, PRO, CO 5/80.

33. Council journal, 27 October 1726, in Saunders, ed., *N.C. Colonial Records*, 2: 643–44.

34. William Bartram, *Travels in Georgia and Florida, 1773–1774: A Report to Dr. John Fothergill*, ed. Francis Harper, p. 146.

35. Court, 25 September 1707, Westmoreland County records, VSL, 54: 74a.

36. Glenn Tucker, *Tecumseh: Vision of Glory*, pp. 19–21.

37. A good starting point for the Creek Confederacy is John R. Swanton, *Early History of the Creek Indians and Their Neighbors*.

38. Günter Wagner, *Yuchi Tales*, p. 25.

39. Charles M. Hudson, *The Catawba Nation*, pp. 1–51.

40. Alexander, "Indian Vocabulary," p. 309.

41. Charles H. Fairbanks, *Ethnohistorical Report on the Florida Indians*, pp. 4, 47–48, 272.

42. A recent sympathetic account of the origin of these Indians is Adolph L. Dial and David K. Eliades, *The Only Land I Know: A History of the Lumbee Indians*, pp. 1–24.

43. William Hartley and Ellen Hartley, *Osceola: The Unconquered Indian*, pp. 110–15.

44. Examples can be found scattered in McDowell, ed., *Documents, Indian Affairs*, 2.

45. Phyllis M. Martin, *The External Trade of the Loango Coast, 1576–*

1870: The Effects of Changing Commercial Relations on the Vili King-dom of Loango, pp. 159–60.

46. Spotswood to Board of Trade, 5 April 1717, in Spotswood, *Letters*, 2: 227; Robert Beverley, *The History and Present State of Virginia*, ed. Louis B. Wright, pp. 38–39; and Byrd, *History of the Dividing Line betwixt Virginia and North Carolina . . . 1728*, in Wright, ed., *The Prose Works of Byrd*, p. 221.

47. John Stewart to William Dunlop, Virginia, 20 October 1693, *SCHGM*, 32 (1931): 172.

48. William O. Tuggle, *Shem, Ham, and Japheth: The Papers of W. O. Tuggle*, ed. Eugene Current-Garcia and Dorothy B. Hatfield, p. 35.

49. Alexander Garden to Bishop of London, Charleston, 4 June 1736, in George W. Williams, ed., "Letters to the Bishop of London from the Commissaries, in South Carolina," p. 239.

50. Eugene D. Genovese, *Roll, Jordan, Roll: The World the Slaves Made*, p. 425.

51. Le Jau to secretary, Goose Creek, 13 June 1710, SPG, mss. A, 5: 342–43.

52. Robert Johnson will, St. George Parish, 5 April 1725, Charleston County wills, 1731–37, SCA, pp. 249–50.

53. John Barnwell to Robert Johnson [1720 ?], *CSP, Colonial*, 31: 307–8.

54. Bartram, *Travels*, p. 11.

55. "Journal of David Taitt's Travels from Pensacola, West Florida, to and through the Country of the Upper and the Lower Creeks, 1772," in Newton D. Mereness, ed., *Travels in the American Colonies*, p. 558.

56. Arthur P. Whitaker, "Alexander McGillivray, 1783–1789," pp. 182–84.

57. Bartram, *Travels*, p. 284.

58. Richard Prize will, 19 May 1710, Charleston County wills, 52: 178.

59. Gilbert, "Eastern Cherokees," p. 203.

60. Theda Perdue, *Slavery and the Evolution of Cherokee Society, 1548–1866*, p. 51.

61. James M. Crawford, *The Mobilian Trade Language*, pp. 4–7.

62. Sturtevant, "Spanish–Indian Relations," pp. 51, 66, and Leonard Bloom, "The Acculturation of the Eastern Cherokee: Historical Aspects," p. 332.

63. Act, 1734, in Hening, ed., *Statutes*, 4: 461.

64. Antonio J. Waring, Jr., *The Waring Papers: The Collected Works of Antonio J. Waring, Jr.*, ed. Stephen Williams, p. 53.

65. Le Jau to secretary, St. James Goose Creek, 4 January 1712, SPG, mss. A, 7, and ibid., St. John's Parish, 25 May 1724, 18: 82.

66. Dennis to secretary, Goose Creek, 3 July 1711, ibid., 6: 143.

67. Bartram, *Travels*, pp. 225–26.

68. Stafford County order book, 1664–1668, in Billings, ed., *Old Dominion*, p. 230; and act for free trade with Indians, 16 April 1691, in Hening, ed., *Statutes*, 3: 69.
69. Picks and Windotts to Dinwiddie, c. June 1752, in Robert Dinwiddie, *Robert Dinwiddie Correspondence Illustrative of His Career in American Colonial Government and Westward Expansion*, ed. Louis K. Koontz, pp. 156–57.
70. Ivor Noël Hume, *Excavations at Rosewell in Gloucester County, Virginia, 1957–59*, p. 172.
71. John Clayton to Dr. Grene, 1687, Add. MSS. 4437, VCRP, reel 546.
72. Stanley A. South, *Exploratory Archaeology at the Site of 1670–1680 Charles Towne on Albemarle Point in South Carolina*, p. 49, and Baker, "Confitachique," p. 168.
73. Kathleen A. Deagan, *Archaeology at the National Greek Orthodox Shrine, St. Augustine, Florida: Microchange in Eighteenth-Century Spanish Colonial Material Culture*, p. 83.
74. Larson, "Historic Guale Indians," p. 136. A candelabrum, which archaeologists surmise was made by mission Indians, is at the Florida State Museum, Gainesville, Florida.
75. Isodoro de León to Manuel de Montiano, Apalachee, 21 May 1745, in Lucy L. Wenhold and Albert C. Manucy, eds., "The Trials of Captain Don Isidoro de León," p. 252.
76. Howard A. MacCord, "Hungar's Neck Trash-Pit, Northampton County, Virginia," p. 59.
77. Ben C. McCary, "An Indian Dugout Canoe, Reworked by Early Settlers, Found in Powhatan Creek, James City County, Virginia," pp. 14–15.
78. "Briefe intelligence from Virginia, 1624," in Purchas, ed., *Pilgrimes*, 19: 209.
79. Edmund Berkeley and Dorothy S. Berkeley, eds., " 'The Manner of Living of the North Carolinians,' by Francis Veale, December 19, 1730," p. 244. The best published source about the black drink is Charles M. Hudson, ed., *Black Drink: A Native American Tea*.
80. For a brief discussion see Hudson, *Southeastern Indians*, p. 499.
81. Frank T. Siebert, Jr., "Resurrecting Virginia Algonquian from the Dead: The Reconstituted and Historical Phonology of Powhatan," in James M. Crawford, ed., *Studies in Southeastern Indian Languages*, pp. 288, 290.
82. Higginbotham, *Old Mobile*, p. 373.
83. Petition of William Leftwich and William Vardeman, 1 July 1785, mss. 2R, 2207b5, VHS.
84. Dinwiddie, *Correspondence*, ed. L. K. Koontz, p. 956.
85. Act, 10 October 1649, in Billings, ed., *Old Dominion*, p. 63.
86. Clemens de Baillou, "Notes on Cherokee Architecture," pp. 25–26,

and Harold R. Shurtleff, *The Log Cabin Myth: A Study of the Early Dwellings of the English Colonists in North America*, pp. 163–85.
87. Ivor Noël Hume, "First Look at a Lost Virginia Settlement."
88. Ivan A. Lopatin, "Origin of the Native American Steam Bath," pp. 982–90.
89. J. Anthony Paredes, "The Emergence of Contemporary Eastern Creek Indian Identity," in Thomas K. Fitzgerald, ed., *Social and Cultural Identity: Problems of Persistence and Change*, p. 72. I am also indebted to conversations with and hospitality extended to me by members of the council of the Creek Nation East of the Mississippi.
90. Michel G. St. Jean de Crèvecoeur, *Letters from an American Farmer*, p. 43.

CHAPTER 11: BR'ER RABBIT AT THE SQUARE GROUND (pp. 248–278)

1. Carter G. Woodson, "The Relations of Negroes and Indians in Massachusetts," p. 45.
2. Brewton Berry, *Almost White*, p. 32.
3. Abraham Jones interview, Alabama, 10 May 1937, *Slave Narratives: A Folk History of Slavery in the United States, from Interviews with Former Slaves, Alabama*, 5: 234.
4. James Fisher narrative, in John W. Blassingame, ed., *Slave Testimony: Two Centuries of Letters, Speeches, Interviews, and Autobiographies*, p. 238.
5. Kenneth W. Porter, "Relations Between Negroes and Indians Within the Present Limits of the United States," p. 319.
6. *St. Petersburg Times*, 31 October 1976.
7. Elias Dawkins interview, Gaffney, S.C., 20 August 1937, *Slave Narratives, S.C.*, 1, part 1: 315. Paul Escott has tabulated the race of slave parents as reported by freedmen in thousands of extant Federal Writers' Project slave narratives. More than 3 percent of the freed slaves related they had pure or mixed Indian parents, while fewer than 1 percent indicated their parents were African. The problem in using or relying on these statistics is that a majority of the former slaves, almost 90 percent, made no specific reference about their parents' race. In any case, it is apparent that the Indian contribution was considerable. Paul D. Escott, *Slavery Remembered: A Record of Twentieth-Century Slave Narratives*, p. 47.
8. Melville J. Herskovits, *The Anthropometry of the American Negro*, pp. 15, 279.

9. August Meier, "A Study of the Racial Ancestry of the Mississippi College Negro," pp. 227–35.

10. Palmer's *Slaves of the White God* is a recent detailed study emphasizing the important role of blacks in colonial Mexico's development.

11. Culpeper's instructions, 6 December 1679, *CSP, Colonial*, 11: 157.

12. Bentley Glass, "On the Unlikelihood of Significant Admixture of Genes from the North American Indians in the Present Composition of the Negroes of the United States." For contrary findings see D. F. Roberts, "The Dynamics of Racial Intermixture in the American Negro: Some Anthropological Considerations," p. 366.

13. Malcolm X, *The Autobiography of Malcolm X, with the Assistance of Alex Haley*, p. 162.

14. Nathaniel Harrison inventory, 15 July 1728, *VMHB*, 31 (1923): 361.

15. Elizabeth Diggs inventory, 13 October 1691, York County records, VSL 4a: 217.

16. *Pennsylvania Journal*, 1 October 1747, in James H. Johnston, "Documentary Evidence of the Relations of Negros and Indians," p. 28.

17. Frank Freeman interview, n.d., in *Slave Narratives, N.C.*, 13 part 1: 321.

18. *Virginia Gazette*, 11 March 1775.

19. This sample is based on more than five hundred slave names, which for the most part are scattered throughout seventeenth- and eighteenth-century South Carolina and Virginia records.

20. Lorenzo D. Turner, *Africanisms in the Gullah Dialect*, p. 177.

21. Accomack County order book, 1671, in Billings, ed., *Old Dominion*, p. 232.

22. Daniel Akehurst, hue and cry, 26 May 1698, in Parker, ed., *N.C. Higher Court Records, 1697–1701*, p. 528.

23. Act, 23 October 1705, in Hening, ed., *Statutes*, 3: 252.

24. Tredwell Bull to secretary, St. Paul's Parish, S.C., 20 January 1715, SPG, mss. A, 10: 90.

25. *S.C. Gazette*, 7 July 1759.

26. Court, 7 August 1706, Accomack County records, 1676–1709, VSL, 79: 75.

27. Martha Allen interview, in *Slave Narratives, N.C.*, 13 part 1: 14.

28. Cyrus H. Gordon, *Before Columbus: Links Between the Old World and Ancient America*, p. 22.

29. John Norris, *Profitable Advice for Rich and Poor. In a Dialogue, or Discourse between James Freeman, a Carolina Planter, and Simon Question, a West-Country Farmer*, pp. 88–95.

30. John Wright mortgage to Samuel Wragg, Jacob Satur, and Joseph Wragg, 15 June 1714, Charleston County, wills, SCA, p. 45.

31. Ann Rowsham's case, 29 April 1717, judgment rolls, court of common pleas, box 10, 57A1, SCA.
32. Uncle Moble Hopson interview, in *Slave Narratives, Va.*, 16: 39.
33. Le Jau to secretary, Goose Creek, 15 September 1708, SPG, mss. A, 4: 430.
34. *Virginia Gazette*, 12 September 1771.
35. Ibid., 3 August 1776.
36. Hartley and Hartley, *Osceola*, pp. 23–25, 116–18; Frank Berry interview, 18 August 1936, in *Slave Narratives, Fla.*, 17: 27–28; and Erik K. Reed, "Fort Moultrie," report, 1968, H2215, SAC.
37. Anna Baker interview, Monroe County, n.d., in *Slave Narratives, Miss.*, 6: 12.
38. Names and numbers of inhabitants, St. George's Parish, S.C., 21 January 1725, SPG, mss. A, 19: 108.
39. William Panton to Lachlan McGillivray, Pensacola, 10 April 1794, in John W. Caughey, *McGillivray of the Creeks*, p. 363.
40. R. Halliburton, Jr., *Red over Black: Black Slavery Among the Cherokee Indians.* For the most part Halliburton uses nineteenth-century evidence to generalize about slavery in the colonial period. His forceful arguments are not necessarily convincing. Perdue in her recent study, *Slavery and the Evolution of Cherokee Society*, p. 144, contends that for some time the Cherokees, because of their noncapitalistic background at first were relatively lenient masters, though eventually they became as harsh as white slaveowners.
41. Roderick Brumbaugh, "Black Maroons in Florida, 1800–1830," paper delivered at Organization of American Historians annual meeting, Boston, 1975, and John M. Goggin, "The Seminole Negroes of Andros Island, Bahamas," p. 206.
42. For a perceptive analysis of slavery in Jamaica see Patterson, *Sociology of Slavery*.
43. Nathan Beauchamp interview, n.d., in *Slave Narratives, Ala.* 5: 26.
44. Genovese, *Roll, Jordan, Roll*, p. 487.
45. Clarence L. Ver Steeg, *Origins of a Southern Mosaic: Studies of Early Carolina and Georgia*, pp. 107–8, 118.
46. Wood, *Black Majority*, pp. 55–62.
47. Julia E. Harn, "Old Canoochee-Ogeechee Chronicles," p. 350, and Frances A. Kemble, *Journal of a Residence on a Georgian Plantation in 1838–1839*, ed. John A. Scott, p. 49.
48. Robert Ascher and Charles H. Fairbanks, "Excavations of a Slave Cabin: Georgia, U.S.A.," p. 8
49. Oral communication, B. Calvin Jones. See also his "State Archaeologists Unearth Spanish Mission Ruins," p. 2.
50. Mr. Johnson testimony, 26 January 1837, in Blassingame, ed., *Slave Testimony*, p. 125.

51. Frank G. Speck, "The Rappahannock Indians of Virginia," pp. 65, 74–76.
52. Martha Richardson interview, Columbia, n.d., in *Slave Narratives*, *S.C.*, 2 part 4: 19.
53. Landon Carter, *The Diary of Colonel Landon Carter of Sabine Hall*, *1752–1778*, ed. Jack P. Greene, 1: 143, 145, 173, 205.
54. Genovese, *Roll, Jordan, Roll*, pp. 232–55, and Donald G. Mathews, *Religion in the Old South*, pp. 185–94.
55. Andrew Bryan to John Rippon, Savannah, 23 December 1800, *JNH*, 1 (1916): 87, and Frances Densmore, "Choctaw Music," p. 120.
56. Newbell N. Puckett, *Folk Beliefs of the Southern Negro*, p. 105.
57. Mac Linscott Ricketts, "The North American Indian Trickster," p. 328, and Tuggle, *Shem, Ham, and Japheth*, pp. 5, 162–63. Alan Dundes, "African Tales Among the North American Indians," p. 218, argues forcefully but not particularly convincingly that the rabbit-trickster was introduced into the South by the relatively few slaves who were imported from East Africa. The rabbit, though not necessarily as a trickster, can be found in folklore of other regions, such as India and Finland.
58. Emmaline Kilpatrick interview, White Plains, Georgia, 8 May 1937, in *Slave Narratives, Ga.*, 12: 12.
59. Examples of the bear's role in Indian folk tradition are in "Fire" and "The Orphan and the Bear" in Swanton, *Myths and Tales*, pp. 122, 192. As a marathon runner, I have complained many times about the bear for "nipping at my heels" or "seizing me tight." I am indebted to John W. Walker of the National Park Service for pointing out the bear's significance among both Indians and Negroes.
60. Melville J. Herskovits, *Life in a Haitian Valley*, p. 224.
61. J. Frederick Fausz, "The Powhatan Uprising of 1622: A Historical Study of Ethnocentrism and Cultural Conflict," pp. 348–49.
62. Ann Matthews interview, Nashville, n.d., in *Slave Narratives*, *Tenn.*, 16: 43.
63. *Georgia Gazette*, 10 January 1770, in *JNH*, 24 (1939): 252.
64. Alexander F. Chamberlain, "Negro and Indian," p. 52.
65. Robert Maule to John Chamberlayne, S.C., 2 August 1711, SPG, mss. A, 7: 363–65.
66. Journal, 12 June 1718, in McDowell, ed., *Journals of Indian Trade*, p. 287.
67. David H. Corkran, *The Creek Frontier, 1540–1783*, p. 73.
68. Perdue, *Slavery and Cherokee Society*, p. 106.
69. The most detailed biographical account is Kenneth W. Porter, "The Negro Abraham," pp. 1–43.
70. Uncle Willis interview, 8 April 1937, in *Slave Narratives, Ga.*, 12

part 4: 169, and James Johnson interview, South Jacksonville, 11 January 1937, in *Slave Narratives, Fla.*, 17: 97.

71. A good treatment of the banjo and minstrelsy is Hans Nathan, *Dan Emmett and the Rise of Early Negro Minstresly*. Nathan implies the instrument came from Africa but unfortunately has little to say about its origins (p. 153). David Evans, "Afro-American One-Stringed Instruments," p. 241, more effectively discusses the use of banjo-like instruments in West Africa. The recent article by Dena J. Epstein, "The Folk Banjo: A Documentary History," pp. 347–71, reviews the evidence and concludes that the banjo's origin still has not been established. She feels an African origin is more likely, however.

72. Densmore, "Choctaw Music," p. 117.

73. Journal, 2 April 1739, in Easterby, ed., *Journal of Commons House*, p. 681.

74. Journal, 10 October 1698, in Salley, ed., *Journals Commons House*, p. 21.

75. Journal, 16 July 1716, in McDowell, ed., *Journals of Indian Trade*, p. 80.

76. James Francis to James Glen, 14 April 1752, in McDowell, ed., *Documents, Indian Affairs*, 1: 250–51, and George Galphin's will, 6 April 1782, Creek Indian Letters, Talks, and Treaties, 1705–1793, part 1, GDAH.

77. Matthew Toole to Glen, Catawba Nation, 13 January 1752, in McDowell, ed., *Documents, Indian Affairs*, 1: 201.

78. Edmund Jenings, proclamation, Virginia, 21 March 1709, CO 5/1316, VCRP.

79. Board of Trade to Spotswood, Whitehall, 28 August 1710, CO 5/1335, VCRP, and journal, 27 April 1710, in McIlwaine, ed., *Executive Journals, Council*, 3: 242–43.

80. Daniel Akehurst, 26 September 1698, colonial court records, misc. papers, 1677–1775, CCR 192, NCA.

81. Court, 3 May 1698, in Parker, ed., *N.C. Higher Court Records, 1697–1701*, pp. 216–17.

82. Journal of proceedings of William Dry, Goose Creek, S.C., SPG, mss. A, 21: 162–70.

83. Gooch to Board of Trade, Williamsburg, 29 June 1729, CO 5/1322, VCRP.

84. ? to Joseph Boone, Carolina, 24 June 1720, *CSP, Colonial*, 32: 57–58.

85. Edmund Gray to John Fallowfield, 15 May 1751, in McDowell, ed., *Documents, Indian Affairs*, 1: 83.

86. Benjamin Quarles, *The Negro in the American Revolution*, p. 174.

87. Laureano de Torres y Ayala to crown, Florida, 9 August 1697, AGI, S.D., 54-5-13, SRNC, reel 9.

88. Journal, 11 November 1698, in Salley, ed., *Journals Commons House*, p. 30.
89. One of Kenneth W. Porter's most valuable articles concerning Negroes among the Seminoles is his "Negroes and the Seminole War, 1835–1842," pp. 427–50.
90. Samuel Mead to Joseah Burchett, Carolina, 27 December 1715, Adm. 1/2095, VCRP.
91. Wood, *Black Majority*, pp. 301–23, stresses the leadership role played by Africans newly arrived from Angola in the Stono Revolt.
92. *Virginia Gazette*, 6 January 1776.

CHAPTER 12: CONCLUSION (pp. 279–290)

1. J. Anthony Paredes and Kenneth J. Plante, "Economics, Politics, and the Subjugation of the Creek Indians: Final Report for National Park Service," pp. 158–64.
2. John Stuart to Board to Trade, Charleston, 2 December 1766, in Saunders, ed., *N.C. Colonial Records*, 7: 281.
3. Eugene P. Southall, personal communication, in *JNH* 11 (1926): 63–64.
4. Emily Mays interview, Griffin, 8 May 1937, in *Slave Narratives, Ga.*, 12: 18.
5. Julia Woodbury interview, Marion, November 1937, in *Slave Narratives, S.C.*, 2: 229–37.
6. J. Leitch Wright, Jr., "Creek–American Treaty of 1790: Alexander McGillivray and the Diplomacy of the Old Southwest," pp. 386, 397.
7. Merrit B. Pound, *Benjamin Hawkins, Indian Agent*, pp. 161–64.
8. Thomas Barton to SPG, Lancaster, 10 November 1766, SPG journal 17: 282–83, and Edmond Atkin, *The Appalachian Indian Frontier: The Edmond Atkin Report and Plan of 1755*, ed. Wilbur R. Jacobs, p. 81.
9. Pertinent abstracts of Marshall's decisions are in Wilcomb E. Washburn, ed., *The Indian and the White Man*, pp. 118–24.
10. Robert T. King, "The Florida Seminole Polity, 1858–1978," p. 158.
11. I discuss European efforts to confederate the western Indians more fully in Wright, *Britain and the American Frontier*.
12. Swanton, *Social Organization of Creek Confederacy*, p. 446, and Baker, "Cofitachique," p. 27.
13. Atkin, *Report*, pp. 64–66.
14. J. Leitch Wright, Jr., "A Note on the First Seminole War as Seen by the Indians, Negroes, and Their British Advisors," pp. 571–74.

Bibliography

I. Manuscript and Document Collections

ATLANTA
Georgia Department of Archives and History
    Creek Indian Letters, Talks, and Treaties
Federal Archives and Records Center
    Records of the South Carolina Court of Admiralty, 1716–32 T309-1
      (microfilm)

COLUMBIA
South Carolina Archives
    John Barnwell map, 1722
    Charleston County wills and miscellaneous records (typescript)
    Court of Common Pleas, judgment rolls
    Miscellaneous records
South Caroliniana Library, University of South Carolina
    John Evans journal, 1702–1715

GAINESVILLE
University of Florida Library
    John B. Stetson Collection
    Indian Oral History Project

LONDON
Public Record Office
    State Paper Office, Foreign 94 (Spain)

MEXICO CITY
Archivo General de la Nación
    Reales cédulas, originales

OTTAWA
Public Archives of Canada
    Claus Papers

RALEIGH
North Carolina Division of Archives and History
    Colonial court records, misc. papers, 1677–1775
    Craven County court records, 1712–1775
    Perquiman's Precinct court records, 1688–1693

RICHMOND
Virginia Historical Society
    Dorothy F. Monroe, "Henry Fleete" (typescript)
    Lee Family Papers
    William Leftwich Papers
Virginia State Library
    Accomack County records
    Charles City County records
    Elizabeth City County records
    Henrico County records
    Northampton County records
    Northumberland County records
    Stafford County records
    Virginia Colonial Records Project (microfilm)
        British Library, Add. MSS. 4437
        Ferrar Papers, Cambridge University
        Ferrar Papers, Magdalen College
        Fulham Palace Papers
        Harley Papers, Loan 29/179 BL
        Lambeth Palace Library
        Public Record Office: Admiralty 1; Colonial Office 1; Colonial
            Office 5; Exchequer 190
        Rawlingson Mss., Bodleian Library
        Society of Antiquities, London
        Writings of George Wilson, Library of Society of Friends
    Westmoreland County records
    York County records

Bibliography

SIMANCAS, SPAIN
Archivo General de Simancas
Estado (England)

TALLAHASSEE
Florida State University Library
Sir Guy Carleton Papers, Public Record Office, London (microfilm)
Society for the Propagation of the Gospel in Foreign Parts, Journal,
Society for the Propagation of the Gospel in Foreign Parts Library, London (microfilm)
Spanish Records of the North Carolina Historical Commission
(microfilm)
Southeast Archeological Center, National Park Service
Historic letters of the Southeast, 16th, 17th, and 18th centuries
Erik K. Reed, "Fort Moultrie," report, 1968, H2215, NPS, SR

WASHINGTON, D.C.
Library of Congress
America, British Colonies
Jeannette T. Connor Collection
Cotton Vespasian, British Library (microfilm)
Records of the States of the United States of America, South Carolina, F (microfilm)
Society for the Propagation of the Gospel in Foreign Parts, mss. A
(microfilm)

II. Newspapers

St. Petersburg Times
South-Carolina Gazette
Virginia Gazette

III. Books and Articles

ABERNETHY, THOMAS P. *Western Lands and the American Revolution.*
New York, 1937.
ADAIR, JAMES. *The History of the American Indians.* Edited by Samuel C.
Williams. Johnson City, 1930.
ALDEN, JOHN R. *John Stuart and the Southern Colonial Frontier: A Study
of Indian Relations, War, Trade, and Land Problems in the Southern Wilderness, 1754–1775.* Ann Arbor, 1944.
ALEXANDER, EDWARD P. "An Indian Vocabulary from Fort Christanna,
1716," *Virginia Magazine of History and Biography* 79 (1971): 303–13.

ALVORD, CLARENCE W., AND LEE BIDGOOD, eds. *The First Explorations of the Trans-Allegheny Region by the Virginians, 1650–1674.* Cleveland, 1912.

ANSTEY, ROGER. *The Atlantic Slave Trade and British Abolition, 1760–1810.* Atlantic Highlands, 1975.

ARBER, EDWARD, AND ARTHUR G. BRADLEY, eds. *Travels and Works of Captain John Smith, President of Virginia, and Admiral of New England, 1580–1631.* 2 vols. Edinburgh, 1910.

ARNADE, CHARLES W. *The Siege of St. Augustine in 1702.* Gainesville, 1959.

ASCHER, ROBERT, AND CHARLES H. FAIRBANKS. "Excavation of a Slave Cabin: Georgia, U.S.A." *Historical Archaeology* 5 (1971): 3–17.

ATKIN, EDMOND. *The Appalachian Indian Frontier: The Edmond Atkin Report and Plan of 1755.* Edited by Wilbur R. Jacobs. Lincoln, 1967.

BAILLOU, CLEMENS DE. "Notes on Cherokee Architecture," *Southern Indian Studies* 19 (1967): 25–33.

BAILLOU, KATHARINE DE, ed. "Oglethorpe's Statement on Christian Pryber," *Georgia Historical Quarterly* 44 (1960): 100–101.

BARBOUR, PHILIP L., ed. *The Jamestown Voyages Under the First Charter, 1606–1609.* 2 vols. London, 1969.

———. *Pocahontas and Her World: A Chronicle of America's First Settlement in Which Is Related the Story of the Indians and the Englishmen— Particularly Captain John Smith, Captain Samuel Argall, and Master John Rolfe.* Boston, 1970.

BARTRAM, WILLIAM. *Travels in Georgia and Florida, 1773–1774: A Report to Dr. John Fothergill.* Edited by Francis Harper. Philadelphia, 1943.

———. *The Travels of William Bartram, Naturalist's Edition.* Edited by Francis Harper. New Haven, 1958.

BERKELEY, EDMUND, AND DOROTHY S. BERKELEY, eds. " 'The Manner of Living of the North Carolinians,' by Francis Veale, December 19, 1730," *North Carolina Historical Review* 41 (1964): 239–45.

BERRY, BREWTON. *Almost White.* New York, 1963.

BEVERLEY, ROBERT. *The History and Present State of Virginia.* Edited by Louis B. Wright. Chapel Hill, 1947.

BILLINGS, WARREN M., ed. *The Old Dominion in the Seventeenth Century: A Documentary History of Virginia, 1606–1689.* Chapel Hill, 1975.

———. "Some Acts Not in Hening's Statutes: The Acts of Assembly, April 1652, November 1652, and July 1653," *Virginia Magazine of History and Biography* 83 (1975): 22–97.

BLANTON, WYNDHAM B. "Epidemics, Real and Imaginary, and Other Factors Influencing Seventeenth Century Virginia's Population," *Bulletin of the History of Medicine* 31 (1957): 454–62.

BLASSINGAME, JOHN W., ed. *Slave Testimony: Two Centuries of Letters, Speeches, Interviews, and Autobiographies.* Baton Rouge, 1977.

Bibliography

BLOOM, LEONARD. "The Acculturation of the Eastern Cherokee: Historical Aspects," *North Carolina Historical Review* 19 (1942): 323–58.

BOLTON, HERBERT E. "Spanish Resistance to the Carolina Traders in Western Georgia (1680–1704), *Georgia Historical Quarterly* 9 (1925): 115–30.

BOSSU, JEAN BERNARD. *Jean Bernard Bossu's Travels in the Interior of North America, 1751–1762.* Edited and translated by Seymour Feiler. Norman, 1962.

BOTHWELL, DICK. "The Earliest Known Americans," Tampa Bay Chapter, Florida Anthropological Society, *Bulletin* 9 (1977), 11–19.

BOYD, MARK F., ed. and trans. "Documents Describing the Second and Third Expeditions of Lieutenant Diego Peña to Apalachee and Apalachicola in 1717 and 1718," *Florida Historical Quarterly* 31 (1952): 109–39.

BOYD, MARK F., HALE G. SMITH, AND JOHN W. GRIFFIN. *Here They Once Stood: The Tragic End of the Apalachee Missions.* Gainesville, 1951.

BRAY, THOMAS. *A Memorial, Representing the Present State of Religion, on the Continent of North-America.* London, 1701.

BRIDENBAUGH, CARL. *Cities in Revolt: Urban Life in America, 1743–1776.* New York, 1955.

BROOKE, CHRISTOPHER. "A Poem on the Late Massacre in Virginia," *Virginia Magazine of History and Biography* 72 (1964): 259–92.

BROWN, ALEXANDER. *The Genesis of the United States.* 2 vols. Boston, 1890.

BRUCE, PHILIP A. *Economic History of Virginia in the Seventeenth Century: An Inquiry into the Material Condition of the People, Based upon Original and Contemporary Records.* 2 vols. New York, 1907.

BULLEN, RIPLEY P. "The Famous Crystal River Site," *Florida Anthropologist* 6 (1953): 9–37.

BUSHNELL, AMY. " 'That Demonic Game': The Campaign to Stop Indian Pelota Playing in Spanish Florida, 1675–1684," *Americas* 35 (1978): 1–19.

BYRD, WILLIAM. *The Prose Works of William Byrd of Westover: Narratives of a Colonial Virginian.* Edited by Louis B. Wright. Cambridge, 1966.

CALDERÓN, GABRIEL D. V. "A 17th Century Letter of Gabriel Diaz Vara Calderón, Bishop of Cuba, Describing the Indians and Indian Missions of Florida." Edited and translated by Lucy L. Wenhold, *Smithsonian Miscellaneous Collections* 95 (1937), no. 16.

CANDLER, ALLEN D., ed. *The Colonial Records of the State of Georgia.* 26 vols. Atlanta, 1904–16.

CARRIER, LYMAN. *Agriculture in Virginia, 1607–1699.* Williamsburg, 1957.

CARTER, LANDON. *The Diary of Colonel Landon Carter of Sabine Hall, 1752–1778.* Edited by Jack P. Greene. 2 vols. Charlottesville, 1965.

CAUGHEY, JOHN W. *McGillivray of the Creeks*. Norman, 1959.

CHAMBERLAIN, ALEXANDER F. "Negro and Indian." *Handbook of American Indians North of Mexico*, edited by Frederick W. Hodge. 2 vols. 2: 51–53. Washington, D.C., 1912.

CHAPMAN, BLANCHE A. *Wills and Administrations of Elizabeth City County, and Virginia, and Other Genealogical and Historical Items, 1610–1800*. Smithfield, 1941.

CLARK, JERRY E. *The Shawnee*. Lexington, Ky., 1977.

CLAYTON, JOHN. "Another 'Account of Virginia,' " edited by Edmund Berkeley and Dorothy S. Berkeley, *Virginia Magazine of History and Biography* 76 (1968): 415–36.

CLOWSE, CONVERSE D. *Economic Beginnings in Colonial South Carolina, 1670–1730*. Columbia, 1971.

Colección de documentos inéditos relativos al descubrimiento, conquista y organización de las antiguas posesiones españolas de ultramar. Segunda serie. 25 vols. Madrid, 1885–1932.

COLEMAN, KENNETH. *Colonial Georgia: A History*. New York, 1976.

CONNOR, JEANNETTE T., ed. and trans. *Colonial Records of Spanish Florida*. 2 vols. DeLand, 1925.

COOK, SHERBURNE F., AND WOODROW BORAH. *Essays in Population History, Mexico and the Caribbean*. Berkeley, 1971– .

CORKRAN, DAVID H. *The Creek Frontier, 1540–1783*. Norman, 1967.

COULTER, E. MERTON. "Mary Musgrove, 'Queen of the Creeks:' A Chapter of Early Georgia Troubles," *Georgia Historical Quarterly* 11 (1927): 1–30.

CRANE, VERNER W. "An Historical Note on the Westo Indians," *American Anthropologist* 20 (1918): 331–37.

———. *The Southern Frontier, 1670–1732*. Durham, 1928.

———. "Thomas Nairne," *Dictionary of American Biography* 13, 379.

CRASHAW, WILLIAM. *A Sermon Preached in London before the Right Honorable the Lord La Warre, Lord Gouernour and Captaine Generall of Virginea, and Others of His Majesties Counsell for That Kingdome, and the Rest of the Aduenturers in That Plantation* . . . . London, 1610.

CRAVEN, WESLEY F. *White, Red and Black: The Seventeenth-Century Virginian*. Charlottesville, 1971.

CRAWFORD, JAMES M. *The Mobilian Trade Language*. Knoxville, 1978.

———. ed. *Studies in Southeastern Indian Languages*. Athens, Ga., 1975.

CRÈVECOUR, MICHEL G. ST. JEAN DE. *Letters from an American Farmer*. London, 1912.

CURTIN, PHILIP D. *The Atlantic Slave Trade: A Census*. Madison, 1969.

DAVENPORT, FRANCES G., AND CHARLES O. PAULLIN, eds. *European Treaties Bearing on the History of the United States and Its Dependencies*. 4 vols. Washington, 1917–37.

Bibliography

DAVIES, KENNETH G. *The Royal African Company.* New York, 1970.

DAVIS, CURTIS C. "A Long Line of Cupbearers: The Earliest Littlepages in America," *Virginia Magazine of History and Biography* 72 (1964): 434–53.

DAVIS, DAVID B. *The Problem of Slavery in the Age of Revolution, 1770–1823.* Ithaca, 1975.

DAVIS, T. FREDERICK, ed. "History of Juan Ponce de Leon's Voyages to Florida, Source Records," *Florida Historical Quarterly* 14 (1935): 5–66.

DEAGAN, KATHLEEN A. *Archaeology at the National Greek Orthodox Shrine, St. Augustine, Florida: Microchange in Eighteenth-Century Spanish Colonial Material Culture.* Gainesville, 1976.

DENEVAN, WILLIAM M., ed. *The Native Population of the Americas in 1492.* Madison, 1976.

DENSMORE, FRANCES. "Choctaw Music," Bureau of American Ethnology, *Bulletin* 136 (1943): 101–88.

DIAL, ADOLPH L., AND DAVID K. ELIADES. *The Only Land I Know: A History of the Lumbee Indians.* San Francisco, 1975.

DICKINSON, JONATHAN. *Jonathan Dickinson's Journal; or, God's Protecting Providence. Being the Narrative of a Journey from Port Royal in Jamaica to Philadelphia between August 23, 1696 and April 1, 1697.* Edited by E. W. Andrews and C. M. Andrews. New Haven, 1945.

DINWIDDIE, ROBERT. *The Official Records of Robert Dinwiddie, Lieutenant-Governor of the Colony of Virginia, 1751–1758, Now First Printed from the Manuscript in the Collections of the Virginia Historical Society.* Edited by R. A. Brock. 2 vols. Richmond, 1883–84.

———. *Robert Dinwiddie Correspondence Illustrative of His Career in American Colonial Government and Westward Expansion.* Edited by Louis K. Koontz. Berkeley, 1951.

DOBYNS, HENRY F. "An Appraisal of Techniques with a New Hemispheric Estimate," *Current Anthropology* 7 (1966): 395–416.

———. *Native American Historical Demography, A Critical Bibliography.* Bloomington, 1976.

DONNAN, ELIZABETH, ed. *Documents Illustrative of the History of the Slave Trade to America.* 4 vols. Washington, 1930–35.

DONNE, JOHN. *The Sermons of John Donne.* Edited by George R. Potter and Evelyn M. Simpson. 10 vols. Berkeley, 1953–62.

DORMAN, JOHN F., ed. *Westmoreland County, Virginia, Records, 1661–64.* Washington, 1972.

DUFFY, JOHN. "Smallpox and the Indians in the American Colonies," *Bulletin of the History of Medicine* 25 (1951): 324–41.

DUNDES, ALAN. "African Tales Among the North American Indians," *Southern Folklore Quarterly* 29 (1965): 207–19.

DUNKLE, JOHN R. "Population Change as an Element in the Historical Geography of St. Augustine," *Florida Historical Quarterly* 37 (1958): 3–32.

EASTERBY, JAMES H., ed. *The Journal of the Commons House of Assembly, 1736– . Columbia, 1951– .

EGMONT, EARL OF. *The Journal of the Earl of Egmont: Abstract of the Trustees Proceedings for Establishing the Colony of Georgia, 1732–1738.* Edited by Robert G. McPherson. Athens, Ga., 1962.

EHRMANN, W. W. "The Timucua Indians of Sixteenth Century Florida," *Florida Historical Quarterly* 18 (1940): 168–91.

ELLIOTT, JOHN H. *Imperial Spain, 1469–1716.* New York, 1964.

EPSTEIN, DENA J. "The Folk Banjo: A Documentary History," *Ethnomusicology* 19 (1975): 347–71.

ESCALANTE FONTANEDA, HERNANDO DE. *Memoir of Dº d'Escalante Fontaneda respecting Florida, Written in Spain, about the Year 1575.* Edited and translated by Buckingham Smith. Miami, 1944.

ESCOTT, PAUL D. *Slavery Remembered: A Record of Twentieth-Century Slave Narratives.* Chapel Hill, 1979.

EVANS, DAVID. "Afro-American One-Stringed Instruments," *Western Folklore* 29 (1970): 229–45.

FAIRBANKS, CHARLES H. *Ethnohistorical Report on the Florida Indians.* New York, 1974.

FEEST, CHRISTIAN F. "Seventeenth Century Virginia Algonquian Population Estimates," *Quarterly Bulletin, The Archaeological Society of Virginia* 28 (1973): 66–79.

FERNÁNDEZ, LEÓN, ed. *Colección de documentos para la historia de Costa-Rica.* 10 vols. Barcelona, 1881–1907.

FITZHUGH, WILLIAM. *William Fitzhugh and His Chesapeake World, 1676–1701; the Fitzhugh Letters and Other Documents.* Edited by Richard B. Davis. Chapel Hill, 1963.

FLEET, BEVERLEY, ed. *Virginia Colonial Abstracts.* Richmond, 1937– .

FLEXNER, JAMES T. *George Washington.* 4 vols. Boston, 1965–72.

FONTAINE, JOHN. *The Journal of John Fontaine, an Irish Huguenot Son in Spain and Virginia, 1710–1719.* Edited by Edward P. Alexander. Williamsburg, 1972.

FORCE, PETER, ed. *Tracts and Other Papers, Relating Principally to the Origin, Settlement, and Progress of the Colonies in North America, from the Discovery of the Country to the Year 1776.* 4 vols. Washington, 1836–46.

FOSTER, LAURENCE. *Negro–Indian Relationships in the Southeast.* Philadelphia, 1935.

FREEMAN, DOUGLAS S. *George Washington: A Biography.* 7 vols. New York, 1948–57.

Bibliography

FRIES, ADELAIDE L., ed. *Records of the Moravians in North Carolina.* 7 vols. Raleigh, 1925–47.

FRYMAN, FRANK B., JR. "Tallahassee's Prehistoric Political Center," State of Florida, Division of Archives, History, and Records Management, *Archives and History News* 2 (1971), no. 3.

FUNDABURK, EMMA LILA, AND MARY DOUGLASS FUNDABURK FORMAN, eds. *Sun Circles and Human Hands: The Southeastern Indians, Art and Industries.* Luverne, 1957.

GALINAT, WALTON C. "The Evolution of Corn and Culture in North America," *Economic Botany* 19 (1965), 350–57.

GANNON, MICHAEL V. *The Cross in the Sand: The Early Catholic Church in Florida, 1513–1870.* Gainesville, 1965.

GARCILASO DE LA VEGA. *The Florida of the Inca.* Edited and trans. by John G. Varner and Jeannette J. Varner. Austin, 1951.

GEARING, FRED. *Priests and Warriors: Social Structures for Cherokee Politics in the 18th Century.* Menasha, 1962.

GEIGER, MAYNARD J. *The Franciscan Conquest of Florida, 1573–1618.* Washington, 1937.

GENOVESE, EUGENE D. *Roll, Jordan, Roll: The World the Slaves Made.* New York, 1974.

GILBERT, WILLIAM H., JR. "The Eastern Cherokees," Bureau of American Ethnology, *Bulletin* 133 (1943): 169–414.

GILLIAM, C. E. "An English Conspiracy Against Wahanganoche, King of Potomac, *circa* 1660," *Quarterly Bulletin, The Archaeological Society of Virginia* 18 (1963): 8–9.

GILLILAND, MARION S. *The Material Culture of Key Marco Florida.* Gainesville, 1975.

GIRAUD, MARCEL. *Histoire de la Louisiane française.* 3 vols. 1953–58.

GLASS, BENTLEY. "On the Unlikelihood of Significant Admixture of Genes from the North American Indians in the Present Composition of the Negroes of the United States," *American Journal of Human Genetics* 7 (1955): 368–85.

GODWIN, MORGAN. *The Negro's and Indian's Advocate, Suing for Their Admission into the Church . . . to Which Is Added a Brief Account of Religion in Virginia.* London, 1680.

GOGGIN, JOHN M. *Indian and Spanish: Selected Writings.* Coral Gables, 1964.

———. "The Seminole Negroes of Andros Island, Bahamas," *Florida Historical Quarterly* 24 (1946): 201–6.

———, AND WILLIAM C. STURTEVANT, "The Calusa: A Stratified Nonagricultural Society (with notes on Sibling Marriage)," in *Explorations in Cultural Anthropology: Essays in Honor of George Peter Murdock.* Edited by Ward H. Goodenough. New York, 1964.

GONZÁLEZ, NANCY L. SOLIEN. *Black Carib Household Structure: A Study of Migration and Modernization.* Seattle, 1969.

GOODWIN, GARY C. *Cherokees in Transition: A Study of Changing Culture and Environment Prior to 1775.* Chicago, 1977.

GORDON, CYRUS H. *Before Columbus: Links Between the Old World and Ancient America.* New York, 1971.

GRAY, ROBERT. *A Good Speed to Virginia, 1609.* Edited by Wesley F. Craven. New York, 1937.

Great Britain, Board of Trade. *Journal of the Commissioners for Trade and Plantations . . . Preserved in the Public Record Office . . . .* 14 vols. London, 1920–38.

———, Historical Manuscripts Commission. *Manuscripts of the Earl of Egmont. Diary of the First Earl of Egmont.* 3 vols. London, 1920–23.

———, Public Record Office. *Calendar of State Papers, Colonial Series.* Edited by W. N. Sainsbury, J. W. Fortescue, C. Headlam, and A. P. Newton. London, 1860–

GREGORIE, ANNE K., ed. *Records of the Court of Chancery of South Carolina, 1671–1779.* Washington, 1950.

GRIFFIN, JOHN W. "Historic Artifacts and the 'Buzzard Cult' in Florida," *Florida Historical Quarterly* 24 (1946): 295–301.

HAKLUYT, RICHARD, ed. *The Principal Navigations, Voyages, Traffiques, and Discoveries of the English Nation.* 12 vols. New York, 1903.

HALE, NATHANIEL C. *Virginia Venturer. A Historical Biography of William Claiborne, 1660–1677.* Richmond, 1951.

HALLIBURTON, R., JR. *Red over Black: Black Slavery Among the Cherokee Indians.* Westport, 1977.

HAMOR, RALPH. *A True Discourse of the Present Estate of Virginia . . . .* London, 1615.

HANDLER, JEROME S. "The Amerindian Slave Population of Barbados in the Seventeenth and Early Eighteenth Centuries," *Caribbean Studies* 8 (1969): 38–64.

———. "Aspects of Amerindian Ethnography in 17th Century Barbados," *Caribbean Studies* 9 (1970), 50–72.

HANKE, LEWIS U. *The Spanish Struggle for Justice in the Conquest of America.* Philadelphia, 1959.

HARING, CLARENCE H. *Trade and Navigation Between Spain and the Indies in the Time of the Hapsburgs.* Cambridge, 1918.

HARIOT, THOMAS. *A Briefe and True Report of the New Found Land of Virginia . . . .* London, 1588.

HARN, JULIA E. "Old Canoochee-Ogeechee Chronicles," *Georgia Historical Quarterly* 15 (1931): 346–60.

HARRINGTON, JOHN P. "The Original Strachey Vocabulary of the Virginia Indian Language," *Bureau of American Ethnology, Bulletin* 157 (1955): 189–202.

HARTLEY, WILLIAM, AND ELLEN HARTLEY. *Osceola: The Unconquered Indian*. New York, 1973.

HENING, WILLIAM W. ed. *The Statutes at Large, Being a Collection of All the Laws of Virginia from the First Session of the Legislature in the Year 1619*. 13 vols. Richmond, 1809–23.

HERNDON, G. MELVIN. "Indian Agriculture in the Southern Colonies," *North Carolina Historical Review* 44 (1967): 283–97.

HERRERA Y TORDESILLAS, ANTONIO DE. *The General History of the Vast Continent and Islands of America, Commonly Call'd, The West-Indies, from the First Discovery Thereof: with the Best Accounts the People Could Give of Their Antiquities . . . .* Translated by John Stevens. 6 vols. London, 1725–26.

HERSKOVITS, MELVILLE J. *The Anthropometry of the American Negro*. New York, 1930.

———. *Life in a Haitian Valley*. New York, 1971.

———. *The Myth of the Negro Past*. Gloucester, 1970.

HIGGINBOTHAM, JAY. *Old Mobile: Fort Louis de la Louisiane, 1702–1711*. Mobile, 1977.

HODGE, FREDERICK W., AND THEODORE H. LEWIS, eds. *Spanish Explorers in the Southern United States, 1528–1543*. New York, 1907.

HORSMAN, REGINALD. *Expansion and American Indian Policy, 1783–1812*. East Lansing, 1967.

HOWARD, JAMES H. *The Southeastern Ceremonial Complex and Its Interpretation*. Missouri Archaeological Society. Memoir 6 (1968).

HUDSON, CHARLES M., ed. *Black Drink: A Native American Tea*. Athens, Ga., 1979.

———. *The Catawba Nation*. Athens, Ga., 1970.

———. *The Southeastern Indians*. Knoxville, 1976.

HULTON, PAUL H., AND DAVID B. QUINN. *The American Drawings of John White, 1577–1590*. 2 vols. London, 1964.

HUMPHREYS, DAVID. *An Historical Account of the Incorporated Society for the Propagation of the Gospel in Foreign Parts, Containing Their Foundation, Proceedings, and the Success of Their Missionaries in the British Colonies, to the Year 1728*. London, 1730.

HURWITZ, SAMUEL J., AND EDITH F. HURWITZ. *Jamaica: A Historical Portrait*. New York, 1971.

JACOBS, WILBUR R. "The Tip of an Iceberg: Pre-Colombian Indian Demography and Some Implications for Revisionism," *William and Mary Quarterly*, 3d ser., 31 (1974): 123–32.

JENNINGS, FRANCIS. *The Invasion of America: Indians, Colonialism, and the Cant of Conquest*. Chapel Hill, 1975.

JENNINGS, JESSE D. *Prehistory of North America*. New York, 1968.

JOHNSON, FRANK ROY. *The Algonquians: Indians of That Part of the New World First Visited by the English*. Murfreesboro, 1972–

JOHNSTON, CHARLES M., ed. *The Valley of the Six Nations: A Collection of Documents on the Indian Lands of the Grand River.* Toronto, 1964.

JOHNSTON, GIDEON. *Carolina Chronicle: The Papers of Commissary Gideon Johnston, 1707–1716.* Edited by Frank J. Klingberg. Berkeley, 1946.

JOHNSTON, JAMES H. "Documentary Evidence of the Relations of Negroes and Indians," *Journal of Negro History* 14 (1929): 21–43.

JONES, B. CALVIN. "Colonel James Moore and the Destruction of the Apalachee Missions in 1704," State of Florida, Division of Archives, History, and Records Management, *Bulletin* 2 (1972): 25–33.

———. "State Archaeologists Unearth Spanish Mission Ruins," State of Florida, Division of Archives, History, and Records Management, *Archives and History News* 2 (1971), no. 4.

JONES, GEORGE F., ed. and trans. *Henry Newman's Salzburger Letterbooks.* Athens, Ga., 1966.

———, AND HERMANN J. LACHER, trans. *Detailed Reports on the Salzburger Emigrants Who Settled in America . . . Edited by Samuel Urlsperger.* Athens, Ga., 1968.

JORDAN, WINTHROP D. *White over Black: American Attitudes Toward the Negro, 1550–1812.* Baltimore, 1969.

KEMBLE, FRANCES A. *Journal of a Residence on a Georgian Plantation in 1838–1839.* Edited by John A. Scott. New York, 1961.

KINGSBURY, SUSAN M., ed. *The Records of the Virginia Company of London.* 4 vols. Washington, 1906–35.

KLINGBERG, FRANK J. "The Mystery of the Lost Yamassee Prince," *South Carolina Historical and Genealogical Magazine.* 63 (1962): 18–32.

KOHLER, TIM A. "Corn, Indians, and Spaniards in North-Central Florida: A Technique for Measuring Evolutionary Changes in Corn," *Florida Anthropologist* 32 (1979): 1–7.

LAND, ROBERT H. "Henrico and Its College," *William and Mary Quarterly,* 2d ser., 18 (1938): 453–98.

LANNING, JOHN T. *The Spanish Missions of Georgia.* Chapel Hill, 1935.

LARSON, LEWIS H., JR. "Historic Guale Indians of the Georgia Coast and the Impact of the Spanish Mission Effort," in *Tacachale: Essays on the Indians of Florida and Southeastern Georgia during the Historic Period.* Edited by Jerald Milanich and Samuel Proctor. Gainesville, 1978.

LAUBER, ALMON W. *Indian Slavery in Colonial Times Within the Present Limits of the United States.* New York, 1913.

LAUDONNIÈRE, RENÉ. *Three Voyages.* Edited and translated by Charles E. Bennett. Gainesville, 1975.

LAURENS, HENRY. *The Papers of Henry Laurens.* Edited by Philip M. Hamer, George C. Rogers, David R. Chesnutt, et al. Columbia, 1968–

Bibliography

LAWSON, JOHN. *Lawson's History of North Carolina.* Richmond, 1937.

LEFLER, HUGH T., AND WILLIAM S. POWELL. *Colonial North Carolina: A History.* New York, 1973.

LE JAU, FRANCIS. *The Carolina Chronicle of Dr. Francis Le Jau, 1706–1717.* Edited by Frank J. Klingberg. Berkeley, 1956.

LEWIS, CLIFFORD M., AND ALBERT J. LOOMIE. *The Spanish Jesuit Mission in Virginia, 1570–1572.* Chapel Hill, 1953.

LONG, ALEXANDER. "A Small Postscript of the Ways and Manners of the Indians Called Charikees," *Southern Indian Studies,* edited by David H. Corkran, 21 (1969): 3–49.

LOPATIN, IVAN A. "Origin of the Native American Steam Bath," *American Anthropologist* 62 (1960): 977–93.

LORANT, STEFAN, ed. *The New World: The First Pictures of America, Made by John White and Jacques Le Moyne and Engraved by Theodore De Bry.* New York, 1946.

LOWERY, WOODBURY. *The Spanish Settlements Within the Present Limits of the United States.* 2 vols. New York, 1959.

LYON, EUGENE. *The Enterprise of Florida: Pedro Menéndez de Avilés and the Spanish Conquest of 1565–1568.* Gainesville, 1976.

McCARY, BEN C. "An Indian Dugout Canoe, Reworked by Early Settlers, Found in Powhatan Creek, James City County, Virginia," *Quarterly Bulletin, The Archaelogical Society of Virginia* 19 (1964): 14–15.

MACCORD, HOWARD A. "Camden: A Postcontact Indian Site in Caroline County," *Quarterly Bulletin, The Archaeological Society of Virginia* 24 (1969): 1–41.

———. "Hungars Neck Trash-Pit, Northampton County, Virginia," *Quarterly Bulletin, The Archaeological Society of Virginia* 27 (1972): 59–64.

McDOWELL, WILLIAM L., JR., ed. *Documents Relating to Indian Affairs.* 2 vols. Columbia, 1958–70.

———. *Journals of the Commissioners of the Indian Trade, September 20, 1710–August 29, 1718.* Columbia, 1955.

McILWAINE, HENRY R., ed. *Executive Journals of the Council of Colonial Virginia.* 5 vols. Richmond, 1925–45.

———. *Journals of the House of Burgesses of Virginia, 1619–1776.* 13 vols. Richmond, 1905–15.

———. *Minutes of the Council and General Court of Colonial Virginia, 1622–1632, 1670–1676.* Richmond, 1924.

McNEILL, WILLIAM H. *Plagues and People.* New York, 1976.

MALCOLM X. *The Autobiography of Malcolm X, with the Assistance of Alex Haley.* New York, 1964.

MARTIN, CALVIN. *Keepers of the Game: Indian–Animal Relationships and the Fur Trade.* Berkeley, 1978.

MARTIN, PHYLLIS M. *The External Trade of the Loango Coast, 1576–1870: The Effects of Changing Commercial Relations on the Vili Kingdom of Loango.* Oxford, 1972.

MASON, CAROL I. "A Reconsideration of Westo-Yuchi Identification," *American Anthropologist* 65 (1963): 1342–46.

MATHEWS, DONALD G. *Religion in the Old South.* Chicago, 1977.

MEIER, AUGUST. "A Study of the Racial Ancestry of the Mississippi College Negro," *American Journal of Physical Anthropology,* new series, 7 (1949): 227–39.

MELLON, KNOX, JR. "Christian Priber's Cherokee 'Kingdom of Paradise,' " *Georgia Historical Quarterly* 57 (1973): 319–31.

MERENESS, NEWTON D., ed. *Travels in the American Colonies.* New York, 1916.

MILANICH, JERALD T. "The Western Timucua: Patterns of Acculturation and Change." In Jerald T. Milanich and Samuel Proctor, eds., *Tacachale.* Gainesville, Fla., 1978.

MILLER, PERRY. "The Religious Impulse in the Founding of Virginia: Religion and Society in the Early Literature," *William and Mary Quarterly,* 3d ser. 5 (1948): 492–522.

MILLING, CHAPMAN J., ed. *Colonial South Carolina: Two Contemporary Descriptions by Governor James Glen and Dr. George Milligen-Johnston.* Columbia, 1951.

MONTAGUE, LUDWELL L. "Richard Lee, the Emigrant, 1613(?)–1664," *Virginia Magazine of History and Biography* 62 (1954): 3–49.

MONTGOMERY, ROBERT. *A Discourse Concerning the Design'd Establishment of a New Colony to the South of Carolina, in the Most Delightful Country of the Universe.* Edited by J. Max Patrick. Atlanta, 1948.

MOONEY, JAMES. "The Aboriginal Population of America North of Mexico," *Smithsonian Miscellaneous Collections* 80 (1928), no. 7.

———. "Myths of the Cherokee," Bureau of American Ethnology, *19th Annual Report, 1897–89.* Washington, 1900.

MORGAN, EDMUND S. *American Slavery, American Freedom: The Ordeal of Colonial Virginia.* New York, 1975.

MORTON, RICHARD L. *Colonial Virginia.* 2 vols. Chapel Hill, 1960.

MOSSIKER, FRANCES. *Pocahontas.* New York, 1976.

MURGA SANZ, VICENTE. *Juan Ponce de León: fundador y primer gobernador del pueblo puertorriqueño, descubridor de la Florida y del Estrecho de las Bahamas.* San Juan, 1959.

NAIRNE, THOMAS. *A Letter from South Carolina; Giving an Account of the Soil, Air, Product, Trade, Government, Laws, Religion, People, Military Strength, etc. of That Province.* London, 1710.

NATHAN, HANS. *Dan Emmett and the Rise of Early Negro Minstrelsy.* Norman, 1962.

NEILL, EDWARD D. *History of the Virginia Company of London, with Letters to and from the First Colony Never Before Printed.* New York, 1968.
———. *Virginia Carolorum: The Colony Under the Rule of Charles the First and Second, A.D. 1625–A.D. 1685* . . . . Albany, N.Y., 1886.
A New Voyage to Georgia, By a Young Gentleman, Giving an Account of His Travels to South Carolina, and Part of North Carolina. To Which is Added, a Curious Account of the Indians, by an Honorable Person, and a Poem to James Oglethorpe, Esq.; on His Arrival from Georgia. London, 1737.
NOËL HUME, IVOR. *Excavations at Rosewell in Gloucester County, Virginia, 1957–1959.* Washington, 1962.
———. "First Look at a Lost Virginia Settlement," *National Geographic* 155 (1979): 735–67.
NORRIS, JOHN. *Profitable Advice for Rich and Poor. In a Dialogue, or Discourse between James Freeman, a Carolina Planter, and Simon Question, a West-Country Farmer.* London, 1712.
NUGENT, NELL M., ed. *Cavaliers and Pioneers: Abstracts of Virginia Land Patents and Grants, 1623–1800.* Richmond, 1934–
ORÉ, LUÍS JERÓNIMO DE. *The Martyrs of Florida (1513–1616).* Edited and translated by Maynard Geiger. New York, 1936.
PACHECO, JOAQUÍN, FRANCISCO DE CÁRDENAS, LUIS TORRES DE MENDOZA, et al., eds. *Colección de documentos inéditos relativos al descubrimiento, conquista, y colonización de las posesiones españolas en América y Oceanía, sacados en su mayor parte, del real Archivo de Indias.* 42 vols. Madrid, 1864–1884.
PALMER, COLIN A. *Slaves of the White God: Blacks in Mexico, 1570–1650.* Cambridge, Mass., 1976.
PAREDES, J. ANTHONY. "The Emergence of Contemporary Eastern Creek Indian Identity," in *Social and Cultural Identity: Problems of Persistence and Change.* Edited by Thomas K. Fitzgerald. Athens, 1974.
———, AND KENNETH J. PLANTE. "Economics, Politics, and the Subjugation of the Creek Indians: Final Report for the National Park Service." Tallahassee, 1975.
PAREJA, FRANCISCO. *Arte de la Lengua Timvqvana compvesto en 1614 por le p^e Francisco Pareja* . . . . Edited by Lucien Adam and Julian Vinson. Paris, 1886.
———. *Francisco Pareja's 1613 Confessionario: A Documentary Source for Timucuan Ethnography.* Edited by Jerald T. Milanich and William C. Sturtevant; translated by Emilio F. Moran. Tallahassee, 1972.
PARKER, IOLA B. "Meadowcroft Dig Continues to Throw Light on Prehistory," *Popular Archaeology* 6 (1977): 6–8.
PARKER, MATTIE E. E., ed. *North Carolina Charters and Constitutions, 1578–1698.* Raleigh, 1963.
———. *North Carolina Higher-Court Records.* Raleigh, 1968–

PARRY, JOHN H. *The Establishment of the European Hegemony, 1415–1715: Trade and Exploration in the Age of the Renaissance.* New York, 1961.

———, AND PHILIP M. SHERLOCK. *A Short History of the West Indies.* New York, 1965.

PASCOE, CHARLES F. *Two Hundred Years of the SPG: An Historical Account of the Society for the Propagation of the Gospel in Foreign Parts, 1701–1900.* 2 vols. London, 1901.

PATTERSON, H. ORLANDO. *The Sociology of Slavery: An Analysis of the Origins, Development and Structure of Negro Slave Society in Jamaica.* Rutherford, N.J., 1969.

PEARCE, ROY H. *The Savages of America: A Study of the Indian and the Idea of Civilization.* Baltimore, 1953.

PEARSON, FRED L., JR. "The Florencia Investigation of Spanish Timucua," *Florida Historical Quarterly* 51 (1972): 166–76.

PERCY, GEORGE. *Observations Gathered out of a Discourse on the Plantation of the Southern Colony in Virginia by the English, 1606.* Edited by David B. Quinn. Charlottesville, 1967.

PERDUE, THEDA. *Slavery and the Evolution of Cherokee Society, 1548–1866.* Knoxville, 1979.

PIKE, RUTH. *Aristocrats and Traders: Sevillian Society in the Sixteenth Century.* Ithaca, 1972.

PORTER, KENNETH W. "The Negro Abraham," *Florida Historical Quarterly* 25 (1946): 1–43.

———. "Negroes and the Seminole War, 1835–1842," *Journal of Southern History* 30 (1964): 427–50.

———. "Relations Between Negroes and Indians Within the Present Limits of the United States," *Journal of Negro History* 17 (1932): 287–367.

POUND, MERRITT B. *Benjamin Hawkins, Indian Agent.* Athens, Ga., 1951.

POWELL, WILLIAM S. "Carolana and the Incomparable Roanoke: Explorations and Attempted Settlements, 1620–1663," *North Carolina Historical Review* 51 (1974): 1–21.

PRIESTLEY, HERBERT I., ed. and trans. *The Luna Papers: Documents Relating to the Expedition of Don Tristán de Luna y Arellano for the Conquest of la Florida in 1559–1561.* 2 vols. Freeport, 1971.

PUCKETT, NEWBELL N. *Folk Beliefs of the Southern Negro.* Chapel Hill, 1926.

PURCHAS, SAMUEL, ed. *Hakluytus Posthumus or Purchas His Pilgrimes, Contayning a History of the World in Sea Voyages and Lande Travells by Englishmen and Others.* 20 vols. Glasgow, 1905–7.

QUARLES, BENJAMIN. *The Negro in the American Revolution.* Chapel Hill, 1961.

QUATTLEBAUM, PAUL. *The Land Called Chicora: The Carolinas Under Spanish Rule, with French Intrusions, 1520–1670.* Gainesville, 1956.

Bibliography

QUINN, DAVID B., ed. *The Roanoke Voyages, 1584–1590. Documents to Illustrate the English Voyages to North America Under the Patent Granted to Walter Raleigh in 1584.* 2 vols. London, 1955.

RANFT, B. MCL., ed. *The Vernon Papers.* London, 1958.

RAWICK, GEORGE P., ed. *The American Slave: A Composite Autobiography. Supplement. Series 1.* 12 vols. Westport, 1978.

RICKETTS, MAC LINSCOTT. "The North American Indian Trickster," *History of Religions* 5 (1966): 327–50.

RIGHTS, DOUGLAS L. *The American Indian in North Carolina.* Winston-Salem, 1957.

ROBERTS, D. F. "The Dynamics of Racial Intermixture in the American Negro: Some Anthropological Considerations," *American Journal of Human Genetics* 7 (1955): 361–67.

ROBINSON, W. STITT, JR. "Indian Education and Missions in Colonial Virginia," *Journal of Southern History* 18 (1952): 152–68.

———. *Mother Earth: Land Grants in Virginia, 1607–1699.* Williamsburg, 1957.

ROOSEVELT, THEODORE. *The Winning of the West.* 4 vols. New York, 1889–96.

ROSS, MARY. "With Pardo and Boyano on the Fringes of the Georgia Land," *Georgia Historical Quarterly* 14 (1930): 267–85.

RUSSELL-WOOD, A. J. R. "Iberian Expansion and the Issue of Black Slavery: Changing Portuguese Attitudes, 1440–1770," *American Historical Review* 83 (1978): 16–42.

SACO, JOSÉ A. *Historia de la esclavitud de los indios en el nuevo mundo seguida de la historia de los repartimientos y encomiendas.* 2 vols. Havana, 1932.

SALAMAN, REDCLIFFE N. *The History and Social Influence of the Potato.* Cambridge, England, 1949.

SALLEY, ALEXANDER S., JR., ed. *Journals of the Commons House of Assembly of South Carolina.* 25 vols. Columbia, 1907–1949.

———. *Journal of the Grand Council of South Carolina.* Columbia, 1907.

———. *Narratives of Early Carolina, 1650–1708.* New York, 1911.

———. *Records in the British Public Record Office Relating to South Carolina, 1663–1710.* 5 vols. Atlanta, 1928.

———. *Warrants for Lands in South Carolina, 1672–1711.* Revised by R. Nicholas Olsberg. Columbia, 1973.

SAUNDERS, WILLIAM L., ed. *The Colonial Records of North Carolina.* 10 vols. Goldsboro, 1886–1890.

SAVELLE, MAX. *The Origins of American Diplomacy: The International History of Angloamerica, 1492–1763.* New York, 1967.

SCHWARTZ, STUART B. "Indian Labor and New World Plantations: European Demands and Indian Responses in Northeastern Brazil," *American Historical Review* 83 (1978): 43–79.

SERRANO Y SANZ, MANUEL, ed. *Documentos históricos de la Florida y la Luisiana, siglos XVI al XVIII*. Madrid, 1912.

The Shaftsbury Papers, and other Records relating to Carolina and the First Settlement on Ashley River Prior to the Year 1676. Edited by Langdon Cheves. *Collections of the South Carolina Historical Society*. Vol. 5. Richmond, 1897.

SHEA, WILLIAM L. "Virginia at War, 1644–1646," *Military Affairs* 41 (1977), 142–47.

SHURTLEFF, HAROLD R. *The Log Cabin Myth: A Study of the Early Dwellings of the English Colonists in North America*. Cambridge, Mass., 1939.

SIEBERT, FRANK T., JR. "Resurrecting Virginia Algonquian from the Dead: The Reconstituted and Historical Phonology of Powhatan," *Studies in Southeastern Indian Languages*. Edited by James M. Crawford. Athens, Ga., 1975.

SIRMANS, MARION EUGENE. *Colonial South Carolina: A Political History, 1663–1763*. Chapel Hill, 1966.

Slave Narratives: A Folk History of Slavery in the United States, from Interviews with Former Slaves. 17 vols. St. Clair Shores, 1976.

SMITH, HALE G. *Documentation Concerning the First Christmas in the United States Presented to the United States Postal Service Commemorative Stamp Committee*. Tallahassee, n.d.

SOLÍS DE MERÁS, GONZALO. *Pedro Menéndez de Avilés, Memorial*. Edited and translated by Jeannette T. Connor. Introduction by Lyle N. McAlister. Gainesville, 1964.

SOUTH, STANLEY A. *Exploratory Archaeology at the Site of 1670–1680 Charles Towne on Albemarle Point in South Carolina*. Columbia, 1969.

———. *Indians in North Carolina*. Raleigh, 1959.

SPALDING, PHINIZY. *Oglethorpe in America*. Chicago, 1977.

SPECK, FRANK G. "The Ethnic Position of Southeastern Algonkian," *American Anthropologist* 26 (1924): 184–200.

———. "The Rappahannock Indians of Virginia," *Indian Notes and Monographs*, Vol. 5, No. 3. Edited by Frederick W. Hodge. New York, 1925.

———. "Some Outlines of Aboriginal Culture in the Southeastern United States," *American Anthropologist* 9 (1907): 287–95.

SPOTSWOOD, ALEXANDER. *The Official Letters of Alexander Spotswood, Lieutenant-Governor of the Colony of Virginia, 1710–1722, Now First Printed from the Manuscript in the Collections of the Virginia Historical Society*. Edited by Robert A. Brock. 2 vols. Richmond, 1882–85.

STOCK, LEO F., ed. *Proceedings and Debates of the British Parliaments Respecting North America*. 5 vols. Washington, 1924–41.

STRACHEY, WILLIAM. *The Historie of Travell into Virginia Britania (1612)*. Edited by Louis B. Wright and Virginia Freund. London, 1953.

STURTEVANT, WILLIAM C. "Notes on the Creek Hothouse," *Southern Indian Studies* 20 (1968): 3–5.

Bibliography

————. "Seminole Myths of the Origins of Races," *Ethnohistory* 10 (1963): 80–86.

————. "Spanish–Indian Relations in Southeastern North America," *Ethnohistory* 9 (1962): 41–94.

SWANTON, JOHN R. "Aboriginal Culture of the Southeast," Bureau of American Ethnology, *42d Annual Report* (1928): 673–726.

————. *Early History of the Creek Indians and Their Neighbors.* Washington, 1922.

————. *The Indians of the Southeastern United States.* Washington, 1946.

————. *The Indian Tribes of North America.* Washington, 1952.

————. *Myths and Tales of the Southeastern Indians.* Washington, 1929.

————. "Religious Beliefs and Medical Practices of the Creek Indians," Bureau of American Ethnology, *42d Annual Report* (1928), pp. 473–672.

————. "Social Organization and Social Usages of the Indians of the Creek Confederacy." Bureau of American Ethnology, *42d Annual Report* (1928), pp. 23–472.

————, JOHN R. FORDYCE, WALTER B. JONES, et al. *Final Report of the United States De Soto Expedition Commission.* Washington, 1939.

SYMONDS, WILLIAM. *The Proceedings of the English Colonie in Virginia Since Their First Beginning from England in the Yeare of Our Lord 1606, Till this Present 1612 . . . .* Oxford, 1612.

————. *Virginia: A Sermon Preached at White-Chappel in the Presence of Many Honourable and Worshipfull, the Adventurers and Planters for Virginia, 25 April 1609.* Amsterdam, 1968.

TAYLOR, EVA G. R., ed. *The Original Writings and Correspondence of the Two Richard Hakluyts,* 2 vols. London, 1935.

TePASKE, JOHN J. *The Governorship of Spanish Florida, 1700–1763.* Durham, 1964.

————. "The Fugitive Slave: Intercolonial Rivalry and Spanish Slave Policy, 1687–1764," *Eighteenth-Century Florida and Its Borderlands.* Edited by Samuel Proctor. Gainesville, 1975.

THOMAS, JONATHAN P., JR. "The Barbadians in Early South Carolina," *South Carolina Historical and Genealogical Magazine* 31 (1930): 75–92.

THOMPSON, HENRY P. *Into All Lands: The History of the Society for the Propagation of the Gospel in Foreign Parts, 1701–1950.* London, 1951.

THOMPSON, STITH. *Motif-Index of Folk-Literature: A Classification of Narrative Elements in Folktales, Ballads, Myths, Fables, Mediaeval Romances, Exempla, Fabliaux, Jest-Books, and Local Legends.* 6 vols. Bloomington, 1955–58.

TIMBERLAKE, HENRY. *Lieut. Henry Timberlake's Memoirs, 1756–1765.* Edited by Samuel C. Williams. Marietta, Ga., 1948.

TINLING, MARION R. G. *The Correspondence of the Three William Byrds of Westover, Virginia, 1684–1776.* 2 vols. Charlottesville, 1977.

TOFFLER, ALVIN. *Future Shock.* New York, 1971.

TUCKER, GLENN. *Tecumseh: Vision of Glory.* New York, 1956.

TUGGLE, WILLIAM O. *Shem, Ham, and Japheth: The Papers of W. O. Tuggle.* Edited by Eugene Current-Garcia and Dorothy B. Hatfield. Athens, Ga., 1973.

TURNER, LORENZO D. *Africanisms in the Gullah Dialect.* Chicago, 1949.

TYLER, LYON G., ed. *Narratives of Early Virginia, 1606–1625.* New York, 1907.

UBELAKER, DOUGLAS H. *Reconstruction of Demographic Profiles from Ossuary Skeletal Samples: A Case Study from the Tidewater Potomac.* Washington, 1974.

United States, Bureau of the Census. *1970 Census of Population, Subject Reports: American Indians.* Washington, 1973.

———, Department of the Interior, National Park Service. *Russell Cave National Monument, Alabama.* Washington, 1967.

VAN EVERY, DALE. *Disinherited: The Lost Birthright of the American Indian.* New York, 1966.

VAUGHAN, ALDEN T. " 'Explusion of the Salvages': English Policy and the Virginia Massacre of 1622," *William and Mary Quarterly* 3d ser., 35 (1978): 57–84.

VERLINDEN, CHARLES. *L'esclavage dans l'Europe médiévale.* 2 vols. Brugge and Gent, 1955–77.

VER STEEG, CLARENCE L. *Origins of a Southern Mosaic: Studies of Early Carolina and Georgia.* Athens, Ga., 1975.

VLACH, JOHN M. *The Afro-American Tradition in Decorative Arts.* Cleveland, 1977.

VLAHOS, OLIVIA. *New World Beginnings: Indian Cultures in the Americas.* New York, 1970.

VOGEL, VIRGIL J. *American Indian Medicine.* Norman, 1970.

WAGNER, GÜNTER. *Yuchi Tales.* New York, 1931.

WALNE, PETER. "The Collections for Henrico College, 1616–1618," *Virginia Magazine of History and Biography* 80 (1972): 259–66.

WARING, ANTONIO J., JR. *The Waring Papers: The Collected Works of Antonio J. Waring, Jr.* Edited by Stephen Williams. Cambridge, Mass., 1968.

———, AND PRESTON HOLDER. "A Prehistoric Ceremonial Complex in the Southeastern United States," *American Anthropology* 47 (1945): 1–34.

WASHBURN, WILCOMB E. *The Governor and the Rebel: A History of Bacon's Rebellion in Virginia.* Chapel Hill, 1957.

———, ed. *The Indian and the White Man.* New York, 1964.

———. *The Indian in America.* New York, 1975.

WEISIGER, BENJAMIN B., ed. *Colonial Wills of Henrico County, Virginia, Part One, 1654–1737.* Richmond, 1976.

WENHOLD, LUCY L., AND ALBERT C. MANUCY, eds. "The Trials of Captain Don Isidoro de León," *Florida Historical Quarterly* 35 (1956): 246–65.

WERTENBAKER, THOMAS J. *Torchbearer of the Revolution: The Story of Bacon's Rebellion and Its Leader*. Princeton, 1941.

WESCOTT, ROGER W. "Bini Names in Nigeria and Georgia," *Linguistics* 124 (1974): 21–32.

WESTON, PLOWDEN C. J., ed. *Documents Connected with the History of South Carolina*. London, 1856.

WHITAKER, ALEXANDER. *Good Newes from Virginia. Sent to the Covnsell and Company of Virginia, Resident in England. From Alexander Whitaker, the Minister of Henrico in Virginia*. London, 1613.

WHITAKER, ARTHUR P. "Alexander McGillivray, 1783–1789," *North Carolina Historical Review* 5 (1928), 181–203.

WILLIAMS, GEORGE W., ed. "Letters to the Bishop of London from the Commissaries in South Carolina," *South Carolina Historical and Genealogical Magazine* 78 (1977): 1–31, 120–47, 213–42, 286–317.

WILLIAMSON, JAMES A. *The Cabot Voyages and Bristol Discovery Under Henry VII; with the Cartography of the Voyages by R. A. Skelton*. Cambridge, 1962.

WILLIS, WILLIAM S., JR. "Divide and Rule: Red, White and Black in the Southeast," in *Red, White, and Black: Symposium on Indians in the Old South*. Edited by Charles M. Hudson. Athens, Ga., 1971.

WILSON, THOMAS, BISHOP OF SODOR AND MAN. *Essay Towards an Instruction for the Indians; Explaining the Most Essential Doctrines of Christianity. Which May Be of Use to Such Christians, as Have Not Well Considered the Meaning of the Religion They Profess; Or, Who Profess to Know God, but In Works Do Deny Him. In Several Short and Plain Dialogues. Together with Directions and Prayers for the Heathen World, Missionaries, Catechumens, Private Persons, Families, of Parents for Their Children, for Sundays, etc.* London, 1740.

WINSTON, SANFORD. "Indian Slavery in the Carolina Region," *Journal of Negro History* 19 (1934): 431–40.

WOOD, PETER H. *Black Majority: Negroes in Colonial South Carolina from 1670 through the Stono Rebellion*. New York, 1974.

WOODMASON, CHARLES. *The Carolina Backcountry on the Eve of The Revolution: The Journal and Other Writings of Charles Woodmason, Anglican Itinerant*. Edited by Richard J. Hooker. Chapel Hill, 1953.

WOODSON, CARTER G. "The Relations of Negroes and Indians in Massachusetts," *Journal of Negro History* 5 (1920): 45–57.

WOODWARD, GRACE S. *Pocahontas*. Norman, 1969.

WRIGHT, J. LEITCH, JR. *Anglo-Spanish Rivalry in North America*. Athens, Ga., 1971.

———. *Britain and the American Frontier, 1783–1815*. Athens, Ga., 1975.

———. "Creek-American Treaty of 1790: Alexander McGillivray and the Diplomacy of the Old Southwest," *Georgia Historical Quarterly* 51 (1967): 379–400.

———. "A Note on the First Seminole War as Seen by the Indians, Negroes, and Their British Advisors," *Journal of Southern History* 34 (1968), 565–75.

———. *William Augustus Bowles: Director General of the Creek Nation.* Athens, Ga., 1967.

———, ed. "William Hilton's Voyage to Carolina in 1662," *Essex Institute Historical Collections* 105 (1969): 96–102.

WROTH, LAWRENCE C., ed. *The Voyages of Giovanni da Verrazzano, 1524–1528.* New Haven, 1970.

ZAVALA, SILVIO A. *Los Esclavos indios en Nueva España.* Mexico City, 1967.

ZUBILLAGA, FÉLIX, ed. *Monumenta Antiquae Floridae (1566–1572).* Rome, 1946.

IV. Unpublished Reports, Papers, and Dissertations

BAKER, STEVEN G. "Cofitachique: Fair Province of Carolina." Master's thesis, University of South Carolina, 1974.

BRUMBAUGH, RODERICK. "Black Maroons in Florida, 1800–1830." Paper delivered at Organization of American Historians Annual Meeting. Boston, 1975.

DOBYNS, HENRY F. "The Historic Demography of Indian North America." Paper delivered at Organization of American Historians Annual Meeting. Atlanta, 1977.

FAUSZ, J. FREDERICK. "The Powhatan Uprising of 1622: A Historical Study of Ethnocentrism and Cultural Conflict." Ph.D. dissertation, The College of William and Mary, 1977.

JURICEK, JOHN T. "Indian Policy in Proprietary South Carolina, 1670–1693." Master's thesis, University of Chicago, 1962.

KING, ROBERT T. "The Florida Seminole Polity, 1858–1978." Ph.D. dissertation, University of Florida, 1978.

MATTER, ROBERT A. "The Spanish Missions of Florida: The Friars Versus the Governors in the 'Golden Age,' 1606–1690." Ph.D. dissertation, University of Washington, 1972.

PEARSON, FRED LAMAR, JR. "Spanish-Indian Relations in Florida: A Study of Two Visitas, 1657–1678." Ph.D. dissertation, University of Alabama, 1968.

REED, ERIK K. "Fort Moultrie." Report, 1968, H2215, Southeast Archaeological Center, National Park Service, Tallahassee.

SNELL, WILLIAM R. "Indian Slavery in Colonial South Carolina, 1671–1795." Ph.D. dissertation, University of Alabama, 1972.

Bibliography

SOUTH, STANLEY A. "Santa Elena on Parris Island South Carolina." Paper delivered at symposium, Spain and the United States. Gainesville, 1979.

WRIGHT, J. LEITCH, JR. "Southern Black Loyalists." Paper delivered at Conference on American Loyalists. St. Augustine, 1975.

Index

Index

Index

Chickasaw Indians, 113, 139, 200, 205, 208, 231
Chicora, province, 35, 36, 102
Chicora, Francisco, 35, 36
Chiefdoms: disintegration of, 51, 230; mentioned, 16
Chiefs: appointed by Spain, 50
Chinquapins, 9, 21
Chippewa Indians, 252
Chisca Indians, 139
Chiskiack, 83
Chiskiack Indians: murdered, 78
Choctaw Indians: drum of, 271; mentioned, 2, 139, 140, 146, 151, 229, 281, 283, 285, 289
Chowan Indians, 92, 188
Chowan River, 230
Chowanoc Indians, 56, 119
Christanna: Indian school and trading post at, 183, 187–88. See also Fort Christanna
Chunky: Indian game, 22
Circumcision, 177
Claiborne, William: Indian trader, 69; patented device to control Indians, 78, 146; campaigns against Indians, 86; family, 110; mentioned, 79, 95, 132, 161
Clan: structure, 9; vengeance, 20, 98, 227–28; effects of alcohol on, 228; mentioned, 17, 238, 282
Clayton, John, 241
Clothing: aboriginal modified, 159; whites adopt that of Indians, 243
Coats: quilted, 83
Cochran, John: death, 123
Cofitachiqui: Queen of, 4, 6, 16, 26; Negroes at, 43; remnants, 96, 119; and Yamasee War, 121; mentioned, 4, 6, 14, 16, 24, 35, 39, 51, 104, 105, 233
Cole, James: slaves of, 274
College at Henricus: lands of, 79; destroyed, 63–64. See also Henricus
Colono-Indian pottery, 240–41, 264
Columbus, Christopher: enslaves natives, 128; voyages of, 29, 31
Columnella pendants, 37
Combahee Indians, 117
Conch shells, 264
Congaree Indians, 23, 119, 124
Congarees: Indians build trading house at, 163
Congo, 146
Congregationalists, 283
Convicts: arrive in Chesapeake Bay, 258
Cook, Sherburne, 24, 31
Cooper, James Fenimore, 11, 245
Cooper, 166
Coosa Indians, 107, 117

Copp, Jonathan: SPG missionary, 211
Copper: from Great Lakes, 14; breast plates, 14, 290; mentioned, 68
Cordwainer, 166
Coree Indians: slaughter of, 140; mentioned, 124, 143
Corn: varieties used by Indians, 6–7. See also maize
Corn Mother, 7
Cortéz, Hernando, 33, 36, 128
Cotachicach Indians, 107
Cotchawesk, 91
Courieurs des bois, 2
Coweta, 214
Cowkeeper, Chief, 145
Cranial deformation, 11, 239
Crashaw, William, 66
Craven, Earl of, 125
Crawshaw, William: a Christian Indian, 179
Crécy, Battle of, 48
Creek Indians: language, 207, 237; description, 222–24, 230–31; rulers, 233; population, 280; hostilities of, 120, 283; twentieth century survivors, 289; mentioned, 16, 110, 114, 119, 130, 142, 144, 195, 224, 226, 235–36, 285. See also Lower Creeks, Upper Creeks
Creek Nation East of the Mississippi, 246
Crèvecoeur, Hector St. John de: views of, 247, 278
Croatoan Indians, 56, 232
Cromwell, Oliver, 180
Crystal River: Indian settlements at, 44
Cuba: population, 31; bishop of, 51; mentioned, 32, 115, 230
Cumberland Island, 264
Cusabo Indians: enslaved, 138; mentioned, 107, 117, 124, 130, 150
Custis, John, 156

Dahlonega, 38
Dale, Thomas, 67, 70, 72
Dances, Indian: 229, 239; mentioned, 21, 22
Darien: maroons of, 274
Dawkins, Elias: denies being an Indian, 250
Deerskins: importance in Indian trade, 93, 110; mentioned, 10, 13
Delaware Prophet, 287
Dennis, Benjamin, 228
De Soto, Hernando: route of expedition, 39; mentioned, 16, 27, 43, 44, 55, 107, 114, 127, 129, 131, 141, 147, 152, 160, 161, 165
Devil's shoestring (Tephrosia), 11
Diseases: introduced by Europeans and

Index

Index

Freeman, Frank: Indian ancestry, 253
French and Indian War, 145, 165, 213, 239, 285
Fundamental Constitutions, 116

Galphin, George: family of, 273; mentioned, 206
Games, Indian, 21
Garcilaso de la Vega, 127
Garvey, Marcus, 248, 262
Geechee: development of, 269
Geneticists: and origins of American Negroes, 251–52
Genovese, Eugene: views of, 263
George I, 193
George, Yamasee Prince: visits England, 193–94; father, 194; mentioned, 222
George Town, 36
Georgia: prohibition of distilled spirits, 171; Indian trade of, 172; founding, 199; boundaries, 200, 203–04; labor supply of, 205; economic role of Indians, 215
Gerrard, Henry: SPG missionary, 192
Ghost Dance: among Plains Indians, 284–85; mentioned, 17
Ginseng, 21, 265
Glass beads, 68–69
Glass, Bentley: genetic study of, 252
Glorious Revolution, 180
Gloucester Co., Virginia, 87
Godwin, Morgan, 181
Gooch, William: and slave insurrection, 274–75
Goose Creek men: quarrel with proprietors, 116; enslave Indians, 138–40; mentioned, 110, 111, 115, 118, 119, 121, 122, 123, 130, 141, 145, 146, 161, 168, 191, 192, 255
Gordillo, Francisco, 33, 35
Gordon, Lord Deane, 222
Gourds: used by slaves, 264
Graffenried, Baron Christoph von, 118–19
Granada, 29
Granaries, 9, 15
Gray, Edmund, 275
Great Awakening, 215
Great Britain: Indian policies of, 285; assumes France's role in North America, 285. See also England
Great Peter, 91–92
Green Corn Ceremony, 7, 11, 19. See also busk
Green Corn dance: and Negroes, 270
Green Spring plantation, 137
Griffin: a mestizo, Mary Musgrove's brother, 214
Griffin, Charles: SPG missionary, 188

Grimke family, 110
Grubbing Hoe Indian, 159
Guadeloupe, 130
Guale Indians: revolt, 51, 64; mentioned, 12, 111, 113, 115, 121, 144, 146
Guale, province: Spanish missions of, 65, 111, 191; mentioned, 24, 27, 102, 163, 200, 202
Guatari: mission at, 43
Guianas: Bush Negroes of, 274
Guinea Company, 68
Gulf Stream, 40
Gullah: development of, 269; mentioned, 253
Gun flints, 221
Gunstocker, Edward, 167
Guy, William: SPG missionary, 193

Hagar, 156
Haiti: prophets of, 268
Hakluyt, Richard, the younger: and Indian labor, 153; mentioned, 54, 57
Haley, Alex: Indian ancestry, 250
Hancock's fort, 83, 120
Hariot, Thomas: views on Indians, 58; mentioned, 59, 153
Harris, Joel Chandler: and Uncle Remus stories, 266–67
Harrison, Nathaniel, 252
Harry: an African slave, 258–59
Hatcher, Edward, 96
Hatcher, Henry, 96
Hatcher, Joseph, 96
Hatcher family, 134–35
Havana, 40, 45, 131
Hawkins, Benjamin: Indian policies, 283
Hawkins, John, 52, 57, 132
Hawkins, William, 132
Headrights: Indians counted, 100, 117
Hearne, Capt. John: brings slaves into Georgia, 203
Heath, Robert: colonization attempts, 103
Hemp, 67
Henrico County: Indian slaves in, 135–36; mentioned, 96
Henricus, 80, 185
Henry VIII: suppressed monastaries, 65; mentioned, 53
Henry of Susa, Cardinal Archbishop of Ostia: views on slavery, 127–28, 284
Henry, Patrick, 100
Herskovits, Melville: anthropometrical survey, 250–51; mentioned, 262
Hickory: a Nottoway Indian, 187
Hill, Col. Edward: expedition of, 77, 87–88; plantation at Westover, 86; mentioned, 90

363

Index

Hillis Hadjo, the Prophet Francis: career, 288

Hilton Head Island, 104

Hilton, William: 1662 voyage, 103; 1663 voyage, 104; mentioned, 138

Hispaniola: Indian population, 24, 31; mentioned, 32, 36, 61

Hitchiti: folk tale in, 150; language, 183, 211; mentioned, 231

Holy Club, 207, 208

Honduras, Gulf of, 145

Hooker, John, 57

Horses: Indians acquire, 166, 224–25; mentioned, 223

Horseshoe Bend, Battle of, 280, 288, 289

Hot house, 15

Houses: description of Indian, 219–20; Indian influence on those of colonists, 245; mentioned, 15

Howard University, 250

Hungarians, 127–28

Hunting: Indians become commercial hunters, 170–172, 220–21; decline of, 288–89; mentioned, 9, 10, 11, 205–06

Huskanaw, 62

Hyde, Gov. Edward: captures Indians, 143; mentioned, 118

Inca Indians, 16, 26, 39

Indentured servitude: terms of Indians extended, 170, 257–58

Ibos, 146

Indian Billey, 170

Indian countrymen, 189, 235

Indians: response to European explorers, 28, 29, 37; title to lands, 54, 99, 100, 116; population, 22, 23, 26, 56, 151, 152; enslaved, 56, 70, 76, 85, 86, 94, 127–29, 134–36, 141, 143, 145–46, 148–49, 215; as artisans and laborers, 12, 152–65, 214; commerce of, 95, 110, 173, 218, 225–27, 234, 288; religious beliefs, 19, 66, 176; dress, 18, 19, 218–19, 169–70; agriculture, 7–9; removal to Oklahoma, 280, 281, 289; patterns of settlement, 15, 16, 81, 280; relations with Africans, 259–61; culture modified, 217–18, 225, 279; sent to West Indies, 44–45, 115, 131; languages, 6, 183; fugitives, 168–69; kinship terms, 18, 212; in twentieth century South, 289; discontent of, 168; hostilities in Virginia, 77–78, 84; 1622 massacre, 74–75; marriages, 20, 190, 234–35, 237; purchase freedom, 169; military tactics, 79–81; fight for Confederacy, 251; description of, 18; and European law, 227–28; modify

white culture, 240; sexual ratios of those enslaved, 258; debts, 173; hostages, 93; land titles, 177. *See also* individual tribes

Ingham, Benjamin: Indian school in Georgia, 208–09

Ingram, David, 51–52

Inquisition, Spanish, 65

Iroquois Indians, 60, 87, 108

Isabella, Queen, 29, 128

Isaw Indians, 107

Israel, Lost Tribe of: reports of among Indians, 177

Isthmus of Panama: Indians of, 26

Jacán: Jesuit mission of, 46, 50–51; mentioned, 28, 41, 43, 55, 59, 89. *See also* Virginia

Jack: an Indian, 164, 169

Jack of Morocco: an Indian, 255

Jack of the Feathers, 268. *See also* Nemattanew

Jack the Fiddler: an Indian, 255

Jackson, Andrew: Florida invasion, 277; mentioned, 78, 91, 120, 268

Jamaica: Indians of, 131; maroons, 274, 277; mentioned, 32, 130, 133, 255

James I, 63, 65

James River, 68, 69, 70, 83, 84, 86, 87, 96, 102, 117

Jamestown: founding, 28; route of ships to, 41; drunken Indians at, 198; fort at, 245; mentioned, 12, 79, 81, 83, 132, 153, 178. *See also* Virginia

Jefferson, Thomas: policies toward Indians, 62, 220; and sericulture, 162

Jeffreys, Col. Herbert, 90

Jesuits, 43, 45, 46, 74

Jews, 30

Jews-harp: Indians adopt, 229, 270–71

Jim Crow Laws, 249

Jimson weed, 21

John the Bowlmaker, 98, 162

Johnson: Gambian-born slave, 264

Johnson, Robert: has Indian wife, 236

Johnson, Robin: Negro owning Indian slaves, 260–61

Johnston, Gideon: Anglican commissary, 182; mentioned, 192, 193, 194, 196

Jones Neck, 79

Jones, Capt. Thomas, 214

Jordan River, 36, 103

Jordan's Point, 79

Kate: Indian listed as Negro, 252

Kate, 156

Kecoughtan, 80, 81

Index

Index

Memphis, 27
Menéndez de Avilés: son of, 41–42; *asiento*, 42; founds St. Augustine, 42; in Cuba, 44–45; and Indian slavery, 131; mentioned, 2, 51, 52, 72, 74, 75, 104, 129
Mennonites, 196
Merrak: an Indian slave, 150, 168
Mestizos (mustees): in Spanish Florida, 51; in Virginia, 73; and Indian trade, 173; definition of, 203, 252, 256; among Indians, 235–36
Metallurgy, 12, 14, 26
Metappin: requests baptism, 180
Methodists, 207, 215
Mexico: population, 24, 129; plague in, 44; African labor in, 251; mentioned, 230
Miami: mission at, 43
Miccosukee Indians: visit Cuba, 284; mentioned, 151
Middle Passage, 130, 137, 248, 256, 265
Middle Plantation (Williamsburg), 83
Middle Temple: masque staged at, 61
Middleton family, 110
Milfort, LeClerc de, 286
Mimi: makes baskets, 262–63
Miranda, María de, 60
Miscegenation, 236–37
Missions, Spanish: Apalachee, 46; Atlantic Coast, 46, 47, 49; South Carolina back country, 46; soldiers at, 47; construction of, 47–48; aboriginal reaction to, 48–50; Indian labor employed, 153; destroyed, 110–11; maize tribute, 159; mentioned, 45, 47, 95, 178, 198
Mississippian Period: influence in Virginia, 68; practice of slavery, 126–27; mentioned, 3, 4, 11, 56, 157, 159, 165, 185
Mobile: Indian slaves at, 152; Apalachees move to, 163, 193; French soldiers at dress like Indians, 243; mentioned, 2, 114, 142, 143, 198, 224
Mobile Indians: language, 113, 254, 286; mentioned, 23
Mohawk Indians: conversion of, 184, 191; visit England 193; mentioned, 87, 195, 283
Mohegan Indians, 11
Monacan Indians, 85
Montero, Father Sebastian, 43
Montesinos, Antonio de, 30
Montgomery, Sir Robert, 200–02
Moon: fertility symbol, 267
Mooney, James, 22–25, 101
Moore, James, Jr.: and Tuscarora War, 120, 121; mentioned, 143
Moore, James, Sr.: attacked St. Augustine,

195; family, 110; Apalachee campaign, 113–14; mentioned, 123, 140, 149, 190, 191, 193, 214
Moors, 30, 127, 128
Moravians, 197, 209
Morgan, Edmund S.: views of Indians, 28; analysis of Bacon's Rebellion, 88; mentioned, 7
Moriscos, 128
Mortars: provenance of, 263
Mortuary practices, 15
Mosquito Indians: and slave trade, 143; in South, 230; mentioned, 146
Mounds: burial, 4; temple, 4, 11, 17, 26, 208–9, 289
Mount Venture, 204
Muklasa Indians, 231, 254
Mulatto: definition, 252, 555–56
Muscle Shoals, 11
Musgrove, John: store, 211; mentioned, 159, 204
Musgrove, Mary: cowpen, 208; youth, 211; land claims, 212–13; mentioned, 203, 204, 209, 214
Music, Indian: influence on Negroes, 270; in twentieth century, 270; mentioned, 22, 229
Musketank, 92
Muskhogean Indians: language, 6; mentioned, 60, 108

Nairne, Thomas: death, 123; aggressive imperialist, 141–42; influence with SPG, 189; mentioned, 191, 192, 194, 196
Names: Christian ones given to Indians, 50; of Spanish Indian slaves, 254
Nanipacana, 40
Nanny, 156
Nansemond Indians, 79, 91, 186, 222
Nansiatico Indians: apprenticed, 157
Nantes, Edict of, 190
Nanticoke Indians: African influence on language, 268; mentioned, 160
Narváez, Pánfilo de: expedition, 38–39; mentioned, 43, 107, 130, 131, 152
Natchez Indians: rebellion, 141; enslaved, 147; join Creeks, 231; movements, 281; mentioned, 2, 4, 16
Natchez Sun, 16, 26, 157
Nativistic religious revivals, 287
Necotowance, 86, 87
Needham, James, 96
Negroes: arrival in America, 43, 44; among Tuscaroras, 118; as factors, 172; conversion of, 190; interpreters, 269–70; rebellions, 275; population, 257; definition of, 252; etymology of

Index

Index

Perquiman's Precinct: Indians baptized in, 195
Persimmons, 21
Pestle: provenance of, 263
Peter: hunts for colonists, 157
Petrine theory, 175
Petroglyphs, 1
Phebe: a "white-Indian woman," 253
Philadelphia: population, 14
Philip II, 58
Philip: an African slave, 274
Pickaninny: etymology of, 268–69
Pictographs, 1
Pidgin languages: Indian influence on, 269
Pigeon wing dance, 270
Pipes: used by whites, 241; mentioned, 7, 12, 162, 242, 267
Plains Indians, 25, 249
Platters, 94
Pocahontas (Rebecca): saves John Smith, 71; meaning of name, 72; in England, 72–73; brothers of, 72; attendant of went to Bermuda, 73; mentioned, 60, 66, 77
Pocotaligo Town, 144
Poisoning: by slaves, 265
Polo, Marco, 29
Ponce de León: expeditions to Florida, 33; mentioned, 1, 32, 46, 54, 129, 130, 131, 217
Pontiac's Rebellion, 286
Population: Indian, 24–25, 280; English in Virginia, 70
Port Royal, South Carolina: Huguenots abandon, 55; description, 104; destroyed, 123; English shipwreck near, 103; mentioned, 2, 112, 193, 194. See also Santa Elena
Potkiak Indians, 91
Potomac Indians: chief of poisoned, 97; king of, 158; mentioned, 85
Potomac River, 83, 87, 95
Pottery: introduction into South, 13; manufacture, 162; mentioned, 3, 12, 94
Powhatan, Emperor: crowned, 63; and 1622 massacre, 64; daughters of, 71–72; death, 75; mentioned, 16, 25, 54, 60, 64, 74, 85, 90, 130, 164
Powhatan Indians: language, 63, 184, 243; possibly refugees from south, 52; artisans rework European wares, 69; trade, 69; whites live among, 73; systems of keeping time, 80; population, 91, 101; 1622 massacre, 76, 77, 80, 83, 85, 89, 99, 117, 125, 132, 154, 178, 179; 1644 massacre, 77, 80, 85, 86, 89, 99, 154, 179, 229; 1646

peace treaty, 86, 87, 89, 92; 1677 peace treaty, 90, 92; mentioned, 4, 10, 11, 12, 24, 56, 66, 80, 94, 127, 132, 134, 154, 162, 179, 252. See also Tsenacommacah
Presbyterian Church: structure of, 196
Priber, Christian: among Cherokees, 197; mentioned, 275–76
Prisoners: whites captured by Florida Indians, 45
Priss: a mulatto, 98, 256
Prize, Richard: Indian wife of, 237
Property: Indian, 18, 237
Prophets: African and Indian, 267–68
Puccoons, 222
Puerto Rico, 32, 131
Pugh, Daniel, 136
Puncheon forts, 245
Purchas, Samuel, 62
Puritan Revolution, 85
Puritans, 54–55, 65

Quakers, 196, 198
Quaque, Philip: visits England, 193
Queen Anne's War: Indian slave raids of, 140; mentioned, 115, 136, 191, 192
Quexos, Pedro de, 35
Quincy, Samuel: marries colonist to Indian, 236

Rabbit: as trickster, 267–68
Rainsford, Giles: SPG missionary among Chowans, 188
Raleigh, Sir Walter, 57, 102, 117, 118
Rappahannock Indians, 97
Rappahannock River, 83
Rattles, 22
Red (war) towns, 234
Religion: Indian and white influence on that of Negro, 265–66
Remus, Uncle, 290
Repartimiento: in Virginia, 67; mentioned, 31, 38, 128, 152–53, 255
Requirement, The, 33
Revolts: Indian and African collaboration, 271–78
Ribault, Jean, 42, 104
Ricahecrians: identification, 87; mentioned, 6, 77, 85, 88, 90, 105, 107
Rice: development of culture in America, 263; mentioned, 159
Richardson, Martha: Indian father made medicine for Negroes, 265
Río de las Palmas, 38
Roanoke, 68, 94, 244. See also wampum
Roanoke Indians, 56, 159

Index

Roanoke Island colony: treatment of Indians at, 57–59; abandoned, 59; fort at, 81; mentioned, 2, 7, 41, 42, 55, 56, 74, 95, 103, 132, 153, 178
Roanoke River, 91
Robin: a Jamaica Indian, 100
Robin: a Pamunkey artisan, 157
Robin: an Indian listed as a Negro, 252
Rolfe, John: marriage, 71–72; death, 73; mentioned, 77, 94
Rolfe, Thomas: in Virginia, 73; mentioned, 71
Roosevelt, Theodore: views on Indians, 55
Rosse: an Indian, 164
Rotunda, 15
Rowsham, Ann: slaves of, 258
Royal African Company, 137–38
Royal Society, 210
Runners: and "Mr. Bear," 267
Russell Cave, 3, 6

Saint Augustine: population, 14; founding, 27; 1702 siege, 140–142; 1740 siege, 213–14; mentioned, 43, 44, 47, 71, 102, 105, 143, 144, 161, 200, 220, 224
Saint Bartholomew Parish: Indian baptized in, 195
Saint Brendan: expedition, 257
Saint Catherines Island: Spanish soldiers at, 111; missions destroyed, 112; mentioned, 212, 213
Saint Domingue, 130, 255
Saint George Parish, South Carolina: census, 260; mentioned, 236
Saint James, Goose Creek Parish, 190
Saint Johns River, 2
Saint Lawrence River, 11
Saint Marks, 220
Saint Mary's River, 113, 200
Saint Paul's Parish, South Carolina: Indian slaves in, 152
Saint Simons Island: attacked, 213; mentioned, 264
Saint Thomas Parish, South Carolina: Indian slaves in, 152
Salem, North Carolina, 197
Salvadore: an Indian, executed, 273
Salzburgers: missionary efforts of, 209–10
Sampa Indians, 107
Sampson: an Indian listed as a Negro, 253
Sandford, Robert: expedition, 104, 105, 107, 138
Sandys, Edwin: reorganizes Virginia Company, 73–74
San Juan, Puerto Rico, 31
San Marcos, Castillo de: Indians help construct, 163; mentioned, 142

Santa Catalina (St. Catherines Island), 47
Santa Elena: Spanish missions at, 46, 103; English ship visits, 52; houses of soldiers, 245; mentioned, 28, 35, 40, 43, 55, 57, 81. See also Port Royal
Santee Indians, 107, 119, 124
Santee River, 36
Santiago, 31
Santo Domingo: founding, 29–30
Sapelo Island, 112, 212
Saponi Indians: Queen of, 188; execution of, 227; description, 232; mentioned, 20, 169, 183, 233
Sarve: school at, 188
Sassafras, 21
Sauna, 245–46
Saunders: a slave, 256
Savannah: founded, 200–201; mentioned, 205
Savannah Indians: destroy Westos, 105; language, 183, 191; join Creeks, 231; mentioned, 107, 108, 110, 119, 121, 138, 139, 140, 172, 184, 190, 191, 194, 195, 208. See also Shawnee Indians
Savannah Town, 161, 195
Sawokli Indians, 231
Sawyers, 166
Scalping: bounties for, 239; of Africans, 272; mentioned, 19, 20, 83, 166, 243–44
Scipio: an African, executed, 273
Scots: and Indian trade, 172
Seamstress: 166
Second Seminole War: abolitionists views toward, 277
Secotan Indians, 56
Seminoles: origins, 145, 232, 238; Africans among, 261, 276–77; mentioned, 47, 150, 151, 224, 233, 283, 289
Semites: possible voyages to America, 176
Seneca Indians, 87, 101, 143, 145, 188
Sepúlveda, Gines de, 30
Serbs, 127
Sericulture, 153, 158, 162, 167, 205
Servants: Indians serve as personal attendants, 164
Seville: population, 128
Sewee Indians, 107, 124, 138
Shackles, 146
Shaftsbury, Earl of, 116
Sharecroppers: Indian, 158
Shawnee Indians: religious revival among, 286–88. See also Savannah Indians
Sherman, William T., 77
Ships: sailing routes, 40–41; wrecks, 40, 41, 55; mentioned, 37
Shirley Hundred, 79
Shoes, Dick, 169

369

Index

Short, Mrs.: buys a Powhatan, 180
Sign language, 286
Silk. *See* sericulture
Silke grasse, 67
Silver: among Indians, 37
Silver Bluff, 4, 206
Simon, 157
Singer: at rituals, 19, 21
Siouan Indians: language, 6; in Virginia, 74; mentioned, 60, 108
Slavery: Indian, 38, 90, 112, 125, 132, 189, 196, 237, 250; African, 132, 202–03; in Georgia, 203–04; institution of, 126–27, 258; fugitives, 134; sexual ratios, 149; slave trade, 173, 221, 281–82; population, 147; code, 97; Christian names given to slaves, 253; Spanish and Portuguese, 254; slave cords, 146
Sloan, Dr. Hans, 210
Smallpox, 25, 26
Smith, John: compiled Powhatan word list, 63; in England, 72; and Indian labor, 154; map of, 79; mentioned, 7, 16, 60, 70, 71, 85, 132, 153, 164, 200
Smith, Rev. Samuel, 210
Society for the Propagation of Christian Knowledge, 197–98
Society for the Propagation of the Gospel in Foreign Parts: missionary efforts among Indians, 194–95, 283; morals of missionaries, 189–90; conversion of slaves, 259; mentioned, 182, 184, 206, 207, 227–28
Sofkee, 223
Somers Islands, 76
Somerset House, 193
Southall, Eugene P., 281
South America, 26, 137
South Carolina: Indian trade, 172, 206; SPG activities, 188; charter, 188; Africans and Indians collaborate in, 274
Southeastern Ceremonial Complex: modern survivals, 290; mentioned, 14, 17, 37, 48, 209
South Sea Bubble, 201
Spain: colonies in West Indies, 31; proposed attack on Carolina, 124–25; mentioned, 201, 202
Spangenberg, Bishop August, 197
Spanish Indians, 232
Spider: Nancy (*anansi*) tales, 267
Spoons, 94
Spotswood, Gov. Alexander: member of SPG, 182; mentioned, 183, 187, 234, 236
Square ground: possibly replaced council house, 238–39; mentioned, 15
Squash, 7

Starving Time, 67
Stenkenocks, 183, 187
Stomp dance: African influence on, 270
Stone implements, 13
Stono Indians: Cacique of, 108; mentioned, 107, 117, 123, 138, 140, 252
Stono Rebellion, 272, 278
Strachey, William: compiled Powhatan word list, 63, 176
Strawberries, Cherokees gather, 239; mentioned, 9, 222
Stewart, John: views on marriage with Indians, 235
Stuart, John: Indian policies, 285
Stuart's Town: destroyed, 113; mentioned, 112, 123, 139
Sue: the bastard of, 156
Sugeree Indians, 119
Sunday: Indian morals on, 180
Sunflowers, 7
Surnames: given to Indians by court, 156
Susan: Indian who "remained a Negro," 250
Susquehannock Indians: fort, 81, 220; migrations, 230; mentioned, 88, 89, 90
Suwannee River, 106
Swanton, John R., 23
Swedes: and log cabin, 244; mentioned, 95
Sweet potato: origins, 223
Swine: Indians acquire, 84, 165
Swiss: immigrants, 118, 119
Symonds, William, 73

Taino Indians, 31
Taitt, David, 236
Tallahassee, Fla.: first Christmas at, 27
Tallapoosas (Upper Creeks), 142
Talomeco, 44
Tama: Yamasee chief of, 122
Tampa Bay, 38, 39
Tampico, 52
Tanning, 12
Tanx (Little) Powhatans, 79
Tappahannock Indians, 79
Tassore, 67
Tastanagi, 150, 233
Tawasa Indians, 143, 146, 231
Taylor, Capt. William: plantation at Chiskiack, 86
Tecumseh: and Indian confederation, 286–88
Temple, Robert, 147
Tenochtitlán, 38
Tequesta Indians, 115, 144, 148, 168
Texas, 44
Textiles, 13
Thirty-nine Articles, 132

Index

Thomas: an Indian, 100
Thomas, Samuel: interested in Yamasees, 191–92
Thorpe, George: and Indian college, 64; mentioned, 65, 66
Tidewater Virginia: population, 25
Timboe: Negro interpreter, 269
Timucuan Indians: language, 49, 50, 238; effects of disease, 218; mentioned, 6, 9, 10, 24, 38, 42, 111, 122, 127, 130, 140, 146, 150, 168, 252
Timucua, province: missions, 176; expeditions against, 115, 144; mentioned; 24, 112, 113, 139, 149, 163
Tithables: Indians counted, 99
Tobacco, 21, 94
Toffler, Alvin: and social mobility, 92
Tomassee, 254
Tomochichi: wife of, 210; in England, 209–10; mentioned, 200, 208, 211, 213
Toonahowi: visits England, 210; death, 215; mentioned, 213
Totems, 18
Totero Indians, 187
Towns: Indian, 14–15
Trade: of Indians in sixteenth century, 41; in seventeenth century Virginia, 68, 74, 93. *See also* peltry trade
Trade jargons, 286
Trail of Tears, 91, 151, 249
Transportation: Indian methods of, 154; penalty of, 98
Treaty of Utrecht, 143
Trent River, 119
Tribes: migrations, 229; composition, 230
Tributaries: in Virginia, 76, 92, 93, 101; in South Carolina, 125; land titles of, 226; mentioned, 93, 225, 282
Trustees (Georgia): and Indian conversion, 199, 206–07; plans for colony, 201–02; opposition to slavery, 203; failure, 213; mentioned, 205
Tsenacommacah: population, 60–61, 76. *See also* Powhatan Indians
Tuckahoe, 9, 222
Tucker, Capt. William: and Potomac River Indians, 83
Turks, 128
Tuscarora Indians: enslaved, 118–20, 144; movements, 121, 143, 281; rivalry with Algonquians, 117; epidemic among, 118; visit Yeardleys, 179–80; hostages of, 186; fort, 220; language, 237; Negroes among, 277; mentioned, 92, 95, 101, 122, 124, 136, 145, 188, 232
Tuscarora War, 117–18, 134, 143
Tuskegee Indians, 231
Tutelo, 183

Uchizes (Creeks), 115
Uktena, 19, 176
United States Indian Claims Commission, 284
Unooneth, 92
Upper Creeks, 113, 281. *See also* Creeks
Usherys, 140
Usufruct, 54, 212, 213, 226, 283–84

Van Every, Dale: attitude toward Indians, 55
Vann, Chief: driven from village, 222
Vann, James, 261
Vann, John: slaves of, 273
Varnod, Francis: SPG missionary, 195
Vera Cruz, 40
Verrazzano, Giovanni da, 28, 59, 60, 61
Villafañe, Ángel de, 40, 46
Virginia: population, 76, 84, 133, 251; hostilities with Indians, 78–79, 83, 273; Indian policies of, 63–64, 66–67, 85, 86, 136; Indian trade, 94, 96, 172; definition of mulatto in, 256; boundary, 91; slave codes, 133–34; mentioned, 56, 124, 126, 137, 181. *See also* Jacán, Jamestown
Virginia (London) Company: establishes Indian college, 64; charter revoked, 67; forced to encourage colonization, 68; mentioned, 61, 153, 162, 171
Virginia Indian Company, 187–88
Vitoria, Francisco de, 30

Waccamaw Indians: and Negro revolt, 275; mentioned, 121
Wahoganoche, the Potomac King, 100
Wall, Mrs. John, 167
Wally, etymology of, 254
Walnuts: Indians gather, 9; bark from tree, 11
Wampum, 13, 92, 95. *See also* peake, roanoke
Wanchese, 56, 57
Wando Indians, 107
Wanniah Indians, 107
Ware Keck, 91
Warfare: Indian manner of, 20, 239
Warm Mineral Springs, 3, 6
War of Spanish Succession, 122
Warrisquoiacke, 79
Washington, George: land speculations, 212; and scalping, 244; mentioned, 21
Wateree Indians, 119, 121
Wattle and daub, 48
Waxhaw Indians, 119, 124
Wayne, Anthony, 78

371

Index

Weanoc Indians: king of, 98, 134; movements, 229; mentioned, 79, 91, 92, 180
Weatherford, William, 261
Weaving, 12, 163
Weetoppen, 134
Weirs, 11, 158
Wesley, Charles: missionary to Georgia, 207–8
Wesley, John: opposition to slavery, 202; missionary to Georgia, 207–8; mentioned, 209, 211, 215
Wesley, Samuel, 207
West Africa: slave trade, 137
West Florida: SPG missionary in, 198, 215. See also Florida
West Indies: slavery, 32, 130, 135, 136, 255, 271; labor shortage, 129, 133; mentioned, 137, 170, 182. See also Antilles
Westo Indians: town of, 107; destroyed, 108; join Creeks, 231; mentioned, 6, 87, 88, 105, 110, 113, 138, 139, 140, 152, 168, 286
Westo River, 105
Wheelwright: 166
Whippings: 121–22
Whitaker, Rev. Alexander: conversion of Virginia Indians, 71; sends wooden idol to England, 176; mentioned, 64, 66
White, John, 2, 5, 7, 8, 9, 10, 11, 59, 153, 244
White (peace) towns, 234
Whitefield, Goerge, 211, 215
Whitelamb, John: hopes to become missionary in Georgia, 207–08
Whonny: an Indian, 203
Wicocons, 91, 92
Wighcocomoco, 100
Wild cherry, 21
Wild oats, 222
Will: an Indian, 169
William and Mary College: founded, 185; mentioned, 186–87, 198
William the Conqueror, 127
Williams, Roger, 61
Williamsburg: population, 14
Williamson, Rev. Atkin, 190
Willoughby, Thomas, 156
Willow bark, 21
Wilmington: population, 14
Wilson, Samuel, 125
Wilson, Thomas, Bishop of Man and Sodor: and Indian conversion, 184; mentioned, 186
Wimbee Indians, 107, 117

Winyaw Indians, 140
Witcheau Indians, 117
Wolf, Chief: distributes cattle, 223–24
Wolstenholme: fort at, 245
Wolves: bounties for, 93, 166
Wood, Abraham, 96, 105, 107, 108, 134, 135
Woodbury, Julia: brother captured, 282
Woodcarving, 13, 167
Woodland Period, 3, 4
Woodmason, Charles, 196
Woodson, Carter: editor *Journal of Negro History*, 248
Woodward, Henry: at Port Royal, 104–05; mentioned, 107, 108, 113, 129, 138, 141, 200
Worcester *v.* Georgia, 284
Wragg family, 110
Wright, John: death, 123; slaves, 258; mentioned, 169
Wyatt, Gov. Francis, 171

Xapiracta, 36
Xoxi, 36, 102

Yamacraw Indians: return to Savannah River, 216; visit England, 210; mentioned, 200, 204, 208, 209, 213, 214
Yamasee Indians: slave raids of, 115, 142, 168; migrations, 111, 124, 200, 229–30; language, 183, 192, 268; enslaved, 122, 145; mariners, 164; absorbed by Creeks, 111; and SPG, 192; effects of disease on, 218; mentioned, 110, 112, 113, 114, 119, 138, 140, 141, 148, 150, 184, 190–91, 195, 214, 231
Yamasee War: influence of Negroes, 277–78; mentioned, 117, 121–25, 135, 143, 144, 193, 194, 196, 286
Yaupon, 21
Yeardley, Francis: Indian trade, 96; Indians visit, 179–80; mentioned, 95
Yeardley, Gov. George, 69
York, Archbishop of, 61
York River, 84, 86, 87, 95
Yorubas, 146
Yuchi Indians, 6, 87, 105, 108, 121, 124, 130, 144, 146, 200, 231

Zambos: emerging population of, 259; as interpreters, 269; as drivers, 272; mentioned, 261

X

E 78 .S65 W74 1981
Wright, J. Leitch 1929-
The only land they knew

DATE			

© THE BAKER & TAYLOR CO.